Crisis and Sustainability

Alessandro Vercelli

Crisis and Sustainability

The Delusion of Free Markets

Alessandro Vercelli
London, UK

ISBN 978-1-137-60068-4   ISBN 978-1-137-60069-1   (eBook)
DOI 10.1057/978-1-137-60069-1

Library of Congress Control Number: 2016958104

Cover illustration: © Johner Images / Alamy Stock Photo

Printed on acid-free paper

This Palgrave Macmillan imprint is published by Springer Nature
The registered company is Macmillan Publishers Ltd. London

For Lorenzo

Preface

The gestation of this book has been very long, overlapping with a significant part of my adult life. Although the process of development occurred
after World War II had been very successful on many accounts, in the
late 1960s a growing number of critics started to question its orientation.
Workers, students, intellectuals, and political parties, influenced by progressive ideas, blamed the Bretton Woods compromise between contrast-
ing economic and social instances for being too conservative. At the same
time, an increasing number of industrialists, bankers, intellectuals (such
as Mises, Hayek, Friedman, and Berlin), and political parties influenced
by conservative liberal ideas blamed the existing policy and institutional
regime for being insufficiently committed to the freedom of people and
markets.

A radical opposition to the status quo emerged in the late 1960s when
students' unrests and workers' strikes culminated in episodes of confron-
tation with governments and police. Though this movement was quite
heterogeneous and often ambiguous, the main goal of the protest was
a radical change of the development process in the direction of a less
authoritarian society, aiming at a stricter democratic control of markets and economic activity. This movement had a significant impact
on community values encouraging individual creativity, sexual liberty,
and anti-authoritarian attitudes towards education and institutions, but
governments and mass media soon severely repressed its equalitarian,

anti-market, and social contents. This favoured a fragmentation of the movement in small groups, and this condemned it to political irrelevance and exposed it to involution processes.

The idea that a change of direction in the process of development was possible and necessary spread in the public opinion, but this had the paradoxical effect of facilitating the triggering of a development trajectory that went in a direction opposite to that advocated by the progressive movement. In the 1970s, a troubled phase of persistent stagflation provided the economic circumstances that justified the urgent implementation of a new development trajectory aiming to shift economic power from the state to the markets. What happened in the 1970s and 1980s looked to most contemporaries just as a frantic and confused sequence of economic troubles: the collapse of the Bretton Woods monetary system in 1971, the two oil shocks in 1973 and 1979, the ongoing stagflation, rocketing interest rates, and the ensuing depression in the early 1980s. This shifted the attention of researchers, workers, political parties, and most intellectuals from the long term of strategic development to the short term of serious overlapping emergencies.

The first unequivocal change of direction clearly perceived by the public opinion was a dramatic U-turn occurred in macroeconomic policy. After a short transition in the 1970s, by the end of the decade, the bulk of the economic profession had shifted from orthodox Keynesian macroeconomics to New Classical Economics advocating and practising a return to the classical economics ousted by Keynes in the 1930s. This produced a U-turn in the policy strategy implemented by most governments, starting from the Mrs Thatcher government since 1979 and the Reagan administration since 1981.

The new model of development unfolded in the following decades maintaining what with hindsight looks a broadly coherent development trajectory. The new paradigm started to be called "neoliberal" in the early 1990s when many observers realised that the new direction taken by the process of evolution of capitalism had some sort of internal and intertemporal consistency. This book adopts this controversial terminology because, as I will argue in Chap. 2, it is descriptively accurate and does not prejudge the contents of the investigation. The exponents of this analytical and political paradigm reject this label and claim that the first goal of their vision is the return to the principles of classical liberalism. However, since they do not deny the necessity of an updating of classical liberalism, the prefix neo- seems to me not necessarily inconsistent with their view. The critics of this vision define it as neoliberal giving to the prefix neo- a different meaning of substantial deviation from the principles of classical liberalism. Therefore, the use of the word does not prejudge its interpretation. I argue in the following chapters that the alleged updating of the classical liberal tradition marks in fact a significant change of direction starting a new development trajectory. This book aims to investigate origins, consequences, and policy implications of the neoliberal trajectory of development.

The introductory chapter explains and justifies the approach chosen in this book to clarify the issues under scrutiny. I adopt an approach of "historical economics" focusing on the interpretation of the co-evolution of facts and theory.

The first part of this book aims to sketch a broad conceptual framework that I believe to be necessary for understanding origins and evolution of the recent crisis.

The second chapter discusses the concepts of liberty and free market focusing on the peculiar version advocated by the neoliberal approach to assess to what extent its idiosyncratic updating of classical liberalism is faithful to the first principles of classical liberalism or reveals a significant change of interpretation. The systematic impact on the development trajectory of the new policy strategy implemented by neoliberal policy makers started becoming manifest in the 1990s and triggered a hot debate on its questionable consequences. At the beginning, the debate focused mainly on the general themes of globalisation and financialisation. We cannot understand the Great Recession and the ensuing Eurocrisis without grasping nature and implications of these two processes whose co-evolution in the recent decades has deeply affected the way in which capitalism works. For this reason, the third and fourth chapters aim to clarify these ambiguous and controversial processes in their origins, evolution, and implications in a long-run perspective. What triggered and shaped the recent episodes of financialisation and globalisation, as the preceding ones after the Industrial Revolution, is a radical change in policy strategy. In industrialised countries, the adoption of a liberal policy strategy around the middle of nineteenth century triggered the first phase of financialisation and globalisation, while the adoption of the neoliberal policy strategy since the late 1970s shaped the main features of the most recent, or second, phase of both financialisation and globalisation.

The third chapter focuses on the meaning, causes, and consequences of the process of globalisation. The new enhanced confidence in the efficiency and fairness of free markets promoted by the emerging neoliberal paradigm contributed to extend free trade across countries leading to a rapid reduction of tariffs and other obstacles to trade leading eventually to the establishment of the World Trade Organisation (WTO) in 1995. I emphasise that the justifications of free trade are surprisingly weak and its implications much more disruptive of social and environmental sustainability than most people believe.

At the same time, the free movement of capital across countries favoured a process of financialisation of the economy that started to attract the attention of scholars and public opinion since the late 1990s. The fourth chapter discusses the causes, meaning, and consequences of this process. The liberalisation of financial markets has been always justified by the idea, endorsed by most economists and experts of finance, that unfettered financial markets are efficient and may greatly contribute to the well-being of people. This thesis found new supporters and new arguments in the 1970s convincing most economists and governments that unfettered financial markets are efficient. This led to a systematic liberalisation of international financial markets that rapidly spurred the so-called Second Financialisation. This process eventually enhanced the importance of finance beyond the level reached by the First Financialisation at the turn of the nineteenth century. The main emphasis of the analysis is on the weakness of the arguments advanced in support of unrestricted financialisation, trying to explain why its negative side effects nurtured the increasing financial instability haunting financialised economies.

The second part of the book aims to reconstruct the neoliberal trajectory from the late 1970s to the Great Recession to assess to what extent the actual implementation of the neoliberal development paradigm maintained its promises and reached its professed goals.

The fifth chapter shows how the unfolding of the neoliberal paradigm eventually led to the subprime financial crisis and to its ensuing degeneration into the Great Recession. The main argument is that the neoliberal model of development proved to be unsustainable from the economic, financial, social, and environmental point of view. The accumulation of side effects produced a growing inflationary bias in the financial system enhanced by the asymmetric monetarism adopted by central banks. In such a fragile situation, the perverse interaction between the housing crisis and the contemporaneous spike in oil and food prices acted as detonator of the crisis. Its first wave, often called "subprime crisis", soon propagated to all areas of finance in the USA and Europe triggering the Great Recession.

The sixth chapter analyses in more depth the financial unsustainability of the neoliberal paradigm and discusses some guidelines for its necessary reform. The implementation of the neoliberal paradigm produced far-reaching structural transformations in finance that changed the way in which the economic and financial system behaves. The focus of the investigation is mainly on the genesis and consequences of shadow banking taking into acount the most important underlying structural changes of finance such as securitisation. In the light of this analysis, this chapter discusses some proposals of reform of the shadow banking system. The focus then broadens to the reform proposals for the entire financial system.

The seventh chapter delves into the environmental unsustainability of the current development trajectory arguing that the neoliberal policy strategy has greatly weakened the efficacy of environmental policy in a delicate conjuncture in which it should be urgently empowered to solve the dire problems of environmental sustainability. The clash between the surge of environmental policy and the surge of neoliberal policy produced a shift from the prevailing use of command and control policy instruments to a systematic use of market-based instruments. The latter proved to be much less efficient than expected. A case in point is the European system of tradable pollution permits (EU ETS) that failed to obtain significant reductions of greenhouse gases emissions. More in general, the environmental policy was unable to invert the trend towards increasing environmental unsustainability, mainly because of an energy system still dominated by the use of fossil fuels, and because of the excessive reliance on market-based instruments. The policy makers may find a durable way out only by implementing a sustainable development model based on a modified technological trajectory. This requires a massive intervention of the state as catalyser of the huge amount of investment required.

The Epilogue focuses on contemporaneous issues that are in rapid flux to draw a few tentative implications from the analysis and policy implications of this book.

The eighth chapter analyses the second wave of the crisis that has occurred in the Eurozone since 2010, arguing that its specific causes have been aggravated by the faulty design of the common currency and its short-sighted management rules.

The ninth chapter discusses further the policy implications of the analysis arguing that the process of deregulation of markets has in fact established a more complex and oppressive regulation system that is substantially ineffective. This depends on a defective conception of liberty, free markets, and collective action endorsed by neoliberal exponents in economics, finance, and politics.

The two Appendixes written by Maria Carmen Siniscalchi aim to complement the arguments of the book related to the evolution of the financial system. The first Appendix is a short compendium of the evolution of financial legislation in the USA, UK, and EU in recent decades. Though this evolutionary process had different characteristics in each of these areas, it followed a similar pattern of deregulation since the early 1980s and subsequent attempts at re-regulation after the Great Recession. The second Appendix is a glossary of financial terms focused on derivatives and other financial instruments particularly linked with the Great Recession.

The complexity of recent financial innovations makes the world of derivatives difficult to understand for people not directly dealing with this kind of financial instruments. This difficulty contributed to a general undervaluation of the importance of finance in the recent crisis. These Appendixes aim to provide the minimum level of background knowledge necessary for understanding the arguments developed in the book without compelling a careful reader to resort to the existing glossaries and compendiums that have different purposes and a different focus.

The scope of the contents of this book is very broad, arguably too broad. This is because its main ambition is that of providing links—conceptual, historical, and causal links—between issues that may seem at first sight unrelated, or only weekly related. In my opinion, this is a necessary step—although by no means sufficient—to work out a full-fledged interpretation of historical events. This conceptual weaving is particularly important for a thorough interpretation of the recent events because the economic, financial, social, and environmental issues have become increasingly interconnected in the last decades. We need a general interpretation, or "vision", to orientate the required in-depth analysis of the single issues discussed in this book and to understand the meaning and the policy implications of their results. I hope thus that researchers involved in the theoretical and empirical analysis of these issues not only in economics but also in other social disciplines will find some useful insights in the conceptual framework sketched in this book. Moreover, I hope that any person with an interest on these issues may find some help to understand better what is going on and why. To this end, I tried hard to keep the understanding of the arguments as much as possible independent from a specific technical background.

London, UK   Alessandro Vercelli

Acknowledgements

The long gestation of this book prevents a complete acknowledgement of all the insights, suggestions, and help received by colleagues, family, and friends.

First, I have to thank my wife, Maria Carmen Siniscalchi, who helped me in all the stages of the drafting of the book, discussing all the main issues, finding relevant contributions, and correcting my drafts. In the final stage, she wrote the two Appendixes. A special thanks also to Sebastiano Cupertino for his help in drafting the figures.

I want to thank, for their help and encouragement, Victoria Chick, Philip Arestis, Jan Toporowski, Giuseppe Fontana, Noemi Levi, Andy Dennis, Hardy Hanappi, Sam Bowles, Tony Norfield, Richard Arena, Theresa Davis, Riccardo Bellofiore, Simone Giansante, Marco Veronese Passarella, Roberto Veneziani, Ernesto Screpanti, Alessandro Spina, Elisa Pannini, and Davide Vercelli.

The final stage of the drafting of this book started in 2011 in coincidence with my engagement as scientific coordinator of the European research FESSUD (Financialisation, Economy, Society and Sustainable Development) for the University of Siena (grant agreement no. 266800 of FP7/2007-2013). The obvious overlapping of the themes and the approach of this book with those of FESSUD immediately reveals how much I owe to all the participants in this research for the stimuli and suggestions I received in the numerous meetings of our common enterprise. A special thanks I owe to the coordinator of this research, Malcolm Sawyers, and my colleagues of the University of Siena who participated in this endeavour: Riccardo Basosi, Simone Borghesi, Costanza Consolandi, Sebastiano Copertino, Massimo Di Matteo, Giampaolo Gabbi, Massimiliano Montini, Serena Sordi, and Silvia Ferrini.

In addition, I wish to thank for comments and suggestions the participants in different seminars held in the same period where I presented preliminary drafts of parts of this book, including the Universities of London (SOAS, City University, and Queen Mary), Kingston, Leeds, Bath, Cambridge, UNAM, Dijon, Lund, Nice, Bilbao, Bruxelles, Rszeszow, Vienna, Siena, Firenze, Arezzo, Pisa, Macerata, Roma, Bergamo, Venice, and Perugia.

Contents

1   Introduction: Approach and Basic Concepts   1

Part I   Globalisation and Financialisation in a Long-Run
         Perspective   29

2   Freedom, Free Markets, and Neoliberalism   31

3   The Globalisation of Markets   63

4   The Evolution of Financialisation   89

Part II The Great Recession: Causes and Consequences   117

5   The Neoliberal Trajectory and the Crisis   119

6   The Neoliberal Financialisation   145

7   Environment and Sustainability   183

Part III   Epilogue   217

8   The Eurocrisis   219

9   Concluding Remarks   247

Appendix 1: The Evolution of Financial Legislation: A Short
              Compendium   269

Appendix 2: Glossary of Financial Terms   291

Author Index   307

Subject Index   315

List of Frequent Abbreviations and Acronyms

ABCP	asset-backed commercial paper
ABS	asset-backed security
ARM	adjustable-rate mortgages
BCBS	Basel Committee on Banking Supervision
BHCA	Bank Holding Company Act
BIS	Bank for International Settlements
CAC	command and control
CDO	collateralised debt obligation
CCP	central counterparty
CDS	credit default swap
CFPB	Consumer Financial Protection Bureau
CFTC	Commodity Futures Trading Commission
CSR	corporate social responsibility
EMH	efficient market hypothesis
EMIR	European Market Infrastructure Regulation
EMS	European monetary system
ESMA	European Securities and Markets Authority
EU	European Union
EU ETS	European Emission Trading System
FCA	Financial Conduct Authority
FDIC	Federal Deposit Insurance Corporation
FIR	financial interrelations ratio
FPC	Financial Policy Committee
FSB	Financial Stability Board

FSOC   Financial Stability Oversight Council
FTT   financial transaction tax
G20   Group of Twenty: G8 plus Argentina, Australia, Brazil, China, India, Indonesia, South Korea, Mexico, Saudi Arabia, South Africa, Turkey, along with the European Union (EU)
G8   Group of Eight: France, the Federal Republic of Germany, Italy, Japan, the UK, the USA, Canada, and Russia (suspended since 2014)
GDP   gross domestic product
GHG   greenhouse gas
GLBA   Gramm-Leach-Bliley Act
G-SIBs   global systemically important banks
ICT   information and communication technology
INDCs   Intended Nationally Determined Contributions
IOSCO   International Organization of Security Commissions
ISDS   Investor-State Dispute Settlement
LIBOR   London Interbank Offered Rate
MBS   mortgage-based securities
MiFID   Markets in Financial Instruments Directive
MMMF   money-market mutual fund
MTF   Multilateral Trading Facility
NAFTA   North American Free Trade Agreement
OCA   optimal currency area
OECD   The Organisation for Economic Co-operation and Development
OFR   Office of Financial Research
OTF   Organised Trading Facility
OTC   over-the-counter
PIIGS   Portugal, Ireland, Italy, Greece, and Spain
PRA   Prudential Regulation Authority
R&D   research and development
REH   rational expectations hypothesis
Repo   sale-and-repurchase agreement
SEC   Securities and Exchange Commission
SIVs   structured investment vehicles
SPV   special purpose vehicle
TARP   Troubled Assets Relief Program
TINA   there is no alternative
TPP   Trans-Pacific Partnership
TTIP   Transatlantic Trade and Investment Partnership
UNFCCC   United Nations Framework Convention on Climate Change
WTO   World Trade Organisation

1

Introduction: Approach and Basic Concepts

1.1 Brief Overview

This book provides a comprehensive interpretation of the neoliberal trajectory of development from its inception in the late 1970s to the US subprime financial crisis that originated the Great Recession and the ensuing Eurocrisis. The approach pursued in this book embeds the argument in a succinct reconstruction of the structural evolution of capitalism after World War II and aims to provide insights on the policy strategy that we should adopt to converge towards a sustainable development trajectory.

The neoliberal development trajectory is not a phase of capitalism characterised by invariant features but a period of accelerated structural change whose consequences turned out to be largely uncontrollable and unpredictable for anyone, including its advocates. What is invariant, at least sufficiently for an unequivocal definition, is the underlying development paradigm defining the goals of the development trajectory and the policy strategy to reach them. The supporters of the neoliberal paradigm do not seem to fear its high potential of "creative destruction", probably because of a deep-seated conviction that unfettered markets cannot be wrong, or at least that intentional collective action cannot beat them.

© The Editor(s) (if applicable) and The Author(s) 2017   **1**
A. Vercelli, *Crisis and Sustainability*,
DOI 10.1057/978-1-137-60069-1_1

This conviction is now particularly surprising in the light of the recent crisis that exhibited an unprecedented disruptive persistence and virulence. What seems evident is that the systematic adoption of a neoliberal policy strategy has opened a very insidious Pandora's box whose ultimate consequences are unpredictable and potentially catastrophic. The urgent need to search for a solution to all these problems is the ultimate motivation for writing this book.

The interpretation of the events advanced in the following chapters radically differs from the interpretation suggested by mainstream economists, policy makers, and mass media, leading to radically different policy prescriptions. As is well known, the standard explanation is that the Great Recession unexpectedly occurred because the subprime financial shock, conceived as essentially exogenous, impinged on a financial system made fragile by excessive sovereign debt. From this interpretation follows a policy strategy that, after the bailout of the financial institutions too big and interconnected to fail, aims to reduce sovereign debt through austerity policies in order to resume the business-as-usual trajectory of development. Though many economists broadly share these ideas, their view is not at all monolithic in significant details of the interpretation and in its concrete policy implications. As an authoritative early survey observed, in the existing literature, the crisis is both overexplained and overdetermined.[1] This assertion captures well what is a crucial shortcoming of the recent literature: the search for *the ultimate* causal factor of the crisis (a single factor, or a very short list of interacting factors). The trouble is that many of these causal factors are mutually correlated, as they are part of a specific socio-economic system having a well-defined economic structure, institutional framework, and policy strategy. Therefore, in order to understand the crisis, we have to forsake causal reductionism and to reconstruct origins and unfolding of the system that produced the conditions of the crisis. This process depends on the actual evolution of structural conditions and policies sustaining a model of development that was believed to be optimal.

The crucial role played in this process by the radical change in policy strategy started in the late 1970s is the consequence of a deep interaction between the evolution of economic facts and the co-evolution of economics. The crisis of the Keynesian paradigm ruling the development trajectory in the Bretton Woods period (1945–1971) prompted the emergence of a new development model, often called neoliberal or neoconservative. After some early alleged successes (disinflation in the early 1980s and subsequent reduction of macroeconomic volatility), the side effects of neoliberal policies became progressively evident: increasing inequality in the distribution of income, stagnation of the real economy, inflationary bias in the financial sector, and growing financial instability.

The policy implications of this book challenge the neoliberal laissez-faire that has been so fashionable in recent times. The narrative told in the following chapters suggests that the multiple causes of the crisis have a common root in the intrinsic unsustainability of the neoliberal development paradigm that has ruled in most countries since the early 1980s. Therefore, the first and foremost policy implication of this book's analysis is that the current policy paradigm must be superseded by a radically different policy strategy fully complying with the principles of sustainability. This book argues that a radical change of paradigm is typical of all great crises. In the past, a radical change in the policy paradigm occurred to exit the crisis in a direction believed to be able to avoid similar disruptions in the future.[2] At the same time, a new development trajectory typically required an apt redirection of the technological trajectory.[3]

In this book, I emphasise the crucial role played by the co-evolution of economics, economic policy, and the real economy in shaping the features of the successive development phases and the interacting technological surges.

1.2   The Approach

The analysis developed in this book is in its essence historical. History does not play a crucial role in the argument in the usual sense of *economic history*, because economic theory is systematically intertwined with it. Moreover, it does not play a crucial role in the sense of *new economic history*, because the statistical and econometric evidence plays a crucial role in the argument but remains in its background and relies on the most dependable secondary sources. The mix of history and theory pursued in this book is similar to that advocated by Kindleberger under the name of *historical economics*. He practised this approach very successfully in his famous book *Manias, Panics, and Crashes* first published in 1978 and then many times updated.[4] Similarly to the approach of Kindleberger, the historical analysis developed in this book is not an end in itself but rather an instrument to build a qualitative—or "literary"—model applicable to the empirical evidence about the most significant "great" crises.

Differently from Kindleberger, however, this book does not work out a general model applied to historical episodes distant in time and space, but a model that aims to focus on the evolution of capitalism and the intertwined evolution of economics and economic policy. In addition, Kindleberger emphasised that different crises have their own specificities, but he did not systematically investigate their underlying evolutionary process.

I wish to emphasise that the actual historical sequences reconstructed in this book are not conceived as mere epiphenomena of a unique grand evolutionary process as in the deterministic varieties of historicism. The evolutionary processes here analysed are dissimilar in different periods and separate areas of the globe, interacting in a very complex way. Periods of progress from a given point of view are periods of regress from a different point of view. Moreover, for a given point of view, regress may follow progress in an unpredictable way.

1.3   Empirical Evidence and Interpretation: The Case of the Phillips Curve

The meaning and implications of theories, theoretical constructs, and models depend on a thorough understanding of their structure. As semiotics and linguistics have since long suggested, concepts and theories may be analysed from three different points of view: the *syntactic* point of view that focuses on the logical structure of the theory (or model), the *semantic* point of view that focuses on its meaning, and the *pragmatic* point of view that focuses on practical and policy implications.[5] In the light of this preliminary distinction, the anatomy of an empirical theory may be subdivided into three main components: pure theory, empirical evidence, and interpretation. Each of these components has a crucial role and is subject to different appraisal criteria. "Pure theory" refers to the logical structure of the theory, ignoring for the time being its semantic and pragmatic implications.[6]

The most sophisticated approaches in science enunciate pure theory in the form of an axiomatic system. A case in point is Debreu's version of general equilibrium theory to which I will refer often in this book.[7] The logical structure of the underlying theory is expressed by a small set of axioms (or hypotheses) and a bunch of propositions derived from them by deduction. In this way, many scientific theories aim to formulate theoretical laws of general validity. In economics, lawlike propositions are very few, and their validity is circumscribed in time and space.

In empirical science, the "pure theory" is interpreted by assigning a precise meaning to each symbol of the axiomatic system by linking them to the empirical evidence. The interpretation of a theory is thus a crucial bridge between pure theory and the empirical evidence and is never univocal. To build one of the possible bridges, we have to work out a model that suggests a possible interpretation of the empirical evidence. In other words, any interpretation is a two-way bridge between theory and facts and can be seen from the point of view of deduction from pure theory to facts or inference from the empirical evidence to a theory.[8]

Coming back to general equilibrium theory, Debreu was fully aware that an axiomatic system may be interpreted in different manners, and he himself exploited this option in a constructive way. The interpreted theory, or model, is then ready to be brought into contact with the available empirical evidence. On the other hand, the empirical inference aims to derive empirical regularities from the available evidence. As is generally accepted today, the results of empirical inference depend on the limitations of the data set and on the researcher's presuppositions.[9] Therefore, empirical regularities cannot have general validity, as their meaning and validity scope depend on the link established by the researcher with a specific theory. A case in point in macroeconomics is the Phillips curve.[10] I choose this example because this model will play an important role in the story I am going to tell.[11]

The eponymous curve is an empirical regularity Phillips detected after having investigated the data sets just made available on prices, wages, and unemployment in the UK in the period 1851–1957. As is well known, this empirical regularity is usually represented by a negatively sloping curve connecting the rate of growth of money wages measured on the vertical axis and the unemployment rate measured on the horizontal axis.[12] This empirical regularity immediately attracted the attention of macroeconomists and policy makers, in part because it seemed remarkably stable over a long period of time, a very rare feature in empirical macroeconomics. As argued above, its meaning and policy implications were dependent on the specific theory to which it was connected. This effort sparked one of the most famous and consequential controversies in macroeconomics. As with all the other controversies of this kind, the crux of the matter was the interpretation of the empirical evidence. Paraphrasing Pirandello's "six characters in search of an author", the Phillips curve was defined as "an empirical regularity in search of a theory".

The first interpretation came from the Keynesians, who were looking for a convincing way to model the monetary implications of their model. Building on Modigliani's standard specification of the labour supply curve and on Phillips' hints,[13] Lipsey soon provided the standard Keynesian interpretation.[14] In this view, the Phillips curve reflects the disequilibrium dynamics of money wages taking into account their downward rigidity. Mainstream Keynesian economists assumed that this regularity was independent of changes in policy and thus interpreted it as a menu of policy choices as if each point of the curve could be a sustainable equilibrium. Therefore, they claimed that policy makers could choose along the curve the combination of inflation and unemployment that best suited social preferences.[15]

Milton Friedman, who was then the main challenger of Keynesian orthodoxy, rejected this interpretation and provided an alternative one with radically different policy implications.[16] He pointed out that the standard Keynesian interpretation of the Phillips curve had to rely on an alleged systematic link between the monetary side of the economy (money inflation) and the real side of the economy (unemployment), violating a basic principle of classical economics: the long-run dichotomy between the monetary and real parts of the economic system. This alternative vision interprets the Phillips curve as a mere synthetic representation of short-term disequilibrium dynamics. Any short-term equilibrium of unemployment based on this dynamic process is by definition temporary and unstable, while only one specific unemployment rate could be consistent with the long-term equilibrium of the system.

Within this conceptual framework, the long-term Phillips curve is just a vertical line crossing the horizontal axis in correspondence with the long-term equilibrium rate of unemployment called the "natural rate of unemployment". Therefore, in Friedman's view, any attempt by policy makers to engineer a lower rate of unemployment was destined to accelerate inflation and progressively shift the short-term Phillips curve upwards because of adaptive expectation dynamics. The policy implications of this interpretation were completely different from those descending from the Keynesian interpretation. Full employment and countercyclical policies were claimed to be counterproductive, being condemned to increase inflation and eventually unemployment beyond the natural rate, in order to normalise the excessive inflation rate. The policy advocated by Friedman relied on the capacity of unfettered markets to establish and maintain the natural rate of unemployment, and on the central bank's capacity to maintain monetary stability by implementing a moderate fixed rate of growth of money supply.[17]

Friedman's interpretation of the Phillips curve managed to gain a rapidly growing consensus among macroeconomists and policy makers because it seemed fully consistent with the contemporaneous empirical evidence. On the contrary, the Keynesian exponents had to introduce exogenous causal factors to reconcile their interpretation with the empirical evidence, but many economists perceived these factors as ad hoc.[18] Therefore, Friedman won the crucial battle over the Phillips curve, and this was a key initial episode in the anti-Keynesian revolution that—in less than a decade—managed to oust Keynesian economics from its hegemonic role in science and policy.

In the late 1970s, a new paradigm took over the hegemonic role in macroeconomics, a paradigm that revived the classical principles in a much more radical way than monetarists themselves, providing the economic foundations to what I call in this book neoliberal policy strategy. Though Friedman's argument based on short-term dynamics affected by adaptive expectation had been remarkably successful, an emerging generation of economists believed that this approach left too much room for an alternative interpretation based on a different specification of the model. The new approach pioneered by Robert Lucas, New Classical Economics, denied any value to disequilibrium analysis and to the distinction between short and long period, and provided new foundations based on the Arrow–Debreu equilibrium model. In this model, the so-called short-run equilibrium is nothing but the long-term equilibrium perturbed by short-run exogenous factors, while expectations are rational and unemployment is always voluntary.[19] In this view, the only role of macroeconomic policy is to design and implement structural reforms meant to make the real market as similar as possible to the perfect competition model.[20]

As this example shows, the interpretation of the empirical evidence is crucial in building a bridge between pure theory and facts, and the way we build this bridge has huge implications for understanding the phenomenon under scrutiny and drawing the correct policy implications. This stage of economic research is the crucial one to provide precise meanings and implications to a certain theory, model, or concept; so it is surprising that its importance is often played down or altogether neglected. In particular, too often the economic arguments disregard a crucial truth: there is never just one univocal interpretation, even when researchers agree on the empirical evidence or on pure theory.

1.4   The Role of Vision in Empirical Science

Typically, any significant theory evolves over time, like a living being. It has a genesis, an evolution, and a decline. To understand the life cycle of a theory, it is of crucial importance to introduce a further structural component: the "vision" underlying the theory and its life cycle, expressing, so to say, its "soul". In particular, the vision plays a vital role in the genesis of a theory, as it provides the basic motivations and fundamental guidelines for its construction. This crucial role is recognised also in natural sciences, where the role played by what I call "vision" is often studied under different names, especially "scientific paradigm"[21] or "research programme".[22]

In economics, Schumpeter rightly emphasised the key role of the "pre-analytic vision" in his monumental history of economic analysis.[23] The language he uses, however, seems to imply that a theory that has reached the maturity stage (that of an analytical model) has an evolution of its own, so that its meaning and implications become independent of the vision. I am inclined to argue that Schumpeter, notwithstanding the terminology adopted (*pre-analytic* vision), does not exclude that the vision may retain a crucial role even in the later stages of the life cycle of a theory when it reaches the stage of full-fledged *analysis*. In any case, in my opinion, this is what a researcher should assume when scrutinising and comparing theories and their evolution. It is important to understand the decisive role of vision in all the stages of research, since it is the fundamental source of interpretation, determining a theory's meanings and policy implications. What follows will be in keeping with this methodological insight.

The inadequacy of the specification of a model as representative of the underlying vision provides the basic motivations and guidelines for its evolution. The decline of a certain vision determines the decadence, and eventually the demise, of the theories and models that it has inspired, and this eventually leads to the adoption of a different vision having dissimilar interpretive and policy implications.

I have to emphasise that many economists do not accept the point of view adopted in this book on the crucial importance of the vision in economics. According to many of them, there is only one possible interpretation of the empirical evidence. The correct interpretation emerges as soon as we connect the available data to the most advanced theory through up-to-date statistical and econometric methods. This point of view leads to the dangerous conviction that "There Is No Alternative" (henceforth TINA): a deeply misleading fallacy that I will call in what follows "TINA fallacy".

According to the alternative point of view adopted in this book, there is never a univocal interpretation of the empirical evidence for three basic reasons: first, the empirical evidence itself is theory-laden;[24] second, there are always several up-to-date theories to which the empirical evidence may be connected; and third, there are different statistical and econometric methods that, once applied to the same empirical evidence, lead to different conclusions. As Popper bluntly asserted, "whenever a theory appears to you the only possible one, take this as a sign that you have neither understood the theory nor the problems it was intended to solve" (Popper 1972, 266). Honest researchers should thus try hard to avoid any form of the TINA fallacy. They should in particular engage in the time-consuming endeavour of giving a critical interpretation of the theory under scrutiny by clarifying under which conditions it is true or untrue. This presupposes a pluralist point of view such as that passionately advocated by John Stuart Mill:

> First, if any opinion is compelled to silence, that opinion may … be true. To deny this is to assume our own infallibility. Secondly, though the silenced opinion be an error, it may, and very commonly does, contain a portion of truth; and since the general or prevailing opinion on any subject is rarely or never the whole truth, it is only by the collision of adverse opinions that the remainder of the truth has any chance of being supplied. Thirdly, even if the received opinion be not only true, but the whole truth; unless it is suffered to be, and actually is, vigorously and earnestly contested, it will, by most of those who receive it, be held in the manner of a prejudice, with little comprehension or feeling of its rational grounds. (Mill 1859, 72)

This famous and oft-quoted excerpt from Mill is worth repeating here for two reasons. First, it is difficult to express the need for an open-minded and pro-active pluralism with better words. Second, this enlightened message epitomises well the best side of classical liberalism that seems to have been lost today. In particular, this book will argue that many advocates of the neoliberal doctrines often rely on the TINA fallacy to defend and promote their point of view, although it is in blatant contradiction with the high liberal principles so well enunciated by John Stuart Mill.

The pluralist approach here advocated does not need to fall into the traps of scepticism or relativism. A serious researcher should choose what believes to be the most robust interpretation and try to convince rational interlocutors of its superiority over the alternative interpretations. He should always be aware that the arguments put forward in support of the preferred interpretation are not compelling demonstrations but just rational arguments meant to persuade rational interlocutors. This was the point of view of Keynes,[25] which was later developed by enlightened epistemologists and philosophers of science such as Toulmin and Perelman.[26]

In the neoliberal period, economics has progressively become less authoritative and more authoritarian: less authoritative for its conspicuous inability to forecast and control the crises and the factors of unsustainability that this book is going to investigate and more authoritarian for its growing addiction to the TINA fallacy. The growing reliance of peer review and education policy on bibliometric methods has greatly incentivised a one-sided approach in economics. Authoritarianism is a typical self-defence of the exponents of a degenerating paradigm. The presumption of many economists unabated by the crushing failures of their discipline seems to confirm that this a real risk in economics.

No doubt, many economists practice their profession with passion and rigour and do not deserve the above criticisms. Still, the instrumental use of economics for political purposes has increased in the recent decades. Whenever a coalition of interests wants the adoption and implementation of an unpopular policy measure, typically it resorts to the TINA fallacy as a powerful argument of persuasion or at least justification: "Science agrees that there is no alternative". What is particularly depressing is that economists themselves too often contribute, as advisors of governments or collaborators of mass media, to justify, or sometimes even promote, the instrumental use of their discipline. I hope that most economists of all tendencies and scientific schools should agree to start a campaign against the instrumental use of their discipline.

In what follows, I will try hard to avoid both scepticism and relativism without falling into the trap of authoritarian science. To this end, I will adopt a precise point of view, the point of view of sustainable development, keeping a critical awareness of its validity conditions.

1.5 Growth and Development: Three Visions

An in-depth understanding of the point of view of sustainable development requires first a clarification of the relationship between "growth" and development. Three alternative visions of this relationship must be sharply distinguished: the mainstream vision, that of sustainable development, and that of "degrowth". In the economic and political language, the meaning attached to the word "growth" without adjective is clear: everyone understands that it means a positive increase of the Gross Domestic Product (GDP) usually measured by its percentage rate of change. What is controversial is the meaning of the word "development".

Every scholar and expert would concede that the concept of development is significantly broader than that of growth as development refers not only to the variations of a particular index of well-being such as the GDP, but also more in general to individual, economic, social, technological, and institutional features that play a crucial role in any historical process. In addition, while growth usually refers to the economy as a whole, any serious analysis of development has to take account of the structural change that characterises any evolutionary process in the economy and society.

The mainstream point of view admits that development has a broader meaning than growth, but believes that, generally speaking, growth is a necessary and sufficient condition of development. This conviction is so robust and widespread that generated a confusing assimilation of the two concepts in economic and political discourse. In mainstream economics, a clear distinction between the two terms is operational only in the case of developing countries that are the concern of a specific specialised branch of economics: development economics. Underlying the distinction between "growth theory" and "development economics" is the analogy with the distinction between adulthood and the previous phases of development of a human being. The latter are perceived as characterised by a rapid structural change converging towards the full-fledged structure of adulthood whose further structural change is believed to be much slower and immaterial for many purposes, to study, for example, its standard physiology and pathology.

The usual confusion between growth and development is justified by a series of arguments rooted in the scholarly literature that provide a specific interpretation to the available empirical evidence. I single out three of the arguments that play a crucial role in buttressing this vision.

The first argument supports the idea that the index of GDP is a reliable measure of well-being. This opinion is clearly unfounded. As is well known since long, GDP accounting neglects many factors that heavily impinge on well-being such as social and environmental externalities or relational goods. On the contrary, it takes into account factors that do not add to well-being of individuals such as the "defensive expenses" that only aim to protect it from negative influences that have already occurred or may occur. The believers in the substantial reliability of GDP accounting maintain that the distortions introduced by the factors neglected, or unduly considered, do not modify substantially the overall picture. On the contrary, since the real markets do not comply with the assumptions of a perfectly competitive market, we should expect significant deviations of their behaviour from that of a competitive market as predicted by general equilibrium theory.[27]

A growing stream of empirical literature on self-reported happiness confirms this conjecture. This literature, started in the 1970s, systematically exploits the growing availability of detailed and articulated time series on self-reported well-being, also called subjective happiness. This literature has provided a wealth of insights on the nature, dimensions, and causes of costs and benefits not registered by the market (also called negative and positive "externalities"). In particular, despite the continuous growth of GDP since World War II, self-reported well-being did not increase in developed countries such as the USA and Japan. Analogously, the continuous improvement of health, as measured by objective comprehensive indexes such as life expectancy, did not translate into more happiness, although most respondents rank health as the main determinant of well-being. Extensive empirical research clarified that the main factors of happiness and health are largely overlapping. GDP is crucial in both cases but only up to a surprisingly low threshold between \$10,000 and \$15,000 per year, after which the main factors affecting happiness and health are social factors (such as inequality, relational goods, education, and unemployment) completely neglected by GDP accounting.[28]

The positive correlation often observed between growth and inequality, for example, in recent decades, deeply questions the widespread assimilation of growth to development. The main defence from this charge relies on an optimist interpretation of an alleged empirical regularity called "Kuznets curve" by the name of the economist who first hypothesised its existence.[29] According to Kuznets, the empirical relationship between inequality and per capita income describes an inverted-U curve. According to his tentative interpretation, while the process of modernisation increases per capita income, it also increases income inequality because the diffusion of the process requires time and determines a massive migration of the population from the countryside where income inequality is low towards industrial towns where the incomes are much more disperse. At a certain point, however, there is a reaction against the growing social disequilibria, leading the government to adopt redistributive measures through progressive taxation, social transfers, and insurance.

Many mainstream economists draw from this conjecture an optimist message. Although the process of modernisation initially increases inequality, one may be confident that eventually the process itself will spontaneously invert its course. Kuznets and his followers found support to this conjecture in the time series referring to the whole nineteenth century up to World War II. While extensive econometric work in the 1960s and 1970s seemed to corroborate the Kuznets' hypothesis, since the 1980s the statistical fit of the new econometric investigations became increasingly poor as the time series progressively incorporated the data reflecting the new phase of increase in income inequality started in the late 1970s. We have to conclude that the spontaneous evolution of markets does not assure the required reduction in inequality, not even in the longer run.[30]

The third argument justifying the assimilation of growth to development relies on an optimist interpretation of the environmental Kuznets curve (EKC), an interpretive hypothesis of the empirical evidence on the correlation between growth and environmental deterioration systematically explored since the early 1990s.[31] This approach claims that, following a pattern similar to that of the Kuznets curve, in many cases the indexes of environmental deterioration increased in the first phase of industrialisation eventually declining after a peak. The advocates of this approach argue that this trend occurs in the case of many environmental pollutants, such as sulphur dioxide, nitrogen oxide, DDT, chlorofluorocarbons, and other chemicals released directly into the air or water.

The standard explanation of this alleged empirical regularity relies on the typical evolution of the productive structure in an industrialising country. Its economy typically develops first the heavy industry that is highly polluting, then the light industry, and finally the sector of services that are progressively less polluting. In addition, they assume that, after a certain threshold, the public opinion exerts a growing pressure on governments in favour of green policies. If the empirical evidence were corroborating the EKC, we should expect that the spontaneous evolution of markets would eventually solve the environmental problems originated in the early stages of industrialisation. Unfortunately, the empirical evidence corroborates to some extent the hypothesis only for a limited number of indicators such as sulphur dioxide that is responsible for acid rain, or particulate matter that is responsible for serious respiratory diseases including lung cancer. In both cases the nexus between cause and effect is clear and direct and calls for effective polices to reduce the emissions of these pollutants.

In other cases, the empirical evidence shows a new wave of environmental deterioration in recent years. A case in point is the concentration of coliform bacteria in freshwater that seems to be the effect of a weakening of policies directed to safeguard the quality of water.[32] Moreover, there is little evidence that the relationship holds true for other aspect of environmental deterioration. For example, energy, land, and resource use do not fall with rising income. While the ratio of energy per real GDP has fallen, total energy use is still rising in most developed countries. In addition, the status of many key ecosystem services provided by ecosystems, such as freshwater provision and regulation, soil fertility, and fisheries, have continued to decline in developed countries. Moreover, some of the most important indicators of environmental deterioration, such as the emission rate of greenhouse gases (GHGs), are continuing to grow without any sign of inversion.[33]

The EKC is thus not general and robust enough to justify optimistic expectations independently of a specific policy strategy. In addition, environmental deterioration depends not only on per capita income but also on other factors, in particular, demographic and technological factors.[34] These examples suggest that the available empirical evidence does not confirm the conviction that growth is, broadly speaking, a necessary and sufficient condition of development.

The second vision on the relationship between growth and development maintains that growth is in general neither a necessary nor a sufficient condition of development. Growth may be consistent with development if, and only if, it complies with a series of sustainability conditions. Sustainability refers to the capacity of a process to be endured, or to be maintained and improved. This term acquired a specialised meaning in ecology where it came to describe biological systems, such as wetlands or forests, which may survive and evolve in healthy conditions without irreversible depletion of resources or deterioration of their environmental qualities. By extension, the "Brundtland Report",[35] commissioned by the United Nations, introduced the neologism "sustainable development" that refers to the long-term well-being of socio-economic systems in the light of the interaction between their economic, environmental, and social conditions.[36]

The third vision rejects both the alternative visions mentioned above. This view regards the negative growth of GDP as a necessary, although by no means sufficient, condition for the well-being of people, at least in developed countries. This point of view rejects the mainstream alternative vision based on the systematic diffusion of consumerism and the unconstrained exploitation of natural resources to maximise the rate of growth. In this view, the mainstream development paradigm is inconsistent with the necessary reduction of the human imprint on the biosphere, while market-oriented technical change is unable to solve the most important environmental and social problems.

This point of view also rejects the second vision. Sustainable development is seen as a contradiction in terms (or an oxymoron) since, contrary to the view maintained here and accepted by many other researchers, development is identified with growth.[37] This point of view may have crept also into the theory of sustainable development and, to the extent, this is true; it is rightly criticised.[38] This criticism, however, does not describe correctly the approach of sustainable development, as here advocated, that sharply distinguishes growth and development. Although the criticisms levelled by degrowth theory against the standard paradigm of unrestrained growth are often convincing, the downsizing of economic activity is neither a necessary nor a sufficient condition of sustainability.

Within the current model of development, degrowth would only make things much worse as the Great Recession and the ensuing Eurocrisis have clearly proved. On the contrary, in a radically different model of sustainable development—such as that advocated in this book—some activities inconsistent with sustainability should contract while other activities should increase their size to strengthen it. Serge Latouche, the main exponent of this approach, has recently made clear that degrowth should not be understood as negative growth but rather as a growth, that is, a plea to shift the attention on the qualitative issues of development.[39] In this interpretation, the analysis and policy implications of this vision largely overlap with those of sustainable development in the version here advocated.

Summing up, the crucial issue is the definition and implementation of a new model of development capable to be fully sustainable even in the long period. Many scientific disciplines and points of view must constructively collaborate to realise this task. To this end, the catalysing concept of sustainable development should be sharply distinguished from the reductionist and misleading concept of growth.

1.6   Sustainable Development, Fairness, and Free Markets

By development, I mean the expansion and deepening of human freedom.[40] This process is not easily measurable as it has many dimensions. A greater availability of capital, goods, and services increases freedom of choice but this is significant only if it relaxes the existing constraints on the access to basic goods (food, health, and home). Once the basic needs are satisfied, much more important becomes the freedom of self-realisation that depends on the social and natural environment.

According to the standard definition of sustainable development suggested by the Brundtland Commission, development is sustainable if it satisfies present-day needs without compromising the capacity of future generations to satisfy their own needs.[41] This definition has robust ethical foundations on a criterion of equity in the distribution of resources between successive generations and within each generation. The *inter-*generational criterion focuses on the conservation of the quantity and quality of environmental goods since the well-being of future generations crucially depends on the state of the biosphere inherited by the preceding generations. The *intra-generational* criterion focuses on the social indexes that reflect distributional equity such as inequality and poverty. Therefore, the definition of sustainable development invites attention on both the environmental and social conditions of sustainability and their interaction.

The ethical foundations underlying the concept of sustainable development are sound and important on their own sake; however, they are strictly linked with far-reaching economic foundations that are rarely made explicit. As the founding fathers of liberalism (such as Smith and Stuart Mill) made clear, the correct functioning of competitive markets presupposes a substantial equality in the starting points of all the participants to market competition. Otherwise, we cannot be sure that the winners of the myriad of overlapping competitions constituting a free market will be the deserving competitors because of their effective performance. This is an obvious, though much neglected, pre-requisite of a genuine competitive market. It is thus also a necessary assumption for the argument that the co-ordination of economic activity through a competitive market maximises the welfare of society.

The equality of initial conditions may seem a utopian requisite; however, what is required by this argument is not absolute equality of income and wealth but only an effective access by everyone to the fundamental economic opportunities. Only in this case the game of market competition is played on a "level playing field". The existing distribution of income is clearly inconsistent with the crucial requisite of a substantially equal access to the relevant economic opportunities, also because in the last three decades income inequality has increased in most countries while the welfare state has been sizeably weakened.[42] A related argument emphasises the negative impact of poverty on the social sustainability of a community. In the absence of adequate help from the community, a person born poor is excluded from higher education and many crucial opportunities so that the potential contributions to his own welfare and that of the community are severely limited.

Also the environmental conditions of sustainability have important economic implications. The pollution of the biosphere reduces the productivity of earth and forests and imposes huge costs to clean up water, soil, and air. The climate change induced by the emissions of GHGs in the atmosphere forces costly defensive interventions to compensate the huge damages and mitigate the expected catastrophic impacts.[43] Finally, there is a vicious circle between social and environmental conditions of sustainability. In particular, since the poor rely mainly on the direct exploitation of natural resources (e.g. traditional biomass for energy), an increase in poverty tends to increase their overexploitation.

1.7   The Life Cycle of Development Paradigms

I define "development trajectory" a process of structural change that broadly maintains a steady direction for a certain time. This usually occurs only for a limited duration lasting no more than a few decades. It is useful to identify the successive trajectories of the development process because each of them has different origins, features, and consequences. The direction pursued by each trajectory depends on the dominant development paradigm that sets the direction of change to improve the well-being of people. Each development paradigm implements its goals by adopting a specific policy strategy believed to be optimal to reach the desired goals, given the existing conditions and constraints.

The consequences of the effective process of development vary through time and determine a sort of typical life cycle of development paradigms. At the beginning, the results of the new paradigm are typically good enough to continue its implementation. The negative side effects gradually emerge and cumulate their disruptive consequences until they trigger a "great crisis", namely a crisis particularly deep and persistent. The blame for the crisis is typically laid on the policy strategy pursued in the preceding phase and thus also on its underlying paradigm rooted in the ruling macroeconomic theory. In such a situation, a new macroeconomic theory emerges and becomes dominant providing the foundations for a new development paradigm and fostering the adoption of a new policy strategy to implement it. This interaction between the evolution of the macroeconomic performance of industrialised countries and the co-evolution of macroeconomics became systematic since the Industrial Revolution in the late eighteenth century and became increasingly effective hereafter.

The historical record shows a recurrent sequence of stages in this evolutionary process. A "great crisis" usually yields a change of paradigm in macroeconomics and, consequently, leads to the adoption of a new policy strategy advocated by the new mainstream paradigm. A serious analysis of each of these historical episodes cannot overlook their peculiarities. Therefore, the interaction between macroeconomic paradigms, policy strategies, and evolution of markets should not be understood as a mechanistic feedback.

For lack of space, the following analysis of development trajectories is bound to be very schematic.[44] I start from the Industrial Revolution occurred at the turn of the eighteenth century and the contemporaneous foundations of modern political economy by Adam Smith. We may interpret *The Wealth of Nations* as a particularly deep and far-sighted expression of the emerging reaction to the crisis of mercantilism brought about by the first Industrial Revolution, a reaction that was in tune with the views and interests of the emerging bourgeoisie.[45] The new Smithian view of free markets as self-regulating mechanisms—managed by a providential (although invisible) hand—had a pervasive impact not only on economic thought but also on the evolution of emerging capitalism. In particular, the liberal policy strategy suggested by this new vision acquired in the subsequent decades a growing influence with decision makers and public opinion, affecting the policies pursued by industrialising countries, particularly since the middle of nineteenth century.

The mild but persistent period of crisis extending from 1873 to 1896,[46] generally called Long Depression, did not question the basic principles of classical liberalism but justified systematic deviations from it and contributed to stimulate a new, more sophisticated, version of the liberal view that I suggest to call "Updated Liberalism". This version of liberalism explicitly rejected the rigid prescriptions of traditional laissez-faire and reconsidered in a more accurate and far-sighted way where the policy makers should fix the boundaries between free market and state. Marshall, Wicksell, and their pupils gave important contributions in this spirit around the turn of the century. However, their new ideas were hardly influential on policy makers who persisted to pay lip service to the traditional laissez-faire prescriptions but in fact were obsequious to the imperialistic ambitions of national policies. This contributed to the outbreak of World War I and eventually to the outburst of the Great Depression started in 1929.

The Great Depression was a much deeper crisis than the preceding ones after the Industrial Revolution, a crisis that produced a radical change of direction in both history of facts and history of thought. The crisis undermined the trust in self-regulating markets favouring the emergence of approaches meant to explain the weakness of the invisible hand and the need of state intervention to restore full employment equilibrium. This set the terrain for the Keynesian Revolution. In the *General Theory* Keynes explained why free markets are unable to self-regulate themselves and why the classical economic theory is unable to cope with this fundamental problem.[47] The new macroeconomic paradigm suggested by Keynes led to a new conception of economic policy in which the state plays a broader role to help the market to maintain or restore full employment equilibrium. The new policy strategy based on Keynesian macroeconomics took a more concrete shape in the troubled 1940s that required a public management of the war economy and of the post-war reconstruction.

When the conditions for growth resurfaced in the early 1950s, the Keynesian theory became the dominant macroeconomic theory. Mainstream Keynesianism, however, sought a synthesis between the ideas of Keynes and those of neoclassical economics. The so-called neoclassical synthesis aimed to bring together Keynes' theory and the updated version of the "classical theory" although the latter had been heavily criticised in his masterwork. This eclectic view maintains that, in principle, the invisible hand should be free to operate. It recognises, however, that the huge macroeconomic failure of involuntary unemployment requires a strategy of policy interventions meant to avoid involuntary unemployment. This policy strategy was synergic with the establishment of the so-called "welfare state" aiming to sustain full employment and redistribute income in favour of the less-advantaged citizens.

This view underlays a period of rapid growth accompanied by a sizeable reduction of poverty and inequality in the 1950s and 1960s, but became increasingly unsustainable because of two related shortcomings. First, it favoured a growing hypertrophy of public expenditure that rapidly increased its share in the GDP of industrialised countries from about 10–20 % in the 1920s to about 40–50 % in the 1970s.

This process went beyond what was necessary to sustain the welfare state and the countercyclical policies to maintain full employment. In addition, it was often accompanied by a progressive increase of bureaucracy, cronyism, and corruption. Second, it exhibited an inflationary bias due to the growing strength of trade unions in a full employment regime. In the 1960s and early 1970s, this bias translated in periodic bouts of wage increases meant to improve, or defend, the share of wages in GDP leading to policy-induced fluctuations. The growing level and dispersion of inflation rates determined by stop-go policies contributed to end the Bretton Woods monetary regime by building up cumulative tensions on the currency exchange rates.

After a period of transition characterised at the same time by stagnation and inflation ("stagflation"), lasting until the late 1970s, a new development paradigm emerged, the neoliberal one, that is still ruling the economy notwithstanding the devastating crisis started in 2007.

Notes

1. See Lo (2012) and the comments by Blyth (2013).
2. Vercelli (2011b).
3. Perez (2002).
4. Kindleberger and Aliber (2011, 6th edition).
5. For a critical application of this tripartition to economics, see Vercelli (1999b).
6. It has been contended that there is no such a thing as a "pure" theory, as any theory, whatever its degree of abstraction, is affected at every stage of its elaboration—implicitly if not explicitly—by its semantic and pragmatic implications (see e.g. Suppe 1977). I agree with this proviso, but I see nothing wrong, in a particular stage of the analysis, with provisionally neglecting, for the sake of analysis, the semantic and pragmatic presuppositions and implications of the argument.
7. Debreu (1959).
8. For the purposes of this book, it is not necessary to enter into the controversial issues raised by the distinction in the empirical inference between induction and abduction.
9. See Popper (1969 and 1972); Suppe (1977).
10. Phillips (1958).
11. See in particular Chap. 5.
12. The Phillips curve is sometimes expressed as a relation between rate of growth of money prices and unemployment. Since money wages and nominal prices are strictly correlated, the two versions of the Phillips curve are very similar, and we need not distinguish them for the purposes of this book.

13. Modigliani (1944).
14. Lipsey (1960).
15. Samuelson and Solow (1960).
16. See in particular Friedman (1968).
17. As a rule of thumb, Friedman suggested a rate of growth of money supply of 2 %, roughly corresponding to the labour productivity growth trend.
18. Some critics likened the allegedly ad hoc introduction of these additional factors to the introduction of epicycles by Ptolemaic astronomers to defend the geocentric theory.
19. The new approach, soon called New Classical Economics, was summarised and motivated by Lucas himself in the collection of his first essays published in the 1970s (Lucas 1981).
20. Vercelli (1991).
21. Kuhn (1962).
22. See in particular Lakatos (1978), and Latsis (1976).
23. Schumpeter (1954).
24. This assertion has been emphasised by epistemologists and philosophers of science. See, for example, the survey of Suppe (1977).
25. See in particular Keynes (1921).
26. See in particular Toulmin (1958) and Perelman (1969).
27. See Chap. 2.
28. See for example the critical survey of this literature by Borghesi and Vercelli (2012).
29. Kuznets (1955).
30. Extensive empirical studies have recently confirmed this opinion. See for example Milanović (2005), Stiglitz (2012), and Piketty (2014).
31. Among the early contributions, see Panayotou (1993); Grossman and Krueger (1993); Selden and Song (1994); and Shafik (1994). For a critical assessment of the literature on the EKC, see for example Borghesi and Vercelli (2008).
32. See for example Borghesi and Vercelli (2008).
33. See in particular IPCC (2014).
34. See for example Borghesi and Vercelli (2008).
35. See WCED (1987).
36. I discuss further this concept in the next section.
37. It is surprising that the advocates of degrowth accept the same meaning of development adopted by mainstream economics. A possible explana-

tion is that the leading advocates of this vision, though critical of mainstream economics, on this crucial point accept its terminology.
38. See Klein (2015) for a series of examples that go in this direction.
39. Latouche (2009).
40. See Vercelli (1998a), and Sen (1999).
41. WCED (1987).
42. See for example Milanović (2005), Stiglitz (2012), and Piketty (2014).
43. IPCC (2014).
44. A more detailed account may be found in Vercelli (2011b).
45. Smith (1776).
46. This periodisation takes into account mainly the UK experience (see e.g. Musson 1959), while in the USA some economic historians restrict the period of crisis to a much shorter time length: 1873–1879 (see e.g. Fels 1949). This crisis was the first truly international economic crisis but had different characteristics and time profiles in different countries. The period was characterised in many countries by persistent price deflation and a significant slowing down of the average rate of growth with a few more limited periods of mild recession. However, the economic and financial turmoil was sufficiently deep and persistent to be called "Great Depression" until the more catastrophic crisis of the 1930s appropriated this name. In the light of the crisis of the 1930s and the recent one started in 2007, the name "Long Depression" attributed to this historical episode sounds more appropriate.
47. Keynes (1936).

Bibliography

Blyth, Mark. 2013. *Austerity. The History of a Dangerous Idea.* Oxford: Oxford University Press.

Borghesi, Simone, and Alessandro Vercelli. 2008. *Global Sustainability. Social and Environmental Conditions.* Palgrave Macmillan: Basingstoke and New York.

———. 2012. Happiness and Health: Two Paradoxes. *Journal of Economic Surveys* 26(2): 203–233.

Debreu, Gérard. 1959. *The Theory of Value: An Axiomatic Analysis of Economic Equilibrium.* New York: John Wiley and Sons.

Fels, Rendigs. 1949. The Long-Wave Depression, 1873–79. *The Review of Economics and Statistics* 31(1): 69–73.

Friedman, Milton. 1968. The Role of Monetary Policy. *The American Economic Review* 58(1): 1–17.

Grossman, Gene H., and Allan B. Krueger. 1993. Environmental Impacts of a North American Free Trade Agreement. In *The Mexico-U.S. Free Trade Agreement*, ed. Peter M. Garber. Cambridge, Mass: MIT Press.

IPCC. 2014. *Fifth Assessment Report—Climate Change 2014: Mitigation of Climate Change*. Geneva Switzerland: Intergovernmental Panel on Climate Change.

Keynes, John Maynard. 1921. *A Treatise on Probability*. London: Macmillan.

———. 1936 [1973]. *The General Theory of Employment, Interest and Money*. (The Collected Writings of John Maynard Keynes. Volume 7). London and Cambridge: Macmillan and Cambridge University Press.

Kindleberger, Charles P., and Robert Z. Aliber. 2011. *Manias, panics and crashes: a history of financial crises*, 6 edn. New York: Palgrave Macmillan.

Klein, Naomi. 2015. *This Changes Everything: Capitalism vs. the Climate. 2014.* London: Penguin.

Kuhn, Thomas S. 1962. *The Structure of Scientific Revolutions*. Chicago: Chicago University Press.

Kuznets, Simon. 1955. Economic Growth and Income Inequality. *American Economic Review* 45: 1–28.

Lakatos, Imre. 1978. *The Methodology of Scientific Research Programmes*. Cambridge: Cambridge University Press.

Latouche, Serge. 2009. *Farewell to Growth*. Cambridge: Polity Press.

Latsis, Spiro J., ed. 1976. *Method and Appraisal in Economics*. Cambridge: Cambridge University Press.

Lipsey, Richard G. 1960. The Relation Between Unemployment and the Rate of Change of Money Wage Rates in the United Kingdom, 1862–1957, a Further Analysis. *Economica* 27: 1–31.

Lo, Andrew W. 2012. Reading about the Financial Crisis: A Twenty-One-Book Review. *Journal of Economic Literature* 50(1): 151–178.

Lucas, Robert E. Jr. 1981. *Studies in Business-Cycle Theory*. Boston, Mass: MIT Press.

Mill, John S. 1859 [1978]. *On Liberty*. Indianapolis, IN: Hackett Publishing.

Milanović, Branko. 2005. *Worlds Apart: Measuring International and Global Inequality*. Princeton, NJ: Princeton University Press.

Modigliani, Franco. 1944. Liquidity Preference and the Theory of Interest and Money. *Econometrica* 12: 45–88.

Musson, Albert E. 1959. The Great Depression in Britain, 1873–1896: A Reappraisal. *The Journal of Economic History* 19(2): 199–228.

Panayotou, Theodore. 1993. Empirical Tests and Policy Analysis of Environmental Degradation at Different Stages of Economic Development. In *Working Paper WP238, Technology and Employment Programme*. Geneva: International Labour Office.

Perelman, Chaïm. 1969. *The New Rhetoric: A Treatise on Argumentation*. Indiana: University of Notre Dame Press.

Perez, Carlota. 2002. *Technological Revolutions and Financial Capital: The Dynamics of Bubbles and Golden Ages*. Cheltenham: Edward Elgar.

Phillips, Alban W.H. 1958. The Relation between Unemployment and the Rate of Change of Money Wage Rates in the United Kingdom, 1851–1957. *Economica* 25: 283–299.

Piketty, Thomas. 2014. *Capital in the Twenty-First Century*. Cambridge Mass: Harvard University Press.

Popper, Karl R. 1969. *Conjectures and Refutations*. London: Routledge.

Popper, Karl R 1972. *Objective Knowledge. An Evolutionary Approach*. New York: Oxford University Press.

Samuelson, Paul A., and Robert M. Solow. 1960. Analytical Aspects of Anti-Inflation Policy. *American Economic Review* 50(2): 177–194.

Schumpeter, Joseph A 1954. *History of Economic Analysis*. Oxford: Oxford University Press.

Selden, Thomas M., and Daqing Song. 1994. Environmental Quality and Development: Is There a Kuznets Curve for Air Pollution Emissions? *Journal of Environmental Economics and Management* 27: 147–162.

Sen, Amartya K. 1999. *Development as Freedom*. New York: Alfred A. Knopf.

Shafik, Nemat. 1994. Economic Development and Environmental Quality: An Econometric Analysis. *Oxford Economic Papers, New Series* 46: 757–773.

Smith, Adam. 1776 [1977]. *An Inquiry into The Nature and Causes of the Wealth of Nations*. Edited by Edwin Cannan. Chicago: University of Chicago Press.

Stiglitz, Joseph E 2012. *The Price of Inequality. How Today's Divided Society Endangers our Future*. New York: W. W. Norton & Co.

Suppe, Frederick. 1977. *The Structure of Scientific Theories*. Urbana, Ill.: University of Illinois Press.

Toulmin, Stephen. 1958. *The Uses of Argument*, Revised edition 2003. Cambridge: Cambridge University Press.

Vercelli, Alessandro. 1991. *Methodological Foundations of Macroeconomics. Keynes and Lucas*. Cambridge: Cambridge University Press.

———. 1998a. Operational Measures of Sustainable Development and the Freedom of Future Generations. In *Sustainability: Dynamics and Uncertainty*, eds. Chichilnisky Graciela, Heal Geoffrey, and Alessandro Vercelli. Dordrecht: Martin Kluwer.

———. 1999b. Coherence, Meaning and Responsibility in the Language of Economics. In *Incommensurability and Translation. Kuhnian Perspectives on Scientific Communication and Theory Change*, eds. Rossini Favretti R., Sandri G., and R. Scazzieri, 351–367. Cheltenham: Elgar.

———. 2011b. Economy and Economics: The Twin Crises. In *The Global Economic Crisis. New Perspectives on the Critique of Economic Theory and Policy*, eds. Emiliano Brancaccio, and Giuseppe Fontana, 27–41. Abingdon and New York: Routledge.

WCED. 1987. *Our Common Future: Report of the World Commission on Environment and Development*. New York: Oxford University Press ("Bruntland Report").

Part I

Globalisation and Financialisation in a Long-Run Perspective

2

Freedom, Free Markets, and Neoliberalism

2.1 Introduction

In this chapter, I wish to provide some necessary background for the arguments I am going to develop in the following chapters. The main concept around which the entire book revolves is that of free market. A thorough clarification of this crucial concept requires a preliminary elucidation of the concept of freedom. No one today questions the pre-eminent value of individual freedom, but this concept is understood in such disparate ways as to support radically different, even opposite, viewpoints on politics and economics.[1] For the purposes of this book, I do not need to stray too far into the meanders of a never-ending debate, but I do have to clarify the meaning that I will attach to this crucial but ambiguous concept.

The subtitle of this book suggests that the belief—some would say faith—in the virtues of free markets that has deeply shaped the economy in the last half-century has been a delusion. This immediately raises a few questions that directly involve the concept of freedom: what are free markets? How can policy authorities intervene without unduly constraining the freedom of individuals? Should they try to enhance it? In what sense and for whom? To what extent and how?

© The Editor(s) (if applicable) and The Author(s) 2017

A. Vercelli, *Crisis and Sustainability*,

DOI 10.1057/978-1-137-60069-1_2

To answer these and related questions, I must first introduce a preliminary discussion of the basic concepts underlying my arguments, beginning with the concept of freedom (Sect. 2.2). I then move on to a critical scrutiny of the concept of free market (Sect. 2.3). In Sect. 2.4, I provide a brief reconstruction of the evolution of economic liberalism with the aim of clarifying the meanings attached to its main varieties. Section 2.5 suggests a definition, as rigorous as possible, of the controversial concept of neoliberalism that is going to play a crucial role in the rest of the book. Section 2.6 discusses the widespread misleading conception of the relationship between state and market as a zero-sum game. Section 2.7 links the results established in this chapter with a few issues I intend to discuss in the following chapters.

2.2   The Concept of Freedom

The well-known legal philosopher Gerald MacCallum convincingly argued that most uses of the liberty concept have a common logical structure. In this view, a rigorous concept of freedom must specify (i) to what agent or group of agents it refers; (ii) the contents of a non-empty set of options concerning what the agent may do or become (positive liberty); and (iii) the boundaries of the above option set defined by constraints that limit what the agent may do or become (negative liberty).[2] Focusing on a single agent, freedom (or liberty) is thus a triadic relationship between the agent, the contents of the option set describing the choices available to the agent, and its boundaries. According to this view, that is very influential in political and legal philosophy, any statement about the freedom or unfreedom of an agent specifies *what* a specific agent or group of agents is free or unfree to do or become, and *from* what constraints it is free or unfree to do or become.[3]

This point of view is consistent with the standard approach of decision theory and analytical economics, where the decision maker chooses the preferred option from a given set of available options. The extension of this option set represents and, under certain assumptions, measures the degree of positive liberty of the agent.[4] It is then possible to study what factors increase or constrain the option set that defines the freedom of the decision makers.

The triadic logical structure of the concept of freedom is of practical interest as soon as it is applied to a specific agent, or group of agents, to analyse the absence or presence of relevant constraints in the light of the available empirical evidence. To do so, the logical structure must be connected to the available evidence in a plausible way according to a specific interpretation, as argued in Chap. 1. Any assertion about liberty is subject to different interpretations, as is true or untrue depending on the definition given to each of the three polarities of the concept.

The crucial interpretive issues refer to the basic distinction between negative and positive liberty. This dichotomy has underlain several influential debates on freedom since World War II. The eminent political philosopher Isaiah Berlin brought this distinction, of Kantian origin,[5] to the forefront of the debate on liberty in an influential essay first published in 1958.[6] The negative liberty of an agent may be defined as *freedom from* specific constraints imposed on his potential or actual actions, while positive liberty may be defined as *freedom to* act for the realisation of the agent's goals.

Also in the case of liberty, we find that the interpretation of a concept plays a crucial role in defining its meaning and pragmatic implications. The preferred interpretation of the concept of liberty depends on the interpreter's political and economic vision and cannot thus be used—as Berlin, Hayek, Friedman, and other liberals and libertarians have done— to justify a particular view of liberty based on negative freedom and reject alternative visions. The only thing one can legitimately do is to provide thorough foundations to the arguments supporting one's interpretation in the hope of convincing the interlocutors of its soundness. I will argue in the next section that a thorough assessment of the pros and cons of free markets involves an analysis of their implications for both negative and positive freedom.

Classical liberalism focused on the negative concept of liberty since its objective was to limit the despotic power of the "Leviathan" (the sovereign supported by its bureaucratic apparatus).[7] From the political point of view, classical liberalism aimed to extend the limitations on the sovereign power introduced with the Magna Charta (1215) and then developed with the expansion of democracy. Early landmark steps in Great Britain were the Habeas Corpus Act of 1679 and the Bill of Rights in 1689 in the period of formation of classical liberalism. From the economic point of view, classical liberalism aimed to restrain the monopoly of economic power that was then managed by the sovereign according to mercantilist principles. The resurgence of liberalism after World War II as exemplified by Berlin, von Mises, Hayek, and Friedman was specifically motivated by the fear of the totalitarian degeneration that had produced the appalling destructions of war and was kept alive by the Cold War. In addition, in the view of conservative liberals, the state's excessive influence on the economy propped up by the systematic adoption of interventionist Keynesian policies and the build-up of the welfare state had progressively eroded citizens' negative liberty. These worries may explain the focus of post-war liberals on negative liberty but, as we will see, do not justify their neglect of positive liberty. For the time being, I observe that the triadic concept of freedom introduced in this section suggests that the opposition between positive and negative liberty emphasised by neoliberal thinkers is prima facie artificial and misleading, as this dichotomy distinguishes two complementary aspects of the concept of liberty rather than two irreconcilable conceptions of it.[8]

2.3   Free Market and Economic Liberalism

There is today a widespread conviction that free markets are the best way to organise economic production and exchange in a contemporary economy. This belief has strong implications for policy and politics, some of which I will discuss in this book. As is well known, the first economist who succeeded in building a robust argument in favour of this thesis was Adam Smith. Liberal ideas had been expressed before the publication of *The Wealth of Nations*, with particular rigour by the Physiocrats under the intellectual leadership of Turgot and Quesnay who exerted a significant influence also on Smith's masterwork.[9] Still, the primacy generally attributed to Smith is well-deserved for a few basic reasons.

First, he succeeded in providing a convincing representation of the working of a competitive market as a self-regulating system—not too dissimilar, as he saw it, from a Newtonian gravitational system—able to reach (or rapidly restore) equilibrium characterised by full employment of resources. This novel view established economics as an autonomous discipline centred on the concept of market.[10]

Second, he argued that a competitive market brings about the optimal allocation of resources that maximises the wealth of people.

Third, he argued compellingly that, contrary to the then-prevailing mercantilist view, these desirable results could be reached through the pursuit of self-interest by egoistic individuals rather than through the interventions of a supposedly benevolent government. To support this argument, he used the suggestive metaphor of the invisible hand, claiming that, although an egoistic economic agent intends only his own gain, "he is in this, as in many other cases, led by an invisible hand to promote an end which was no part of his intention … by pursuing his own interest he frequently promotes that of the society more effectually than when he really intends to promote it" (Smith 1776 [1977], vol. IV, 477).[11]

In modern economics, the most cogent support for Smith's invisible hand parable comes from the so-called "fundamental theorems of welfare economics".[12] The first of these theorems demonstrates that the equilibrium of every competitive economy is "Pareto efficient" in the sense that no one can be made better off without someone being made worse off. The second theorem proves that every Pareto efficient resource allocation can be attained through a competitive market mechanism provided that we choose the appropriate initial distribution. Both theorems are thus about the efficiency of a competitive market system evaluated by separating, through the specific concept suggested by Pareto, the issue of efficiency from the issues related to the distribution of resources among economic agents. This approach conveys the illusion of providing an "objective" measure of efficiency but has significant costs; in particular, the implications regarding inequality are altogether neglected. For example, if allocation B improves the payoff of one agent without affecting that of the other agents as compared to an initial allocation A, then B is considered to be more efficient than A, even though the distribution of resources is more unequal. This example shows that the scope and meaning of these theorems must be accurately examined, because the way in which they are understood deeply affects the interpretation of most economic models and their policy implications.

The advantage of having theorems as a foundation of the famous Smith's invisible hand assertion is that they allow a deep understanding of the conditions under which this assertion is true. These conditions are extremely strict and articulated. I need not list all of them to buttress my arguments. I will mention here only the conditions that play an active role in this book.

(a) The fundamental theorems of welfare economics demonstrate the efficiency of markets in terms of Pareto's very particular definition of efficiency. The decision to use this concept of efficiency is not just a matter of method-ological taste. Let us suppose that each round of market allocation, given an initial distribution of resources, leads to a more unequal distribution, as suggested by significant theoretical insights and extensive empirical evi-dence.[13] In this case, the classical liberal principle of equal liberty would call for iterated redistributive action on the part of the state to maintain a fair distribution of resources.[14] In these theorems, the market is assumed to be perfectly competitive. All agents are thus price takers, and no one can affect the prices and quantities established by the market process. Real markets are certainly not competitive in this sense because large firms can, and often do, manipulate the market by exercising their market power to their own advantage. This may also be true of rich families or other groups or coali-tions that can exert a significant influence on market processes through the political process.

(b) The outcomes of the market process also depend on assumptions regarding decision makers. In the general equilibrium models that provide the ana-lytic foundations for the theorems, agents are attributed characteristics quite different from the real-world ones. They are assumed to be fully ratio-nal in the sense that they correctly forecast the future value of the relevant variables, apart from the impact of stochastic shocks which by definition cannot be predicted (in other words, the agents entertain "rational expecta-tions"). This implies that all the agents have access to complete information, and there is thus no asymmetric information. Empirical evidence shows that this assumption is significantly counterfactual. Expectations, even on average, are not rational.[15]

(c) Markets must be complete; this is a stringent requirement of market effi-ciency.[16] For this condition to be true, any article of trade should be exchangeable at any time. Future markets, however, exist only for financial assets and standardised commodities (petrol, gold, and grains) for a limited number of future dates. Some economists have claimed that, although real markets are seriously incomplete, they could be completed by issuing ad hoc Arrow–Debreu securities.[17] However, as is generally recognised, this technique may reduce incompleteness but cannot dream of eliminating it.

(d) There are no externalities (costs or benefits not spontaneously registered by the market). Whenever this condition is violated and externalities are present, market resource allocation is inefficient unless the externalities are "internalised" through taxes or tradeable permits that force the market to take account of external costs and benefits.[18] The trouble with this solution is that it is extremely difficult to detect and measure market externalities in any concrete situation.

(e) Exchanges are not affected by transaction costs that would introduce a form of time irreversibility. Violation of this condition would be inconsistent with the necessary flexibility of the substitution processes required by this sort of model.

(f) There are no public goods.[19] Public goods are typically undersupplied in a perfectly competitive market because additional individuals may benefit from them without paying their cost, and it is impossible to exclude any individual from enjoying them.

(g) The perfect competition assumption entails the full employment of all available resources, including labour. Persistent unemployment is inconsistent with all the standard varieties of general equilibrium that assume either that the system is always in equilibrium or that full employment equilibrium is stable even in the short term.

(h) Agents operate in an environment characterised by weak uncertainly comparable to that associated with games of chance. The players do not know the outcome of the game, but do know the possible outcomes and their probabilities. This allows the application of the usual theory of (additive) probability, and of the standard decision theory based on the maximisation of expected utility. In the real market, uncertainty is often much more profound, because agents do not know all the possible outcomes. Uncertainty can thus be often represented only by a non-additive probability distribution or a plurality of probability distributions (strong uncertainty); in some cases, uncertainty cannot be sensibly represented by any sort of probability distribution at all (radical uncertainty).[20]

Though the above list of counterfactual assumptions underlying the invisible hand theorems is incomplete, it is sufficient to show that they are hardly consistent with the belief that Smith's invisible hand actually operates in reality. We could conclude that in the real markets, the invisible hand is invisible because it does not exist,[21] or is so weak that it is easily coerced by multinational corporations and banks too big to be subject to the market discipline. In any case, we have to keep in mind throughout this book that the chasm between real markets and the perfect competition market is vast and not easily bridged.

The existence of a gap between real markets and the perfect competition market model is universally recognised, albeit with different emphases and implications. Opinion is divided in particular on two crucial issues that will be discussed below. Considering this "market gap", can any version of the general equilibrium model be applied to the real world? Are real markets, unlike the general equilibrium model, liable to persistent disequilibria leading, for example, to structural unemployment, hyperinflation, crisis and depression?

To the first question, whether a general equilibrium model may be applied to the real world, mainstream economics gives an affirmative answer. Moreover, according to Lucas who shaped the methodological paradigm of contemporary macroeconomics, only models thoroughly microfounded in the Arrow–Debreu equilibrium model can be accepted as sound.[22] And what about the "market gap"? Mainstream economics provides two basic answers. The first defence was developed mainly by Friedman who maintained that in science, the realism of hypotheses does not matter, provided that the model worked out on the basis of these hypotheses predicts empirical outcomes better than rival models.[23] This "instrumentalist" point of view has been criticised even in natural science where the predictability test is much more easily and convincingly implemented. In any case, the predictive performance of mainstream economics has always been poor in turbulent times, as the recent crisis has made evident to the general public. Mainstream economists, however, have a second defence line that acts as a powerful protective belt to their research programme.[24] Since, as mentioned above, sound macroeconomics must be rigorously microfounded in general equilibrium theory to be coherent, intelligible and useful for policy,[25] the shortcomings of existing models—in particular the unbridged market gap—cannot question this research programme but are merely a stimulus to build a better generation of models. This argument raises complex methodological issues that will be resumed in the following sections and chapters. For the moment, I will limit myself to observing that this argument makes this research programme non-falsifiable, contrary to a widely accepted requisite of sound science.[26]

To the second question, whether real markets are liable to persistent disequilibria, mainstream economists have given a substantially negative answer, rooted in two basic arguments. First, what appears to be a persistent disequilibrium is in fact the consequence of exogenous shocks due mainly to policy errors. Whenever it is difficult to deny the existence of a market failure, as in the case of the Great Depression or the recent subprime crisis and the ensuing Great Recession, the justification is found in what I have called the "market gap". The remedy on the causes of the crisis relies thus on structural reforms meant to reduce the market gap through a policy based on deregulation and privatisation. This argument builds a second formidable protective belt around the neoliberal research programme, making it even more non-falsifiable. In this view, any market failure is ascribed to weak structural reforms that were unable to eliminate the market gap.

According to the economists who are critical of mainstream economics, each of the conditions of validity of the invisible hand assertion is—when violated—a source of market failure. And what is worse, these market failures are strictly interrelated and come together:

> Information problems often provide part of the explanation of missing markets. In turn, externalities are often thought to arise from missing markets: if fishermen could be charged for using fishing grounds—if there were a market for fishing rights—there would not be overfishing. Public goods are sometimes viewed as an extreme case of externalities, where others benefit from my production of the good as much as I do (Stiglitz 2000, 85).

Summing up, the desirability and implications of free markets crucially depend on the interpretation of both pure theory and available empirical evidence. The usual interpretation of the two fundamental theorems of welfare economics is that they confirm Smith's metaphor of the invisible hand: in this view, given a distribution of resources, a perfectly competitive market leads to the most efficient allocation of resources and thus to the maximisation of the agents' well-being. The fact that these conclusions are confirmed by specific theorems is taken as a sign of the rigour of the argument, giving it an unquestionable and inescapable scientific weight. However, this is not the only possible interpretation and, put in these simplistic terms, is profoundly misleading. An alternative interpretation could legitimately lead to the opposite conclusion: generally speaking, the real markets, being so different from a perfectly competitive market, realise neither the optimal allocation of resources nor the maximisation of agents' well-being. In principle, only collective action could correct the distortions of real markets and push the economy towards the optimal position.

As for observed market failures, two interpretive stances are possible: either they confirm the intrinsic shortcomings of unfettered real markets, or they suggest that the structural reforms advocated by the neoliberal paradigm have not been implemented with the necessary energy and consistency. After the Great Depression, the first interpretation prevailed, leading to the open-minded and moderate kind of liberalism that ruled in the Bretton Woods period (1950s and 1960s), while after the recent Great Recession, the second interpretation prevailed. In the rest of the book I will discuss which of these interpretations is more convincing.

2.4   Varieties of Economic Liberalism: Evolution and Suggested Definitions

In the preceding sections, I sought a common denominator to the main usages of the concepts of freedom and free market. It is much more difficult to find a common denominator to the concepts of liberalism (that I discuss in this section) and neoliberalism (that I discuss in the next section). As for liberalism, very few scholars have dared to provide one univocal definition.[27] The only common denominator one may find is that, in all varieties of liberalism, freedom is normatively basic, so any limitation of freedom, especially through coercive means, must be thoroughly justified. We might call this the *Fundamental Liberal Principle*.[28] The different varieties of liberalism then disagree on what is freedom and what sort of policy intervention may be justified.

According to a widespread view, economic liberalism began with Adam Smith (1776) and was further developed by classical economists, in particular Ricardo and Stuart Mill. It is called *classical* (economic) liberalism not only because this distinguished group of scholars originated a prestigious and influential tradition, "classical" in that sense, but also because the underlying theory is usually called "classical economics".[29] The main policy implications of this approach can be summed up by the statement "the government should abstain from any sort of intervention in the economy unless there is a sound reason to do so." This basic prescription leads to a critical version of laissez-faire that is constrained by the limits of real markets. However, the actual policy strategy adopted by liberal governments—which I call "real liberalism", echoing the usual distinction between socialism and "real socialism"—has often tended towards an unrestrained and uncritical version of laissez-faire, although this approach has never been supported by the main classical exponents.[30]

In the second half of the nineteenth century, the most influential liberal economists reacted to the then-fashionable form of unrestrained laissez-faire and its dire consequences by more stringently defining the market limits and the consequent limitations of laissez-faire policies. This change of emphasis emerges clearly in the writings of the most influential liberal economist of that period, John Stuart Mill.[31] He believed that the capacity for autonomous action was the fruit of learning and education, and that this capacity could be developed with the help of supportive institutions. A similar criticism of unrestrained laissez-faire is found in Marshall's writings:

> Free competition, or rather, freedom of industry and enterprise, was set loose to run, like a huge untrained monster, its wayward course. The abuse of their new power by able but uncultured businessmen led to evils on every side; it unfitted mothers for their duties, it weighed down children with overwork and disease; and in many places it degraded the race. (Marshall 1890, 9)

Marshall was therefore attracted by the opportunity to bring "free enterprise somewhat under control, to diminish its power of doing evil and increase its power of doing good" (ibid., 10). At the turn of the century, this new, milder version of economic liberalism was developed mainly by Marshall (1890), Wicksell (1898), and their pupils and followers. In particular Pigou, Marshall's most influential academic pupil, built on his mentor's concept of externality to point out an important source of microeconomic market failures providing a fully justified motive for public intervention meant to internalise externalities.[32] This approach, which later became the basis for environmental policy, was often called new liberal or, after the end of World War II, neoliberal, especially in Germany. I prefer to call it "updated liberalism" to avoid confusion with the meaning assumed by neoliberalism since the late 1970s, and to stress the continuity between this version of liberalism and classical liberalism. Updated liberalism frames its arguments in terms of neoclassical economics, the new version of mainstream economics since the 1970s.

A much more radical innovation came from Marshall's most influential pupil, John Maynard Keynes, who explained the Great Depression of the 1930s in terms of a macroscopic market failure: involuntary unemployment. This was a major deviation from one fundamental idea of classical liberalism, the ability of the market to self-regulate. However, this point of view can still rightly be called liberal, because the deviations from the usual liberal prescriptions are circumscribed and fully justified in terms of liberal basic principles and updated economic theory. In other words, the boundary between free markets and the state is shifted in the direction of a greater role for collective action, whenever its intervention is convincingly justified, but the default policy prescriptions remain liberal, as in classical liberalism.[33] The Keynesian revolution does not imply the demise of open-minded liberalism, but rather of laissez-faire.[34] Keynes' theory was legitimately considered by most pupils and followers as a perfected form of liberalism, or "modern liberalism".

After the war, a growing number of economists challenged the compatibility of Keynesian theory with the basic tenets of liberalism.[35] Finally, in the 1970s, as a reaction to persistent stagflation, a growing number of anti-Keynesian economists brought about a counter-revolution aiming to restore the principles of liberalism based on an updated form of neoclassical economics called New Classical Economics.[36] This new kind of liberalism and its supporting economic theory rapidly became main-stream. Critics immediately pointed out that this new vision, and its consequent policy strategy, was quite different from that advocated by classical liberalism. To stress this difference, they labelled it neoliberalism.

2.5 Neoliberalism: Evolution and Definitions

The word "neoliberalism" and the related modifier "neoliberal" started to be used with a meaning similar to the current one since the late 1970s. Its mentions have then exponentially increased in the last three decades also in the scholarly literature.[37] Notwithstanding a growing concern for the appropriateness of its use, the increasing success of the word neoliberalism and its underlying concept has not subsided. The concept has been criticised for being vague, equivocal, partisan, value-charged, and misleading.[38] These complaints raise issues of contents and terminology. I address first the issues relating to the contents of the concept. I start my investigation by suggesting three nested definitions of neoliberalism showing that this concept is not necessarily vague and equivocal. I will then discuss some controversial issues concerning the meaning and implications of neoliberalism in the light of the suggested definitions.

As I mentioned before, the basic distinction that has underlain most debates on freedom since World War II is between negative and positive liberty.[39] The eminent political philosopher Isaiah Berlin extensively discussed this dichotomy in an influential essay, first published in 1958, that triggered a heated debate. In my opinion, the crucial distinction between classical liberalism (from Locke to Stuart Mill) and neoliberalism (in its recent use) depends on the fact that classical liberalism was concerned with both the negative and positive liberty of citizens and economic agents, while neoliberalism focuses exclusively on the concept of negative liberty and rejects the value of positive liberty or its relevance for ethics and policy. This is my suggested definition of what I call the *weak* form of neoliberalism underlying all its most significant variants since the late 1970s.

Most critics of neoliberalism generally focus, implicitly or explicitly, on the neglected aspects of positive liberty conceived as self-determination and self-realisation of individuals (or groups of individuals such as social classes or communities). Liberty of individuals in this positive acceptation might benefit from state interventions of a kind stigmatised by neoliberals as intolerable limitation on individual liberty. I am ready to concede that the founding fathers of liberalism focused mainly on the defence of negative liberty as they were worried by the excessive interference of an authoritarian state with individuals' freedom. However, they also explicitly emphasised the importance of individuals' positive liberty, generally referred to with the word "autonomy" of Kantian ascendancy, and constructively explored how the state could enhance it.

The *standard* version of neoliberalism assumes a further crucial condition. Though in principle negative liberty may be affected by intentional or unintentional interferences, only the intentional interferences of other individuals are considered relevant for ethics, politics, and policy. For example, Berlin asserted that the coercion of negative liberty "implies the deliberate interference of other human beings within the area in which I could otherwise act. You lack political liberty or freedom only if you are prevented from attaining a goal by other human beings".[40] This standpoint excludes economic circumstances from being relevant to liberty. Market conditions, as Smith made clear, are the unintended consequences of a myriad of decisions taken by the economic agents. Therefore, the standard view of neoliberalism denies any legitimacy to full employment, countercyclical, redistributive, or social insurance policies, although they are meant to relax economic conditions that may severely limit the freedom of individuals. This is the ultimate foundation for rejecting Keynesian and welfare state policies such as those practised in the Bretton Woods period. Since the late 1970s this standard version of neoliberalism has been very influential and has inspired extensively both political programmes and policy strategies.

Critics of neoliberal views believe such a restriction to be ad hoc or arbitrary. I wish to emphasise, however, that the neoliberal approach does not necessarily exclude policy interferences on the intentional decisions of specific economic agents whenever the latter are believed to undermine the negative liberty of other agents. Cases in point are the monopolistic and oligopolistic practices, the market manipulations in finance, the intentional opacity of balance sheets, and so on. On the contrary, also this sort of policy interference—meant just to curb the intentional disruptive interferences of economic agents upon other economic agents—is excluded by what I call the "strong" form of neoliberalism, because in this view only the interference of the state is considered relevant for ethics and policy. In this view, state interventions in the economy and society should thus be limited as much as possible. This implicitly justifies the existing, very unequal, distribution of positive liberty among individuals and ends up by endorsing the current trend of growing inequality.

My nested definitions of neoliberalism (weak, standard, and strong neoliberalism) show that this concept is not necessarily vague or equivocal. What about the other complaints against the use of this concept? A further crucial objection is that the advocates and supporters of the neoliberal paradigm refuse this name as an expression of a partisan point of view. They claim that their ideas and consequent actions are just aiming to revert to "classical liberalism", or to genuine "liberalism". Therefore, as they claim, they do not need a different name whose adoption would thus be unfounded and misleading. Most neoliberal exponents do not deny that this tradition of thought has to be updated, but claim that their suggested updates do not alter the substance of classical liberalism. This objection leads to another objection. Since only the critics of neoliberalism adopted this concept, its meaning has become increasingly value-charged and partisan.[41] Therefore, in this view, the use of this concept would prejudge the issues under scrutiny.

To these two linked objections I respond that the belief that there is a coherent continuity between classical liberalism and so-called neoliberalism is unfounded. If by classical liberalism we mean the vision of the founding fathers of liberalism from Locke to Stuart Mill, we can easily ascertain that they refuse the idea that only negative liberty is significant for ethics and policy. They share two crucial principles that are instead rejected by most neoliberal exponents. The first one is often called "Lockean proviso".[42] This principle—expressed in modern language—maintains that, though the privatisation of a public good limits the liberty of the excluded citizens, it is nevertheless acceptable if it improves the management of this good and does not make anyone worse off.[43]

The second principle to be respected according to classical liberalism has been called "principle" or "law" of equal liberty. This basic moral rule, first enunciated by Locke,[44] has been interpreted and reformulated in different ways. In all its versions it shows a concern of classical liberalism for a fair distribution of rights not only in the negative sense of the word (e.g. the *habeas corpus* principle) but also in its positive sense of active inclusion of all citizens in the economic and political process (for example political rights). Most liberal democracies, under the influence of the "modern liberalism" of Beveridge and Keynes,[45] provide their citizens with publicly funded education, healthcare, social security, and unemployment benefits in the assumption that all citizens have a positive right to a minimal amount of these goods and services. On the contrary, neoliberal policies focus on negative rights and strive to progressively reduce the scope of the positive rights inherited from the past.[46] Neoliberal exponents often share on this issue the point of view of libertarians who believe that positive rights do not exist until they are created by contract.

Another crucial difference between classical liberalism and neoliberalism concerns the value of democracy. Classical liberals consider democracy a crucial instrument and goal of their vision. Ricardo, for example, maintained that democracy is "the means of depriving interests of privileged influence" (Dixon 2008, 237). He was thus favourable to "extend the right of voting for Members of Parliament to every class of the people" (Ricardo 1817, 503), because "the people, if left to the unrestricted exercise of their choice … act wisely and prudently" (ibid., 289).[47]

On the contrary, the advocates of neoliberalism look often uncommitted to democracy.[48] Hayek, for example, bluntly uttered: "I must frankly admit, that if democracy is taken to mean government by the unrestricted will of the majority, I am not a democrat, and even regard such government as pernicious and in the long run unworkable" (Hayek 1979, 39).[49] The neoliberal policy strategy aims to shift power from political to economic decision makers, from collective action to individuals' action, from the state to markets, and consequently from the legislative and executive authorities to the judiciary.[50] In this view, whenever the democratic process undermines or slows down the implementation of the required neoliberal reforms, or is alleged to threaten the negative liberty of the individuals or market freedom, democracy has to be enfeebled or suspended and replaced by the rule of technocrats or ad hoc legal instruments. Political rights are positive rights that empower the positive liberty of all citizens, while their exercise may jeopardise the negative liberty of some citizens, mainly the wealthiest and most powerful ones.

In the light of the preceding analysis, I may address now the terminological objection. The adjective "neoliberal" came into use at the end of the nineteenth century with a meaning completely different from the current one. It was then used to designate a more moderate version of classical liberalism that aimed to relax the traditional policy prescriptions based on strict laissez-faire principles, what I suggested to call "updated liberalism".[51] This terminology, as an alternative to "ordo-liberalism", became particularly popular in Germany in the period between the two World Wars. The ordo-liberals sought to sever the freedom of individuals to compete in the marketplace from the negative freedom from state intervention.[52] They argued in particular that a laissez-faire policy suffocates genuine competition favouring the progressive concentration of market power. The same point of view was revived, with more success, after World War II as the mainstream point of view inspiring the policy strategy pursued by the German government under the leadership of Ludwig Erhard. In academic articles and book reviews published in the 1950s and 1960s, ordo-liberalism was most often associated with the "Freiburg School" and economists such as Eucken, Röpke, and Rüstow.

In the same period, the word neoliberalism took on positive overtones not only in Germany but also elsewhere, especially in Latin America, where many economists and policy makers adopted it as an inspiration to overcome the shortcomings of traditional laissez-faire policies. However, in the 1970s the word underwent a radical change of meaning suddenly assuming negative overtones. Boas and Gans-Morse argue convincingly that in Latin America the watershed between these two radically different meanings was the 1973 Pinochet coup in Chile and post-coup government's adoption of a new policy strategy along the lines advocated by the so-called "Chicago Boys".[53] Many critics of this U-turn in economic policy started to call "neoliberal" the new policy strategy with a new negative meaning. This sudden mutation of meaning rapidly spread around the globe to designate the change of policy strategy adopted by most governments since the late 1970s.

Notwithstanding the viral success of this new use of the term neoliberalism, its meaning has been insufficiently clarified. One reason for this anomaly lies in the strong, unprecedented convergence of policy strategies towards the neoliberal paradigm in most developed countries and many developing countries. The meaning of the word looked thus quite clear from the intuitive and pragmatic point of view, as well as in terms of its underlying economic theory (often called "macroeconomic consensus" to underline an alleged wide convergence on its foundations). I believe, however, that a rigorous use of the concept requires an explicit in-depth clarification of its meaning. In this section, I provided three nested definitions of neoliberalism as a first step in this direction.

As for the charge of the partisan use of the term neoliberal, in my opinion nothing prevents its rigorous use. The word neoliberal, after all, is in itself neutral, as is consistent with both main interpretations of its meaning and implications: an updated version of the liberal tradition, as claimed by its supporters, and an extreme—possibly distorted—version of this tradition, as claimed by most critics. We can then leave to rigorous arguments the specification ex post of its positive or negative implications for the issue under scrutiny.

In any case, it is difficult to find a better name because, to the best of my knowledge, the alternative terms have all acquired negative political overtones, as is the case with the two main terminological candidates to indicate the same concept: neoconservative or Washington consensus policies. In addition, the use of the word "neoconservative" obscures the fact that neoliberal policies have also been advocated by parties considered progressive not only by their exponents but also by many commentators and voters. Analogously, the use of the expression "Washington consensus" policies may suggest the idea that the new orthodoxy has been established through some sort of a covered agreement reached by a few powerful diplomats and politicians in the inaccessible chambers of the Washington institutions rather than through a much more complex process involving civil society and public opinion.[54] Therefore, I decided—after some hesitation—to use systematically in this book the word neoliberalism and the underlying concept as here defined.

2.6   The Misleading Zero-Sum Game Between State and Market

The neoliberal focus on the negative freedom of individuals, coupled with the neoliberal emphasis on the state's constraints to individual liberty, has led to a widespread adoption of the misleading dichotomy between state, seen as the expression of collective action, and market, seen as the expression of free initiative of individuals. This dichotomy plays a crucial role in the economic and political debate, especially in the coverage of mass media. From the institutional point of view, the relationship between markets and state is presented as one of substitution rather than complementariness. For example, privatisation measures are generally justified as a way to transfer economic power from the government to the market. However, in the real world "markets and governments are opposites only in the sense that they form two sides of the same coin" (Rodrik 2011, 237). Markets necessarily require state-supported institutions to function properly. These institutions are established by the state, are then directly or indirectly regulated by policy makers, and must be continuously supervised by public agencies. First of all, the legal system must be sufficiently developed and reliable to ensure the "rule of law". Sophistication and reliability of the legal system are necessary features not only to protect private property, as all varieties of liberals have always emphasised, but also to ensure the enforcement of contracts, to regulate money circulation, and to assure the smooth flowing of trade. Finally, open-minded liberals recognise also that the state has the duty "to preserve the legitimacy of markets by protecting people from the risks and insecurities markets bring with them".[55] The welfare state was conceived by Beveridge and Keynes as a fundamental instrument to save market capitalism.[56] Their opinion is now challenged by neoliberal exponents, but their criticism ignores the crucial function of the "welfare state" in promoting the positive liberty of all the citizens. Also the empirical evidence supports the thesis of the complementariness between state and market. For example, David Cameron, a well-known Yale political scientist, argued in an empirical study that the size of the public sector in countries having comparable levels of development may be explained by the importance of trade in their economies.[57] In his view, more developed international trade requires a more effective support of public institutions.

The neoliberal dichotomy between state and market plays a particularly misleading role in any discussion about the correct distribution of economic power between the two poles of the dichotomy. In this perspective, the exercise of economic power is seen as a zero-sum game between the state and the market. Therefore, under the two neoliberal assumptions mentioned above, the protection of individuals' liberties requires a shift of power from the state to the market. This view, however, overlooks the third fundamental player in the game in a real market: the private firm.[58] This player should never be confused with the market, as often happens, because the firm manages its economic power according to rules that are radically different from those of both the state and the market.[59] The state is a hierarchical institution where the source of power is supposed to be the parliament that has been democratically elected by the citizens, while the decisions of the parliament are implemented and enforced by the government. In its pure competitive form, the market is a horizontal institution where all the participants (including the firms) are devoid of discretionary power and are coordinated by the price system to efficiently allocate resources. The firm, as was argued long ago by Coase, is completely different from the other two main players in the economic power game. It is obviously different from the state, although its hierarchical power structure is reminiscent of that of the state with shareholders playing the role of the ultimate source of power, while the top management plays a role of governance analogous to that of government in the state. And it is also different from the market, because the allocation of resources inside the firm is intentional and not impersonal, though affected by market forces.[60]

The confusion between firms and market would be in part justified only if the firms operating within a certain market were a myriad of very small price-taker firms, completely devoid of market power as well as of discretionary autonomy in the management of internal resources. In this case—that is, the case contemplated by the standard model of perfect competition—firms would take decisions by passively adapting to the will of the invisible hand which would be fully independent of individual firms' decisions. In a real market, firms' decisions and performances are certainly significantly affected by the market, but they retain a largely autonomous power in the management of internal resources and, in the case of biggest firms, in manipulating the market itself to their own advantage.

To support the desired shift of economic power from the state to the market, in reality from the state to private firms, neoliberal exponents, backed by mass media and political parties, have since the late 1970s strengthened their propaganda regarding market efficiency versus state inefficiency. As for the efficiency of real markets, the arguments put forward to support this thesis are questionable, as I argued above. It is surprising that this opinion is still so strong after the Great Recession and the ongoing Eurocrisis. The relative inefficiency of the state, however, is easier to sustain because of the higher opacity of firms as compared to that of the state. The general public does not know enough about the activity of the state, notwithstanding all the legal and political safeguards typical of democracy, but they know much less about the activity of private firms. The result is that the mass media continuously denounces the inefficiencies and shortcomings of public services (such as instruction, education, and health) that are of particular direct interest of all the citizens, suggesting that the privatisation of these sectors would greatly improve their own well-being.

These systematic campaigns succeeded in heightening citizens' mistrust, even rage, against the state. They were abetted by the fact that every citizen has some direct experience of the consequences of inefficiency and corruption in the public sector, while the consequences of inefficiency and corruption in the private sector are only indirect for most people. Very few people, for example, have a direct experience of the huge consequences of scams such as that perpetrated by Volkswagen and other car makers on CO_2 emissions,[61] or by major banks on London Interbank Offered Rate (LIBOR).[62] Moreover, a thorough understanding of their negative consequences for society requires abstract reasoning and access to detailed information on global warming and finance, which are beyond the capabilities of most citizens. No one takes any notice of corporate unfairness and corruption unless one judge opens a case and a mass media report on it. Thus, the comparison between the shortcomings of the market and those of the state is heavily weighted against the state. And, after all, who corrupts state officials? Typically, private firms.

Political party propaganda exploits and intensifies this distorted assessment of the relative merits of the state and the market. Pro-market politicians—which are the majority these days—know very well that to criticise the inefficiency and corruption of the state is very popular with the electorate. It is also very easy to contribute to these and other shortcomings of public administrations and agencies. This led to a vicious circle: reductions in public expenditures contribute to reducing further the efficiency of services provided by the state, confirming its inefficiency and apparently justifying further cuts. This vicious circle, maintained by neoliberal governments since Mrs Thatcher went into power in the UK in 1979, has greatly worsened the quality of vital services such as those provided by the education and health systems, strengthening the case for their privatisation (see Chap. 5).

The misleading nature of the dichotomy between state and market is clearly revealed, in my opinion, by the following thought experiment.[63] The main pragmatic motivation underlying the adoption of neoliberal policies since the late 1970s has been the urgency to shift economic power from the inefficient and corrupt state to the efficient and fair market in order to empower the invisible hand. Looking back with hindsight to the last decades, we see instead a progressive empowerment of large multinational corporations and their visible hands, while real markets do not seem to be more competitive now than in the late 1970s. Economic power has shifted neither to citizens who are increasingly aware that they are living in post-democratic regimes where their will is systematically disregarded, nor to the state as representative of citizens' interests.[64] The real winners in this massive redistribution of power are the shareholders and top managers of large multinational corporations, and the politicians and technocrats who support their interests. The vicious circle between the increasing power and wealth of a few private subjects and top public subjects (government officials, legislators, and top-level technocrats) yielding to their goals in their own interest, has led to a progressive concentration of power and wealth.

In principle, the individuals should be the ultimate source of power of the three basic institutions that manage the most important economic decisions: state, firms and the market. They should exert power on the state as citizens, on the firms as stakeholders and on the market as consumers, savers, and investors. However, the real power of most citizens has been progressively declining in recent decades. In the following chapters, I aim to explain why, and what conditions need to be established to restore their power.

2.7   Concluding Remarks

In this chapter, a pivotal theme has emerged that will be a persistent leitmotiv throughout the book: the evolution of capitalism has produced a growing contradiction between substantive democracy and a narrow view of freedom centred on negative freedom. The contradiction between democracy and the incautious and instrumental enhancement of positive freedom has long been stigmatised as an excuse for state despotism. Neoliberal philosophers and economists have disseminated the illusion that the problem could be easily solved by rejecting the very concept of positive freedom while focusing instead on negative freedom. This solution of the dilemma, implicit in the laissez-faire policies implemented in the nineteenth century, had already been perceived as a delusion in the second half of the same century, determining a gradual change of position on the part of the most enlightened and farsighted liberal intellectuals (such as John Stuart Mill), and prompting innovative ideas among successive generations of economists (in particular Marshall and his pupils Pigou and Keynes).

After World War II, there was a revival of liberalism based on a stricter concept of negative liberty, often called neoliberalism. The fear of despotism had been rekindled by the emergence of totalitarian states during the inter-war period. A few economists and intellectuals (including Mises, Hayek, Berlin, and Friedman) extended this fear to the prevailing policy strategies adopted after the war that were focused on enhancing positive liberty. They stigmatised thus as detrimental to personal liberty the policy strategy of Keynesian inspiration implemented in the Bretton Woods period. At the beginning, the exponents of this point of view had little public support, but the latter grew progressively in the 1950s and 1960s. Public opinion shifted its prevailing orientation in the 1970s in consequence of stagflation, which cast serious doubt on the basic tenets of modern liberalism. This led to an anti-Keynesian counter-revolution which, by the late 1970s, brought about a radical change in macroeconomics and policy strategy in a neoliberal direction. Neoliberalism was characterised by profound mistrust of state intervention in the economy and by an unbounded trust in the ability of unfettered markets to solve in the best possible way all the weighty problems of economics and society. I argue in the following chapters that the outcome of this change in orientation was quite different from what had been hoped and predicted.[65] This book aims to provide a coherent picture of facts and their causes based on the fundamental values of freedom, democracy, and sustainability.

Notes

1. In this book, I will use the terms freedom and liberty interchangeably. Some authors have suggested a distinction of meaning between them, but such proposals have never caught on (see e.g. Dworkin 2011). In any case, only the English language has two different words for the concept, one of Latin origin (*libertas*) and one of German origin (*freiheit*), and this would prevent a straightforward translation of a dual definition into another language.
2. MacCallum (1967).
3. Carter (2012).
4. See Vercelli (1998a), and the literature there cited.
5. Kant's concept of "autonomy" has a clear kinship with the concept of positive liberty (see e.g. Johnson 2014). The distinction between negative and positive liberty plays a crucial role in a famous lecture delivered in 1880 by T. H. Green on "Liberal Legislation and Freedom of Contract" (Green 1895). Green, an influential exponent of "Oxford Idealists", defines positive freedom as "a power or capacity of doing or enjoying something worth doing or enjoying" (quoted in Skinner 1974, 23). In his opinion, the state may play a crucial role in promoting the positive liberty, or self-realisation, of citizens through education.
6. 'Two Concepts of Liberty' was Berlin's inaugural lecture in 1958 as Chichele Professor of Political and Social Theory at Oxford University. My references are to the second version published by Berlin (1969).

7. Hobbes (1651) introduced the term Leviathan to argue the need for a somewhat despotic power to keep the war of 'everyone against everyone' under control.
8. See Sect. 1.5.
9. Smith (1776).
10. See Skinner (1974).
11. As is well known, the actual meaning of Smith's metaphor of the invisible hand is controversial. I do not need to enter into this sort of philological issues in this book. I assume here the usual interpretation.
12. See, for example, Stiglitz (2000, 55–75).
13. I am not aware of any compelling demonstration that an unfettered competitive market tends to increase inequality, but this conjecture is plausible enough to require a continuous focus on income distribution. From the theoretical point of view, I should mention that it is quite likely that the participants in the market game who have greater access to resources and opportunities are more likely to win market competitions. This is so also because some of them have the means to manipulate outcomes either directly by using their market power, or indirectly by lobbying or bribing the executive and legislative powers. From the empirical point of view, the correlation between the adoption of increasingly market-friendly policies since the late 1970s and the subsequent progressive increase of inequality suggests a likely causal relation.
14. See Sect. 1.5.
15. See for example Vercelli (1991).
16. The competitive equilibrium in an incomplete market is generally "constrained suboptimal" (Geanakoplos and Polemarchakis 1986).
17. An Arrow–Debreu security is a contract that pays one unit of a currency if a particular state occurs at a particular time in the future and pays nothing in all the other states.
18. Pigou (1920).
19. As is well known, a public good is a good that is non-excludable and non-rivalrous in the sense that individuals cannot effectively exclude other individuals from its use, while the use by one individual does not reduce its availability to others.
20. For a non-technical survey of recent advances in decision theory under uncertainty see for example Vercelli (1999a).
21. See in particular Stiglitz (1991).
22. See Lucas (1981) and Vercelli (1991) for a critical discussion of Lucas's research programme.

23. Friedman (1953).
24. I use here the expression "research programme" and "protective belt" in the sense suggested by Lakatos (1978). In this view, a research programme provides a framework within which research can be conducted on the basis of "first principles" which are shared by those involved in it (the "hard core" of the research programme). Typically, a research programme tries to survive as long as possible by relying on ad hoc arguments called "protective belt" to safeguard the "hard core" from being refuted.
25. Lucas (1981).
26. See for example Popper (1969).
27. A significant exception is Gray (1995) but his definition is too focused on political philosophy to be of help in this book.
28. Gaus (1996, 162–166).
29. I am thus not using the meaning introduced by Keynes (1936), who conflates classical economics with neoclassical economics.
30. For an accurate survey of these issues, see Robbins (1952).
31. According to Miller, "Mill's view is that capitalist economies should at some point undergo a 'spontaneous' and incremental process of socialisation, involving the formation of worker-controlled 'socialistic' enterprises through either the transformation of 'capitalistic' enterprises or creation *de novo*" (Miller 2003, 213). Mill considered this kind of socialist orientation, sometimes called "utopian socialism", to be fully consistent with the basic liberal principles (ibid.).
32. Pigou (1920).
33. Vercelli (2010).
34. The mainstream form of liberalism dominating policy strategies in the Bretton Woods period was given several names: 'modern liberalism', 'social liberalism' or 'equalitarian liberalism', depending on the country and the focus on different exponents or aspects of this new paradigm.
35. Suffice it to mention here Mises (1962), Hayek (1960), and Friedman (1953, 1960, 1968).
36. See in particular Lucas (1981).
37. Boas and Gans-Morse (2009).
38. See for example Thorsen and Lie (2007).
39. See retro Sect. 2.2.
40. Berlin (1969, 122). Hayek (1960) is another eminent example of this point of view.
41. See for example Boas and Gans-Morse (2009).

42. The phrase "Lockean proviso" was coined by the political philosopher Robert Nozick (1974).
43. In the words of Locke, the "appropriation of any parcel of land, by improving it … [should not give] any prejudice to any other man, since there was still enough and as good left… For he that leaves as much as another can make use of does as good as take nothing at all. Nobody could think himself injured by the drinking of another man, though he took a good draught, who had a whole river of the same water left him to quench his thirst." Locke (1690, *Chapter V, paragraph 33*).
44. Locke (1690).
45. This sort of liberalism is also called "social liberalism".
46. See for example Gaus et al. (2015).
47. The relationship between Ricardo and democracy is thoroughly clarified in Dixon (2008).
48. See for example Harvey (2005); Saad-Filho and Johnston (2005).
49. It is interesting to compare the quotation from Ricardo with that from Hayek and notice the radically different view towards *unrestricted* democracy. This does not imply that neoliberal exponents are against democracy in all its meanings, or that they share the same views on democracy. Nevertheless, most of them are comfortable with diminutive conceptions of democracy that imply a subordination to market self-regulation. A further clarification of this important but intricate issue goes beyond the scope of this book.
50. Thorsen and Lie (2007, 15).
51. See retro Sect. 2.4.
52. Boas and Gans-Morse (2009, 146).
53. Boas and Gans-Morse (2009, 149).
54. See Mirowski and Plehwe (2009), and Mirowski (2014).
55. Ibid., 19.
56. See in particular Beveridge (1942) and Keynes (1936).
57. See Cameron (1978), and the comments by Rodrik (2011, 16–19).
58. Borghesi and Vercelli (2008).
59. Ibid.
60. Coase (1937).
61. Warner (2015, 121–133).
62. Bariviera et al. (2015).
63. I refer collectively to the following arguments as "thought experiments", notwithstanding their reference to empirical evidence, because I do not

attempt here to support my opinions with empirical evidence systematically collected and interpreted using state-of-the-art statistical and econometric techniques. Such an attempt would be very interesting but extremely
difficult. To the best of my knowledge, reliable literature of this kind is
missing.

64. Crouch (2004).

65. The contradiction between negative freedom and democracy has increased
greatly in the neoliberal era. Sovereignty has progressively shifted from citizens and their representatives to markets, more accurately to private firms
and their cronies, limiting both individual liberty and democratic control
of most citizens. The trilemma between freedom, democracy, and globalisation brilliantly enunciated by Rodrik (2011) is none other than an expression of the growing contradiction between a misconceived defence of
negative freedom and genuine democracy determined by the recent process
of financialisation and globalisation (see Sect. 9.6).

Bibliography

Bariviera, Aurelio F., María B. Guercio, Lisana B. Martinez, and Osvaldo
A. Rosso. 2015. The (In)visible Hand in the Libor Market: An Information
Theory Approach. *The European Physical Journal B* 88(8). doi:10.1140/epjb/
e2015-60410-1.

Berlin, Isaiah. 1969. Two Concepts of Liberty. In *Four Essays on Liberty*, ed.
Isaiah Berlin, London: Oxford University Press. 2002, 118–172.

Beveridge, William. 1942. *Social Insurance and Allied Services*. (The Beveridge
Report.) London: Cmd 6404, HMSO.

Boas, Taylor C., and Jordan Gans-Morse. 2009. Neoliberalism: From New
Liberal Philosophy to Anti-Liberal Slogan. *Studies in Comparative
International Development* 44: 137–161.

Borghesi, Simone, and Alessandro Vercelli. 2008. *Global Sustainability. Social
and Environmental Conditions*. Palgrave Macmillan: Basingstoke and
New York.

Cameron, David R. 1978. The Expansion of The Public Economy: A
Comparative Analysis. *American Political Science Review* 72(4): 1243–1261.

Carter, Ian. 2012. Positive and Negative Liberty. In *The Stanford Encyclopaedia of
Philosophy* (Spring 2012 Edition), ed. Edward N. Zalta, http://plato.stanford.
edu/archives/spr2012/entries/liberty-positive-negative/. Retrieved 5 April 2016.

Coase, Ronald H. 1937. The Nature of the Firm. *Economica*, New Series 4(16):386–405.

Crouch, Colin. 2004. *Post-democracy*. Chichester: John Wiley and Sons.

Dixon, William. 2008. Ricardo: Economic Thought and Social Order. *Journal of the History of Economic Thought* 30(2): 235–253.

Dworkin, Ronald. 2011. *Justice for Hedgehogs*. Harvard: Harvard University Press.

Friedman, Milton. 1953. The Case for Flexible Exchange Rates. In *Essays in Positive Economics*, ed. Milton Friedman, 157–203. Chicago: University of Chicago Press.

———. 1960. *A Program for Monetary Stability*. New York: Fordham University Press.

———. 1968. The Role of Monetary Policy. *The American Economic Review* 58(1): 1–17.

Gaus, Gerald F. 1996. *Justificatory Liberalism: An Essay on Epistemology and Political Theory*. New York: Oxford University Press.

Gaus, Gerald F., Courtland, Shane D., and David Schmidtz. 2015. Liberalism. In *The Stanford Encyclopaedia of Philosophy* (Spring 2015 Edition), ed. Edward N. Zalta. http://plato.stanford.edu/archives/spr2015/entries/liberalism/.

Geanakoplos, John D., and Heraklis M. Polemarchakis. 1986. Existence, Regularity and Constrained Suboptimality of Competitive Allocations When the Asset Structure is Incomplete. In *Uncertainty, Information and Communication: Essays in Honor of K.J. Arrow*, vol. 3, eds. W.P. Heller, R.M. Starr and D.A. Starrett, 65–95. New York: Cambridge University Press.

Gray, John. 1995. *Liberalism*, 2 edn. Buckingham: Open University Press.

Green, Thomas H. 1895. *Lectures on the Principles of Political Obligation*. London: Longmans, Green, and Co.

Harvey, David. 2005. *A Brief History of Neoliberalism*. Oxford: Oxford University Press.

Hayek, Friedrich A 1960. *The Constitution of Liberty*. Chicago: University of Chicago Press.

——— 1979. *Law, Legislation and Liberty. Volume 3: The Political Order of a Free People*. London: Routledge & Kegan Paul.

Hobbes, Thomas. 1651 [2010]. Leviathan: Or the Matter, Forme, and Power of a Common-Wealth Ecclesiasticall and Civil, ed. Ian Shapiro. Yale: Yale University Press.

Johnson, Robert. 2014. Kant's Moral Philosophy. *The Stanford Encyclopaedia of Philosophy* (Summer 2014 Edition), ed. Edward N. Zalta. http://plato.stanford.edu/archives/sum2014/entries/kant-moral/.

Keynes, John Maynard. 1936 [1973]. *The General Theory of Employment, Interest and Money*. (The Collected Writings of John Maynard Keynes. Volume 7). London and Cambridge: Macmillan and Cambridge University Press.

Lakatos, Imre. 1978. *The Methodology of Scientific Research Programmes*. Cambridge: Cambridge University Press.

Locke, John. 1690 [1982]. *Second Treatise of Government*. Edited by Richard Cox. Arlington Heights, Ill.: Harlan Davidson.

Lucas, Robert E. Jr. 1981. *Studies in Business-Cycle Theory*. Boston, Mass: MIT Press.

MacCallum, Gerald C. Jr. 1967. Negative and Positive Freedom. *Philosophical Review* 76: 312–334.

Marshall, Alfred. 1890. *Principles of Economics*. London: Macmillan.

Miller, Dale E. 2003. Mill's 'Socialism'. *Politics, Philosophy and Economics* 2(2): 213–248.

Mirowski, Philip. 2014. The Political Movement that Dared not Speak its own Name: The Neoliberal Thought Collective Under Erasure. Working Paper No.23. INET.

Mirowski, Philip, and Dieter Plehwe, eds. 2009. *The Road from Mont Pelerin: The Making of the Neoliberal Thought Collective*. Cambridge, Ma: Harvard University Press.

Mises, Ludwig von. 1962. *The Free and Prosperous Commonwealth: An Exposition of the Ideas of Classical Liberalism*. Princeton, NJ: Van Nostrand.

Nozick, Robert. 1974. *Anarchy, State, and Utopia*. New York: Basic Books.

Pigou, Arthur C. 1920. *The Economics of Welfare*. London: Macmillan.

Popper, Karl R. 1969. *Conjectures and Refutations*. London: Routledge.

Ricardo, David. 1817 [1951–73.] *Principles of Political Economy and Taxation*. In *The Works and Correspondence of David Ricardo*, vol. V, eds. David Ricardo, Piero Sraffa. Cambridge: Cambridge University Press.

Robbins, Lionel. 1952. *Theory of Economic Policy in English Classical Political Economy*. London: Macmillan.

Rodrik, Dani. 2011. *The Globalisation Paradox*. In *Why Global Markets, States, and Democracy Can't Coexist*. Oxford: Oxford University Press.

Saad-Filho, Alfredo, and Deborah Johnston. 2005. *Neoliberalism—A Critical Reader*. London: Pluto Press.

Skinner, Andrew S. 1974. *Adam Smith and The Role of the State*. Glasgow: University of Glasgow Press.

Smith, Adam. 1776 [1977]. *An Inquiry into The Nature and Causes of the Wealth of Nations*. Edited by Edwin Cannan. Chicago: University of Chicago Press.

Stiglitz, Joseph E. 1991. The Invisible Hand and Modern Welfare Economics. *Working Paper No. 3641 National Bureau of Economic Research.* Cambridge, MA.

Stiglitz, Joseph E 2000. *Economics of the Public Sector.* New York: W. W. Norton & Co.

Thorsen, Dag E. and Amund Lie. 2007. What is Neoliberalism? Unpublished Manuscript. Department of Political Science, University of Oslo.

Vercelli, Alessandro. 1991. *Methodological Foundations of Macroeconomics. Keynes and Lucas.* Cambridge: Cambridge University Press.

———. 1998a. Operational Measures of Sustainable Development and the Freedom of Future Generations. In *Sustainability: Dynamics and Uncertainty,* eds. Chichilnisky Graciela, Heal Geoffrey, and Alessandro Vercelli. Dordrecht: Martin Kluwer.

———. 1999a. The Recent Advances in Decision Theory under Uncertainty: A Non-technical Introduction. In *Uncertain Decisions: Bridging Theory and Experiments,* ed. Luigi Luini. Dordrecht: Kluwer.

———. 2010. Mr. Keynes and the 'liberals'. In *Keynes' General Theory after Seventy Years,* eds. Robert Dimand, Robert Mundell, and Alessandro Vercelli, 63–90. Basingstoke and New York: Palgrave Macmillan.

Warner, Carolyn M. 2015. Sources of Corruption in the European Union. In *Routledge Handbook of Political Corruption,* ed. Paul Heywood, 121–133. New York: Routledge.

Wicksell, Knut. 1898. *Interest and Prices.* English Translation 1936. New York: Sentry Press.

3

The Globalisation of Markets

3.1   Introduction

Economic globalisation is the extension of free markets to the international economy. It is thus not at all surprising that, at least after the Industrial Revolution, the ups and downs of globalisation typically overlap with those of free trade, following the fluctuating appeal of free markets for policy makers and public opinion. This is particularly true if the liberal stance supporting free market and free trade focuses on the negative freedom of economic agents as liberalism, especially neoliberalism, has often been inclined to do. In this case, the dominant wisdom disregards or plays down the negative externalities of laissez-faire, and globalisation may thrive unimpeded. In particular, the neoliberal policy strategy pursued in recent decades has significantly accelerated the process of economic globalisation as is confirmed by a significant indicator: global trade grew from around the equivalent of 40 % of world GDP in 1992 to over 50 % in 2009.[1]

If the invisible hand succeeds to optimise the allocation of resources within national markets, the same should happen at the international level. Why should the invisible hand hesitate to cross national boundaries? Although

© The Editor(s) (if applicable) and The Author(s) 2017   **63**
A. Vercelli, *Crisis and Sustainability*,
DOI 10.1057/978-1-137-60069-1_3

this looks fully convincing in intuitive terms, a sound analytical extension of the modern version of the invisible hand theorems to the world economy is by no means a trivial endeavour. The trouble is that the international markets are characterised by a further set of serious deviations from the assumptions underlying the perfect competition model. The segmentation of the global market in national markets brings about and nurtures these deviations.[2] The segmentation of markets is a serious problem also at the national level, since it impedes the market mechanism to equalise local costs and prices undermining efficiency. In the case of the international economy, however, the segmentation in national economies is particularly deep and entrenched in the deep structural differences (cultural, institutional, technological, and political) that distinguish the national economies.

Let us consider the case of a de-industrialising region within a nation. A first crucial difference is that workers may migrate easily from the declining region to another region benefitting from internal free movement of production factors. That is how, for example, southern states in the USA adjusted to the industrial dominance of the north.[3] The national government may implement a second response by engaging in transfer payments in favour of the citizens adversely affected. Other policies may be adopted since a nation shares a common set of regulations (in labour, product, and capital markets). Trust in the re-equilibrating virtues of national policies may be excessive but, in any case, no one can entertain a similar hope within the global markets. This explains why, since long, there is a specialised literature that argues in favour of free trade emphasising its benefits for all the countries involved in this policy despite the significant structural differences between them.

In the first part of this chapter, I reconstruct the evolution of market globalisation as a necessary background to my successive analysis. I start from the Industrial Revolution identifying the broad profile of the process and its articulation in two surges of globalisation divided by an intermediate period of de-globalisation (Sect. 3.2). Sections 3.3 and 3.4 investigate the specific features, respectively, of the First and Second Globalisation. Section 3.5 discusses the main arguments in favour of or against globalisation analysing the co-evolution of history of facts and history of economic analysis with specific reference to the theory of free trade. Section 3.6 focuses on the issue of cross-country mobility of production factors.

Section 3.7 concludes by observing that the arguments produced so far in favour of free trade are surprisingly weak and maintaining that the freedom of people should always be the ultimate priority.

3.2 Globalisation after the Industrial Revolution

Globalisation is a popular word often used in a loose way. We cannot say anything significant on globalisation unless we assign a clear meaning to this fuzzy concept. Let us start from the observation that, consistently with its etymology, globalisation indicates a process of territorial expansion of a certain entity that extends its reach, at least in principle, to the entire globe. Globalisation in this sense may be political, economic, or cultural. We may detect since ancient history a tendency towards the territorial expansion of political entities to accumulate power, wealth, influence, and knowledge. This led to the constitution of empires, long-distance trade routes,[4] and the propagation of beliefs systems: religions, philosophical and scientific schools, and ideologies believed to be superior to the alternatives. Some scholars called "archaic globalisation" these early examples of territorial expansion.[5] However, the analogies between archaic and modern globalisation should not cloud the deep differences. The "globe" had then a different, much more limited, meaning.

Sometimes, the territorial expansion succeeded to unify a significant part of the "civilised" world, deserving in this metaphoric sense the name of globalisation (let us just mention the Empire built by Alexander the Great, the Roman Empire, and the Muslim Empire). However, Empires did not last long. The excessive extension of Empires typically led to a fragmentation in parts preluding to their downfall. Alexander's Empire was divided after his death into unstable kingdoms ruled by "Diadochi"; the Roman Empire was articulated in provinces and eventually dichotomised in the Eastern and Western parts; the Muslim Empire was fragmented in caliphates; and so on. Typically, the different articulations of a certain Empire often fought each other for supremacy while proved unable to withstand the pressure of outside aggressions. This led to the downfall of empires and the recomposition of territories in new empires.

In the historical episodes recalled above, we may well trace the germs of modern globalisation. However, we can speak of globalisation in a proper sense only after the period of worldwide explorations in the sixteenth and seventeenth centuries that originated the modern meaning of "global" as referring, in principle, to the whole earthly globe. Because of the progressive globalisation of the international transport system and the early stages of trade globalisation, in the seventeenth and eighteenth centuries, the world trade started to expand at an average rate of about 1 % per year.[6] In this period, consistently with the mercantilist doctrine, national states promoted and supported foreign trade to build up significant and persistent surpluses believed to be a crucial ingredient of their power and wealth. This result was sought not only with the traditional means of war and diplomacy but also by chartering private corporations such as the British East India Company (founded in 1600), often described as the first multinational corporation, or the Dutch East India Company (founded in 1602). A few historians called "proto-globalisation" the slow but steady increase of world trade in these centuries.[7]

Only after the Industrial Revolution, we can speak of globalisation in the modern sense of the term. Within this broad secular process, we have to distinguish two separate waves. The first era of modern globalisation extended from early nineteenth century (after the final defeat of Napoleon in Waterloo and the ensuing Congress of Vienna in 1815) to 1914 (just before World War I) and was characterised by an unprecedented growth of the world trade at an average rate of almost 4 % per year.[8]

The intermediate period from the beginning of World War I to the end of World War II is a period of de-globalisation as wars and the Great Depression pushed the countries affected by these catastrophic events towards a more inward-looking, sometimes fully autarkic, policy orientation. The resumption of trade and growth during the "roaring 1920s" was too short-lived to invert the declining trend. Only at the end of World War II, the process of globalisation started a new persistent surge generating a second wave that has not yet exhausted its momentum, notwithstanding a growing opposition in the public opinion and the recent Great Recession started in 2007.

The second era of globalisation is quite different from the first one. In both cases, private firms implemented economic globalisation with the active support of their country of origin, but the relationship between the economic and political sides of globalisation has significantly changed through time. In the first surge, the economic globalisation was still under the strict control of the state, although private economic interests increasingly influenced the policies pursued by policy makers. In the second wave, the protagonists of globalisation were the multinational corporations that, with increasing ease, succeeded to orientate public policies in their favour and to exploit public resources in their self-interest.

The evolution of globalisation in the last two centuries has been characterised by a continuous process of structural change that a too simple periodisation risks to misrepresent. To avoid as much as possible a distortional representation, we have to distinguish at least two sub-phases in both surges of globalisation.[9]

3.3 The First Globalisation

Within the first wave of globalisation, we have to distinguish a first phase, initiated at the end of the Napoleonic wars (1815) and extending up to about the middle of the century, from the second phase that ended with the breakdown of the Gold Standard at the beginning of World War I. In the first phase, the rapid diffusion of industrialisation and technical change pushed the vigorous acceleration of globalisation. This unprecedented process of continuous structural change affected in particular the transport system that rapidly reduced costs also of long-distance trade. In this period, contrary to a widespread conviction, free-trade policies were not yet a significant factor in the modernisation process, since systematic free-trade policies began to materialise only at the end of this phase.

In the UK, the most advanced country of the period, the change of direction of economic policy was clearly signalled by the repeal in 1846 of the Corn Laws adopted in 1815 to protect domestic landowners' interests by imposing restrictions and tariffs on imported grains. In the same period, the UK started to sign free-trade agreements with other countries.[10] However, this process of transition to free trade was limited and short-lived: "even though we think of the nineteenth century as an era of free trade, Britain is the only large economy that maintained open trade policies for any length of time. The United States put up very steep tariffs on manufactured imports during the Civil War and kept them high throughout the century. The major continental powers in Europe were unhesitant converts to free trade only for a short period during the 1860s and 1870s" (Rodrik 2011, 26).

The overvaluation of the role of free trade in the First Globalisation depends on the fact that the rhetoric of free trade had then, as still has now, a currency much broader than genuine free-trade policies. Honest free-trade agreements should be symmetrical and affect in the same way imports and exports of all the countries involved. On the contrary, during the nineteenth century, free-trade arguments often aimed to justify and enforce asymmetric "agreements" between core countries and periphery countries. These agreements typically were imposed to eliminate, or at least reduce, any sort of obstacle to the exports of core countries favouring at the same time cheap imports of raw materials from periphery countries. This was a crucial component of the colonialist policies pursued by big powers from Napoleonic wars to the end of World War II.

Summing up, the First Globalisation was an era dominated not by genuine free trade but from what we could call "forced free trade", or "freed trade", where trade was systematically "liberated" from obstacles raised by periphery countries and disliked by core countries. A case in point is the treatise of Balta Limani signed by Britain with Ottoman Turkey in 1838 to force it to restrict import duties to a maximum of 5 % and abolish import prohibitions. A particularly cynical use of free-trade arguments in the interest of a core country was the Opium war (1838–1842) fought by Britain to force China to liberalise the imports of goods from the British Empire including opium that had been prohibited to safeguard the health of the local population.

The timid process of convergence towards a full-fledged free-trade regime started in the middle of the nineteenth century was soon the victim of one of its consequences: the adoption of the Gold Standard by a growing number of countries to reduce currency-exchange risk that jeopardised the international flows of goods and capital.[11] The consequences of the extension of the Gold Standard regime were in part unexpected by its supporters. The scarcity of gold contributed to trigger the so-called Long Depression (1873–1896) that was characterised by a mild but continuous deflation of prices and a marked slowdown in the rate of growth in globalising countries. This persistent depression greatly increased unemployment and poverty in many countries, particularly in agriculture and domestic manufacturing.[12] The crisis affected less the international capital movements as the Gold Standard favoured their cross-country flows increasingly motivated by mere speculation. This shifted the balance of power from agriculture and manufacture to finance accelerating the First Financialisation.[13] In particular, the crisis accelerated the process of concentration of capital both in the real sector, where oligopolies progressively increased their influence and, in the financial sector, where a few big banks emerged in many countries as catalysers of investment allocation and policy strategies.

The interests of big oligopolies and banks relied in this period on the imperialist policies pursued by the great powers that often set aside free-trade policies in favour of more direct means of persuasion. However, the clash between the conflicting interests of great powers led to World War I that ended the first wave of globalisation triggering a process of de-globalisation. This process followed the sudden demise of the Gold Standard regime in 1914. A similar fate hit with a short delay the process of financialisation that suffered from the reduced international capital mobility and the missing support by the Gold Standard. In this new environment, the international economic system could not cope with the growing disequilibria in the balance of payments. The rigidity of currency exchange rates had become increasingly inconsistent with the diverging dynamics of productivity and real wages in countries having different degrees of industrialisation and technological dynamism. This led to growing structural surpluses or deficits under the pressure of rapid and dis-homogeneous technological change and differential involvement in the war.[14]

Only at the end of World War II, the process of globalisation could resume a growing trend. This was facilitated by the adoption of the Gold Exchange Standard, a new monetary regime that significantly reduced the rigidity and asymmetries of the traditional Gold Standard. As in the first surge, the process of financialisation followed with a short time lag the resumption of globalisation and the revival of an ordered monetary system (see Chap. 4).

3.4   The Second Globalisation

Within the Second Globalisation, we have to distinguish two sub-periods: the Bretton Woods phase (1944–1971) and, after a brief transition process in the 1970s, the neoliberal phase (from about 1979 to the present). The differences between the two sub-periods of the Second Globalisation are highly significant and will be at the centre of the analysis pursued in the rest of the book. The second part of the book will focus on the neoliberal era, namely on the development trajectory starting from the crisis of the Bretton Woods era and lasting up to now. Here we anticipate just a few broad differences that distinguish these two phases of the Second Globalisation from the preceding phases and one from the other.

The world that emerged after World War II was committed to free trade much more than during the first surge of globalisation. We can see two main reasons behind the unprecedented success of free trade: (a) the conviction that the alternative instruments of competition between countries (such as colonialism and imperialism), massively deployed during the First Globalisation, would lead to new devastating wars and (b) the growing influence acquired by economics that had succeeded to coalesce a widespread consensus on the desirability of free markets and free trade.

The favourable attitude towards free trade that is common to both recent phases of globalisation has radically different foundations and policy implications in the Bretton Woods phase and in the neoliberal phase. In both cases, the desirability of free trade is a corollary of the belief in the superiority of free markets over alternative institutional arrangements, but the attitude towards free markets changed sharply in the rapid transition from the first to the second phase that occurred in the 1970s.

The Bretton Woods phase conformed to the conviction that, although markets should be as free as possible, policy makers should regulate and supervise them taking into account their intrinsic limits. In the second phase, the neoliberal revolution started in the early 1970s spread the idea that the limits of real markets and their failures depend exclusively, or at least preponderantly, on the interference of public regulators and supervisors in the market processes (see Sect. 3.5). This change of attitude had far-reaching implications that changed radically the policy strategy, the model of development, and its social and environmental features.

3.5   The Free-Trade Doctrine

The free-trade doctrine is one of the few fields were the agreement of economists is almost universal. Many distinguished economists have often repeated this opinion. Gregory Mankiw, for example, asserted in his popular blog that "few propositions command as much consensus among professional economists as that open world trade increases economic growth and raises living standards" (Mankiw 2006). A host of surveys and polls confirms this opinion. For example, in a 2006 survey of American economists (83 responders), "87.5 % agree that the U.S. should eliminate remaining tariffs and other barriers to trade" and "90.1 % disagree with the suggestion that the U.S. should restrict employers from outsourcing work to foreign countries" (Whaples 2006).

Notwithstanding this wide consensus, systematically advertised and sponsored by mass media, a large part of the public opinion has always remained unconvinced about the merits of free trade. This is true even in a country such as the USA whose governments have supported free trade by any means since long. For example, nearly 70 % of the respondents to a survey undertaken in the USA in the late 1990s advocated limiting imports.[15] The recent Great Recession did not help to convince a recalcitrant public opinion: "the proportion of respondents in an NBC/Wall Street Journal" poll saying globalization has been good for the U.S. economy has fallen precipitously, from 42 percent in June 2007 to 25 percent in March 2008" (Rodrik 2011, xiv).

The economists played a crucial role in endowing policy makers with, allegedly "scientific", arguments to justify the adoption of free-trade measures in front of a reluctant public opinion. These measures have been typically cherished by creditors and net exporter big business but not by workers and farms. Did the economists succeed in finding robust general arguments in favour of free trade? Many qualified economists have recently argued that the answer should be negative.[16]

Adam Smith, the founding father of economic liberalism, played an important role also as an influential advocate of free trade. Its specific argument in support of free trade is rather rudimentary as it focuses mainly on the beneficial division of labour between countries based on their absolute advantage in the production of specific goods. This is an immediate implication of one of the fundamental propositions of his economic system: the positive correlation between the extension of the market and division of labour, which allows increasing productivity of factors through specialisation and scale economies. In this view, free trade has effects equivalent to technological progress. If a country can obtain a certain quantity of a good by buying it from abroad instead of producing it at a higher cost at home, why should the government put obstacles to it through tariffs and quotas? It would be like refusing technical progress by raising obstacles to the adoption of a more efficient machine. Other economists before Smith had already worked out similar arguments in favour of free trade, sometimes in a more compelling way.[17] However, Smith was much more influential also because in the meantime the industrial revolution had progressed in a substantial way and with it the influence of the interests in favour of free trade. In addition, he was the first to present the argument in favour of free trade as a natural corollary of the advantages of free markets that he first argued in a systematic and convincing way. Smith's argument, however, had a few shortcomings.

Although the analogy with technical progress suggests that free-trade benefits all traders, this is literally true only if the technological level reached by trading countries is comparable. Otherwise, the technologically advanced country could have an absolute advantage in most sectors with the only likely exception of raw materials and agriculture whose production costs depend mainly on natural scarcity and climate.[18] With his theory of comparative advantage, David Ricardo ingeniously circumvented this objection. Ricardo was able to show that, by specialising in the productive activities exhibiting a comparative advantage, all countries could gain from foreign trade even if one of them were more productive than the other countries in the production of all goods.[19] Free trade allows thus a process of international division of labour that exploits the relative (rather than absolute) advantages of countries whatever their ultimate cause (natural, cultural, institutional, and so on).[20]

The modern versions of the theory of free trade rely on general equilibrium. This approach allowed further refinements in the theory of comparative advantages. In particular, Heckscher and Ohlin clarified the crucial role of factor endowments.[21] In this view, a country has a comparative advantage in producing the good that uses intensively the abundant production factor. Therefore, a country exports goods that use its abundant factors intensively and imports goods that use its scarce factors intensively.[22]

Samuelson observed that the theory of comparative advantage "is probably the only proposition in economics that is at once true and non-trivial" (quoted in Rodrik 2011, 50). Notwithstanding this and many other similar authoritative endorsements, the comparative advantage argument suffers from a series of weak points. The models of free trade have the same shortcomings of the free-market models discussed in the preceding sections as they are all expressed in terms of general equilibrium theory. However, the limitations of general equilibrium theory descending from its assumptions are much more constraining in the case of free-trade theory.

First, standard models ignore transaction costs including transport costs that are so crucial in international trade. Ricardo and Stuart Mill already recognised this weak point, underlining that transport costs may outweigh the potential gain from trade. There is no doubt, however, that the progressive reduction of transport costs since the Industrial Revolution has reduced the significance of this objection favouring the process of globalisation.

The standard models assume also the perfect mobility of production factors within countries, although not across countries, as they assume that free trade will reallocate factors of production from sectors with comparative disadvantage to sectors with comparative advantage. If this mechanism does not work well, the reallocation of resources brought about by free trade is bound to produce unemployment. This reveals a further weakness in standard free-trade models: the assumption that full employment always prevails. I have emphasised this crucial shortcoming already in the models arguing in favour of free markets (see Sect. 2.3), but in the context of international trade this assumption has further crucial implications. Since emerging and declining industries have different productivity levels, the more productive industries will create fewer jobs than the less productive. In the absence of perfect factors mobility, at least within the country under scrutiny, this would produce structural unemployment. In the real world, the costs of factors mobility are significant, taking into account the sunk costs of investments in plants and machinery and the huge costs associated with the retraining and relocation of labour. This is a reason for protecting 'nascent industries' from fully liberalised international trade during the period in which new firms should pay a high cost of entry into the market.

A further important limitation of the free-trade argument relates to the fact that the standard theory of comparative advantage assumes constant returns to scale while manufactured products are often characterised by increasing returns to scale. As critics of free trade pointed out, "with increasing returns, the lowest cost will be incurred by the country that starts earliest and moves fastest on any particular line. Potential competitors have to protect their own industries if they wish them to survive long enough to achieve competitive scale" (Galbraith 2008, 68–69).

In the presence of scale economies, nations that reach large-scale production in an industry will be successful simply because they were first.[23] This justifies the "infant industry argument" first formulated by Alexander Hamilton and Friedrich List at the beginning of the nineteenth century. This argument has far-reaching consequences. It means that the international division of production depends not only on the spontaneous industrial history of countries but also on the more or less far-sighted policies of their governments.[24]

Another distorting feature of free-trade models is the usual assumption of perfect competition in international markets. In the real world, big multinational corporations succeed to manipulate markets and policy makers in their own interest.

The assumption of absence of externalities is a further crucial assumption that biases the argument in favour of free trade. Goods produced in a country with laxer environmental standards are relatively cheaper. Under these circumstances, free trade boosts the exports of pollution-haven countries but increases the imports of more environmentally virtuous countries disincentivising the adoption of higher environmental standards and deteriorating further the global environment.

Another significant externality is the consequence of "technological spillovers", which occur when technological progress in a particular industry benefits not only its own stakeholders but also other economic agents that do not contribute to its profits. Subsidised foreign competitors may undermine the survival of an industry that generates technological spillovers because the price system does not accurately reflect all the value produced and its origin. This process of adverse selection affects efficiency and may slow down the pace of technological progress.

As the previous discussion shows, comparative advantage theory relies on a static approach that greatly undermines the robustness of its arguments. For example, international factor mobility can alter nations' relative factor abundance changing the distribution of comparative advantages. A longer-run evolutionary perspective shows that it pays to invest in strategic emerging industries even if this would imply a sacrifice of short-term efficiency. In other words, the "infant industry" exception to free trade does not apply only to developing countries but also to any developed country that wishes to keep its economy up to date with the evolution of technology.

The factors contributing to long-term growth are multiple and very complex and are affected by path dependency and positive externalities that are ignored by the standard theory of comparative advantage. This is a major reason why nations that have openly rejected this theory as a guide to policy, like Japan and China, have been so successful in recent decades.

The most compelling criticism of free trade has to do with its distributive consequences that most advocates of free trade have ignored or underplayed. The standard model of international trade shows that, by eliminating any obstacle to trade (e.g. a tariff), a country has a net gain. The trouble with this result is that not everyone gains from liberalisation measures. Free-trade advocates, however, contend that, in the long run, these losses will be reabsorbed, and most people will be better off. This optimistic belief is not supported by compelling arguments. On the contrary, Stolper and Samuelson (1941) proved long ago that a part of society is bound to suffer long-term losses from free trade. What is worse, the order of magnitude of the redistribution effect is generally much greater than the aggregate net gain. For example, Rodrik found that in the USA a move to complete free trade would redistribute $50 for any dollar of aggregate net gain.[25]

To conclude this section, it is interesting to see how free-trade theory co-evolved with globalisation. In the century preceding World War I, world trade experienced a continuous vigorous growth that was broadly consistent with comparative advantage theory as it was based mainly on the marked differences between developed countries exporting manufactured goods and developing countries mainly exporting natural resources. Core countries forced this pattern of "freed trade" through colonialist and imperialist policy strategies.[26] The theory of comparative advantages, however, neglected a factor that played a crucial role already in that period: increasing returns in the form of localised external economies that strongly influenced intra-national trade.[27] This aspect of international trade increased progressively in importance at the turn of the century stimulating the development of the Heckscher-Ohlin model. The First Globalisation exhausted its momentum with World War I, and trade declined until the end of World War II, retaining to some extent the character of trade promoted by comparative advantage. When trade resumed its growth starting the Second Globalisation, trade between countries exchanging similar goods became increasingly important. This explains why in this period the so-called "new trade theory" based on increasing returns emerged and was so successful. However, in the most recent period—broadly coinciding with the second phase of the Second Globalisation— international trade has been again dominated by comparative advantage: "with the rise of China and other low-wage economies, we seem once again to be in a comparative advantage world, in which countries with very different resources export very different goods" (Krugman 2009, 11). The co-evolution of globalisation and trade theory shows how dependent is trade theory on the vagaries of globalisation and how much globalisation relies on the, allegedly sound, arguments provided by economists.

3.6   Cross-Country Movements of Productive Factors

Most arguments concerning free trade depend on the assumptions concerning the cross-country mobility of productive factors. According to the Heckscher-Ohlin model, cross-country movements of productive factors act as a substitute for trade of goods and services.[28] However, as we have seen in the preceding section, the assumptions of this model are unlikely to hold true in the real world so that what the model really does is to contribute to explain why the substitution between factors of production and commodities is incomplete. Consequently, we should consider the cross-country movements of productive factors from the point of view of their specific constraints, motivations, and implications. This section briefly discusses their desirability and their main effects.

Migration flows are a crucial cause and consequence of globalisation and deeply affect the functioning of global markets. International labour mobility, though, is a particularly contentious issue. Traditional international economic theory maintains that the elimination of the barriers to labour mobility would lead to the equalisation of wages across countries and would thus contribute to economic efficiency. Classical liberalism supported this analysis and succeeded to influence policy makers in many countries to adopt its prescriptions. Smith emphasised that a free market requires the free movement of people. In the Chap. X of the first book of *The Wealth of Nations*, Smith's sharp criticism of the Elizabethan Poor Law of 1601 makes clear the importance he attached to this requisite.[29] He argued that, by assigning poor people to a specific parish to obtain the required support, the law prevented the necessary mobility of people from the areas characterised by excess supply of labour to those characterised by excess demand of labour, jeopardising equilibrium in the labour market and national prosperity.[30]

The exponents of classical liberalism had in mind mainly the movement of labour within a single country that in the eighteenth century and early nineteenth century was still impeded by any sort of constraints including local duties and binding laws such as the Poor Law. However, the cross-country mobility of labour has similar causes and effects, and this induced classical liberalism to consider favourably also cross-country migrations. In consequence of this attitude, improving transport facilities and falling costs relative to wages, the First Globalisation was characterised by huge migratory flows that contributed to reduce the gap between developed and developing countries. This tendency gathered momentum in the second phase of the First Globalisation that was still influenced on this specific issue by liberal principles (1850–1914). In this period, about the 10 % of the world population was migrating, much more than the 3 % of the Second Globalisation. At the turn of the century, one million people a year migrated to the new world. Most migrants in this period were pushed by poverty, hunger, and unemployment and pulled by the hope in better job opportunities.

The Second Globalisation by contrast has been characterised by a generalised adoption of anti-immigration laws that greatly reduced the cross-country mobility of labour, while the mobility of capital was completely liberalised. Neoliberal exponents and policy makers believed that the complete liberalisation of capital movements could surrogate a reduced cross-country mobility of the labour force. This led in many areas, and in particular in Europe, to an extensive delocalisation of productive processes in foreign countries with lower wages or laxer protection of trade unions rights and environmental constraints. The severely constrained mobility of labour coupled with the complete mobility of capital contributed to shift the balance of power from labour to capital in many developed countries. During the Second Globalisation, immigration was not so much determined by economic motivations as in the first one, but by the desire to escape war, violence, persecution, and environmental disasters. Since this book focuses on economic globalisation, the following chapters will not consider migration flows in all their dimensions but only insofar as they interacted with the functioning of global markets.

As for the role of capital, we have to distinguish between cross-border movement of real capital (expenditure in plants and machinery) and of financial capital. The traditional theory of comparative advantage requires the assumption that real capital is not significantly mobile between nations. David Ricardo, for example, believed that capital does not move easily from one country to another because of the enhanced insecurity of its control and "the natural disinclination which every man has to quit the country of his birth and connections, and entrust himself, with all his habits fixed, to a strange government and new laws" (Ricardo 1817, 83). As he put it in his standard example of the trade in English cloth for Portuguese wine:

> It would undoubtedly be advantageous to the capitalists of England, and to the consumers in both countries, that under such circumstances, the wine and the cloth should both be made in Portugal, and therefore that the capital and labour of England employed in making cloth should be removed to Portugal for that purpose. (Ibid.)

In his opinion, however, this would not be advantageous for workers in England, and since most consumers are also workers, there is no guarantee that under free-trade English citizens would gain more in the former capacity than they would lose in the latter. The process of globalisation has made obsolete Ricardo's assertions on the mobility of capital taking into account that trade and foreign direct investment motivate a small percentage of global capital flows as compared with rapidly growing financial flows. In addition, the Second Globalisation shifted the balance between financial flows to support the real economy and those to earn speculative gains in favour of the latter. While still in the early 1980s foreign direct investment constituted the 90 % of cross-border capital flows, this percentage has become less than 10 % in consequence of the amazing growth of speculative flows.

A crucial feature of traditional free-trade theory is that it ignores financial flows across countries that are so important in the financial globalisation of the last decades. The trouble is that in traditional theory comparative advantages depend on the fact that countries face different costs for producing goods. Therefore, if prices do not reflect correctly these costs, the market mechanism is bound to produce distortionary results.

Summing up, during the First Globalisation, the massive migration of workers played the role of last-resort equaliser. Notwithstanding their significant impact on the global markets, the growth of inequality was only slowed down. During the Second Globalisation, cross-border capital movements were supposed to play the role of last-resort equaliser but the growth of inequality did not relent; on the contrary, inequality that had subsided since World War 1 started to grow again. We may find one reason for growing inequality in the progressive decline of foreign direct investment on the total of capital flows. In addition, the multinational corporations that implemented foreign direct investment in peripheral countries kept much of the profits in the core countries of origin.[31]

3.7   Concluding Remarks

The preceding brief critical survey on the properties and desirability of free trade suggests that the arguments produced so far in favour of free trade are surprisingly weak. A growing number of economists share this opinion but they are still a minority in the profession.[32] This raises the puzzling question of why most economists are such enthusiastic supporters of free trade, despite the arguments in its favour are so weak. In my opinion, this depends on the deep-seated rooting of the free-trade doctrine in the typical vision of most economists. It seems obvious that any free act of trade is bound to advantage all the traders for the simple reason that the agreement to trade is voluntary and traders are in general not masochist. If this is true for any single act of trade, why should it not be true for a sum of them? Or, indeed, the sum of all of them? Unfortunately, for all its intuitive appeal, this apparent truism is strongly misleading because it does not take into account three insidious pitfalls: the fallacy of composition, the distributive effects of trade, and market externalities.

Moreover, the concept of freedom underlying free trade is ambiguous and misleading. This is revealed by a typical apology of free trade claiming that the case for free trade ultimately is a moral one since it has to do with people's freedom to act as they wish.[33] This view does not take into account the freedom of people damaged by free trade. Free-trade advocates focus on freedom as mere freedom of choice between the elements of a given set of available options, whatever are the number and variety of these options, disregarding the factors that shape the range and contents of these sets.[34] They take into account, and stigmatise, only the constraints on individual liberty imposed by the state. If we accept this shallow concept of freedom, often restricted to its negative dimension (see Chap. 2), even the choice of giving a thief the purse in exchange of life rather than both life and purse could be defined as free, although this abnormal and extreme reduction of the option set depends on the thief itself. More in general, whenever a trader manipulates the option set of other traders to draw an advantage, the above concept of freedom is misleading. In addition, this is true also in the ubiquitous case of indirect and unintentional restriction of the freedom of single economic units brought about by the market.

The second pillar of the economist's vision that biases the typical economist in favour of free trade is the belief that its alleged superiority is nothing but an obvious extension to the international level of the presumed superiority of free markets over alternative institutional arrangements of the economic activity in a country. However, the set of circumstances under which free trade within a nation is undesirable is a small subset of the circumstances under which free trade between nations is undesirable. As Rodrik clearly explains:

> This is not because the economic logic that drives commerce within a country is different. It is because there are many more degrees of freedom in both the way that a region adjusts to trade and in the possibilities of governmental response … The defining characteristic of a national market is that it is deeply embedded in a set of social and political institutions—a common legal and regulatory framework provided by the nation-state. The international market is at best weakly embedded in transnational arrangements, and the arrangements that do exist such as the WTO and bilateral investment treaties are commercial rather than fully-fledged political/redistributive/regulatory arrangements. (Rodrik 2015)

Though I agree with Rodrik that the case for free trade is significantly weaker than the case for free markets, I argued in the preceding chapter that the case for free market itself is not as strong as Rodrik himself seems to believe in this passage.

I wish to emphasise that the critical attitude taken on free trade in this book is not motivated by the desire of defending protectionism in its usual narrow meaning of defence of specific national interests through tariffs or quotas and other obstacles to foreign trade. A country should be open, as much as possible, to foreign goods, services, productive factors, technology, and cultural influences, unless there are sound reasons to act otherwise, reasons that policy makers have to ponder case by case with the maximum care. Nevertheless, this open attitude should never undermine the general interests of citizens of all countries involved in international trade and their rights to self-determination and democratic management of internal issues. In particular, the liberalisation of cross-country movements of goods, services, and productive factors as supervised by the WTO and treaties such as those underlying the NAFTA (North American Free Trade Agreement), the European common market, the institution of the Euro, the TTIP (Transatlantic Trade and Investment Partnership), and so on should never limit the citizens' right to choose a model of development and to ensure its social and environmental sustainability. The adoption of this principle may imply constraints to the free movement across countries of material and financial flows. This is why we should never consider free trade and free capital movements as rigid dogmas to be applied by technocrats with a limited accountability. We should always keep in mind that the freedom of people, rather than the freedom of markets, should be the ultimate priority.

Notes

1. Love and Lattimore (2009).
2. See retro Sect. 1.3.
3. Rodrik (2015).
4. Obvious examples are the silk and spices routes connecting the Middle Ages China with the Middle East.
5. See for example Martell (2010).
6. O'Rourke and Williamson (2004).
7. Hopkins (2003).
8. O'Rourke and Williamson (2004), and Eichengreen (2008).
9. An insurmountable problem with any periodisation of this kind is that each country followed a specific trajectory characterised by its own peculiarities. The periodisation here suggested refers to an ideal type of the most advanced countries, mainly the UK in the nineteenth century and the USA after World War II.
10. Particularly significant was the Cobden-Chevalier agreement with France signed in 1860 that reduced French duties on most British manufacturing goods and British duties on French wine and brandy.
11. The UK adopted a full-fledged Gold Standard regime only with the Bank Charter Act of 1844 that gave the Bank of England the monopoly in the issuance of new notes fully backed by gold. This example was soon followed by many of its colonies and a few other countries.
12. In what has been defined the most famous speech in American political history, William J. Bryan expressed efficaciously the sentiments of large parts of the US population against the Gold Standard, claiming that the supporters of Gold Standard " will search the pages of history in vain to find a single instance in which the common people of any land ever declared themselves in favour of a Gold Standard … this was a struggle between the idle holders of idle capital and the struggling masses who produce the

wealth and pay the taxes of the country ... Having behind us the commercial interests and the laboring interests and all the toiling masses, we shall answer [the demand for a Gold Standard] by saying ... you shall not crucify mankind upon a cross of gold" (Bryan 1896).

13. This is the first persistent episode of financialisation after the Industrial Revolution (see Chap. 4).
14. Notice the analogy with the Eurocrisis that will be discussed in Chap. 8.
15. Rodrik (2011, 51).
16. See for example Rodrik (2011), and Driskill (2012).
17. A case in point is Henry Martin who published anonymously in 1701 a tract that anticipated many of the arguments produced later by the economists to advocate free trade; in particular, he developed the analogy between liberalisation and technical progress in a more explicit and persuasive way than Smith himself (Martin 1701; see the comments in Maneschi 2002, and Rodrik 2011).
18. As Galbraith maintains, "countries doomed by climate and history to produce bananas, coffee, or cocoa and little else are invariably poor. Why? First, the demand for their products is inelastic: when supply increases worldwide, the price falls, and with it national income. Second, they suffer from diminishing returns ... Third, a country with just one major cash export will lack a cushion in other products when fashion or technology turns against their specialty. Conversely, diversification pays. Countries with the capacity to diversify across multiple industries are far more likely to weather export demand shocks or insurgent competition from (say) China than those that commit themselves to a single industry or product line. Diversifiers are also better placed to take advantage of new technical opportunities, since by diversification they develop expertise in a range of products and processes" (Galbraith 2008, 70).
19. A thorough understanding of the theory of comparative advantage requires a clarification of the concept of opportunity cost. Opportunity costs measure the loss of output of a good brought out by an increase in the production of another. Trade will occur as long as the opportunity cost differs across countries. If the opportunity cost of a good is less than the international price, then a country will export that good; if the opportunity cost of a good is greater than the international price, then that country will import that good.

20. Stuart Mill (1844) refined further the argument showing that the gain from trade divides between the trading countries in proportion to the demand for imported goods expressed by each of them.
21. Ohlin (1933).
22. This causal nexus may lead to an excessive specialisation of developing countries. Galbraith (2008, 68–69) recalls a tragic example of the risks of overspecialisation as advocated by a narrow interpretation of the free-trade doctrine: "Ireland during the 1800s gives a tragic example of the dangers of specialization. When the union with Great Britain was formed in 1800, Irish textile industries protected by tariffs were exposed to world markets where England had a comparative advantage in technology, experience and scale of operation which devastated the Irish industry. Ireland was forced to specialize in the export of grain while the displaced Irish labour was forced into subsistence farming and relying on the potato for survival. When the potato blight occurred the resulting famine killed at least one million Irish in the worst famine in European history." According to Cecil Woodham-Smith, an historian who is considered the main authority on the subject, "the Irish peasant was told to replace the potato by eating his grain, but Trevelyan [assistant secretary to HM Treasury administrating famine relief] once again refused to take any steps to curb the export of food from Ireland" and wrote, on 3 September (1946), "do not encourage the idea of prohibiting exports … perfect free trade is the right course" (Woodham-Smith 1962, 49, 100, and 118).
23. This is one of the arguments supporting protection for the "infant industry", an argument that may be found already in Mill (1848). Mill maintained that certain additional conditions must also be met in order to justify protection that in any case should be temporary. He specifically mentioned the potential for learning by doing and maturing into an industry viable without protection. Subsequently, Charles Francis Bastable (1891) added another condition requiring that the cumulative net benefits accruing from the protected industry exceed the cumulative costs of protection. Together, these conditions are known as the Mill–Bastable Test.
24. See for example Gomory and Baumol (2001).
25. Rodrik (2011, 57–58).
26. See retro Sect. 3.3.
27. Krugman (2009, 3).
28. See Ohlin (1933). In this view, in the absence of trade barriers, factor prices tend towards a common equilibrium even when productive factors cannot move freely across countries. On the other hand, in the absence of barriers

to productive factors, mobility, goods, and services prices converge towards a common equilibrium, even when goods and services cannot move freely across countries.

29. Smith (1776).

30. According to the original version of the law, the parishes had the duty to take care of their own poor with their own funds. To avoid as much as possible this use of their scarce funds, many churches tried to convince their poor to move to other parishes. However, they needed to settle in the new parishes for 40 days before they had legal rights. In addition, to discourage further the migration of the poor, James II required people to submit notice in writing that they intended to move. In any case, the poor who decided to migrate moved towards the richest churches rather than where the excess demand of labour was higher. Smith concludes his detailed analysis by asserting that the Poor Law is the cause of the unequal distribution of wages and employment across England jeopardising the prosperity of the country. Ricardo and Malthus addressed similar criticisms to the Poor Law.

31. In the second part of the book, I will discuss further reasons of growing inequality. For a comprehensive analysis of this issue, see Piketty (2014).

32. Important recent exceptions are Rodrik (2011), and Driskill (2012).

33. Rodrik (2011, 64).

34. I am inclined to call this shallow concept of freedom as "department store freedom" since in this case the range of options may be measured by the number of goods on the shelves and their variety (avoiding double counting). The Venn diagram often used to represent this kind of freedom is based on a similar spatial intuition. For a brief critical survey of this literature, see for example Vercelli (1998a).

Bibliography

Bastable, Charles F. 1891 [1921]. *The Commerce of Nations*, 10 edn. London: Macmillan and Co.

Bryan, William J. 1896, July 9. Speech to the Democratic National Convention, *Official Proceedings of the Democratic National Convention Held in Chicago, Illinois, July 7, 8, 9, 10, and 11*, Logansport, Indiana: 226–234.

Driskill, Robert. 2012. Deconstructing the Argument for Free Trade: A Case Study of the Role of Economists in Policy Debates. *Economics and Philosophy* 28: 1–30.

Eichengreen, Barry. 2008. *Globalizing Capital: A History of the International Monetary System*, 2 edn. Princeton and Oxford: Princeton University Press.

Galbraith, James K. 2008. *The Predator State: How Conservatives Abandoned the Free Market and Why Liberals Should Too*. New York: Free Press.

Gomory, Ralph E., and William J. Baumol. 2001. *Global Trade and Conflicting National Interests*. Cambridge, Mass.: MIT Press.

Hopkins, Antony G. 2003. *Globalization in World History*. New York City (NY): Norton.

Krugman, Paul. 2009. The Big Zero. Op-ed, *The New York Times*, Dec. 27.

Love, Patrick, and Ralph Lattimore. 2009. *International Trade: Free, Fair, and Open?* Paris: OECD Publishing.

Maneschi, Andrea. 2002. The Tercentenary of Henry Martin's Considerations upon the East-India Trade. *Journal of the History of Economic Thought* 24(2): 233–249.

Mankiw, Gregory N. 2006. Outsourcing Redux. In *Greg Mankiw's Blog: Random Observations for Students of Economics*, May 7. http://gregmankiw.blogspot.co.uk/2006/05/outsourcing-redux.html. Retrieved 2 February 2016.

Martyn, Henry. 1701 [1954]. *Considerations upon the East-India Trade*, reprinted in *Early English Tracts on Commerce*, ed. J. McCulloch, 541–595. Cambridge: Cambridge University Press.

Martell, Luke. 2010. *The Sociology of Globalization*. Cambridge: Polity Press.

Mill, John S. 1844. *Essays on Some Unsettled Questions in Political Economy*. London: Longmans, Green, Reader, and Dyer.

Mill, John S 1848. *Principles of Political Economy with Some of their Applications to Social Philosophy*. London: John W. Parker.

Ohlin, Bertil. 1933. *Interregional and International Trade*. Cambridge, MA: Harvard University Press.

O'Rourke, Kevin H., and Jeffrey G. Williamson. 2004. Once More: When Did Globalisation Begin? *European Review of Economic History* 8: 109–117.

Piketty, Thomas. 2014. *Capital in the Twenty-First Century*. Cambridge Mass: Harvard University Press.

Ricardo, David. 1817 [1951–73.] *Principles of Political Economy and Taxation*. In *The Works and Correspondence of David Ricardo*, vol. V, eds. David Ricardo, Piero Sraffa. Cambridge: Cambridge University Press.

Rodrik, Dani. 2011. *The Globalisation Paradox*. In *Why Global Markets, States, and Democracy Can't Coexist*. Oxford: Oxford University Press.

———. 2015. Trade within versus between nations. *Dani Rodrik's weblog, Unconventional Thoughts on Economic Development and Globalization*, September 18, http://rodrik.typepad.com/dani_rodriks_weblog/2015/09/trade-within-versus-between-nations.html. Retrieved 20 September 2015.

Smith, Adam. 1776 [1977]. *An Inquiry into The Nature and Causes of the Wealth of Nations*. Edited by Edwin Cannan. Chicago: University of Chicago Press.

Stolper, Wolfgang F., and Paul A. Samuelson. 1941. Protection and Real Wages. *Review of Economic Studies* 9: 58–73.

Vercelli, Alessandro. 1998a. Operational Measures of Sustainable Development and the Freedom of Future Generations. In *Sustainability: Dynamics and Uncertainty*, eds. Chichilnisky Graciela, Heal Geoffrey, and Alessandro Vercelli. Dordrecht: Martin Kluwer.

Whaples, Robert. 2006. Do Economists Agree on Anything? Yes! *The Economists' Voice* 3(9): 1–6.

Woodham-Smith, Cecil. 1962. *The Great Hunger, Ireland 1845–1849*. New York: Harper and Row.

4

The Evolution of Financialisation

4.1 Introduction

The neoliberal policy strategy adopted in most countries since the early 1980s triggered a process of development characterised by a trend of growing globalisation and financialisation.[1] The preceding chapter discussed the origins and impact of globalisation. This chapter aims to provide the necessary background on the meaning, causes, and consequences of financialisation. The insights that will emerge from this preliminary analysis will help us to understand what happened in the recent decades.

In the neoliberal era, the importance of finance has progressively increased assuming a position of pre-eminence in the production and distribution of economic resources. A host of quantitative indexes and qualitative observations confirms this tendency. From the quantitative point of view, a particularly significant index is the Financial Interrelations Ratio (FIR) suggested by Goldsmith to measure the degree of financial development reached by a country in a certain stage of its economic evolution.[2] The FIR measures specifically the degree of financial intermediation of a certain economic system, namely it is the ratio between the liabilities of the financial corporations and the sum of the liabilities of all the other

A. Vercelli, *Crisis and Sustainability*,
DOI 10.1057/978-1-137-60069-1_4

sectors. The FIR started to increase after the post-war Reconstruction, but until the 1970s finance continued to conform to the regulatory and supervisory rules introduced in the 1930s and did not play a crucial role in driving the process of accumulation. Since the late 1970s, the FIR accelerated reflecting the change in policy strategy implemented by the new neoliberal orientation of policy makers. The impact of the process goes much beyond this quantitative change affecting the behavioural rules of economic agents and deeply transforming the trajectory of development. The index is subject to country-specific short-run fluctuations that depend mainly on the fluctuations of the real economy and the institutional setting. Other indexes, such as the share of GDP produced by the financial sector, also showed a significant increase in the relative weight of finance since the late 1970s. These examples suggest, however, that the existing quantitative indexes do not capture the main features of financialisation and its consequences, as they are unable to reflect the growing importance of financial motives in other sectors of the economy such as that of non-financial firms and households. The importance of the process of financialisation crucially relates to the qualitative features of agents' behaviour increasingly affected by financial constraints and motivations.

The neoliberal financialisation is an idiosyncratic historical process that we have to understand in all its specificities. A merely historicist approach, however, risks blurring the causal relations behind a smokescreen of historical details. To understand the main causes and consequences of neoliberal financialisation, it is useful to investigate whether it is possible to find analogies in preceding historical episodes. Historical analogies point out to similar causes helping one to detect them in the dark forest of historical specificities. This is what this chapter intends to do.

Section 4.2 discusses to what extent, and in what sense, financialisation is a recurring phenomenon. This approach suggests a tentative explanation of the main common causes underlying different episodes of financialisation. The investigation focuses on the two most recent episodes of financialisation after the Industrial Revolution. These are the so-called "First Financialisation" that occurred at the turn of the nineteenth century and the so-called "Second Financialisation" that occurred at the turn of the twentieth century. The historical evidence shows that these episodes of rapid financialisation alternated with periods of slower, sometimes even receding, financialisation (or de-financialisation). This begs the question whether the fluctuations of financialisation occurred around a trend or not. Section 4.3 argues that we can detect a secular tendency towards financialisation. This tendency is very slow and manifests itself in diverse ways in different countries and historical periods. However, the progressive steps of financialisation have a common root in the nature of financial innovations underlying them. Financialisation-enhancing innovations aim to increase the agents' flexibility of choice as this improves their expected returns. Section 4.4 discusses the dark side of the process of financialisation from the point of view of sustainability. Section 4.5 emphasises that the deep but abstract analogies between different episodes and stages of financialisation should never cloud the crucial differences between them. A thorough analysis of the process of financialisation must always combine a careful investigation of both analogies and differences. This section will restrain to some hints at the structural differences between the two most recent episodes of financialisation. A more detailed analysis of the Second Financialisation will follow in the second part of this book, mainly in Chap. 6. The concluding section of this chapter (Sect. 4.6) briefly summarises the pros and cons of the process of financialisation from the point of view of sustainability.

4.2   Financialisation as a Recurring Phenomenon

Most economic historians agree that the recent process of financialisation is just the latest instance of a sequence of similar historical episodes. This suggests the conjecture that financialisation is in some sense a recurrent phenomenon. In order to analyse analogies and differences between different episodes and stages of financialisation, we need a preliminary definition broad enough to encompass all the instances we want to compare. To this end, I suggest to define financialisation as a *process of evolution of money that progressively increases its influence in the economy and society*.[3] This definition requires a few specifications. First, this definition uses the word "money" in its broadest acceptation that includes also credit and finance.[4] Second, money does not refer here only to a mere quantity that can be created, multiplied, hoarded, and utilised as a mean of exchange and deposit of value; it refers also to its role as institution, shaping the forms of exchange and accumulation, determining the viability and efficiency of economic transactions. Finally, let me emphasise that money, as defined above, is in its essence a network of social relations that mediates between the members of a society through impersonal and unintentional links that blur their personal links but deeply affect their actions.

This clarification on the meaning of money is important because the reduction of its complex meaning to its quantitative meaning has been a source of widespread misunderstandings that have unduly lessened the importance of money and clouded the significance of financialisation. This sort of quantitative reductionism has characterised since long the mainstream approach of economics to money as soon as the early monetary theory started to be based on the "quantitative theory of money".[5] The underlying equation of exchange established simple quantitative relations between the principal aggregate variables (money supply, its velocity of circulation, and the indexes of prices and income) under the explicit assumption of invariance of money as technology, institution, and social relation. The extraordinary success of this first rudimentary quantitative model contributed to convince most mainstream economists that money is just a veil blurring the vision of the real economy without affecting it in a substantial way.[6] Even many heterodox economists played down the importance of money in the conviction that the monetary forms of exchange and production were just a superstructure of the real economy without a decisive autonomous influence on the underlying structure. This opinion implies a reductionist approach to money different from that accepted by mainstream economics but convergent towards a common undervaluation of its crucial role.

As soon as we assume the broader definition of money adopted in this chapter, we are in a position to understand analogies and differences between distinct episodes of financialisation. Economic historians mention various spells of financialisation since the discovery of the new world, culminating with two long episodes of unprecedented intensity: a first surge of financialisation from about 1880 to 1929 that is often called First Financialisation and a second surge from about 1980 up to now that is often called Second Financialisation. Which are the factors that trigger and sustain these historical episodes? Let us investigate three main explanations that do not necessarily exclude each other.

According to the first one, financialisation is a reaction to economic and political decline. From the economical point of view, a typical causal explanation of Marxian ascendancy points out that a declining rate of profit in the real economy encourages the search for higher or additional profits in finance.[7] A more articulated variant of this point of view sees financialisation as an escape from the malfunctioning sphere of production towards the more profitable sphere of circulation.[8] The basic idea is that monopolistic capital produces a growing surplus that is increasingly difficult to realise. In the 1970s, the traditional methods of surplus absorption (such as unproductive consumption and military expenditure) became insufficient for many firms that thus sought a solution in the process of financialisation that channelled the extra surplus in the speculative activities of finance.

Turning now to the political point of view, a declining hegemonic power typically compensates the fading political influence through a proactive management of credit made possible by the capital accumulated in financial form in the previous period. We find this idea already in Marx who in his analysis of the so-called primitive accumulation reconstructs an historical sequence showing that the declining commercial power typically becomes the principal lender to the emerging commercial power. In this way, the declining country prolongs its prosperity and political influence by exploiting the capital accumulated in financial form in the period of their commercial hegemony. In the seventeenth century, declining Venice supported with financial capital the emergence of Holland as manufacturing power; declining Holland supported in a similar way the rise of England in the eighteenth and nineteenth centuries; and declining England supported with abundant loans the surge of the USA in the twentieth century.[9] Analogously, Braudel detected two waves of financialisation before the Industrial Revolution: the first wave when the Genoese withdrew from commerce and specialised in finance establishing a symbiotic relation with the kingdom of Spain that offered military protection in exchange of abundant credit for their exploration of new commercial routes.[10] The second wave occurred after 1740 when the Dutch withdrew from international trade to become the bankers of Europe.

After the Industrial Revolution, the nexus between political decline and financialisation becomes even more evident. According to the well-known social scientist Giovanni Arrighi, the First Financialisation is a response to the decline of the British Empire, while the Second Financialisation relates to the decline of the American hegemony.[11] Analogously, the political commentator Kevin Phillips argued in a best-selling book that financialisation preluded to the collapse of Empires in history. Examples are the Roman Empire, Habsburg Spain in the sixteenth century, the Dutch trading Empire in the eighteenth century, and the British Empire in the nineteenth century. He claims that the ongoing financialisation of the US economy, if unchecked, preludes to the collapse of its hegemony.[12]

In my opinion, any explanation of the episodes of financialisation that relies mainly on the economic and political decline of the financialising country is partial and potentially misleading. First, financialisation is an international phenomenon, and its analysis cannot be restricted to a single country. This is not to deny that financialisation assumes dissimilar characteristics in distinct countries in consequence of their different institutional and policy features. However, we may understand not only the analogies but also the peculiarities of financialisation only in the light of its global evolution. Second, while financialisation slows down the decline of the previously dominant country, it accelerates the takeover of the emerging country. If, from the supply side, financialisation is typical of a declining country, from the demand side, the growing importance of finance in a country is a sign of its emergent success. There is no contradiction in this observation since financialisation is, in its essence, a catalyst of accelerated structural change. Since structural change produces losers and winners, losers associate it with decline while winners associate it with progress. Therefore, to connect financialisation mainly with decline is misleading as soon as this point of view is extended to the whole process and all its actors. In particular, the First Financialisation has been interpreted as a sign of irreversible breakdown, or "highest stage" of capitalism.[13] This point of view reappeared also in reference to the Second Financialisation after the Great Recession. However, both the First and the Second Financialisation are basically periods of accelerated structural change. Whether the new stage is better or worse than the preceding stage, and whether the direction of change is sustainable or not, it is a much more complex issue that has to consider all the significant aspects of the process.

A different approach relates financialisation not to economic and political decline but to "long waves". In this view, the episodes of financialisation emerge in a specific phase of recurring long-run fluctuations. These phases are characterised by rapid structural change that may be progressive or regressive according to the point of view and the specific circumstances. The "long waves" of these fluctuations are not regular cycles but exhibit recurrent qualitative features that require an explanation as they have a significant impact on the evolution of the economy and society. The existence of long waves in history has been noticed since long. In modern economics, a systematic analysis of long-run fluctuations started with Kondratieff who detected in the empirical evidence long, irregular fluctuations lasting from 48 to 60 years, and discussed their possible causes originating a rich literature.[14] Schumpeter endorsed the existence and significance of Kondratieff cycles and provided the most influential causal account. According to Schumpeter, long cycles reflect the sequence of technological paradigms originating from recurrent industrial revolutions.[15] His followers, often called with the collective name of "neo-Schumpeterian school", have further developed the analysis of the technological trajectories broadening its scope by integrating the technological dimension with the economic, institutional, and policy dimensions of capitalist evolution.[16] This book will refer mainly to the version of Carlota Perez whose recent contributions are particularly relevant for the subsequent analysis.[17]

According to the neo-Schumpeterian approach, the evolution of capitalism is characterised by a sequence of technological paradigms triggered by a technological revolution. In the installation phase of a new technological paradigm, financial capital leads the process of economic growth because it provides the necessary structural flexibility that makes possible the rapid structural change occurring in the economy and in society itself. This is a phase characterised by "creative destruction" to use the evocative image suggested by Schumpeter.[18] Typically, the excessive and unfettered flexibility in the real economy accompanied by growing financial instability leads to a great crisis such as the Great Depression (1929–1939) or the Great Recession (2007–2009). After a prolonged period of economic turbulence that may extend up to a decade or more, a healthier phase of growth typically emerges. In this phase, the existing technological paradigm deploys in a more harmonic way with the help of a policy strategy and institutional setting better calibrated to the new techno-economic paradigm. In this period of "creative construction", typically financial capital steps back, and productive capital resumes the lead of the growth process.[19]

In this view, the First Financialisation was instrumental to the installation of a new technological trajectory based on the systematic use of oil as principal energy source, the development of automobile, and mass production, while the Second Financialisation was instrumental to the installation of a new technological trajectory based on the installation of the information and communication technologies (ICT). The first period of creative destruction led eventually to the Great Depression, while the second one led to the Great Recession. It is interesting to observe that this technological perspective connects the episodes of financialisation not to decline but to the most dynamic part of the process of development. This phase is by no means an idyllic process. The installation of a new technological paradigm produces a process of accelerated structural change that implies the rapid "destruction" of obsolete economic activities, the dislocation of production, and the impoverishment of workers and social classes trapped in the old activities. These periods are often characterised by increasing poverty and inequality leading to social turmoil and political upheavals but cannot be defined simply as periods of decline. As for the desirability of financialisation, one has to evaluate the nature and direction of structural change from the point of view of specific ethical and political values. The point of view adopted in this book is that of sustainability (see Sects. 1.6 and 7.6).

As we have seen, according to the neo-Schumpeterian school, the evolution of capitalism is characterised by a sequence of *technological paradigms*, each of which has its own life cycle. According to a different, but complementary, point of view, the evolution of capitalism is characterised by a sequence of *development paradigms*, each of which has its own life cycle.[20] A development paradigm is a view of the direction that structural change should pursue to improve the well-being of people in a sustainable way. Each paradigm is rooted in a macroeconomic paradigm, namely a vision of how the economy works. We may detect in the history of capitalism a succession of macroeconomic paradigms each of which justifying and sustaining a policy strategy believed to be optimal. Since the Industrial Revolution, we may observe an alternation of macroeconomic paradigms more open to free markets and free trade with macroeconomic paradigms that enhance the constraints to the spontaneous working of markets.[21] The adoption of a policy strategy of the first kind spurs globalisation and financialisation, while the adoption of a policy strategy of the second kind slows down, sometimes even reverses, the trend of globalisation and financialisation.

The common root of globalisation and financialisation contributes to explain why these two processes exhibit a strict empirical correlation at least since the Industrial Revolution. As we have seen in Chap. 3, the First Globalisation broadly overlaps with the First Financialisation,[22] while the Second Globalisation surged together with the Second Financialisation in the late 1970s. The focus on the evolution of policy strategies points to a further important causal factor whose role is often neglected or underplayed: the role of economic thought and its underlying political ideologies in the evolution of capitalism. The dominant policy strategy is typically based on the dominant macroeconomic paradigm. Therefore, when a great crisis occurs, a rapidly growing number of critics laid the blame on the policy strategy ruling in the period preceding the crisis, and indirectly on the macroeconomic paradigm inspiring such a policy strategy. This leads to the adoption of a new macroeconomic paradigm supporting a new policy strategy believed to be able to overcome the shortcomings of the preceding orthodoxy. The new policy strategy seems to work well in the short period also because its advocates tailored it to solve the problems manifested by the crisis. In the longer period, new anomalies emerge that cumulate their effects until a new great crisis occurs.

We may use this conceptual framework to clarify the causes and consequences of the First and Second Financialisation. The critics of traditional liberalism immediately laid the blame for the Great Depression on the previous mainstream policy strategy based on the laissez-faire recommended by classical economics. This produced a paradigm change rendering Keynesian macroeconomics the new dominant view underlying a new policy strategy. This led to the adoption of much stricter rules of financial control, regulation, and supervision that determined the sudden decline of the First Financialisation. The new policy strategy supported a period of unprecedented prosperity characterised by high growth rates, full employment, monetary and financial stability. A few anomalies started to emerge in the late 1960s and led to a new great crisis in the 1970s characterised by stagnation and inflation (stagflation). The critics of the Keynesian paradigm immediately blamed the existing policy strategy for these economic failures and advocated an updated form of classical economics (self-defined New Classical Economics) supporting a new policy strategy often called neoliberal. This new policy environment was instrumental to a rapid development of the Second Financialisation.

The evolution of policy strategies is broadly synchronised with the evolution of technological trajectories by the crucial impact that the great crises have on both. This produces a co-evolution between technological surges and macroeconomic paradigms keeping in mind that, in principle, the life cycle of macroeconomic paradigms has, broadly speaking, a half-cycle lag relatively to the life cycle of a technological trajectory. Typically, a great crisis does not start a technological trajectory but ends the phase of its installation, while it starts the life cycle of a new policy paradigm. Of course, the co-evolution between technological and development trajectories is affected by direct interactions between these two processes that have been largely ignored so far in the literature. In what follows, I will provide some hints of this interaction. On one hand, as has been often recognised, the waves of technological progress in the field of transport had a crucial impact on the process of globalisation and thus also of financialisation. On the other hand, the ruling development paradigm affects the way in which a certain technological paradigm is installed and deployed. In particular, Chap. 7 will argue that the neoliberal policy paradigm drove the installation of the ICT paradigm in a direction inconsistent with sustainability. After the crisis, we should aim to deploy the potential of the ICT in a different direction that could contribute to the implementation of a sustainable trajectory. This may happen, however, only if a sustainable development paradigm will supersede the neoliberal paradigm of development.

4.3   Financialisation as a Long-Run Tendency: The Driving Role of Financial Innovations

I have argued so far that we can detect in history a series of episodes of financialisation exhibiting substantial differences but also significant analogies. We may wonder whether these fluctuations of financialisation occur around a sort of long-run trend or not. This section aims to suggest that there is a secular tendency towards financialisation that is intrinsic in the evolution of market relations. This daring assertion requires a few preliminary qualifications. The tendency towards growing financialisation has been quite irregular, often interrupted, and reversed and has been diversified in time and space because financialisation is affected by cultural, material, and political conditions which vary in different times and areas.[23] Still, if we compare a recent episode of de-financialisation, such as the period of Bretton Woods, with an earlier period of financialisation, such as the Venetian one in the Renaissance period, we see immediately—as is obvious—that the importance of banks and financial markets was then much less prominent than in recent times. The contemporaries perceived the novelties introduced by the process of financialisation and were impressed by the unprecedented importance of money, credit, and finance. For example, in the *Merchant of Venice*, Shakespeare represented in a vivid way a few dire human implications of the contemporaneous process of financialisation but could not even imagine to what extremes the process would have brought the humankind in the future.[24]

The development of market relations progressed in history in a complex, non-linear, and unsteady way. Still we can detect a progressive tendency towards a growing opposition between the use value of goods and their exchange value. The genesis and development of money are rooted in this process of separation of exchange value from the use value of goods and services. In the end, money transforms itself from mere means of exchange to ultimate end of the exchange to accumulate more and more value. Credit becomes a crucial permissive condition of investment and accumulation of capital. The accumulation of financial capital eventually loses its role of support to the accumulation of real capital and becomes the self-referential goal of accumulation.[25]

This tendency towards financialisation took millennia to develop in a slow, complex, and often contradictory, way also because in the past different reasons contributed to repress it: religious, political, ethical reasons, and so on.[26] This contributes to explain the fluctuations of the process. The tendency towards financialisation decelerated, sometimes even declined, when the repression became tougher as, for example, in the Bretton Woods period (1945–1971), while it accelerated when financial repression was relaxed given birth to the episodes of financialisation proper (e.g. in the neoliberal era from 1980 up to now).

The assertion that we can detect a secular tendency towards increasing financialisation should not be interpreted as an "iron law" of history but as the unintended result of a myriad of monetary and financial innovations adopted at the micro level just because they were expected to increase the utility or returns of the innovators. Other agents soon adopted the successful innovations spreading them in the market. The reason why this decentralised and chaotic innovation process produced a general upward tendency is that most monetary and financial innovations have something in common: they increase the flexibility of choice of economic agents. In other words, a financial innovation increases the range of available options between which the innovator may choose. This increases in principle his liberty of choice and economic power. In addition, a larger option set correlates with higher expected returns because one or more of the new options may dominate the pre-existing options. Rigorous decision theory and portfolio selection theory confirmed the existence of a positive correlation between flexibility and expected returns.[27]

A significant early example of flexibility-enhancing innovation is the introduction of money as general means of exchange. Whatever was the historical origin of money, the adoption of a medium of exchange accepted by all would-be traders in a certain community or geographic area overcame the strictures of "double coincidence of wants" that were severely limiting the range of possible exchanges based upon barter. In consequence of this innovation, the set of potential exchanges became in principle universal, that is encompassed all tradable goods and services within the area where money was accepted as currency or legal tender. Further monetary innovations aimed to enlarge this area or the convertibility with currencies accepted in other areas increasing further the exchange flexibility of would-be traders.[28]

More in general, the main virtue of money as medium of exchange is its liquidity. Liquidity has a static dimension depending on the range of exchange options that it allows in a certain moment, and an inter-temporal dimension related to the range of exchange options that it allows in the future.[29] Most financial innovations aim to create liquidity or to transform its time profile. The basic idea is again very simple. Money has the advantage of liquidity but in normal circumstances it does not involve economic returns, differently from other financial assets that earn returns originated in the commercial and industrial activity to which they contribute. A first category of financial innovations aims to give credit to commercial and industrial entrepreneurs to start and sustain their businesses. This originated specific financial institutions, commercial banks, that managed deposits of money given by savers and created liquidity for the investors. These financial innovations increased the option set of investors allowing their immediate investment, as well as the option set of savers transforming their barren liquidity in interest-earning saving deposits. In particular, as emphasised by Schumpeter, the credit to innovators endowed the economy of the necessary structural flexibility that feeds the process of economic development.[30]

The flexibility of the economy has been traditionally limited by the fact that the capital assets necessary for a commercial and industrial activity are strongly illiquid. An epoch-making financial innovation removed this obstacle by introducing the joint-stock company based on the fragmentation of the ownership of the company's real capital in a number of shares that are marketable, and are thus much more liquid than the real capital that they represent. This technique of securitisation of the real capital systematically extended since the 1970s to any sort of real assets, increasing further their liquidity and the structural flexibility of the economic system (see Chap. 6). We may interpret also the set of innovations related to the recent emergence of shadow banking as a way to increase the liquidity and flexibility of large operators contributing to increase the structural flexibility of the system.[31]

4.4   Financialisation and Sustainability

The features of the process of financialisation that we have examined so far put it in a light that seems more benign than sinister. As we have seen, through an uninterrupted sequence of financial innovations, decision makers have progressively increased the range of options to their disposal. This contributed to their economic freedom and to their power of control on economic resources. Can we conclude that financialisation significantly contributed to the well-being of the human lot? The answer is mixed. The innovators adopt the flexibility-enhancing financial innovations underlying the process of financialisation because, from their own microeconomic point of view, they expect to enhance their returns. Unfortunately, these innovations imply external costs that adversely affect the economic system. In particular, the increased flexibility of the system enhances its instability producing financial bubbles and crises. This trade-off was already clear to Keynes:

> Decisions to invest in private business of the old-fashioned type were … decisions largely irrevocable, not only for the community as a whole, but also for the individual. With the separation between ownership and management which prevails to-day and with the development of organised investment markets, a new factor of great importance has entered in, which sometimes facilitates investment but sometimes adds greatly to the instability of the system. (Keynes 1936, 150–151)

If we keep in mind this trade-off, we cannot be sure that financialisation improves the performance of the system. The increase in micro efficiency that justifies the adoption of a financial innovation in a certain firm, once imitated, may contribute to systemic instability that could trigger a process of debt-deflation leading to recession and a wave of bankruptcies that could eventually involve also the business of the innovator.

The second general effect of financialisation is that of increasing the uncertainty characterising economic decisions. The flexibility of financial decisions greatly enhanced by financialisation makes expectations extremely unstable and subject to contagion. For example, the Stock Exchange greatly enhances the flexibility of investment decisions because gives a frequent opportunity to investors to revise their investment commitments but, at the same time, increases the systemic instability of the economy by making expectations volatile.[32] In such an environment, expectations rely on a conventional valuation that is liable to change suddenly because of new information altering the mood of decision makers.

The third general consequence of financialisation relates to its significant distributive effects. In the absence of suitable institutional and political constraints, a small minority of financiers, rentiers, and complacent politicians reaps the advantages of enhanced economic freedom.

The joint effects of these dark sides of financialisation make the unfettered process of financialisation inconsistent with sustainable development in all its principal dimensions. The increasing inequality in the distribution of income is inconsistent with social sustainability. The market trickle-down mechanisms proved to be too weak to compensate this tendency.[33] The strong, sometimes radical, uncertainty on the expected returns of investment discourages its implementation, especially in the real economy. The growing dominance of exchange value maximisation over use-value within an increasingly shorter time horizon distorts investment by shifting it from the real to the financial sector. This depresses in particular the investment required to assure the environmental sustainability of development (see Chap. 6).

4.5 Differences Between First and Second Financialisation

So far, I focused mainly on the analogies between different episodes of financialisation. This preliminary investigation justified the view here adopted that the process of financialisation is a recurring phenomenon. The ensuing analysis of the fluctuations of financialisation suggested that they occur around a secular trend of increasing financialisation. This view of financialisation may offer a useful background for a thorough analysis of the specificities of each single episode of financialisation. This is what I intend to do in the second part of the book which is about the most recent episode of financialisation, often called Second Financialisation. To pave the way for this investigation, this section hints at some significant differences between

First and Second Financialisation. The variegated nature of financialisation makes difficult a simple comparison between them. We may build, however, an ideal-type of the First Financialisation and one of the Second Financialisations aiming to capture in abstract terms some features that are broadly common in Europe and in the USA in about the same period.

A difference that is often emphasised is that the First Financialisation is bank-based while the Second Financialisation is market-based.[34] At the turn of the nineteenth century, a few major investment banks became so powerful to play almost the role of private planning authorities.[35] At the turn of the twentieth century, financial markets became so powerful to manage not only the financial system but also the entire economy. This view is not altogether groundless but requires a few important qualifications. The importance of banks during the First Financialisation is often overemphasised under the influence of Hilferding who generalised his experience of bank-based German and Austrian capitalism, while, in contemporaneous Anglo-Saxon capitalism, financial markets played a greater role.[36]

Second, there is no doubt that in the Second Financialisation financial markets increased their size and power to an unprecedented level (for a more detailed analysis, see Appendix 1 and Appendix 2). They were spurred by the rocketing increase of an alphabet soup of new securities (such as asset-backed securities and credit default swaps), the direct participation of new financial institutions (such as hedging funds, money market funds, and special purpose vehicles), and the indirect participation of new subjects (non-financial firms, individuals, and households). Third, it is also true that, in this period, banks weakened their traditional role of intermediation between savers and investors. However, in the Second Financialisation, megabanks played a crucial role in shaping and managing financial markets. A case in point is that of the over-the-counter (OTC) derivative market. Its amazing growth from irrelevance in the 1980s to a value of about US$700 trillion in 2011 seems at first sight a sign of the growing dominance of financial markets in financial decisions. However, a more in-depth analysis shows that "banks are the pillar of contemporary derivatives markets both as market-makers … and as organizers of the basic structure of derivatives markets " (Lapavitsas 2013, 6–7). OTC derivatives play the role of banking instruments, as 15 to 20 dealer banks control their trading at the global level (ibid., 8).

The power exerted by banks on financial markets is so pervasive that they could systematically manipulate to their advantage crucial variables such as the LIBOR,[37] namely the interest rate at which derivatives are valued and traded. Big financial banks control financial markets directly also by other means in blatant contrast with the principles of free markets. The manipulation of the ratings of crony agencies and the systematic use of "creative accounting" are further significant examples of deliberate distortion of the market mechanisms on which market efficiency is supposed to rely. Finally, big banks control financial markets indirectly through governments and regulators. Therefore, the crucial difference is that in the Second Financialisation big banks exerted their power in a more indirect and opaque way, making much more arduous their regulation and supervision.

The second significant difference relates to the kind of influence exerted by finance on the real economy through two main causal channels. The first channel of influence depends on the cash-in-advance constraint that characterises any monetary economy. Finance has always exerted a crucial permissive power able to condition political and economic decisions. For example, the kingdom of Castile could not have started the ambitious policy of exploration of new ways of international trade without the abundant loans conceded by Genoese bankers. Later on, in the mercantilist period, the megabanks assumed a crucial role in supporting and conditioning the colonialist and imperialist policies of the most powerful states. This kind of power exerted by finance was thus already existent much before the Industrial Revolution, but became more systematic and influential thereafter when credit became a crucial support of great part of industrial investment. During the First Financialisation, big banks playing the role of coordination and orientation of capitalistic decisions started to exert this sort of power in a more systematic way.[38] During the Second Financialisation, finance extended its influence to the choices of non-financial firms, households, and individuals not only as far as their viability is concerned but also in reference to their contents. This is because the logic of choices of any subject in any field has become more and more influenced by the financial paradigm of portfolio selection within a time horizon as short as that typical of financial decision making.[39] Because of this powerful tendency, the choices consistent with sustainability became increasingly non-competitive with short-term profit maximising alternatives since the former typically imply immediate costs and significant benefits only in a relatively distant future.

A third important difference has to do with the role of central banks. During the First Financialisation, the central banks were still weak as in the UK or absent as in the USA so that their role was still limited or altogether inexistent.[40] On the contrary, the central banks acquired increasing power during the Second Financialisation playing the role of interface between the financial system and policy makers. They became thus the ultimate regulators of liquidity and financial behaviour in the economic system. The measures taken in many countries since the early 1980s to implement the so-called "independence" of central banks progressively weakened the influence of policy makers, regulators, and supervisors whenever financial markets deemed uncongenial their interventions. Central banks assumed thus the role of pivot of the financial system playing a crucial role in the promotion and coordination of the Second Financialisation. In this period, central banks reacted immediately to any inflationary symptom detected in the real economy with restrictive monetary measures, while they did not intervene to check asset inflation but flooded the financial system with liquidity whenever the upward trend of asset prices got out of steam.[41] This monetary policy introduced a bias in the economy in favour of the financial system favouring the process of financialisation. The investors interpreted this monetary policy as an implicit insurance to financial investment crowding out industrial investment.[42] The higher profits earned by financiers and rentiers sustained to some extent aggregate demand in the real economy but not enough to compensate for the declining profits and wages in the industrial sector. Profit earners reinvested a significant part of their higher incomes in the financial system, further contributing to financialisation and strengthening in this way the stagnation tendency observed in the real economy. Therefore, we should not consider financialisation simply as a symptom of the tendencies of Monopoly Capital,[43] but as a crucial determinant of the capitalist evolution and its laws of motion.[44]

A fourth crucial difference between the First and the Second Financialisation relates to the strategy of expansion of capital investment. In the period characterised by the First Financialisation, private investment sought mainly a territorial expansion in new areas supporting the imperialist and colonialist policies of their home countries. During the Second Financialisation, private investment tried to expand not only in peripheral territorial areas devising new—more opaque—forms of colonialism and imperialism, but also at home in the fields presided by the welfare state. The systematic privatisation of health, education, and social security services (including pensions) implemented this strategy in most countries since the late 1970s (see Chap. 5). In particular, the policy rules adopted in the Eurozone to manage the common currency and the austerity policies adopted during the Eurocrisis contributed to dismantle the welfare state in the EU (see Chap. 8). The progressive occupation of the spaces presided by public expenditure in the Bretton Woods period is playing during the Second Financialisation a role similar to that played by traditional colonialism and imperialism during the First Financialisation.

4.6   Concluding Remarks

Mainstream economics sees financialisation as a physiological process meant to increase market efficiency. In this view, any attempt at conditioning or limiting the process would produce inferior results. The Keynesian view that was mainstream in the Bretton Woods period saw financialisation as a process having both physiological and pathological aspects. Other streams of heterodox economics focused on pathological aspects of financialisation that cannot be easily mended or mitigated within a capitalist system. The suggested policy recipes vary with the theoretical framework and the normative objectives but their analysis goes beyond the scope of this chapter.

According to the vision sketched in this chapter, financialisation is a contradictory process. The financial innovations underlying the process of financialisation tend to expand the freedom of the economic agents that adopt them. In principle, this expanded freedom could improve the well-being of all the citizens. However, in the absence of apt institutional and policy constraints, a small minority of financiers, rentiers, and complacent politicians reaps the advantages of enhanced freedom. This distributive bias has been a crucial cause of the Great Recession and the ensuing Eurocrisis.[45] The advocates of the neoliberal policies that have brought about the Second Financialisation claimed that more inequality would have strengthened the incentives to growth, while in the longer run the extra income so produced would have percolated to all the citizens through a trickle-down mechanism. An extensive interdisciplinary empirical literature has demonstrated that inequality does not provide incentives to improve the effort of individuals while it significantly jeopardises their health and well-being.[46] Moreover, whether there is an effective trickle-down mechanism or not depends on the nature of the specific innovation and the institutional and political environment. In most cases, spontaneous redistributive mechanisms of this kind proved to be insufficiently effective to avoid increasing inequality.[47] In the absence of effective redistributive policies, the inequality continued to increase undermining social sustainability. In addition, the growing obsession for the maximisation of exchange value within an increasingly shorter time horizon jeopardised also environmental sustainability since the latter is a very long-term objective focused on use values and deep-seated ethical principles (see infra Chap. 7).

The deep conflict between unfettered financialisation and sustainability does not imply that the actual process of financialisation is bound to undermine sustainability in all its dimensions. This is so because the actual process of financialisation has always been deeply affected by cultural, religious, and political constraints meant to preserve as much as possible the human, social, and environmental values of sustainability. A thorough assessment of the long-term impact of financialisation on sustainability has thus to be assessed period by period and location by location taking account of the specific institutional and policy constraints. Financialisation showed its destructive potential mainly in periods of economic and political decline when the arguments of financiers and rentiers became more persuasive for a broad audience seeking remedies against stagnation, while the counterarguments became weaker being identified with the declining status quo. However, decline was just one aspect of a process of radical and accelerated structural change catalysed by financialisation. In addition, in the short period, the acceleration of financialisation succeeded to slow down the decline of profits, growth, and hegemonic power. This convinced many observers of the therapeutic virtues of financialisation but this proved to be true only in the short period. The liberalisation of finance increased financial profits, while the increasing wealth and income of financiers and rentiers supported for a while aggregate demand. The sort of relief from stagnation, however, proved to be insufficient in the longer period because the propensity to consume of this wealthy layer of society is significantly lower than that of the layers damaged by the more unequal redistribution of income.

I will suggest in the second part of this book and in Chap. 8 that in the Second Financialisation the pathological aspects exceeded the alleged advantages. In this period, the systemic negative externalities happened to be much bigger than the advantages accruing to a minority of wealthy and powerful economic agents. In particular, it led to an unprecedented concentration of wealth and income that produced a vicious circle with a parallel concentration of power undermining sustainability in all its dimensions: economic (unemployment), social (poverty and inequality), and environmental (pollution, scarcity, and climate change). Moreover, what is worse, this vicious circle is undermining democracy itself. We must be aware that, without a substantive form of democracy, we cannot hope to solve persistently any of the problems emphasised in this book.

Notes

1. In this book, I do not use the term "development" with positive overtones, as it often happens in common parlance. I use the term "development" rather than "growth" whenever the focus of the analysis is not restricted to the quantitative increase of GDP but extends to the structural and qualitative changes that accompany and underlie it. On this point, see retro Sect. 1.5.
2. See Goldsmith (1969 and 1985).
3. This suggested definition is reminiscent of the well-known definition of Epstein (2002, 2): "Financialization refers to the increasing importance of financial markets, financial motives, financial institutions, and financial elites in the operation of the economy and its governing institutions, both at the national and international levels."
4. This definition is obviously consistent with a money theory of credit but does not mean to be in conflict with a credit theory of money (see e.g.

Schumpeter 1934), also because the two points of view do not necessarily exclude each other. In particular, the assertion supported by archeologic evidence that credit systems "*preceded* the invention of coinage by thousands of years" (Graeber 2011) does not necessarily collide with the definition of financialisation and the approach to its analysis here pursued, because—however and whenever the credit was originated—a sequence of financial innovations made it increasingly embedded in the working of markets.

5. In the modern interpretation, the quantitative theory of money is a particular causal interpretation of the equation of exchange, an identity that equates the amount of money in circulation M multiplied by its velocity of circulation V, with the real value of aggregate transactions T (in modern language the real output), multiplied by the index of prices P. According to the usual assumptions of the quantitative theory of money (exogeneity of money supply and short-period invariance of V and T), an increase in money supply translates into a proportional increase of the price index.

6. See for example Pigou (1949).

7. See for example Brenner (2006).

8. This approach has been worked out by scholars associated with the Monthly Review in a series of stimulating books and papers. See in particular Baran and Sweezy (1966), Magdoff and Sweezy (1987), Bellamy Foster (2006 and 2008), and Bellamy Foster and Magdoff (2009).

9. Marx (1867 [1976]). For a recent assessment of the process of financialisation in the USA since 1860, see Philippon (2008).

10. Braudel (1982).

11. Arrighi (1994).

12. Phillips (2006).

13. See for example Lenin (1916).

14. See Kondratieff (1922 [2004]). An assessment of the extensive literature may be found in Goodwin, Di Matteo, and Vercelli (1989).

15. Schumpeter (1939).

16. See for example Freeman and Louçã (2001).

17. See in particular Perez (2002).

18. Schumpeter (1934).

19. See for example Schumpeter (1934), and Perez (2012).

20. Vercelli (2011b).

21. Borghesi and Vercelli (2008).

22. The breakdown of the Gold Standard on the eve of World War I had a stronger and more immediate effect on international trade rather than on

financialisation, while the impetuous recovery of growth and trade in the roaring 1920s gave a further impulse to financialisation but was too short-lived to reverse the trend of international trade.

23. Financialisation, similarly to globalisation, has been defined as "variegated" to emphasise its temporal and spatial differences (Brown, Veronese Passarella, and Spencer 2013). There is an obvious relation between the varieties of financialisation and the varieties of capitalism as studied, for example, by Hall and Soskice (2001).

24. Since the beginning, a few critics of Shakespeare accused him of anti-Semitism for his vivid but ungenerous depiction of the character of Shylock, the Jew moneylender. This accusation is questionable in the light of the complex character of Shylock and his eloquent self-defence. What is certain, however, is that the relationship between Shylock and Marcello depicts well the conflictual relationship between financial capital and commercial capital in Venice in the late Renaissance (or in Amsterdam, or London, in the same period). The ambiguous and clumsy mediation of this conflict by the public authorities suggests that they perceived the importance of both forms of capitalism but were unable to regulate and supervise their interaction.

25. The co-evolution of financialisation and economic theory is discussed in Vercelli (2013–2014).

26. See in particular Polanyi (1944), and Graeber (2011).

27. See for example Vercelli (1998b and 1999a).

28. Before continuing this reasoning on financial innovation, I have to consider a possible objection. The modern historiography, anthropology, and ethnography of primitive money underline that a barter economy never existed and money evolved rather from state debt (see Graeber 2011, and the literature there cited). The updated knowledge on the origins of money is consistent with the view on financial innovations sketched in this section. A full-fledged barter economy could never exist exactly because its excessive rigidity would have prevented any persistent commitment deriving from division of labour. The emergence of money as generalised means of exchange and reliable deposit of value clearly relates to the much greater choice flexibility allowed by it as compared to alternative technologies of exchange.

29. See Hicks (1983), and Jones and Ostroy (1984).

30. Schumpeter (1934).

31. See for example Gorton and Metrick (2010 and 2012). Section 6.5 will resume and develop this argument.

32. Keynes (1936, 151).
33. Stiglitz (2012).
34. See for example Orléan (2009 and 2014).
35. Hilferding (1910).
36. Lapavitsas (2013, 61).
37. See Sect. 6.6.
38. This point has been first emphasised by Hilferding in his famous essay (1910) that influenced many subsequent writers and political leaders, including Lenin (2010).
39. This was already clear to Keynes who in the Chap. 17 of the *General Theory* tried to give ultimate foundations of his new macroeconomic theory in terms of portfolio choices (Keynes 1936). Here, as elsewhere, Keynes perceived the importance of a tendency that would have played a much greater role in the future.
40. As is well known, the US Federal Reserve was established in 1913.
41. I suggest calling "asymmetric monetarism" this policy inaugurated by Greenspan in the late 1980s and soon imitated by most other central bankers, because it complies with the traditional rules of monetarism in reference to the real system but not to the financial system. I will analyse these issues in Chaps. 5 and 6. On the concept of financial inflation, see Toporowski (2000 and 2005).
42. See for example Orhangazy (2007), and Cecchetti and Kharroubi (2013).
43. On this issue, see for example Bellamy Foster (2008).
44. See for example Palley (2007), and Lapavitsas (2013).
45. See infra Chaps. 5, 6, and 8.
46. See for a critical survey of this literature Borghesi and Vercelli (2012).
47. Stiglitz (2012).

Bibliography

Arrighi, Giovanni. 1994. *The Long Twentieth Century: Money, Power and the Origins of Our Times*. New York: Verso.

Baran, Paul A., and Paul M. Sweezy. 1966. *Monopoly Capital*. New York: Monthly Review Press.

Bellamy Foster, John. 2006. Monopoly-Finance Capital. *Monthly Review* 58(7): 1–14.

————. 2008. The Financialization of Capital and the Crisis. *Monthly Review* 59(11): 1–19.

Bellamy Foster, John, and Fred Magdoff. 2009. *The Great Financial Crisis: Causes and Consequences*. New York: Monthly Review Press.

Borghesi, Simone, and Alessandro Vercelli. 2008. *Global Sustainability. Social and Environmental Conditions*. Palgrave Macmillan: Basingstoke and New York.

————. 2012. Happiness and Health: Two Paradoxes. *Journal of Economic Surveys* 26(2): 203–233.

Braudel, Fernand. 1982. *The Wheels of Commerce, Civilization and Capitalism 15th–18th Century*. Berkeley: University of California Press.

Brenner, Robert. 2006. *The Economics of Global Turbulence*. London: Verso.

Brown, Ellen. 2013. *The Public Bank Solution*. Baton Rouge: Third Millennium Press.

Brown, Andrew, Marco Veronese Passarella, and David Spencer. 2015. The Nature and Variegation of Financialisation: Across-Country Comparison, FESSUD Working Paper Series No 127.

Cecchetti, Stephen G., and Enisse Kharroubi. 2013. Why Does Financial Sector Growth Crowd Out Real Economic Growth. Bank for International Settlements, available online at https://evbdn.eventbrite.com/s3-s3/eventlogos/67785745/cecchetti.pdf. Retrieved 18 March 2016

Di Matteo, Massimo, Richard M. Goodwin, and Alessandro Vercelli, eds. 1989. *Social and Technological Factors in Long Term Fluctuations*. New York: Springer.

Epstein, Gerald A. 2002. *Financialization, Rentier Interests, and Central Bank Policy*. Manuscript: version 1.2. Amherst, MA: Department of Economics, University of Massachusetts.

Freeman, Chris, and Francisco Louçã. 2001. *As Time Goes By. From the Industrial Revolutions to the Information Revolution*. Oxford: Oxford University Press.

Goldsmith, Raymond W. 1969. *Financial Structure and Development*. New Haven, CT: Yale University Press.

———— 1985. *Comparative National Balance Sheets*. Chicago: The University of Chicago Press.

Gorton, Gary B., and Andrew Metrick. 2010. Regulating the Shadow Banking System. *Brookings Papers on Economic Activity* 2: 261–297.

————. 2012. Securitized Banking and the Run on Repo. *Journal of Financial Economics* 104: 425–451.

Graeber, David. 2011. *Debt: The First 5,000 Years*. Brooklyn, NY: Melville House Publishing.

Hall, Peter A., and David Soskice. 2001. *Varieties of Capitalism. The Institutional Foundations of Comparative Advantage.* Oxford: oxford University Press.

Hicks, John. 1983. Liquidity. In *Collected Essays on Economic Theory*, vol 2, ed. John Hicks, 238–247. Oxford: Basil Blackwell.

Hilferding, Rudolf. 1910 [1981]. Finance Capital. A Study of the Latest Phase of Capitalist Development. London: Routledge.

Jones, Robert A., and Joseph M. Ostroy. 1984. Flexibility and Uncertainty. *The Review of Economic Studies* 51(1): 13–32.

Keynes, John Maynard. 1936 [1973]. *The General Theory of Employment, Interest and Money.* (The Collected Writings of John Maynard Keynes. Volume 7). London and Cambridge: Macmillan and Cambridge University Press.

Kondratieff, Nikolai. 1922 [2004]. The World Economy and its Conjunctures During and after the War. eds. Yuri V. Yakovets, Natalia A. Makasheva. Trans. V. Wolfson. Moscow: International Kondratieff Foundation.

Lapavitsas, Costas. 2013. *Profiting Without Producing. How Finance Exploits us All.* London: Verso.

Lenin, Vladimir I. 1916 [2010]. *Imperialism, the Highest Stage of Capitalism.* London: Penguin Classics.

Magdoff, Harry, and Paul M. Sweezy. 1987. *Stagnation and the Financial Explosion.* New York: Monthly Review Press.

Marx, Karl. 1867 [1976]. *Capital*, Vol. 1. London: Penguin Books.

Orhangazy, Özgür. 2007. Financialization and Capital Accumulation in the Non-Financial Capital Sector. A Theoretical and Empirical Investigation of the U.S. Economy: 1973–2003. In *Working Paper Series 149.* University of Massachusetts at Amherst: Political Economy Research Institute.

Orléan, André. 2009. *De l'euphorie à la panique: Penser la crise financière.* Paris: Édition de la Rue d'Ulm.

———. 2014. *The Empire of Value. A New Foundation for Economics.* Cambridge, MA: MIT Press.

Palley, Thomas. 2007. Financialization: What It Is and Why It Matters, *Working Paper No. 525*, The Levy Economics Institute of Bard College.

Perez, Carlota. 2002. *Technological Revolutions and Financial Capital: The Dynamics of Bubbles and Golden Ages.* Cheltenham: Edward Elgar.

———. 2012. Why IT and the Green Economy are the Real Answer to the Financial Crisis. Green Alliance Blog, 19 March. http://www.green-alliance.org.uk/uploadedFiles/Publications/reports/InsideTrack_30_web_spreads.pdf

Philippon, Thomas. 2008. The Evolution of the US Financial Industry from 1860 to 2007: Theory and Evidence. *NBER Working Paper* No. 13405.

Phillips, Kevin P. 2006. *American Theocracy: The Peril and Politics of Radical Religion, Oil, and Borrowed Money in the 21st Century*. London: Penguin Books.

Pigou, Arthur C 1949. *The Veil of Money*. London: Macmillan.

Polanyi, Karl. 1944. *The Great Transformation*. New York: Farrar & Rinehart.

Schumpeter, Joseph A. 1934 [1911]. *The Theory of Economic Development*, English Translation of the second edition. Cambridge, Mass.: Harvard University Press.

———. 1939. *Business Cycles: A Theoretical, Historical and Statistical Analysis of the Capitalist Process*. New York, NY: McGraw-Hill.

Stiglitz, Joseph E 2012. *The Price of Inequality. How Today's Divided Society Endangers our Future*. New York: W. W. Norton & Co.

Toporowski, Jan. 2005. *The End of Finance: The Theory of Capital Market Inflation, Financial Derivatives and Pension Funds Capitalism*. London: Routledge.

———. *Theories of Financial Disturbance. An Examination of Critical Theories of Finance from Adam Smith to the Present Day*. Cheltenham: Edward Elgar.

Vercelli, Alessandro. 1998b. Uncertainty and Environmental Policy. In *Sustainability: Dynamics and Uncertainty*, eds. Chichilnisky Graciela, Heal Geoffrey, and Alessandro Vercelli. Dordrecht: Martin Kluwer.

———. 1999a. The Recent Advances in Decision Theory under Uncertainty: A Non-technical Introduction. In *Uncertain Decisions: Bridging Theory and Experiments*, ed. Luigi Luini. Dordrecht: Kluwer.

———. 2011b. Economy and Economics: The Twin Crises. In *The Global Economic Crisis. New Perspectives on the Critique of Economic Theory and Policy*, eds. Emiliano Brancaccio, and Giuseppe Fontana, 27–41. Abingdon and New York: Routledge.

———. 2013–14. Financialisation in a Long-Run Perspective. *International Journal of Political Economy* 42 (4):19–46.

Part II

The Great Recession: Causes and Consequences

5

The Neoliberal Trajectory and the Crisis

5.1   Introduction[1]

This chapter argues that the recent global crisis is the direct consequence of a development paradigm that is unsustainable from the economic, financial, social, and environmental point of view. Such a model became progressively dominant since the late 1970s when the neoliberal policy strategy started to become hegemonic at the world level.[2]

The increasing flexibility of labour market and the progressive dismantlement of the welfare state progressively increased income and wealth inequality, causing a growing polarisation among social classes that has undermined social cohesion.[3] In addition, this process reduced the purchasing power of middle and lower classes and increased the poverty plague also in several industrialised countries (*social unsustainability*). This tendency brought about a downward trend of aggregate demand that contributed to slow down the growth rate in many countries (*economic unsustainability*). The increasing indebtedness of the economic agents that has contributed to sustain their demand[4] and the rapid financialisation of the economy that has progressively increased the contribution of finance to income formation partially offset this tendency. This sort of "doping"

© The Editor(s) (if applicable) and The Author(s) 2017
A. Vercelli, *Crisis and Sustainability*,
DOI 10.1057/978-1-137-60069-1_5

of aggregate demand, however, was not sufficient to keep the growth rate of industrialised countries at the same level experienced during the Bretton Woods era (1945–1971), a period that was characterised by a predominant Keynesian policy strategy.[5] In addition, the rapid increase of private and public debt and the hypertrophy of finance have undermined the financial stability of the system. Severe financial crises, that were absent during the Bretton Woods period, reappeared during the 1970s and progressively increased their frequency, intensity, and geographical extension (*financial unsustainability*).[6]

The monetary policy aimed to sustain the value of financial assets pursued by the Federal Reserve under Greenspan (1987–2006) and his successor Bernanke (2006–2014), and then adopted by most other central bankers, managed to moderate the adverse effects of financial instability, though only in the short term. At the same time, however, this policy favoured the spread of ever-increasing speculative bubbles that transferred into the future the risks of the growing financial fragility up to the outburst of the recent global crisis.

The deep and persistent financial turmoil, originated by the subprime crisis in 2007, and the consequent recession of the real economy are thus the result of a deleterious interaction between different dimensions of unsustainability. The financial crisis, in its turn, has remarkably worsened many social and economic sustainability indicators generating a vicious circle that became increasingly difficult to reverse. The *environmental unsustainability* of the existing development model greatly reinforced the recent crisis. While the speculative bubble of the real estate sector started to deflate in the USA, the oil price rapidly increased from less than $50 per barrel in 2005 to a new record of about $150 in spring 2008. This provoked a rise in the production costs of all goods (particularly of food). The central banks reacted to the consequent cost inflation with a significant increase in the discount rate that raised the loans' interest rate. This undermined the borrowers' capacity to comply with mortgage payments, compelling many of them to sell their house or to default. The consequent collapse of the housing market sank the price of mortgage-based derivatives triggering a contagion process in the financial system.

This analysis calls for a systematic revision of the current development paradigm towards a more sustainable direction. We urgently need a radical redirection of the development trajectory to get out of the present crisis and start up a new development phase.

The structure of this chapter is as follows. Section 1 discusses the origins of the Second Financialisation underlying the neoliberal trajectory. I distinguish then and briefly analyse four successive phases of the neoliberal trajectory, the Monetarist Disinflation: 1979–1987 (Sect. 5.3), the Roaring 1990s: 1987–2000 (Sect. 5.4), the Zero Years: 2000–2007, and the Genesis of the Great Recession: 2007–2009 (Sect. 5.5).[7] Section 5.6 discusses the propagation mechanism of the crisis. The final remarks in Sect. 5.7 discuss the relationship between the neoliberal model of development and its sustainability in the light of the preceding narrative.

5.2 The Origins of the Second Financialisation

While the First Globalisation started to decelerate since 1914 in consequence of the collapse of the Gold Standard and the inception of World War I, the First Financialisation outlived the changed economic environment for a few further years until the 1929. The Great Depression eventually triggered a process of de-financialisation that hardened in the USA with the approval in 1933 of the "Glass-Steagall Act" to recover a more efficient control of finance.[8] The financial service industry strongly resisted these new measures of regulation and control considering them instruments of "financial repression", an emotionally charged phrasing meant to stress their allegedly illiberal nature. However, the Great Depression greatly undermined the economic and political power of banks to such an extent that their massive support to the sharp criticisms iterated by liberal economists and politicians only succeeded to water down some important details of the law. Nevertheless, the pressure exerted by this systematic resistance to the Glass-Steagall Act and the haste to reach an approval in the parliament explain why a few serious loopholes remained in the law. These loopholes have been subsequently exploited by the financial institutions to get round its provisions (see Appendix A).

After the approval of the Glass-Stegall Act in the USA and similar laws of finance repression elsewhere, a movement advocating the re-liberalisation—seen by someone as "liberation"—of finance immediately started, but war interrupted it. In such a situation of emergence, the financial industry could not dare to question the priority of war issues over all other issues. Finance had to play the role of crucial instrument to "pay for the war", and this required subordination to the political and military goals of the government.[9] Analogously, at the end of the war, the finance service industry had to interpret in the best possible way its crucial instrumental role of support to the reconstruction of the national economies.

As soon as these emergencies were over, the financial industry resumed at full steam the efforts to regain a greater autonomy from the state. In the 1950s and 1960s, the rapid and steady growth of the real economy progressively increased the demand for the financial services of banks, favouring the progressive growth of their economic and political power. The period of Bretton Woods was thus a period of steady but moderate financialisation that did not alter significantly the role of banks in the economy. The expansion of their activity beyond the boundaries fixed by the containment legislation approved in the 1930s was very slow for a host of reasons. First, the Glass-Steagall Act had coupled constraints on financial activity with constraints on competition in the financial sector, concerning in particular the freedom of entry in the market. This assured the incumbent financial institutions the steady earning of low-risk oligopolistic profits.[10] In addition, the existing controls on capital movements slowed down the expansion of the financial business abroad restricting the international competition. The growth of GDP was so buoyant in developed countries that it was difficult to convince the public opinion, its political representatives, and policy makers that it was wise to change the rules of the game established in Bretton Woods period. In that period, the financial service sector experienced an unprecedented degree of stability while its support to the real economy looked adequate. If the financial "repression" had confined finance in a prison, as some exponents of this sector continued to maintain, it was no doubt a "prison dorée". This reduced the willingness, or at least the determination, of finance to fight an unrestrained "liberation war" against public control and supervision.

The economic and political environment changed radically since 1971 when President Nixon declared unilaterally the inconvertibility of dollar with gold. This far-reaching move not only ended the monetary regime established in Bretton Woods but also initiated a rapid transition to a radically different policy strategy that will eventually take over since the end of the 1970s. This act of deregulation of the international monetary system also changed the attitude of finance and the attitude towards finance. The exponents of the financial service industry immediately adopted the mantra of markets deregulation and, in a period of economic turmoil, easily succeeded to convince the policy makers that the liberalisation of finance was a particularly urgent objective. Its implementation was progressive and became systematic since the early 1980s. The main argument iterated by the advocates of financial deregulation was that the constraints to competition adopted in the Bretton Woods period had significantly reduced the efficiency of financial markets. Academic finance endorsed this change in policy strategy arguing that unfettered financial markets are efficient.[11] Some foresighted economist pointed out that there was a trade-off between efficiency and stability but most finance experts and policy makers claimed that the efficiency of financial markets was the main goal to pursue since its advantages exceeded its potential disadvantages.

The period of deep economic turmoil started in the early 1970, soon called with the name of "stagflation" to emphasise the unusual and distressing coexistence of stagnation and inflation, offered the occasion to forsake the policy strategy that had dominated the Bretton Woods period.

5.3   The "Monetarist Disinflation"

The "Great Stagflation" of the 1970s triggered a profound crisis of the policy strategy pursued in the Bretton Woods period and, consequently, of the macroeconomic theory underlying its foundations. The critics led by the monetarists under the leadership of Milton Friedman interpreted the high and accelerating inflation as the consequence of an increasing inflationary bias introduced in the system by the countercyclical Keynesian policies aiming to keep full employment.[12] In this view, the ensuing empowerment of trade unions resulted in a money-wage dynamics inconsistent with monetary stability, trade equilibrium, and balanced budget. The progressive adaptation of expectations to this growing inflationary bias explains the increasing correlation between inflation and unemployment leading to stagflation. Therefore, in this view, the ultimate cause of the growing economic distress leading to stagflation was the Keynesian macroeconomic paradigm justifying and promoting an excessive interference of the state with the working of markets.

Based on this analysis, the critics of the Keynesian policies claimed that the policy makers might find a solution of this conundrum only by giving back to the market the responsibility of economic choices reverting to the traditional liberal policy principles. This called for a policy strategy based on the privatisation of public goods and activities and the systematic deregulation of markets. A corollary of this new policy orientation was the progressive dismantlement of the so-called welfare state that, in this view, implies an excessive interference of collective action with the markets, an unwise empowerment of disadvantaged people, and a plethoric public expenditure undermining the budget equilibrium. The neoliberal revolution of the 1970s was a crucial stage of the co-evolution of development paradigms, policy strategies, and macroeconomic theory as sketched in Sect. 1.7.

The government of Mrs Thatcher, appointed UK Prime Minister in 1979, was the first government to adopt a neoliberal policy strategy. Her groundbreaking leadership was soon followed in the USA by the Reagan administration and then in rapid sequence by most other countries. We can thus take 1979 as a conventional starting point of the neoliberal development trajectory.[13] We may distinguish four phases: the Monetarist Disinflation: 1979–1987, the Roaring 1990s: 1987–2000, the Zero Years: 2000–2007, and the Great Recession: 2007–2009 (triggering the Eurocrisis since 2010).

The first and foremost problem that required an urgent solution was that of stagflation that had haunted many developed countries in the 1970s. The new Chair of the FED Paul Volcker (1979–1987), under the influence of monetarism,[14] immediately adopted a very restrictive monetary policy meant to curb inflation and inflationary expectations.[15] Inflation, which had peaked in the USA at 13.5 % in 1981, subsided to 3.2 % by 1983. Policy makers obtained this result at the cost of inducing a severe recession of the real economy that lasted until the 1983 in the USA and a few more semesters in other industrialised countries.

A robust and widespread recovery started in the second half of the 1980s in consequence of significant policy-induced structural changes in the economy, that were going to characterise the neoliberal cycle from then on. The neoliberal governments exploited the situation of weakness of trade unions induced by the sharp increase of unemployment to implement a radical reform of labour markets and industrial relations. The main goal pursued was the systematic deregulation of labour markets in order to reach a level of flexibility consistent with the neoliberal tenets of competitive markets. This policy modified the structural characteristics underlying the Phillips curve shifting it downwards and reducing its slope.[16] The supporters of the neoliberal paradigm argued that this implied the elimination of the inflationary bias in the real economy attributed to the Keynesian policies. For a couple of decades, the rate of inflation in the real economy remained low even in periods of boom making superfluous the adoption of restrictive policy interventions such as those that had triggered the stop-and-go fluctuations of the Keynesian era. This in turn contributed to reduce the variability of time series giving the illusion of a steadier growth regime (later called "Great Moderation").

The neoliberal policy strategy, however, obtained these apparent successes at the cost of serious "side effects" that became increasingly evident with time. We mention in this section only the main social effects that started to emerge almost immediately, while the other collateral effects became evident only in successive phases of the neoliberal development trajectory. The first side effect concerns the inequality in the distribution of income that is a crucial condition of social sustainability. In most countries, in particular within the OECD, the trend of inequality that had slightly diminished in consequence of the welfare state policies pursued in the Bretton Woods period started to increase again since the late 1970s or early 1980s.[17] The neoliberal policy strategy fed this new tendency by promoting a reduction—sometimes even inversion—of fiscal progressivity, the dismantlement of the welfare state, and the enhanced flexibility of labour markets decoupling labour productivity increase from real wages increase. Technological innovations and a radical change in the international division of labour may have contributed to increase inequality, but also these factors were clearly correlated with the new policy strategy and the kind of globalisation promoted by it.[18] Many neoliberal economists have contended that the reduction in inequality is a questionable target as more inequality could give incentives to more personal effort and thus to enhanced productivity and higher growth. On the contrary, an extensive literature has recently shown that the negative impact of inequality on well-being is quite substantial.[19]

The second main social side effect was the increase in poverty also in many developed countries. Subtle and controversial problems of measure blur the hot debate on the relationship between globalisation and poverty. In what follows, I will adopt the definition suggested by the World Bank classifying as poor any person whose income does not exceed the mean value of $2 per day.[20] This measure of poverty is certainly quite rough, but is useful to give a first idea of its long-run evolution. No one denies that its reduction must be an important target of policy, but the prevailing view maintains that what we really need to conquer poverty is a higher rate of growth.[21] In this view, the process of modernisation accelerated growth to an unprecedented level and sustained its trend throughout two centuries. This explains why the percentage of the poor over the world population steadily declined from more than 95 % in the second decade of the nineteenth century to less than 50 % in the last decade. Projecting this decline in the future, the optimists believe that the process of modernisation supported by globalisation and financialisation is more than halfway to solve the problem of poverty. The trouble is that in the last two centuries the number of the poor continued to grow from about 1 billion in the second decade of the nineteenth century to about 3 billion.[22] The poor ratio on the world population declined mainly because the latter increased on average at a double rate. In any case, the extrapolative projection into the future of the declining trend of poverty ratio would eliminate poverty only after other two centuries or so. However, projections of this kind are not reliable as the relevant trends depend on many factors that we cannot easily predict. The subprime crisis, for example, and the ensuing Great Recession have greatly increased in many countries the number of the poor beyond the trend. Moreover, taking account of the decelerating demographic growth, we cannot exclude that the poor ratio will start to increase again.

Contrary to a widespread conviction,[23] the increase in inequality since the beginning of the industrialisation era played a crucial role in the increase of poverty. Bourguignon and Morisson (2002, 733) argued: "had the world distribution of income remained unchanged since 1820, the number of poor people would be less than 1/4th than it is today and the number of extremely poor people would be less than 1/8th of what is today."

Further increase of the poor and malnutrition occurred in consequence of the Great Recession. The poverty rate has increased also in developed countries recently reaching 12.7 % of population in Italy, 14.0 % in Spain, and 17.9 % in the USA.[24] In addition, extensive empirical research documented a progressive deterioration of the "social capital" on which the well-being of people crucially depends.[25]

The social collateral effects contribute to explain what could be defined "economic unsustainability" as revealed by the slowdown of the trend of GDP growth. The increasing inequality and poverty affected the trend of private expenditure explaining its slowdown in the period 1980–2012 as compared to that of the period 1950–1979.[26] This slowdown mainly occurred in the OECD countries rather than in developing countries less intoxicated by the neoliberal policy strategy. Different private decisions and policy measures tried to counteract this tendency. In particular, households increased their indebtedness in the attempt to keep their life standards. Many governments encouraged to some extent this behaviour by supporting the purchase of the first house for any family. In addition, most governments tried to support the rate of growth even at the cost of increasing public debt, even when this was in sheer contrast to neoliberal principles.[27]

Since the late 1970s, another trend changed its sign. The ratio between public debt and GDP, which in the G7 countries had progressively diminished from the high post-war levels (more than 70 %) to a much more manageable levels (about 40 % in the middle 1970s), started to increase again in the late 1970s. Just before the crisis, the trend breached the 80 % threshold and then rapidly increased beyond 100 % in consequence of the crisis (see Fig. 5.1). The G20 countries exhibited a similar behavioural pattern, though in a less marked way (ibid.).

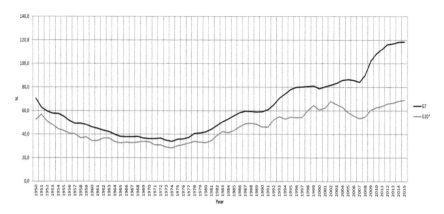

Fig. 5.1 Government Debt in G7 and G20 countries (as % GDP). *Source*: author's elaboration of IMF database (see Abbas et al. 2011, 2014)

The empirical evidence shows then that the trend of public debt diminished in the Bretton Woods period characterised by the construction of the welfare state and full employment Keynesian policies and turned upwards again when these policies were abandoned in favour of neoliberal policies. This observation questions the widespread prejudice supported by governments, international organisations, and mainstream mass media that overgenerous social security transfers was the ultimate cause of the sovereign debt crisis.

An important factor of this inversion relates to the growing independence of central banks from Treasury directives. This explains their growing reluctance to continue to act as "buyers of last resort" of Treasury bonds as in the Bretton Woods period, when banks had to step in to buy unsold tranches of bonds that otherwise would have been sold at an excessive interest rate. In many countries, the banking system advocated this new orientation as an occasion to increase profits. Specific legislative measures implemented in the early 1980s the independence of central banks strongly supported by the monetarist principles of monetary policy neutrality.

A case in point is that of Italy that sanctioned in 1981 the so-called "divorce" between Treasury and Bank of Italy. Most other countries took similar measures in the 1980s and 1990s. In the same mood, the Statute of the European Central Bank (ECB), approved in 1998, does not admit the direct buying of sovereign debt. The new orientation of central banks in the neoliberal era contributed significantly to the increase of public debt reducing seigniorage revenues and increasing the rate of interest to refinance debt. In the meantime, the slowdown of GDP growth rate contributed to increase the ratio between debt and GDP. Finally, drawing inspiration from neoliberal principles, many governments did not hesitate to reduce the taxes paid by corporations and rich people at the cost of increasing the burden of debt.

Typically, the reduction of social and security expenditure supposed to compensate the reduction of revenues did not prove to be sufficient and motivated further cuts in the welfare provisions. For example, during Regan's presidency, the annual deficits averaged 4.2 % of GDP after inheriting an annual deficit of 2.7 % of GDP in 1980 under President Carter, so that the public debt rose from 26.1 % GDP in 1980 to 41.0 % GDP by 1988.

5.4 The Roaring 1990s

Since 1987, the structural changes in the real economy made possible the adoption of a new monetary policy first introduced and pursued by the new Chairman of FED Alan Greenspan (1987–2006). Also in this case, a change in theory preceded the change in policy. In the early 1980s, mainstream macroeconomics shifted from the "monetary equilibrium business cycle" approach suggested by Lucas to the "real business cycle approach" suggested by Kydland and Prescott, reversing the causal relation between supply of money and the real economy.[28]

In the light of the new macroeconomic approach, Greenspan took profit of the flattening of the Phillips curve starting to validate with an accommodating monetary policy a persistent increase in the price of financial assets without fearing a surge of inflation. The advocates of this new policy strategy believed that it could prop the growth of GDP not only because it favoured the expansion of the financial sector, but also because the higher income of financiers and rentiers could enhance the demand of real goods. This new policy alchemy seemed to work for a while, leading to a period of sustained growth in many countries. Many observers called this period with the evocative name of "Roaring 1990s".[29] Unfortunately, the analogy with the "roaring 1920s" was not limited to wording since, also in this case, the excessive euphoria led to a global financial crisis, indeed two of them, the second of which starting in 2007 proved to be as devastating as the Great Depression.

Many operators and finance experts often referred to this new monetary policy with the evocative name of "Greenspan put".[30] I prefer to call it "asymmetric monetarism" for two reasons. First, it implied the setting of a floor to the price of financial assets without establishing an analogous ceiling. Second, it aimed to avoid inflation in the real sector but not necessarily in the financial sector.[31]

Most commentators hailed this new monetary policy as a stroke of genius, ignoring its dangerous side effects that became increasingly evident with time. In fact, an inflationary bias in finance eventually replaced the inflationary bias observed in the real economy during the Bretton Woods period and blamed upon Keynesian policies. This new inflationary bias determined different but not inferior pathological effects. First, this sort of asymmetric monetarism produced growing distortional effects altering the relative price, risk, and expectations of financial, as compared to real, investment. Second, it produced an environment conducive to financial bubbles, because the economic units were encouraged to augment their indebtedness by the implicit insurance on financial returns, and this brought about an increasing financial fragility of the economy. The shift of investment from the real to the financial sector induced a tendency towards stagnation in the real economy that the wealth effect originated in the financial sector and the increasing indebtedness of economic units could only partially compensate. The progressive slowdown of the growth rate of the real economy encouraged many governments to indulge on measures favouring the indebtedness of households to sustain aggregate demand and to rely at the same time on unorthodox deficit spending policies (as in the case of the Reagan and Bush administrations). The interaction between the increasing financial fragility of the private economic units and of the public administration led to a growing number of increasingly deep financial crises.

According to an accurate econometric study, of the 18 main financial crises identified by Kaminsky and Reinhart (1999) in the second half of the past century, three occurred in the second half of the 1970s, seven in the 1980s, and eight in the 1990s. They were not yet global crises, since they were circumscribed to a particular institution (the hedge fund Long-Term Capital Management in 1998), sector (the US saving and loan associations in 1984), or country (Italy in 1990, the UK in 1991, Japan in 1992, and so on). All these episodes happened after specific acts of deregulation confirming the decisive role played by the neoliberal policy strategies in the observed growth of financial instability.[32] The Asian crisis occurred in 1997 may be considered as the first post-war global financial crisis (as it hit also the USA and Japan) but its centre was not in the core of the system. Only at the beginning of the new millennium, the increasing financial instability led to devastating global crises centred in the core of the system.

Contemporary observers, however, focused on the reduction in volatility of business cycles fluctuations as exhibited by crucial economic variables such as GDP growth and unemployment in the period 1987–2007. The advocates of neoliberal policies called this phenomenon "great moderation" and advertised it as a great success of the new policy strategy.[33] The great moderation was the joint consequence of the flattening of the Phillips curve forced by the neoliberal reforms of the labour market and the new monetary policy introduced by Greenspan. Higher employment rates in periods of boom did not translate into higher wages and inflation, while generous injections of liquidity in the financial system promptly thwarted the decline of financial values. Minsky was one of the few economists who understood in real time that this short-term stabilisation was cumulating increasing financial instability to become virtually irrepressible in the longer period.[34] As a matter of fact, the widespread conviction that the economic and financial performance had become more predictable and better controllable by policy authorities induced many economic units to be less concerned about capital reserves and liquidity positions reducing their risk awareness and increasing their indebtedness. This delusional belief encouraged a further increase in the financial fragility of economic units.

5.5 The "Zero Years" and The Genesis of the Great Recession

The process of increasing financial instability culminated in the "Zero Years" of the new millennium when two major global crises originated from within the core of the system.[35] First came the *new economy* (or "dot-com") crisis in 2000–2002. This deep crisis was a serious warning of a major disaster approaching, but very few observers took seriously its structural causes gravid with devastating consequences. Moreover, also in this case, the accommodating monetary policy implemented by the FED succeeded to thwart the crisis sooner than expected. This apparent success further strengthened the confidence in the omnipotence of the invisible hand astutely supported by the Greenspan's visible hand.

In consequence of the dot-com crisis, speculation shifted from immaterial ICT goods to brick-and-mortar goods. The ensuing swelling bubble of the real estate sector gradually built up a crucial triggering factor of the second, much more devastating, global crisis.[36] The crisis of subprime mortgages and adjustable rate mortgages (ARM) in the USA played the role of detonator of the crisis. The slowdown of housing prices in the second half of 2006 did not worry most operators who expected a salutary soft landing. This economic factor, however, interacted with a host of financial, environmental, and policy factors that impinge on the ultimate sustainability of the neoliberal model of development.

The price of oil increased from $63 in December 2006 to $147 in July 2008 triggering a process of cost inflation fed by an analogous spike of food price. Notwithstanding the inflationary surge was moderate and independent of excessive demand, and despite the emerging crisis, central banks reacted as usual by tightening monetary policy. In particular, the FED did not hesitate to increase the discount rate from 2.00 % in May 2004 to 6.25 % in August 2008. This increased significantly also the mortgage rates pushing into insolvency most holders of subprime mortgages and adjustable-rate mortgages (ARM). The ensuing foreclosures rapidly drove the housing prices downwards.

We observe in this period a perverse interaction between financial, economic, and environmental problems (in particular, those related to the energy system based on fossil fuels) that makes clear the unsustainability of the neoliberal growth regime. This interaction brought to an end the era of "great moderation", that claimed to have tamed the Keynesian inflationary bias haunting the real economy in the late Bretton Woods period. This belief proved to be delusional. The neoliberal model of development ended up by being haunted by a dual inflationary bias. To the inflationary bias in the financial sector discussed in Sect. 5.4, one more was added in the real sector, a bias not related to wages (as in the Bretton Woods era) but to the price of natural resources. This tendency has been partly masked by the ongoing recession, the North Africa and Middle East turmoil, the rapid increase of non-conventional fossil fuel (in particular fracking oil and gas), and other temporary factors. However, despite all these countervailing factors, energy-driven cost inflation is likely to accelerate with a sustained and persistent recovery of the world economy jeopardising its viability.

The huge efforts after the subprime crisis to bail out the financial institutions believed to be "too big to fail" have significantly worsened both deficits and debt in most countries hit by the financial crisis. On the contrary, in the "Zero Years" preceding the subprime crisis, there is no evidence of a significant increase of deficit and debt ratio.[37] There is thus no reason to consider the excessive sovereign debt as the immediate cause (triggering factor) of the crisis. It has been rather a factor of its propagation, particularly in the Eurozone, but only in consequence of the massive bailout of distressed financial institutions and the unwise adoption of severe austerity policies.[38]

5.6 The Propagation of the Crisis

The structural causes underlying the propagation mechanisms of the crisis have increased further its destructive potential. In the Bretton Woods period, the propagation mechanism was strong mainly within the real side of the economy as it was rooted in the conflict about income distribution leading to stop-and-go fluctuations, accelerating inflation, and eventually stagflation.

Since the late 1970s, a deep transformation of the propagation process is detectable, as contagion starts to proceed mainly through the financial side of the economy. This structural change occurred in consequence of the profound transformations of the financial system often summarised with the label of "Second Financialisation".[39] The neoliberal policies systematically pursued since the late 1970s aimed to liberalise the sector of finance that policy makers had strictly regulated and controlled in the Bretton Woods period. The liberalisation of cross-country capital flows in the 1980s was a crucial driver of the process of globalisation. This process produced a growing global interconnection among decision makers in economics and finance, and this strengthened the mechanisms of contagion. In this new environment, the sudden awareness of an excessive financial exposition immediately triggered the fire sale of assets to reduce indebtedness. This abated the price of assets and increased further the indebtedness ratio inducing new rounds of hurried sales of assets (including the strategic ones) in a climate of growing panic. This process of debt-deflation in the financial sector soon triggered a second mechanism of propagation in the real sector.[40] The reduction of demand of real goods and services, consequent to the generalised flight to safety and the ensuing negative wealth effect, sank the price of assets and the supply of goods, increased unemployment, and reduced further the expenditure in the real sector. The process of globalisation increased the connectedness of economic units also at the international level by enhancing the strength and rapidity of the propagation process.

The interconnection between financial units via their balance sheets and market interaction has progressively increased in the neoliberal era in consequence of the systematic process of securitisation. As Minsky pointed out, there is a symbiotic relation between the globalisation of the world's financial structure and the securitisation of financial instruments.[41] In addition, the process of securitisation was encouraged by the illusion that a bank could transfer the risk of credit to the market in the belief—endorsed by many mainstream economists—that "the market knows better".[42] However, this proved only partially true,[43] and only at the cost of increasing systemic risk. In addition, this illusion encouraged moral hazard as no one felt the responsibility of thoroughly evaluating the value and risk associated to the decision of holding an asset or security. This attitude encouraged imprudent and predatory practices such as those observed in the process of mortgage origination. In the end, financially fragile banks and economic units propagated the systemic crisis much more rapidly than in the Bretton Woods era.[44]

The process of securitisation was instrumental to the emergence and development of shadow banks, that is, "financial intermediaries that conduct maturity, credit, and liquidity transformation without explicit access to central bank liquidity or public sector credit guarantees" (Pozsar et al. 2010, 2).[45] The subprime mortgage crisis started as a bank run within shadow banking.[46] In addition, the shadow banking system extended systemic risk and financial fragility in an opaque way as shadow banks typically rely on off-balance-sheet operations.

The first wave of the financial earthquake propagated very rapidly from the US mortgage sector to all the US financial system through mortgage-based derivatives and collateralised debt obligations (see Appendix 2). The wave almost immediately propagated also abroad in consequence of the globalisation of the financial system. The impact proved to be particularly devastating in the Eurozone where the peculiar design of the euro showed all its weaknesses (see Chap. 8). The big budget deficits due mainly to the huge public help offered to a virtually broke banking system without any condition were the excuse for the forced adoption of austerity policies that were particularly tough and devastating in the weaker countries of the EU, so-called PIIGS (i.e. Portugal, Ireland, Italy, Greece, and Spain). The systematic pressure of speculation on sovereign debt in the weaker countries of the Eurozone paralysed the protest of the citizens deeply hit by the consequences of these policies. The fragility of financial institutions believed to be "too big to fail" was transferred to the public balance sheets. The financial institutions so rescued did not show any gratitude and actively contributed to a systematic campaign against the unsustainable generosity of the welfare state: "finance was rescued, only to turn and bite its rescuer" (Lapavitsas et al. 2012, 2). This was one of the causes of the Eurocrisis (see Chap. 8).

5.7   Concluding Remarks: The Unsustainability of the Neoliberal Model of Development

I argued in this chapter that the neoliberal model of development is unsustainable from the economic, financial, social, and environmental points of view. Its alleged successes in the early 1980s, in particular the rapid disinflation and the flattening of the Phillips curve, were obtained through a harsh redistribution of income and power from workers to entrepreneurs and from the poor to the rich. The neoliberal policy makers sought greater flexibility in labour markets and industrial relations by increasing the precariousness of jobs and by reducing the rights of workers. What neoliberal advocates considered a success for the economy as a whole, and was certainly a success for most entrepreneurs and shareholders, was instead an epoch-making defeat for blue and white collars that started the decline of the middle and lower classes. Moreover, this alleged success from the point of view of macroeconomic performance materialised only at the cost of serious side effects that in the longer period would have provoked the outbreak of the recent crisis. First, the transfer of power from labour to capital soon translated in an analogous transfer of income and wealth within most OECD countries and many developing countries adopting similar policies. The indexes of inequality in the distribution of income started to increase since the late 1970s and continued the upward trend until now. In addition, the increasing inequality often reflected growing poverty also in the richest countries (including the USA and many European countries). The neoliberal policies systematically violated the basic conditions of social sustainability during all the period. This failure had a significant impact also on economic sustainability as measured by the growth of GDP. The stagnation of the aggregate income of middle and lower classes consequent to the increase in inequality and poverty brought about a persisting stagnation of aggregate consumption. Since also the aggregate investment in the real economy tended to subside in consequence of financialisation, the ensuing stagnation in aggregate private expenditure tended to slow down the rate of growth. The increasing indebtedness of households and the growing contribution of finance to GDP were insufficient to compensate for the downbeat factors. In addition, the growing contribution of the FIRE sector (Finance, Insurance and Real Estate) to GDP came at the cost of increasing financial fragility and systemic risk. The process of financialisation also undermined the environmental sustainability by crowding out the investment from the real sector and by enhancing the short-termism of economic choices including those referring to investment. The consequence was that the investment necessary for greening the economy has been insufficient; in particular, the investment in research and development (R&D) necessary to promote environmental innovation has been inadequate. Big banks continued to finance the huge investment in the field of fossil fuels (infrastructures, new exploration, plants of transformation, etc.) by profiting also of the public incentives still higher than in the field of renewable energy sources. The investment in the field of renewable energy typically divides in a myriad of small amounts distributed on the territory. Banks considered this sort of investment much less appealing for its small contribution to their returns on equity.

The neoliberal policies produced a perverse interaction between social, financial, economic, and environmental problems. This brought to an end the era of "great moderation" claiming to have overcome the inflationary bias of the Bretton Woods period originating in the market for labour and in the distributive struggle between workers and entrepreneurs. A dual inflationary bias eventually haunted the neoliberal regime: one in the financial sector in consequence of financialisation and the asymmetric monetarism practised by central banks and another one in the real sector because any acceleration of growth exerts a further pressure on overexploited natural resources. The ensuing increase in the price of oil and other scarce natural resources brings about cost inflation that motivates the adoption of more restrictive monetary policies destined to chock off growth.

We should not interpret the spike of oil price in the period 2005–2008 as the consequence of an erratic shock, but rather as the signal of an unsustainable energy system, largely based on the use of exhaustible and polluting fossil fuels that are the main cause of the ongoing climate change process.[47] Most studies estimate that conventional oil production should reach its peak in the near future, thus forcing the economies along the declining part of the so-called Hubbert curve.[48] Of course, an increase in the production of non-conventional fossil fuel can provide the missing supply. A case in point is the sharp increase in production of oil and natural gas in the USA through the unconventional, and controversial, technique of fracking, increase that promises to recover the energetic independence of this country. The trouble is that this and the other techniques of production of unconventional fossil fuel have significant external costs. Therefore, in the absence of appropriate policy measures that may speed up the necessary transition towards the systematic use of renewable energy sources, the sensitivity of oil price (and that of its substitutes) to demand increases is likely to become a serious obstacle to the sustainability of a business-as-usual economic recovery. An expected increase in aggregate demand would affect the oil price leading to a significant surge of cost inflation, and consequently of the rate of interest, that would hinder and possibly interrupt economic recovery.

In the past, decision makers have typically found a durable escape from a great crisis through a radical change of direction in the development trajectory based on a new development model. In fact, at least in the last 150 years, a development trajectory has always started after a great crisis as a response to it. The mainstream opinion typically laid the blame of the crisis on the preceding model of development. In such a situation, innovative thinkers and reformist policy makers are stimulated to work out a new model of development in the conviction that it could overcome the shortcomings of the preceding model.[49] Therefore, as soon as the new model became hegemonic, a new trajectory started to implement it in the best possible way. This is what happened after the last three great crises. The reaction to the Great Depression led to the abandonment of the previous laissez-faire policy strategy considered responsible for the crisis and to the adoption of a Keynesian policy strategy. The Great Stagflation of the 1970s led to the abandonment of the Keynesian policies and the adoption of a neoliberal policy strategy that proved to be much more unsustainable than the traditional liberal strategy. The reaction to the Great Recession instead, after a brief and instrumental revival of the Keynesian and Minskyan policy approaches, did not lead so far to the much-needed radical change of direction in the development trajectory. On the contrary, the dominant policy reaction led, particularly in the

Eurozone, to a more extreme and rigid version of the neoliberal model of development that is further worsening its unsustainability.

The transition to a different trajectory of development crucially depends on the size and structure of investment. This transition requires a significant increase of investment in the real economy to promote an environment-friendly economy, the sustainability of towns, and transports, as well as the health, education, and culture of citizens. All these goals require a recovery of public and private investments in a radically different direction with respect to that prevailing in the last three decades. We have thus to radically change route rather than persevering in the old business-as-usual policy strategy that jeopardises the well-being of most individuals worldwide.

Notes

1. This chapter heavily borrows from a preceding work of mine (Vercelli 2015).
2. See Borghesi and Vercelli (2003 and 2008), and Vercelli (2012).
3. See for example Milanović (2005), Piketty and Saez (2006), Rothstein and Uslaner (2005).
4. The increasing indebtedness affected both the private and public sectors though with a distinct time profile in different countries.
5. See in particular Cameron and Wallace (2002).
6. See for example Kaminsky and Reinhart (1999), Stiglitz (2010 and 2012), and Krugman (2012).
7. The crisis did not end in 2009 but shifted its focus in Europe since the end of 2009. I postpone to Chap. 8 the discussion of the crisis in the Eurozone (or Eurocrisis).
8. See Appendix A.1. Most other developed countries soon adopted similar measures with similar effects.
9. Keynes (1940).
10. Gorton (2010).
11. On the concept of financial market efficiency, see Sect. 6.2.
12. Keynesian and Monetarists fought the decisive battle on the battleground of the Phillips curve. See retro Sect. 1.3 for a more detailed account of this crucial episode that paved the way to the adoption of a neoliberal policy strategy since the late 1970s.

13. Another reason for choosing this conventional starting year is the adoption by the newly appointed chairman of FED, Paul Walker, of a strict monetarist policy soon imitated by most other central banks.
14. The traditional monetarism of Friedman and the new version worked out by Lucas had different foundations but had similar policy implications.
15. Lucas provided in the early 1970s more rigorous foundations to the monetarism of Friedman. The new approach suggested by Lucas, based on stochastic general equilibrium theory and the adoption of the rational expectations hypothesis, became soon the standard approach of neoliberal macroeconomics. This approach was retained also when the original monetarism was abandoned by adopting the perspective of the "real business cycle" (Kydland and Prescott 1982). On these issues, see Lucas (1981) and the critical comments in Vercelli (1991).
16. See retro Sect. 1.3.
17. See for example Milanović (2005), Borghesi and Vercelli (2008), and Piketty (2014).
18. In many developing countries that deviated from neoliberal precepts, this did not occur. A case in point is Brazil after 2003.
19. See for example Stiglitz (2012), and Borghesi and Vercelli (2012).
20. In this brief discussion of the long-run behaviour of this particular World Bank indicator, I ignore the recent changes introduced by the World Bank in the Purchasing Power Parity (PPP) conversion factors.
21. See for example Bhagwati (2004).
22. Bourguignon and Morisson (2002).
23. A recent version is the "Bhagwati hypothesis" (Bhagwati 2004).
24. OECD (2016).
25. See for example Bartolini and Sarracino (2011).
26. Maddison (2004).
27. A case in point is the Reagan administration that resorted often to deficit spending to sustain the rate of growth.
28. Kydland and Prescott (1982).
29. See Krueger and Solow (2002), and Stiglitz (2003).
30. During Greenspan's chairmanship (1987–2006), when the stock market fell more than a certain limited threshold, the FED reacted by lowering the Federal funds rate to force downward the market interest rate and restore as soon as possible the confidence of financial markets. Bernanke (2006–2014) pursued a similar policy also called "Bernanke put". In addition, the quantitative easing interventions introduced since 2007 further strengthened this sort of monetary policy mainly focused on the support of the financial sector.

31. The previous flattening of the Phillips curve made possible the adoption of this new monetary policy suggesting that an increase in aggregate demand brought about by asset inflation and the ensuing wealth effect did not imply more inflation in the real sector.

32. Kaminsky and Reinhart (1999).

33. James Stock and Mark Watson (2002) introduced the catchphrase "great moderation" that was brought to the attention of the wider public by Ben Bernanke (then member, and since 2007 chair, of the Board of Governors of the Federal Reserve System) in a speech at the 2004 meeting of the Eastern Economic Association (Bernanke 2004).

34. See in particular Minsky (1982 and 1986).

35. Krugman (2009) suggested to call the first decade of the millennium the "Big Zero decade" not so much for descriptive reasons (two zero after the 2) but because in it "we achieved nothing and learned nothing … none of the optimistic things we were supposed to believe turned out to be true".

36. This bubble was particularly oversize in the USA, the UK, and Spain.

37. This is particularly true in the Eurozone. See Chap. 8.

38. Chapter 8 will discuss this issue at more length.

39. In Chap. 4, I analysed the process of financialisation in a long-run perspective until the First Financialisation occurred at the turn of the nineteenth century. In Chap. 6, I will analyse in more depth the Second Financialisation started in the 1970s and leading to the recent crisis.

40. See in particular Fisher (1933), and Minsky (1982 and 1986).

41. Minsky maintained that "securitization leads to the creation of financial paper that is eminently suitable for a global financial structure … globalization requires the conformity of institutions across national lines and in particular the ability of creditors to capture assets that underlie the securities" (Minsky 2008, 2–3).

42. Greenspan authoritatively endorsed this belief (see e.g. Greenspan 2007).

43. See infra Sect. 6.5.

44. See in particular Adrian and Shin (2010).

45. Examples of shadow banks "include finance companies, asset-backed commercial paper (ABCP), conduits, structured investment vehicles (SIVs), credit hedge funds, money market mutual funds, security lenders, limited-purpose finance companies (LPFCs), and the government-sponsored enterprises (GSEs)" (Pozsar et al. 2010, 2).

46. See Sect. 6.4.

47. Borghesi and Vercelli (2008 and 2009).

48. Hirsch et al. (2005).

49. Vercelli (2011b).

Bibliography

Adrian, Tobias, and Hyun S. Shin. 2010. The Changing Nature of Financial Intermediation and the Financial Crisis of 2007–2009. *Annual Review of Economics* 2: 603–618.

Abbas, Ali S. M., Belhocine Nazim, El-Ganainy Asmaa, and Mark Horton. 2011. Historical Patterns of Public Debt—Evidence From a New Database. *IMF Economic Review* 59(4):717–742. https://www.imf.org/external/np/seminars/eng/2010/eui/pdf/AB.pdf. Retrieved 4 February 2016.

Abbas, Ali S. M., Blattner Laura, De Broeck Mark, El-Ganainy Asmaa, and Malin Hu. 2014. Sovereign Debt Composition in Advanced Economies: A Historical Perspective. IMF Working Paper WP/14/162. New York: IMF. http://www.imf.org/external/pubs/ft/wp/2014/wp14162.pdf. Retrieved 4 February 2016..

Bartolini, Stefano, and Francesco Sarracino. 2011. Happy for How Long? How Social Capital and GDP relate to Happiness over Time. Working Paper No 2011–60. Luxembourg: CEPS/INSTEAD.

Bernanke, Ben S. 2004. The Great Moderation. Remarks by Governor Ben S. Bernanke at the Meeting of the Eastern Economic Association, Washington, DC. http://www.federalreserve.gov/BOARDDOCS/SPEECHES/2004/20040220/default.htm. Retrieved 11 January 2016.

Bhagwati, Jagdish. 2004. *In Defence of Globalization*. New York: Oxford University Press.

Borghesi, Simone, and Alessandro Vercelli. 2003. Sustainable Globalisation. *Ecological Economics* 44(1): 77–89.

———. 2008. *Global Sustainability. Social and Environmental Conditions*. Palgrave Macmillan: Basingstoke and New York.

Borghesi Simone, and Alessandro Vercelli. 2009. Greenhouse Gas Emissions and the Energy System: Are Current Trends Sustainable? In *International Journal of Global Energy Issues*, Special Issue on 'Energy Efficiency, Environmental Performance and Sustainability', 32 (1–2):160–174.

Borghesi, Simone, and Alessandro Vercelli. 2012. Happiness and Health: Two Paradoxes. *Journal of Economic Surveys* 26(2): 203–233.

Bourguignon, François, and Christian Morisson. 2002. Income among World Citizens: 1820–1992. *American Economic Review* 92(4): 727–744.

Cameron, Gavin, and Christopher C. Wallace. 2002. Macroeconomic Performance in the Bretton Woods Era and After. *Oxford Review of Economic Policy* 18(4): 479–494.

Fisher, Irving. 1933. The Debt-Deflation Theory of the Great Depression. *Econometrica* 1: 337–357.

Gorton, Gary B. 2010. *Slapped by the Invisible Hand: The Panic of 2007*. New York: Oxford University Press.

Greenspan, Alan. 2007. *The age of turbulence: Adventures in a new world*. New York: Penguin Press.

Hirsch, Robert L., Bezdek, Roger, and Robert Wendling. 2005. *Peaking Of World Oil Production: Impacts, Mitigation, & Risk Management*. ("Hirsch Report"). Washington, D.C.: Science Applications International Corporation/ U.S. Department of Energy, National Energy Technology Laboratory.

Kaminsky, Graciela L., and Carmen M. Reinhart. 1999. The Twin Crises: The Causes of Banking and Balance-of-Payments Problems. *American Economic Review* 89(3): 473–500.

Keynes, John Maynard. 1940. *How to Pay for the War: A Radical Plan for the Chancellor of the Exchequer*. London: Macmillan.

Krugman, Paul. 2009. The Big Zero. Op-ed, *The New York Times*, Dec. 27.

———. 2012. *End this depression now!* New York: W. W. Norton and Co.

Krueger, Alan B., and Robert Solow, eds. 2002. *The Roaring Nineties*. New York, NY: Russell Sage Foundation.

Kydland, Finn E., and Edward C. Prescott. 1982. Time to Build and Aggregate Fluctuations. *Econometrica* 50(6): 1345–1370.

Lapavitsas, Costas, et al. 2012. *Crisis in the Eurozone*. London: Verso.

Lucas, Robert E. Jr. 1981. *Studies in Business-Cycle Theory*. Boston, Mass: MIT Press.

Maddison, Angus. 2004. *The World Economy: Historical Statistics*. Paris: OECD.

Milanović, Branko. 2005. *Worlds Apart: Measuring International and Global Inequality*. Princeton, NJ: Princeton University Press.

Minsky, Hyman P. 1982. *Can "It" Happen Again? Essays on Instability and Finance*. Armonk, NY: Sharpe.

——— 1986. *Stabilizing an Unstable Economy*. New Haven and London: Yale University Press.

——— 2008 [1987]. Securitization. Handout Econ 335A. In Levy Archives. Published as *Policy Note* 2, The Levy Economics Institute.

OECD. 2016. Poverty rate (indicator). doi: 10.1787/0fe1315d-en (Accessed on 01 March 2016).

Piketty, Thomas, and Emmanuel Saez. 2006. The evolution of top incomes: a historical and international perspectives. *American Economic Review* 96(2): 200–205.

Piketty, Thomas. 2014. *Capital in the Twenty-First Century*. Cambridge Mass: Harvard University Press.

Pozsar, Zoltan, Adrian, Tobias, Ashcraft, Adam, and Hayley Boesky. 2010. Shadow Banking, Federal Reserve Bank of New York Staff Report No. 458, revised 2012.

Rothstein, Bo, and Eric M. Uslaner. 2005. All for all: Equality, Corruption, and Social Trust. *World Politics* 58(1): 41–72.

Stiglitz, Joseph E 2003. *The Roaring Nineties*. New York: W. W. Norton & Co.

———— 2010. *Freefall: Free Markets and the Sinking of the Global Economy*. New York: W. W. Norton & Co.

———— 2012. *The Price of Inequality. How Today's Divided Society Endangers our Future*. New York: W. W. Norton & Co.

Stock, James H. and Mark W. Watson. 2002. Has the Business Cycle Changed and Why?. In *NBER Macroeconomics Annual 2002* 17:159–227, ed. Mark Gertler, Kenneth Rogoff.

Vercelli, Alessandro. 1991. *Methodological Foundations of Macroeconomics. Keynes and Lucas*. Cambridge: Cambridge University Press.

————. 2011b. Economy and Economics: The Twin Crises. In *The Global Economic Crisis. New Perspectives on the Critique of Economic Theory and Policy*, eds. Emiliano Brancaccio, and Giuseppe Fontana, 27–41. Abingdon and New York: Routledge.

————. 2012. *Sustainability*. In the *Wiley-Blackwell Encyclopaedia of Globalization*, vol. 4, ed. George Ritzer, 1941–1952.

————. 2015. The Neoliberal Trajectory, the Great Recession and Sustainable Development. *International Papers in Political Economy*, issue on "Finance and the Macroeconomics of Environmental Policies", ed. Philip Arestis and Malcolm Sawyer, 37–73.

6

The Neoliberal Financialisation[1]

6.1 Introduction

This chapter investigates some causes and consequences of the second surge of financialisation after the Industrial Revolution (often called Second Financialisation; see Chaps. 4 and 5). I resume here the analysis started in Chap. 4 that extended the long-term analysis of financialisation up to its collapse induced by the Great Depression in the 1930s. In particular, this chapter intends to complement the analysis of the genesis and causes of the Great Recession by examining in more depth the role of finance during the crisis and the policy implications of the recent evolution of finance.

An immense literature has extensively discussed this topic. A host of contributions to a hot debate may be found in academic journals, mass media, blogs, policy briefs, and so on. The prevailing orientation of the debate followed a path that proved to be highly misleading. In a first phase (2007–2009), under the pressure of a widespread rage and indignation for the questionable behaviour of financial institutions, the public opinion considered them and their regulators as the main culprit of the disaster. A second phase followed in which mass media and policy makers

© The Editor(s) (if applicable) and The Author(s) 2017
A. Vercelli, *Crisis and Sustainability*,
DOI 10.1057/978-1-137-60069-1_6

progressively de-emphasised the role of finance. A series of causes contributed to the emergence of this new attitude: the successful diversion of attention from finance to sovereign debt and corruption, the opacity of the continuing massive support to distressed financial institutions through unorthodox means (such as quantitative easing), and the urgency of the real problems (such as unemployment, stagnation, inequality, and poverty) that seemed at first sight only remotely linked to finance.

The academic literature contributed to the current undervaluation of the role of finance under the influence of deeply rooted prejudices. Mainstream economics, consciously or unconsciously, has been—and still often is—victim of the deep-seated a priori that money and finance are not much more than a "veil" concealing the view of economic fundamentals (technology, tastes, and endowment of resources). Another source of undervaluation of finance, though based on completely different foundations, is the idea entertained by many heterodox economists that money and finance belong to a superstructure of capitalism that ultimately depends on an underlying economic and social structure. The practical convergence of these two paradigmatic visions, coupled with a massive lobbying of the financial institutions, explains why the urgent need for a radical reform of the financial system, though maintained by most voices after the peak of the crisis in the autumn 2008, has progressively lost momentum. Policy makers produced many proposals but did very little so far, as they continued to postpone and water down the most ambitious reforms (see Appendix 1).

In this chapter, I start from a different standpoint that I have justified in Chap. 4: finance cannot be neatly severed from the real economy as a separate sector or level of reality; it is just one aspect of financialised capitalism contributing in an essential way to its dynamics. We can isolate in vitro this specific aspect for the purpose of analysis only as a preliminary step towards a more comprehensive synthesis. This view implies that a radical reform of finance is urgent because it is a necessary, though by no means sufficient, condition for the implementation of a new sustainable model of development.

This chapter aims to blaze a trail in the thick forest of the debate on the role of finance in the recent crisis trying to connect theory and facts.

To this end, I start from a critical presentation of the mainstream views on finance and financial crisis that happen to be based on the assumption of asymmetric information. The identification of a few fundamental shortcomings in this variegated and influential mainstream theory will indicate the way to pursue for understanding better the role of finance in the financial crisis. This assessment should clarify also how to reform finance to stabilise the economy and assure a rapid convergence towards a trajectory of sustainable development.

The structure of this chapter is as follows. Section 6.2 briefly surveys the changes in finance theory since the 1970s that provided the foundations to the new policy strategy of neoliberal inspiration. The implementation of the latter produced far-reaching structural transformations in finance that changed the way in which the economic and financial system behaves. Section 6.3 outlines the genesis of shadow banking hinting at the most important underlying structural changes of finance such as securitisation. Section 6.4 investigates some significant consequences of the rise of shadow banking. Section 6.5 discusses some proposals of reform of the shadow banking system. In Sect. 6.6, the focus broadens to the reform proposals for the entire financial system. The concluding remarks in Sect. 6.7 wrap up the previous analysis of the shortcomings of neoliberal deregulation in finance.

6.2   The Neoliberal Revolution in Finance

The neoliberal revolution in economics and finance that burst in the late 1970s paved the way for a radical change in policy strategy. As for its genesis, at the turn of the 1950s, a bifurcation occurred in mainstream economics between a "fundamentalist" approach adopting the rational expectations hypothesis (REH) and the efficient market hypothesis (EMH) on one side and, on the other side, a behavioural approach adopting broader and more flexible theoretical assumptions strictly rooted in the empirical observation of actual behaviour.

The emerging tension between the two camps was already visible "in vitro" at the Graduate School of Industrial Administration at Carnegie Mellon in the late 1950s and early 1960s. A group of first-rate researchers (including three future Nobel laureates: Modigliani, Muth, and Simon) interacted there on the role of rationality in decision making. Simon reacted to the excessive reliance on agents' rationality in economics starting an alternative research programme based on bounded rationality.[2] On the contrary, Muth focused on the lack of rationality characterising the existing models of expectations formation and worked out a formal concept of expectations fully complying with uncompromising economic rationality: the REH.[3]

Herbert Simon advocated a behavioural approach committed to the observation of actual economic behaviour without too strict a priori axioms and too narrow disciplinary boundaries. Muth on the contrary argued that the assumption of REH provided the foundations for a more coherent and systematic focus on economic fundamentals.

The behavioural approach advocated by Simon promoted a systematic interaction between economists, psychologists, and other social scientists giving birth to the interdisciplinary sub-disciplines of "behavioural economics", "behavioural finance", and "experimental economics". The fundamentalist approach suggested by Muth provided instead crucial building blocks to a new view in mainstream economics that materialised in different variants (such as new classical economics, monetary equilibrium business cycle, real business cycle, and endogenous growth theory). For this to happen, however, the REH, at the beginning applied exclusively to microeconomics and partial equilibrium, had to combine its insights with those of the EMH that directly referred to the properties of free markets. In the early 1970s, Lucas was the first to combine the "genes" of the EMH and the REH starting a radical mutation of macroeconomics in a fundamentalist direction. The EMH provided a new view of the self-regulating properties of markets promising to give a more rigorous and constructive view of the "invisible hand" first evoked by Smith and then cherished and developed by neoclassical economists. The REH provided in its turn a powerful analytic bridge between this vision of markets and the Arrow–Debreu probabilistic version of general equilibrium theory.[4]

Both branches of "respectable" economics have subsequently flourished in the academia and in the research offices of international institutions, central banks, and governments, inspiring the decision strategies of big private operators and the policy rules of policy makers. Behavioural economics and finance have been particularly popular with practitioners while many policy makers were keen to adopt fundamentalist economics and finance to exploit their implications in favour of laissez-faire.

The EMH represents the centrepiece of neoclassical finance theory, being for quite a long time the dominating view on the functioning of financial markets. According to Fama, the intellectual leader of this approach, the conditions for market efficiency are the absence of transaction costs and the assumption that all information is freely available to all agents, which means that all agents agree on the implications of available information for current and future stock prices.[5] Based on these assumptions, the EMH maintains that at any point in time stock prices fully reflect all available information about individual stocks and about stock market as a whole. Therefore, nobody can earn returns higher than market returns.[6]

Fama assembled a comprehensive review of theory and evidence of market efficiency and proposed a classification of forms of market efficiency. The weak form of the EMH claims that prices fully reflect the information implicit in the sequence of past prices; the semi-strong form asserts that prices reflect all relevant information that is publicly available, while the strong form asserts that market prices fully reflect the information known to any agent. Since then, these three categories have become the standard foundations of market efficiency.

The assumptions underlying the EMH characterise mainstream research and policy since the late 1970s. Although the single research programmes adopting some version of these assumptions may differ in a significant way (as is the case of "monetary business cycle" vs "real business cycle" models), they have in common the idea that, generally speaking, real markets are efficient and allocate in the best possible way the existing resources maximising the well-being of the economic agents. This implies that economic and financial markets should be "perturbed" as little as possible by legal regulation, public interventions, and strict supervision. The exponents of mainstream economics and finance often do not deny that the working of real markets is subject to "frictions" that may occasionally bring about significant welfare losses. The new classical economists, however, tend to blame the excessive and mis-conceived interference of public authorities, while the new Keynesians advocate a more coherent interventionist policy strategy.

The streams of macroeconomics accepting the EMH and the REH are often called "fundamentalist" because they believe that a correct predic-tion of economic and financial behaviour should rely on market funda-mentals (endowments, preferences, and technology). The new Keynesian school instead on the significant role of market frictions (such as asym-metric information, price rigidities, oligopolistic practices, and transac-tion costs); however, the acceptation of the two hypotheses mentioned above implies that market frictions, as suggested by the terminology itself, play a secondary role as compared to market fundamentals. This explains why the Keynesian economists that are closer to the original message of Keynes, such as the post-Keynesian economists, reject both hypotheses.

We have to emphasise that the assumptions of fundamentalist macro-economics are very demanding. In particular:

(i) Only equilibrium positions are analysed, while disequilibrium positions and dynamics are disregarded as irrelevant and irrational.[7]
(ii) The agents are unboundedly rational and therefore always able to maximise their utility function.
(iii) Time is fully reversible; this excludes the significance of any sort of evolu-tion, time dependency, and even transaction costs.
(iv) Uncertainty has an impact on the agents' decisions only in its weakest meaning, as it is represented and analysed through fully reliable additive probability distributions.

These crucial assumptions imply that money and credit do not play any significant role as institutions affecting the way in which the system works. They are seen as a mere "veil" blurring the contours of economic phenomena without affecting them, and this is reaffirmed not only for the long period as in traditional neoclassical macroeconomics, but also for the short period.

As for the policy implications of this paradigm, we observe an evo-lution from a monetarist point of view supporting the Friedman's idea that discretionary monetary policy implies a suboptimal growth, to a non-monetarist point of view that reverses the causal direction between money and the real economy. The monetarism "mark 2" of Lucas, based on his "monetary equilibrium business cycle", inspired the restrictive policies of central banks in the late 1970s and early 1980s first introduced by Paul Volcker, Chairman of the Federal Reserve from 1979 to 1987. The "real business cycle" approach inspired the new monetarist policy introduced by Greenspan and carried on by his successor Bernanke and most other central bankers.[8] I suggest calling the new monetary policy "asymmetric monetarism" as it aims to fight inflation with the usual severity in the real sector but provides the financial system with all the liquidity needed to sustain a trend of steady appreciation of financial assets. This asymmetry became extreme after the subprime crisis particularly in the Eurozone when the rigid monetarism in the real sector carried on by austerity policies was coupled with a continuous over-generous provision of liquidity to the financial sector.

The mainstream point of view based upon the EMH and REH sees the process of financialisation, even in the last three decades, as a physiological process to the extent that the market has managed it without interference of regulators and supervisors. The supporters of macroeconomic and financial fundamentalism did not change opinion after the financial crisis and the ensuing Great Recession since they lay the blame on the excessive and misguided interference of regulators and supervisors. They maintained in particular that policy makers should never intervene to bail out virtually bankrupted banks, as this would encourage moral hazard. More in general, since fundamentalist economists are in favour of a strict form of laissez-faire, they are against the adoption of more rigorous rules of regulation and supervision of finance.

The point of view of behavioural economics and finance on the process of financialisation, the recent crisis, and their policy implications is much more difficult to assess. While the behavioural approach succeeded to conquer growing spaces in academic research and to some extent in academic curricula, its impact on policy has been much more limited. Two basic factors may explain this asymmetry:

(a) Fundamentalist economists are quite homogeneous from the point of view of theory, method, and policy, while behavioural economists have in common not much more than a critical attitude towards fundamentalist principles but divide in a myriad of heterogeneous research programmes having diverging policy implications.

(b) The policy prescriptions of fundamentalist macroeconomics are in tune with the neoliberal orientation of policy makers and ruling classes, while the policy prescriptions of the behavioural approaches are more diversified and often inconsistent with laissez-faire.

In particular, we cannot say that the behavioural economists have a common point of view, not even a prevailing one, on the explanation of the process of financialisation, its consequences, and its possible alternatives. This approach, however, offers a vision and a few useful instruments to understand better the fallout of the financialisation process on real people who are characterised by peculiar cognitive features, emotions, and social and ethical preferences. By assuming the behavioural point of view, we can therefore get useful insights on the human and social implications of financialisation from the viewpoint of sustainable development.

The sustainability of development, on the contrary, is almost completely beyond the boundaries of fundamentalist economics and finance since

(i) economic sustainability is generally conceived in a very restrictive way as mere steady growth of GDP (notwithstanding the well-known shortcomings of such distorting measure of well-being);

(ii) environmental sustainability is restricted to the internalisation of externalities (whose role is often played down on the basis of the Coase theorem);[9] and

(iii) social sustainability is restricted to the distribution of per capita GDP (believed to be hardly modifiable by policy).[10]

Both mainstream economics and orthodox finance theory explain, and pretend to predict, economic and financial behaviour as a rational response to market signals. It is therefore natural to look at banking and financial crises in terms of information and incentives. However, if we look at the economic system in this way, namely from the point of view of general equilibrium theory, the supply of loanable funds should match perfectly well the demand of credit directly in the market, guaranteeing the smooth and efficient working of the system without requiring any need of financial intermediation. Therefore, to explain the anomalies of financial behaviour (including the frequent episodes of panic), this approach has to resort to some significant deviation from the assumptions that financial markets are efficient and perfectly competitive. In the last decades (since the early 1970s), the crucial deviation from the perfect competition model, introduced to justify the prominent role of banks in the economy, is the acknowledgment of the ubiquitous impact of sizeable asymmetric information in financial markets. Mainstream economists and experts of finance used this assumption to explain many stylised facts observed in financial markets such as banking panics, financial crises, and their propagation mechanisms.

The asymmetric information approach recognises a significant impact of the financial side of a given economy on the dynamic behaviour of the economic system (denied by traditional general equilibrium theory) by focusing on the different quantity and quality of information available to parties in financial contracts. In particular, this approach assumes that borrowers have better information than lenders about their genuine financial position and the viability of their investment projects. The ensuing information asymmetry is likely to produce significant deviations from optimal equilibrium.[11] This depends, first, on adverse selection as asymmetric information provides a relative advantage to bad quality borrowers (often called "lemons" in this literature) over good quality borrowers who could withdraw from the market.[12] Since lenders are unable to discriminate correctly between bad and good borrowers, they charge an average rate of interest that, taking account of the effective risk, is too high for good borrowers and too low for bad borrowers. The ensuing distortions of investment imply more systemic risk for the economy as a whole, less aggregate investment, and thus more financial instability and less growth. Lenders react by further increasing the average rate of interest; the latter, however, results in greater adverse selection as well as in credit rationing.[13] The higher interest rate would not equilibrate the market even in the case of excess demand for loans but, on the contrary, would further increase disequilibrium. This cumulative out-of-equilibrium process may easily lead to a credit crunch and possibly to a collapse of financial markets.[14]

The exponents of the asymmetric information approach claim that this cumulative process contributes to explain the recurrence of financial fluctuations and their occasional degeneration in episodes of severe financial crisis.[15] Moreover, the additional moral hazard brought about by an increment of asymmetric information is likely to reinforce the distortional impact of adverse selection. Since lenders cannot easily ascertain the quality of the projects of borrowers, the latter have incentives to engage in projects which increase the expected profits but also the risk of default.

The asymmetric information approach has provided an influential explanation of the prominent role of banks in financial markets. In this view, their main role lies in their ability to reduce asymmetric information mitigating many problems raised by adverse selection and moral hazard. In particular, according to the traditional model of banking, often called "originate-to-hold", banks have an expertise in collecting information about the reliability of borrowers. They exploit their lower cost of monitoring as compared to individuals and more efficient enforcement of restrictive covenants.[16] This advantage is enhanced by long-term customer relationships such as those entertained by local commercial banks with their clients.

The asymmetric information approach recognises that market mechanisms cannot easily solve the problems produced by asymmetric information. In this view, the main market remedy for the lender relies in the request that the borrower provides adequate collateral for the loan that may safely cover the value of the loan in case of default. This solution, however, requires that the value of the collateral be information-insensitive so that it retains its value also in case of unexpected developments of the financial conditions of the borrower or the economy at large. This requires the intervention of specific institutions able to create information-insensitive debt. The private institutions that play this crucial role are banks. Therefore, they also play an active role in the endogenous process of money creation that provides liquidity to the system whenever is needed. Unfortunately, banks play fairly well this role only when the markets are healthy and not when some sort of pathology develops.

The asymmetric information approach provides many clues not only for explaining the existence and the crucial role of banks in the economy, but also for explaining financial fluctuations and their recurring degeneration into serious, sometimes devastating, financial crises. The causal mechanisms, briefly reviewed above, are liable to trigger cumulative processes bringing about recurring fluctuations and, under particular circumstances, a financial collapse. Analogously, a stock market crash lowers the value of collaterals enhancing adverse selection and moral hazard, and this is likely to lead to financial disruption.[17] Any reduction in the net worth of borrowers may induce serious financial distress because they have less to lose by engaging in moral hazard activities to defend the declining net worth.[18] An autonomous increase in asymmetric information or a negative shift of expectations may induce or reinforce one or more of the financial vicious circles. In all these cases, the vicious circle generated by asymmetric information eventually leads to a reduction of investment transmitting the crisis to the real economy.

6.3   The Genesis of Shadow Banking

Shadow banking gradually emerged since the early 1970s as cause and consequence of deep structural changes in the financial system. The main specific drivers of this ongoing process were, from the supply side, a continuous flow of flexibility-enhancing financial innovations and deep regulatory changes that aimed to liberalise banks and financial markets from any form of pressing regulation, control, and supervision.[19] A second impulse came from the demand of collateral for financial transactions that incentivised the surge of securitisation and the systematic use of repurchase agreements (**repos**) as a money-like instrument for big financial institutions. Supply and demand forces found a benign support from the visible hand of court decisions and regulatory innovations that allowed securitisation and gave repos a privileged treatment under the bankruptcy code.

This complex of factors produced a progressive decline of the traditional banking model as shaped by the containment laws of the 1930s and by the Bretton Woods policy rules. Federal Reserve flow of funds data confirm that the ratio of off-balance-sheet to on-balance-sheet loan funding grew from about zero in 1980 to over 60 % in 2007.[20] However, we should not interpret this evolutionary change as a mere process of substitution between old and new banking model, because the relationship between these two models is a very complex one that is based at the same time on competition and complementarity. Commercial banks increasingly suffered from a growing competitive challenge exerted by non-banks and their products both from the asset side of their balance sheets (junk bonds, commercial paper, exotic derivatives, and so on), as well as from their liability side (in particular **money-market mutual funds [MMMF]**).[21]

Commercial banks reacted to the progressive fall of their deposits and declining profitability by seeking new profit opportunities in the emerging shadow sector contributing to its further development. On the other hand, strong complementary links developed between commercial banks and shadow institutions. Commercial banks started to manage short-term liquidity through shadow banking (securitised repo market), while the shadow institutions relied on commercial banks as ultimate source of liquidity (see Appendix A1). This complex interaction between commercial banks and shadow institutions is what makes so difficult to understand the impact of shadow banking on financial fragility and contagion. For the same reason, the control, regulation, and supervision of such a system is an unsolved problem.[22] A way out in the right direction requires a radical change of perspective.

The collapse of the Bretton Woods system started a process of transformation of finance in the direction of a growing importance of financial markets. This determined the progressive success of market-based financial institutions such as institutional investors, pension funds, and mutual funds. The focus of this chapter is restricted to a particular category of market-based financial institutions often called shadow banks since they perform banking functions outside the regulatory purview of banks, so to say in the shadows.[23] This terminology immediately caught up also in academic circles notwithstanding reiterated criticisms. The success of this terminology is rooted in the fact that the word "shadow" immediately evokes a few features of this form of banking that make it elusive and uncontrollable. First, it is based on off-balance-sheet operations that make difficult their control and supervision. Second, it relies on complex and variable procedures that render its economic implications quite opaque for public opinion, policy makers, and even most operators. Finally, shadow banking often intentionally enhances opacity by resorting to offshore financial centres. However, what is most confusing in this terminology is not so much the first word "shadow" but the second word "banking", especially when it is used to indicate specific financial institutions. Though these institutions perform functions traditionally performed by traditional banks, they have characteristics sharply distinct from those of traditional banks.[24]

Since any definition of shadow banks based on the definition of their function is intrinsically ambiguous, the literature indulges in extensional definitions offering lists of financial institutions, instruments, and contractual arrangements that go under the name of shadow banks. For example, according to Gorton and Metrick, "in its broadest definition, shadow banking includes such familiar institutions as investment banks, money-market mutual funds, and mortgage brokers; some rather old contractual forms, such as sale-and-repurchase agreements (repos); and more esoteric instruments such as asset-backed securities (**ABS**s), collateralised debt obligations (**CDO**s), and asset-backed commercial paper (**ABCP**)."[25] This and other similar lists of shadow banks define simply a residual category, to complement that of regulated commercial banks.[26] In this section, I just wish to investigate why and how some of these financial entities emerged and started to interact as a coherent system. To this end, I focus only on a selected subset of shadow institutions that have become prominent in the shadow banking system and have played a crucial role in the transmission of the financial crisis.

Among the market-based financial institutions that started to erode the traditional role of commercial banks, money-market funds (MMFs) played a particularly important role since the 1970s. They were a response to the interest rate ceilings on demand deposits established by the Regulation Q (see Appendix A1). Unsurprisingly, they started to grow in response to the sharp increase in the rates of interest induced in the late 1970s by the monetarist policy of the FED under the leadership of Paul Volcker (see retro Chap. 5). In consequence of the ensuing increase of deposit costs, MMFs took off in the mid-1980s. Their assets grew from

$76.4 billion in 1980 to $1.8 trillion by 2000, and reached a peak of $3.8 trillion in 2008.[27] The main reason of their success was their promise of maintaining the $1 share price that gave the investors an illusion of security equivalent to that of bank deposit accounts. However, as long as money market funds have implicit, cost-free government backing, they will have a cost advantage over insured deposits.[28]

A crucial building block of shadow banking was the process of securitisation. As is well known, securitisation is the process by which an issuer, typically a bank, sells loans into the capital markets. The bank sells large portfolios of loans to **special purpose vehicles (SPVs)**, which finance these purchases by selling securities in the capital markets divided into tranches ranked by seniority and differently rated. The process of securitisation thus selects loans that a traditional originating bank would have held on the balance sheet until maturity to create securities immediately marketable via the off-balance-sheet SPV.

Securitisation has a long pedigree but its role started to become crucial in the 1970s, because this process was fully coherent with the emergent market-based finance. An early example of its success in the neoliberal era is the introduction and rapid growth of **mortgage-based securities (MBS)**. Starting in the 1980s, the process of securitisation spread to other income-producing assets: commercial mortgages, auto loans, or credit card debt obligations (or other non-debt assets-generating receivables). In the last decade the scope of securitisation extended beyond the traditional self-liquidating assets (such as mortgages, bank loans, or consumer loans), to a wider variety of asset types, including home equity loans, lease receivables, and small business loans.

The process of securitisation progressively transformed the traditional "originate-to-hold" model of banking into a new "originate-to-distribute" model. In the traditional model, banks provided loans to their clients, holding the right to receive the ensuing cash flows. Therefore, within this model, banks have strong incentives to assess the problems raised by asymmetric information, and this contributes to a beneficial reduction of systemic risk and to a significant increase in the efficiency of financial markets. In the "originate-to-distribute" model, banks originate loans to distribute them by selling them in the secondary loan market.

In this model of banking, originating banks have lower incentives to screening their borrowers increasing asymmetric information and systemic risk.

Shadow banking grew out of a symbiotic integration of two forms of banking: the wholesale securitisation system and the repo market. For large depositors, repos can act as a substitute for insured demand deposits. The introduction of deposit insurance in 1934 has been very successful in avoiding bank runs because retail investors felt reassured by this form of insurance. However, with deposit insurance capped at $100,000 per account, institutions with large cash holdings such as pension funds, mutual funds, states and municipalities, and non-financial companies lack easy access to safe, interest-earning, short-term investments. The shadow banking system provides a solution to this problem since it offers a safe investment that earns interest and, similarly to a demand deposit, retains the flexibility of using the cash when needed.

Repo agreements may play a role similar to that of insured demand deposits because they obtained a special status under the US Bankruptcy Code.[29] A depositor, for example, can unilaterally terminate its repo with an insolvent bank and sell the collateral. Without this protection, a party to a repo contract would be just another creditor waiting for the conclusion of the bankruptcy proceedings. In addition, the operators can rehypothecate repo collaterals reusing them in another transaction with an unrelated third party.

As the Bank for International Settlements (BIS) has pointed out, this results in high levels of "velocity" in repo markets.[30] This occurs when a single piece of collateral is used to settle a number of contracts on the same day. It allows the daily repo trading volume to exceed the outstanding amount of collateral, as participants are able to borrow and lend a single piece of collateral repeatedly over the course of a day. Rehypothecation thus creates a multiplier process for collateral, similar to the more familiar money multiplier.

The repo market is not only a deposit market, since repos are used also for a series of other crucial purposes, such as to hedge derivative positions, to "short" positions in securities markets, or to enhance leverage. For all these reasons, a few experts maintain that the repo market has become the core of the financial system.[31]

6.4   Contagion and Propagation

According to the mainstream point of view, the crisis has been the consequence of the emergence of a new model of banking characterised by significant microeconomic advantages but generating at the same time negative externalities for the system as a whole. The incentives of banks to assess accurately the reliability of borrowers, the soundness of their investment projects, and the risks involved in each specific transaction became significantly weaker since they are not residual claimants on these loans. In particular, the balance sheets of banks adopting the new paradigm become less reliable since the process of securitisation is largely based on off-balance-sheet transactions through SPVs or other conduits established ad hoc. This further contributes to feed asymmetric information in the market strengthening the vicious circle.

Financial institutions and policy authorities have adopted this analysis soon after the inception of the crisis.[32] In April 2008, the authoritative Joint Forum endorsed this view of the emerging financial crisis: "under the "originate-to-distribute" model, banks frequently no longer have significant retained exposures, nor have they necessarily retained the personnel specializing in workouts who can steer creditor negotiations" (Joint Forum 2008, 20).[33]

In this view, the originate-to-distribute model of banking creates "severe incentive problems, which are referred to as principal-agent problems … in which the agent (the originator of the loans) did not have the incentives to act fully in the interest of the principal (the ultimate holder of the loan). Originators have every incentive to maintain origination volume, because that would allow them to earn substantial fees, but they had weak incentives to maintain loan quality" (Mishkin 2008).

An alternative influential view of the origin and deployment of the Great Recession utilised asymmetric information theory in a different way focusing on the relationship between securitisation and contagion in the shadow banking system.[34] The basic idea is that the US financial crisis started in 2007 has many significant analogies with the banking panics of the past. In the recent crisis, a similar panic originated within the shadow banking system when an unexpected exogenous shock (slowdown of housing prices followed by their significant reduction) affected first the MBS market in the early 2007 and then, since August 2007, the whole banking system.

This alternative point of view, worked out by Gorton and his collaborators, relies on a different understanding of the nature of both traditional banking and shadow banking. It is worthwhile to consider this approach in some detail because it helps to clarify some crucial shortcomings of the mainstream point of view and, at the same time, of the financial system itself. In this view, the essence of banking is not intermediation between savers and investors, since their mutual relation—especially in financialised capitalism—depends on financial markets. In this view, the specific role of banking is instead that of creating a special kind of debt immune to adverse selection by privately informed traders. This sort of "informationally insensitive" debt was originally limited to demand deposits. However, the latter are of no use to large institutions (such as firms, banks, hedge funds, and corporate treasuries), which may need to deposit large amounts of money for a short period.[35] They "deposit" instead their short-term liquidity in the sale and repurchase (repo) market. As we have seen above, these deposits are "insured" by collateral, including in a growing percentage securitised products. The depositor may reuse the collateral by "rehypothecation" that plays a role similar to writing cheques with analogous multiplicative effects. This sort of collateral plays for large financial institutions the role of a "currency" that creates "deposits" of money on call (mostly overnight), and may "circulate".

The progressive growth of repo market stimulated the parallel growth of wholesale securitisation to satisfy its growing need of collateral. This kind of debt in normal conditions is largely informationally insensitive and has thus an information advantage over corporate debt since the latter is subject to speculation on information about the corporation performance.

The main trouble with shadow banking is the fact that its peculiar "deposits" give the illusion of being information-insensitive being "insured" by the market through the process of collateralisation. However, the crisis of 2007 revealed that such illusion is mistaken. The collaterals proved to be information-insensitive only in periods of financial tranquillity but became suddenly information-sensitive, and highly so, as soon as the crisis burst. The behaviour of repo haircuts clearly betrays the sudden loss of confidence in the information-insensitiveness of collateral.[36]

The haircut has been zero until early July 2007 showing a widespread trust in the information-insensitiveness of collateral in the US repo market; however, after the housing shock that started to affect the value of mortgage-related assets, the haircut began to be perceived as a systemic event. By the end of 2007, the average repo haircut on structured debt had reached in the USA the significant level of 9 %. In 2008, it increased rapidly from 10 % in January to 15 % in June, reaching 24 % in August, and jumping to 46 % after the bankruptcy of the Lehman Brothers.[37] We may interpret the increasing haircut as "withdrawal" of repo deposits from banks and its continuous and rapid increase to unprecedented values as a bank run in the repo market. In this view, the run on repo was analogous to previous banking panics. Earlier bank runs happened because deposits were not insured; the recent run in the repo market happened when the depositors discovered that their deposits were in fact only partially and very imperfectly covered by the value of collaterals. This led to a sort of "lemon market" in which everyone needs to produce information to trade making it highly illiquid.[38] What is worse, much of the required information was not available, in particular about where the exposures to the shock were actually located. The ensuing panic inevitably paralysed all the interbank market.

The effective practice of securitisation shows that, contrary to expectations, transfer of risk from the banks originating loans to investors is only partial. Systemic risk and asymmetric information increase as risk spreads in an opaque way over much larger categories of subjects participating in the chain of loans securitisation. None of these subjects retains significant incentives to assess the risk of securitised loans but this is by itself insufficient to explain the banking panic triggered by the subprime crisis.

The process of securitisation has become a crucial component of "shadow banking", conceived as a parallel banking system interacting with the traditional one but having a certain degree of autonomy. According to the first official reaction to the crisis, "shadow banking" is a degeneration of the traditional banking system that in principle should be contained. According to the alternative point of view of Gorton, the repo market is a parallel banking system utilised by large institutions that plays a crucial role in finance and should thus be adequately controlled and regulated rather than contained.

In my opinion, each of the two main variants of the asymmetric information approach captures some significant features of the recent evolution of the banking system and, in particular, of the 2007–2009 bank panic. However, both branches suffer from the limitations of the common trunk from which they are branching.

The financial crises depend not only on asymmetric information but also more in general on the nature and degree of systemic uncertainty, whether the latter is asymmetric or not. Asymmetric information is a significant and ubiquitous source of uncertainty but it is not the only one. The spreading of risk across a plurality of unknown and unknowable subjects emphasised by both branches of asymmetric information theory implies by itself that uncertainty over the value and risk of securitised assets is strong (not representable through additive probability distributions) or radical (we just do not know). In addition, information and uncertainty do not exhaust the causes of financial crises and their propagation. This is a common shortcoming of all the branches of the asymmetric information approach.

The crucial concept that banking is in its essence creation of information-insensitive debt contributes to the understanding of the recent banking practices but is too narrow. The meaning and implications of banking should be analysed in all its dimensions. Although new information is an important category of potential shocks, other important shocks have a different nature. In particular, those triggered by the interaction between the balance sheets of economic units are not information shocks but the consequence of market interactions reflected by accounting figures.

Information-sensitiveness is a concept akin to that of financial fragility: in both cases, a small perturbation is sufficient to change the behaviour of a financial entity.[39] Minsky refers this concept to economic units or to the economic system as a whole. The financial fragility of a unit depends on the degree of shock-sensitiveness of its portfolio of assets, while the financial fragility of the system depends on that of the single units and the features of their interconnectedness.

This interaction may be understood only by delving in the processes of contagion focusing on the propagation of the financial crisis from the mortgage-related assets to the entire finance and then to the whole economy. The shock that triggered the crisis (the slowdown of the price of housing at the turn of 2006, followed by its reduction, at first mild and then precipitous) affected at first only the subprime assets classes whose value significantly declined. Since early 2007, the financial markets show also a progressive deterioration of subprime-related assets classes and firms.[40] Subprime mortgage originations in 2005 and 2006 amounted to $1.2 billion, a remarkable sum that would not have been sufficient per se to trigger a systemic crisis in a large country such as the USA. The systemic event reflected by the collapse of other asset classes normally unrelated with subprime assets started only in August 2007 when average repo haircuts, that were still about zero until then, started to rise. The crisis became systemic because no one knew where the increased risk related to mortgage asset classes was located. When most economic agents started to believe that this risk had breached the safety threshold set by the decision makers, the consequent panic spread to the banking system as a whole. Therefore, the problem is not only asymmetric information but also a widespread deep lack of information suffered by decision makers. The ultimate causes of the crisis are rooted into the strong uncertainty affecting the choices, while asymmetric information is only an aspect of it.

The run on repo deposits triggered a well-known process of propagation experienced in all preceding financial crises, at least the most serious ones: a variant of the Fisherian process of debt deflation as updated by Minsky.[41] The main dealers found increasingly difficult to refinance their positions and found themselves overindebted; in order to reduce their indebtedness, they had to sell part of their assets, even those that were originally unrelated to mortgage collateral. The market values of all these assets progressively declined compelling the main dealers of securitised products in the repo market to downsize their activity. This vicious circle eventually propagated to all the economic units holding financial assets, and their herd behaviour produced a significant loss of their value. This process of slow but progressive build-up of bank panic emerged in August 2007 and became progressively more intense, culminating in September 2008.

6.5   Regulation of Shadow Banking

The two main branches of the asymmetric information approach discussed above have radically different policy implications. The "hold-to-distribute" hypothesis points to the correction of the most significant shortcomings of the new model of banking, aiming to mend the distortions of securitisation and shadow banking. The polar star of the required policies should be the elimination of asymmetric information through requisites of transparency and disclosure. The opinions differ, however, on which are the most efficacious and urgent measures to be adopted to reach this goal. In principle, these measures should go in the direction of an effective discipline of securitisation and the request that the balance sheets of banks rigorously register all the operations, including those that are currently off-balance sheet. Although, at the start of the subprime crisis, the policy authorities seemed inclined to endorse this version of the mainstream approach, they have been so far reluctant, or unable, to push with the necessary energy towards the implementation of reforms strongly opposed by powerful financial lobbies. The policy measures adopted so far seem to rely on the combination of two strategies that financial markets are inclined to tolerate. First, central banks provided, and still provide, plenty of liquidity to banks by keeping very low interest rates and by implementing quantitative easing strategies. According to the asymmetric information approach, this strategy should counteract the increase in asymmetric information brought about by the crisis. Second, OTC derivatives trading should be moved to exchanges and clearing houses relying on their self-regulation mechanisms (see Appendix 1 and 2).

The Dodd-Frank Act included many provisions relevant to shadow banking (see Appendix A1). In particular, hedge funds should now register with the Securities and Exchange Commission (SEC), while the Federal Reserve should regulate all systemically important institutions. In addition, retail lenders should be subject to federal-level regulation through the new Consumer Financial Protection Bureau housed within the Federal Reserve (see Appendix A1).

According to Gorton, these measures of shadow banking regulation are useful but incomplete on the most important points concerning the regulation of MMMFs, securitisation, and repos.[42] In this alternative view, the modifications of the model of traditional banking and its distortions are not the crucial cause of the bank panic of 2008 for three basic reasons. First, the process of securitisation, contrary to the intentions, did not succeed to transfer much of the risk of loans from the originators (banks) to the buyers (investors). Along the subprime chain, many operators have suffered significant losses including originators and underwriters such as Option One, Ameriquest, New Century that went bankrupt, and megabanks such as Citibank, UBS, and Merrill Lynch that suffered billions of write-downs.[43] In particular, the originators retained a number of direct risks because loans are stored before they are securitised, then they are transferred to the underwriters that have to store the MBS tranches and, in later stages of the process, dealer bankers underwriting the CDOs also have to store securitisation tranches. Second, originators of loans (in particular mortgages) keep a participation in returns or losses that may accrue from the loans originated due to servicing rates and retained interests. In particular, some banks keep the most senior portions of CDOs on their balance sheets. Third, the existence of implicit contractual arrangements between buyers of tranches and the structured investment vehicle (**SIV**) sponsor led some SIV to take these items back onto their balance sheets.[44]

Therefore, according to Gorton, the solution is not that of forcing everything back on balance sheets since this would not solve the crucial problem: the scarcity of reliable information-insensitive collateral. A better solution in his opinion would be the adoption of a series of measures meant to create charter value and information-insensitive debt. This is possible only through a strict regulation of whatever subject plays the role of banking (including the emission of securitised products and the creation of repo deposits). This view suggests the introduction of the following measures:

(i) Senior tranches of securitisation products should be insured by the state.

(ii) Government, not rating agencies, should supervise and examine banks, including their activity of securitisation.

(iii) Entry into securitisation should be limited, and any firm that enters into this activity should be considered as a "bank" and subject to supervision.

Points (i) and (ii) are instrumental to the creation of more reliable informationally insensitive debt, while point (iii) creates value for the production of information-insensitive debt. Contrary to the standard objection raised against the measures recommended under (i) and (iii), their adoption would not encourage moral hazard since the latter would be discouraged by the fear of compromising a valuable charter; on the contrary, as shown by the history of banking in the USA, moral hazard develops in a climate of unfettered competition as a way to defeat competitors.

The policy implications drawn from this analysis of the recent banking panic go in a sensible direction: in order to re-establish a period of financial stability, we have to sacrifice the myth of perfect competition. In the 1970s and 1980s, it was customary to discuss about the trade-off between efficiency promoted by more competition and financial stability promoted by strict regulation and severe supervision in the quest of the right balance between these two objectives. In the 1980s, the Gordian knot was cut in the direction of competition and efficiency in the illusion that the evolution of banking, finance theory, and regulation would have avoided an increase in financial instability. The result was that financial instability progressively increased as witnessed by a growing number of severe financial crises experienced in the last three decades.[45] As for efficiency, there are hardly any signs of improvement, particularly in the sector of support to the real economy, since in the recent decades trading and speculation—that were more profitable in the short period and seemed less risky—crowded out credit for firms and households. In addition, the progressive disappearance of the charter value of banks brought about by the systematic deregulation of financial markets, contrary to what was expected, encouraged moral hazard, predatory lending, and corporate irresponsibility.

The policy perspective advanced by Gorton is questionable, however, in its unqualified defence of shadow banking. In his view, the latter should be strictly regulated but not repressed. This seems in contradiction with his own theoretical assumptions. If the ultimate problem is asymmetric information, shadow banking is a crucial part of the problem since, as he himself recognises, "there are no official measures of the size of the repo market, or repo haircuts or rates. There are no data on the identity of repo market participants … there are no official measures of collateral usage in derivatives or settlement. There are no official measures on securitization. The shadow banking system was, as they say, 'off the radar screen'" (Gorton 2009, 42).

How is it possible to regulate the shadow banking if all the relevant data are missing or unreliable estimates? How could airport traffic operators regulate traffic and keep safety without a radar? How could regulators supervise banking without an access to reliable balance sheets? How reliable may be considered balance sheets if off-balance-sheets posting is a legitimate and systematic practice? In addition, complete transparency is necessary to complete the information of all the agents to overcome excessive liquidity preference and other anomalies typical of strong uncertainty and to avoid asymmetric information.

6.6   Towards a Sustainable Finance

Proposals of financial reform at the national and international levels are abundant. Their number multiplied in consequence of the recent crisis. Any serious reform of the financial system has to combine a series of policy measures in a coherent way and in the right sequence. We cannot think of designing and implementing effective reforms in a piecemeal fashion. What is required is a package of mutually consistent and synergic measures. To this end, we have to clarify the nexus between the different measures suggested. A preliminary step in this direction is some sort of classification of the existing reform proposals. I adopt a classification articulated in three hierarchical categories.[46]

Level one reforms aim to improve the stability and safety of the existing financial system without affecting its size, scope, and autonomy. The reforms introduced after the beginning of the crisis belong to this category. This is, for example, the case of the reforms approved in the USA (in particular the Dodd-Frank Act), in the UK, and in the EU after the peak of the crisis.[47] Governments and international institutions often pay lip service to the need to mitigate systemic risk by re-regulating financial markets. According to the official view, however, policy makers and supervision authorities should keep regulation within limits as strict as possible, avoiding "a 'rush to regulate' that could impose excessive and inefficient regulation and stifle financial innovation" (IMF 2009, 4). The results obtained by this ambiguous, if not contradictory, reform strategy have been so far rather meagre (see Appendix 1).

Level two reforms are much more ambitious as they aim to downsize the financial system and limit its excessive power by redesigning a more healthy relationship with the real sector. The reforms introduced in the USA by the Glass-Steagall Act of 1933 to counteract the Great Depression and its structural causes belong to this category of reforms.[48] We could classify in this category also some of the measures proposed by the incumbent policy makers noticing that so far they did not implement most of them in practice. A case in point is the "financial transaction tax" proposed by the European Commission in 2009 that, after a complex and controversial procedure, is expected to find its first application in the near future in a few Eurozone countries. This measure would contribute to downsize the most speculative part of finance (trading in derivatives and high-frequency finance). In any case, a level three reform should adopt this measure as part of a comprehensive package (this issue will be resumed later).

Another example is the institution of a cap to leverage as suggested by the IMF: "a measure akin to the equity/asset ratio but with enhanced sensitivity to off-balance sheet exposures should be introduced in the capital framework as an upper bound to constrain excessive leverage in the upswing" (IMF 2009, 13). This measure would contribute to downsize the financial activity hitting the most risky operations. The implementation of this sort of measure, however, is difficult because "the monitoring and management of systemic leverage proved to be difficult, owing to the increased use of off balance sheet vehicles, the growth of leverage among systemically important NBFIs, and the increasingly complex web of exposures to other financial institutions" (ibid., 16). For this reason, or pretext, the implementation of this measure is still under study.

Level three reforms are the most ambitious as they aim to push the financial system to assume a propulsive role in the transition to a sustainable development trajectory. They presuppose level two reforms, as they could not have an influence on an untamed financial system. We badly need this level of reforms to get out of the crisis in a persistent way.

I start my reasoning on the reform of the financial system by observing that the arguments put forward in this book suggest that the financial system is unable to self-regulate. This assertion refers not only to the inability shown by the financial system to remain close to equilibrium or to recover stability when perturbed by external causes, but also to its tendency to self-destabilise for endogenous reasons.[49] It refers also to its lack of adequate motivations and capabilities to support the real economy keeping in mind the well-being of all citizens.

First, the automatic mechanisms of self-regulation inbuilt in the market have a much more limited scope than many mainstream economists assert and policy makers believe. In particular, the market mechanisms of stabilisation work only in quiet times but collapse when panic develops. This is true of the law of supply and demand itself. An excess of demand of financial assets increases their price but this often increases further their demand for speculative reasons rather than reducing it as in the real economy.[50] The vicious circle between dynamics of asset prices and their expectations nurtured a sequence of financial bubbles of increasing intensity also because the asymmetric monetarism practised by central banks validated these sort of extrapolative expectations (see Chap. 5). In addition, big banks often manipulate in their own interest also the variables that are responsive to the usual demand and supply mechanism.

The case of the systematic manipulation of LIBOR is a significant case in point.[51] Megabanks (such as Barclays, UBS, Citigroup, Bank of America, Royal Bank of Scotland, and JP Morgan) have been recently accused of manipulating the LIBOR rate of interest to their advantage. In 2012, the US Department of Justice started a criminal investigation into LIBOR abuse. In consequence of this and other investigations, some of these banks have already been condemned to pay big fines. The distortionary consequences on the allocation of resources performed by the financial system have been huge, keeping in mind that the LIBOR rate underpins approximately $350 trillion in derivatives and loans.[52] Andrew Lo, Professor of Finance at MIT, asserted that this scandal dwarfs by orders of magnitude any financial fraud in the history of markets.[53]

Finally, a competitive equilibrium can persist only if there are no obstacles to the entry into the market and the exit from it. The growing requisites for operating in the financial market strengthened by the Basel III Accord constitute a formidable barrier to entry since they heavily affect the viability of small banks. This determined the growing disappearance of small banks and encouraged the ongoing process of concentration in the financial services industry. Therefore, the big financial institutions are more and more "too big and interconnected to fail". They are also too big to be prosecuted and thus to be regulated. Finally, they are becoming too big to be bailed out. What credibility has the hypothesis of efficiency of financial markets under these conditions?

Second, financial institutions claim that, whenever a potential market failure is detected, it is in their interest to reach an agreement on the rules to be followed to avoid, or at least mitigate, the risks. This explains why, since the 1970s, the regulation of financial institutions has been progressively weakened in the belief that it would have been substituted by more effective self-regulation. The growing independence of central banks from the governments made them more and more dependent on the view and desiderata of financial institutions. Though central banks are perceived as public institutions, they became increasingly independent of incumbent governments. In addition, many of them are private or mixed institutions with a very low degree of accountability and are heavily influenced by the prevailing interests of financial institutions. In consequence of this, also the most prestigious international financial institutions, such as the Basel Committee on Banking Supervision (BCBS), are strongly influenced by the financial system.[54] The same is true of other consultative, but influential, regulatory institutions such as the Financial Stability Board or International Organization of Securities Commissions (IOSCO).[55]

Third, according to the neoliberal point of view, the deterioration of corporate social responsibility (CSR) observed in the financial system can be checked by the self-regulation of financial institutions. However, the CSR initiatives can have an impact only if the stakeholders take account in their choices of the CSR standards reached by potential suppliers of goods and services.[56] Since this feedback effect is very weak, CSR self-regulation may only complement the legal regulation and should not be taken as a pretext to weaken legal regulation.

The examples briefly discussed in this section converge towards the same conclusion. Since the financial system is unable to self-regulate itself, it has to be regulated by independent decision makers who have to be fully accountable to all citizens. Since the behaviour of the financial system has deep influences on the well-being of all the citizens, regulators have to be selected by all the electors through a sound, not too indirect, democratic process. In words that are more concrete, the financial system has to be re-regulated by public decision makers who must be fully accountable to all citizens also on these specific choices. Accountability presupposes full transparency of financial firms. This crucial requisite is inconsistent with the direction pursued by the financial system that has become increasingly opaque. This reasoning suggests some broad outlines to keep in mind to move towards a serious reform of the financial system.

First, a credible reform must downsize the dimensions of financial institutions. This is a priority; otherwise, they would retain the power to impede, or at least heavily water down, any significant reform of the financial system. This is what we have seen after the peak of the crisis. In particular, mega-banks have been able to dilute and postpone the most significant provision contained in the first draft of the Dodd-Frank Act: the so-called "Volcker rule" forbidding proprietary trading (see Appendix 1). Analogously, mega-banks succeeded to water down and defer two significant proposals put forward by the European Commission: the adoption of a cap to leverage and of a financial transaction tax.

The adoption of a cap to leverage would be much more effective than a floor to liquidity or a higher capital requirement. While the latter measures may be useful in tranquil times or to counteract mild crises, their protection against insolvency would rapidly disappear in a severe crisis leading to a Minsky meltdown.[57] In addition, for a given risk propensity of decision makers, more liquidity and capital would just encourage more leverage. On the contrary, a cap to leverage would act as an effective ceiling to excessive indebtedness preventing insolvency. Most financial institutions, however, resist tenaciously the introduction of a leverage cap perceived as an unwelcome limitation to their freedom.

Turning now to the second example, the European Commission proposed in 2010 the adoption of a European Transaction Tax (EU FTT).

This tax would cover all transactions that involve European firms, no matter whether these transactions take place within the EU or elsewhere in the world. The ensuing endless controversies, instigated by the powerful lobby of financial institutions, watered down the initial proposal and postponed many times the commencement of its application.[58] The official proposal suggested a differentiated model, taxing shares and bonds at a rate of 0.1 %, and derivative contracts at a rate of 0.01 %. According to the European Commission, this could approximately raise €57 billion every year. Much of the revenue would go directly to member states. The EU would retain only a part of the tax, an increase that would be offset by reductions in national contributions. The effects of the introduction of this tax have been particularly controversial. An official study by the European Commission suggests that a flat 0.01 % tax would raise between €16.4 billion and €43.4 billion per year, or 0.13 % and 0.35 % of GDP. If the tax rate were increased to 0.1 %, total estimated revenues would amount to a value between €73.3 billion and €433.9 billion (0.60 % and 3.54 % of GDP). The European Commission expects the EU FTT to have the following main impacts on financial markets:

(i) Up to a 90 % reduction in derivatives transactions
(ii) Slightly negative or positive effect on economic growth depending on the design of the EU FTT
(iii) An effective curb on automated high-frequency trading
(iv) A small increase in capital costs, which could be mitigated by excluding primary markets for bonds and shares from the tax

Griffith-Jones and Persaud estimated a positive effect on economic growth of at least €30 billion until 2050 based on a reduction of the probability of the financial crisis of 5 %.[59]

A serious level-two reform of the financial system requires the abandonment of the taboo that banks should necessarily be private. A public bank, owned and managed by the citizens through administrators appointed by the state or a local government entity, may receive a particular mandate in the interest of all the community. In this case, the profits may return to the community, used to reduce taxation, or to finance additional investment in its interest. In particular, a public bank may issue credit at low cost, or no cost, in the direction desired by the community, including public and private institutions. An interesting example in the USA is the century-old public Bank of North Dakota that supports a network of local small community banks enabling them to comply with regulatory requirements such as asset to loan ratios and deposit to loan ratios.[60]

The standard objections to level two reforms such as those mentioned above seem at first sight compelling:

(a) Banks will have lower profits and turnover.
(b) Therefore, they will pay fewer taxes.
(c) They will have to sack their employees.
(d) They will eventually migrate abroad where regulation is laxer.

No government today and very few political parties (generally marginal and hardly influential) resist arguments of this sort after many years of stagnation, high unemployment, and soaring public deficits. However, these arguments are flawed because make an implicit business-as-usual assumption. In a different model of development, complying with the requisites of sustainable development, the reduction of profits, turnover, employment, and contribution to GDP of financial institutions thriving mainly on speculation could be offset by a higher contribution of the real economy in the direction of sustainable development. In this view, the migration abroad of a megabank prone mainly to speculation would bring more benefits than harm if a network of efficient local banks adequately supported by one or more public banks or public institutions provides the credit to the real economy.

This outline of a radical reform of the financial system may seem today outrageously utopian because the one-dimensional vision that is mainstream today has convinced most people that there is no alternative to the existing unfettered evolution of financialised capitalism, but history has often falsified the extrapolative projections of the current trends into the future.

6.7   Concluding Remarks

The self-regulation of financial markets may succeed to avoid bank runs in tranquil times but not when the economic agents start to fear that the entire system is insolvent. Therefore, in 1934, the policy makers took the crucial decision of re-regulating the banking system according to strict rules providing bank deposits with public insurance. This new policy regime inaugurated a "quiet period" in US banking that lasted many decades. The number of US bank failures, that had increased to the appalling number of about 4000 per year just before this courageous and controversial decision, suddenly dropped to a number very close to zero that was maintained until the early 1970s. This unprecedented degree of financial stability relied not only on public deposits insurance but also on a severe regulation of the banking system:

(i) Segregating commercial banking from investment banking (Glass-Steagall Act, 1933)
(ii) Limiting the entry in the market by rationing in each area banking charters
(iii) Introducing a strict supervision, compulsory balance sheet disclosure, and interest rate ceilings on deposits (Regulation Q)

These measures combined the strictures of severe regulation and close supervision with the provision of a more valuable bank charter. This policy strategy reduced the freedom of choice of bank managers and the degree of competition between banks but at the same time greatly increased the stability of the financial system. It is likely that what was lost in efficiency because of the policy constraints on competition was more than compensated by the huge positive externalities accruing from financial stability.

The deregulation of financial markets progressively implemented since the 1970s, in accordance with the neoliberal policy view, caused bank charter values to decline. The growing competition also from non-banks (e.g. MMMFs) induced banks to reduce capital, increase risk, and rely on financial innovation. The systematic process of securitisation and the rapid growth of shadow banking intervened as a response of the banking system to the new policy environment to preserve the returns on equity in banking. Unfortunately, as we have seen, shadow banking was more profitable for banks but much more vulnerable to panic since the system of market insurance through collateral turned out to be not at all panic-proof.

The neoliberal policy strategy adopted since the late 1970s determined an acceleration of the process of financialisation started in the period of Bretton Woods. The ensuing increase of the weight of finance had a great impact on the economic system and society. This went much beyond the increase of quantitative indexes such as the share of employment and GDP in the financial service industry sector. It affected the views and motivations of all economic agents including those operating in the non-financial sector or households themselves. This process has been cause and effect of a deep and far-reaching transformation not only of the financial system but also of capitalism itself.

As for the structural transformation of the financial system, while in the Bretton Woods era the basic structure of the financial system remained remarkably invariant within the constraints imposed by the policy authorities, in the neoliberal era the structure of the system underwent a process of rapid transformation led by a continuous flow of financial innovations. A picture of the financial system would thus be different according to the moment in which it is shot. What is fairly well-defined and substantially invariant, however, is the direction of this process of structural change from a bank-based system to a market-based system. This produced a shift of decision power from banks directly regulated and supervised by the policy authorities to increasingly deregulated and unsupervised financial markets. This trend apparently shifted the decision power from the particularly influential top management of the biggest banks to the impersonal power of markets. The latter acts as a sort of "shadow" or elusive power because it looks altogether impersonal, and therefore uncontrollable, to its subjects.

Since Adam Smith, this impersonal and overwhelming form of power is often depicted as exerted by a providential "invisible hand" that maximises the well-being of economic agents. This view is in our case deeply misleading because a few powerful decision makers manipulate these markets and orientate their evolution: top management of great banking conglomerates, institutional funds, central banks, multinational organisations such as the IMF and the World Bank, and governments of the most powerful countries. The fact that the power in the neoliberal era is exerted indirectly through the market makes more difficult the democratic control of the financial system because the invisible but shadowy hand of the market conceals the visible hands of a powerful minority that ultimately takes the crucial decisions.

Notes

1. In this Chapter the use of bold fonts signals the first occurrence of a financial term defined in the Glossary of Financial Terms (Appendix 2).
2. See in particular Simon (1957).
3. Muth (1961).
4. See in particular Debreu (1959).
5. Fama (1970).
6. Fama (1970, 383).
7. Vercelli (1991).
8. Kydland and Prescott (1982).
9. See Coase (1960).
10. Bhagwati (2004).
11. See for example Mishkin (1991, 70–71).
12. Akerlof (1970).
13. Stiglitz and Weiss (1981).
14. Mankiw (2006).
15. See for example Mishkin (1991, 71).
16. Diamond (1984).
17. See in particular Calomiris and Hubbard (1990).
18. Bernanke and Gertler (1989).
19. See retro Chap. 4.
20. Gorton and Metrick (2010, 265).
21. See Appendix 1.
22. See in particular Omarova (2011).
23. McCulley (2007).
24. Some of them are so different that generate terminological paradoxes, as in the case of "non-bank banks" often mentioned in the literature (see Appendix 2).
25. Gorton and Metrick (2010, 261–262).

26. See Adrian et al. (2010) for a survey of the literature, and Nesvetailova (2014) for a classification of definitions.
27. Gorton and Metrick (2010, 269).
28. Gorton and Metrick (2010 and 2012).
29. The legal infrastructure facilitating the use of repos as money has evolved as their volume has grown. In the USA, the 1978 Bankruptcy Code and the Federal Deposit Insurance Act provided exemptions for certain kinds of financial contracts. In 1984, the Bankruptcy Code was amended to allow parties to a repo to liquidate collateral without the counterparty going into bankruptcy.
30. BIS (1999, 7–8).
31. See for example Comotto (2010).
32. For example, according to Gorton (2010, 28), "all the major bank regulators and central bankers appear to subscribe to this view, though their views have differences and nuances."
33. The Joint Forum includes the BCBS, the IOSCO, and the International Association of Insurance Supervisors.
34. See in particular the contributions of Gary Gorton and his collaborators: Gorton (2009 and 2010), Gorton and Metrick (2010 and 2012).
35. Gorton (2009, 3–4).
36. As Gorton (2009, 30) clarifies: "when the depositor deposits money, the collateral may involve a 'haircut' or margin. The haircut is the percentage difference between the market value of the pledged collateral and the amount of funds lent. For example, a haircut of 5 % means that a "bank" can borrow $95 for each $100 in pledged collateral. A haircut further protects the depositor against the risk of borrower default by the 'bank'. The size of the haircut reflects the credit risk of the borrower and the riskiness of the pledged collateral".
37. Gorton (2009, 33).
38. Gorton (2009, 37).
39. Vercelli (1991 and 2011a).
40. See Gorton (2009, 31).
41. Fisher (1933) and Vercelli (2013/2014).
42. Gorton (2010, 262).
43. Gorton (2010, 28).
44. Gorton (2010, 31).
45. Reinhart and Rogoff (2009).
46. SOMO (2015).

47. See Appendix 1.
48. See section A1 of Appendix 1.
49. Minsky (1982 and 1986).
50. Orléan (2009 and 2014).
51. The LIBOR is an average interest rate calculated through submission by the leading banks in London of the interest rate paid to borrow from other banks. Since 2007 a growing evidence accumulated that many of these banks manipulated the required information to make substantial profits on their huge portfolios whose value was linked to LIBOR (see Snider and Youle 2010), or to appear more creditworthy than they were.
52. O'Toole (2012).
53. Cited in O'Toole (2012).
54. The BCBS is a committee of banking supervisory authorities established by the central banks of the Group of Ten in 1974.
55. The Financial Stability Board brings together senior policy makers from ministries of finance, central banks, and supervisory and regulatory authorities, for the G20 countries plus four other key financial centres—Hong Kong, Singapore, Spain, and Switzerland. In addition, it includes international bodies, including standard-setters and regional bodies like the ECB and European Commission.

    The IOSCO is the worldwide association of national securities regulatory commissions, such as the SEC in the USA, the Financial Services Authority in the UK, and about 100 other similar bodies.
56. Borghesi and Vercelli (2008).
57. Vercelli (2011a).
58. A framework proposal, supported only by 11 EU member states, was eventually approved by the European Parliament in December 2012 and by the Council of the EU in January 2013, to be introduced on 1 January 2014. Further opposition required the drafting of a new proposal to be introduced in January 2016. However, participating member states have failed to reach a consensus on the introduction of the EU FTT following a meeting of European Finance Ministers on 9 November 2015. There are still major disagreements on the scope of the tax and how it should be levied. In addition, some countries are making special requests that will inevitably prolong the process of convergence towards an agreement. Its commencement is thus likely to be further postponed.
59. As Griffith-Jones and Persaud (1912, 6) rightly remind, "the growth costs of crises are massive. For example, Reinhart and Rogoff (2009) estimate

that, from peak to trough, the average fall in per capita GDP, as result of major financial crises, was 9 %. The Institute of Fiscal Studies (2011) has recently estimated that for the UK, when comparing the real median income household income in 2009–2010 with 2012–2013, the decline has been 7.4 %."

60. Brown (2013).

Bibliography

Adrian, Tobias, Adam B. Ashcraft, Hayley Boesky, and Zoltan Pozsar. 2010. Shadow Banking. In *Staff Reports 458*. New York: Federal Reserve Bank.

Akerlof, George A. 1970. The Market for 'Lemons': Quality Uncertainty and the Market Mechanism. *Quarterly Journal of Economics* 84(3): 488–500.

Bernanke, Ben S., and Mark Gertler. 1989. Agency Costs, Net Worth, and Business Fluctuations. *The American Economic Review* 79(1): 14–31.

Bhagwati, Jagdish. 2004. *In Defence of Globalization*. New York: Oxford University Press.

BIS. 1999. *Implications of Repo Markets for Central Banks. Report of a working group of the Committee on the Global Financial System*. Basle: Bank for International Settlements.

Borghesi, Simone, and Alessandro Vercelli. 2008. *Global Sustainability. Social and Environmental Conditions*. Palgrave Macmillan: Basingstoke and New York.

Brown, Ellen. 2013. *The Public Bank Solution*. Baton Rouge: Third Millennium Press.

Calomiris, Charles W., and R. Glenn Hubbard. 1990. Firm Heterogeneity, Internal Finance, and 'Credit Rationing'. *Economic Journal* 100: 90–104.

Coase, Ronald H 1960. The Problem of Social Cost. *Journal of Law and Economics*. 3(3): 1–44.

Comotto, Richard. 2010. *A White Paper on the Operation of the European Repo Market, the Role of Short-Selling, the Problem of Settlement Failures and the Need for Reform of the Market Infrastructure*. Zurich: International Capital Market Association, European Repo Council.

Debreu, Gérard. 1959. *The Theory of Value: An Axiomatic Analysis of Economic Equilibrium*. New York: John Wiley and Sons.

Diamond, Douglas W. 1984. Financial Intermediation and Delegated Monitoring. *Review of Economic Studies* 51: 393–414.

Fama, Eugene. 1970. Efficient Capital Markets: A Review of Theory and Empirical Work. *Journal of Finance* 25: 383–417.

Fisher, Irving. 1933. The Debt-Deflation Theory of the Great Depression. *Econometrica* 1: 337–357.

Gorton, Gary B. 2009. Information, Liquidity, and the (Ongoing) Panic of 2007. *American Economic Review, Papers and Proceedings* 99(2): 567–572.

Gorton, ———. 2010. *Slapped by the Invisible Hand: The Panic of 2007*. New York: Oxford University Press.

Gorton, Gary B., and Andrew Metrick. 2010. Regulating the Shadow Banking System. *Brookings Papers on Economic Activity* 2: 261–297.

Griffith-Jones, Stephany, and Avinash Persaud. 2012. Financial Transaction Taxes. Paper Prepared for—and Presented to—the Committee on Economic and Monetary Affairs of the European Parliament in 6th February 2012.

———. 2012. Securitized Banking and the Run on Repo. *Journal of Financial Economics* 104: 425–451.

IMF. 2009. Lessons of the Financial Crisis for Future Regulation of Financial Institutions and Markets and for Liquidity Management Prepared by the Monetary and Capital Markets Department. http://www.imf.org/external/np/pp/eng/2009/020409.pdf. Retrieved 18 November 2015.

Joint Forum. 2008. *Credit Risk Transfer. Developments from 2005 to 2007*. April 2008.

Kydland, Finn E., and Edward C. Prescott. 1982. Time to Build and Aggregate Fluctuations. *Econometrica* 50(6): 1345–1370.

Mankiw, Gregory N. 2006. Outsourcing Redux. In *Greg Mankiw's Blog: Random Observations for Students of Economics*, May 7. http://gregmankiw.blogspot.co.uk/2006/05/outsourcing-redux.html. Retrieved 2 February 2016.

McCulley, Paul A. 2007. Teton Reflections. *PIMCO Global Central Bank Focus*. https://www.pimco.com/insights/economic-and-market-commentary/global-central-bank-focus/teton-reflections. Retrieved 2 February 2016.

Minsky, Hyman P. 1982. *Can "It" Happen Again? Essays on Instability and Finance*. Armonk, NY: Sharpe.

———. 1986. *Stabilizing an Unstable Economy*. New Haven and London: Yale University Press.

Mishkin, Frederic S. 1991. Asymmetric Information and Financial Crises: A Historical Perspective. In *Financial Markets and Financial Crises*, ed. R. Glenn Hubbard, 69–108. Chicago: The University of Chicago Press.

———. 2008. Leveraged Losses: Lessons from the Mortgage Meltdown. Speech at the U.S. Monetary Policy Forum, New York, NY, February 29, 2008.

https://www.federalreserve.gov/newsevents/speech/mishkin20080229a.htm. Retrieved 7 April 2016.

Muth, John F. 1961. Rational Expectations and the Theory of Price Movements. *Econometrica* 29(3): 315–335.

Nesvetailova, Anastasia. 2014. A Crisis of the Overcrowded Future: Shadow Banking and the Political Economy of Financial Innovation. *New Political Economy* 20(3): 431–453.

Omarova, Saule T 2011. From-Leach-Bliley to Dodd-Frank: The Unfulfilled Promise of Section 23A of the Federal Reserve Act. *In North Carolina Law Review* 89: 1685–1769.

Orléan, André. 2009. *De l'euphorie à la panique: Penser la crise financière*. Paris: Édition de la Rue d'Ulm.

———. 2014. *The Empire of Value. A New Foundation for Economics*. Cambridge, Mass.: MIT Press.

O'Toole, James. 2012. Explaining the Libor interest rate mess. *CNNMoneyInvest* (July 10, 2012). http://money.cnn.com/2012/07/03/investing/libor-interest-rate-faq/. Retrieved 3 February 2016.

Reinhart, Carmen M., and Kenneth S. Rogoff. 2009. *This Time is Different, Eight Centuries of Financial Folly*. Princeton and Oxford: Princeton University Press.

Simon, Herbert. 1957. A Behavioral Model of Rational Choice. In *Models of Man, Social and Rational: Mathematical Essays on Rational Human Behavior in a Social Setting*, ed. Herbert Simon. New York: Wiley.

Snider, Connan A., and Thomas Youle. 2010. Does the LIBOR Reflect Banks' Borrowing Costs? Available at SSRN: http://ssrn.com/abstract=1569603 or doi: 10.2139/ssrn.1569603. Retrieved 3 March 2016.

SOMO, Centre for Research On Multinational Corporations. 2015. *Overview of the Reforms of the Financial System*

Stiglitz, Joseph E., and Andrew M. Weiss. 1981. Credit Rationing in Markets with Imperfect Information. *American Eonomic Review* 71(3): 393–410.

The Institute for Fiscal Studies. 2011. Poverty and Inequality in the UK: 2011. IFS Commentary C118. London: The Institute for Fiscal Studies.

Vercelli, Alessandro. 1991. *Methodological Foundations of Macroeconomics. Keynes and Lucas*. Cambridge: Cambridge University Press.

———. 2011a. A Perspective on Minsky Moments: Revisiting the Core of the Financial Instability Hypothesis. *Review of Political Economy* 23(1): 49–67.

———. 2013–14. Financialisation in a Long-Run Perspective. *International Journal of Political Economy* 42 (4):19–46.

7

Environment and Sustainability

7.1   Introduction

In the previous chapters, I have argued that the neoliberal policy strategy, as implemented since the late 1970s, fostered the adoption of a development model that has proved to be unsustainable in all its main dimensions. In addition, by comparing the neoliberal era (since the late 1970s) with the preceding "Keynesian" era (during the Bretton Woods period), I pointed out that all the main dimensions of sustainability deteriorated in the second period with the only exception of some specific indexes of environmental sustainability. I also underlined the growing interaction between the environmental dimension and the other dimensions of sustainability. In this chapter, I wish to discuss in more depth the sustainability of the neoliberal model of development from the environmental point of view.

The prima facie correlation between the surge of environmental policy and the surge of neoliberal policies is at first sight puzzling. While the trajectory of the neoliberal paradigm mounted and spread in the 1980s and 1990s, a contemporaneous surge in environmental policy materialised since the early 1970s. The government of industrialised countries adopted systematic environmental policies in the 1970s for the first time

© The Editor(s) (if applicable) and The Author(s) 2017   **183**
A. Vercelli, *Crisis and Sustainability*,
DOI 10.1057/978-1-137-60069-1_7

in history. Developing countries followed in the two successive decades. Unfortunately, this wave started to lose momentum in the late 1990s and progressively receded by fits and starts in the new millennium. This backlash mounted notwithstanding the growing scientific evidence on the dramatic unsustainability of the existing model of development made evident, above all, by climate change and its increasingly alarming projections.

Despite all its shortcomings and its recent decline, the environmental policies pursued by developed countries obtained a few remarkable successes since its inception. However, a growing number of economists and politicians started to question the gravity and urgency of environmental problems, as well as the measures taken to tackle them.[1] They claimed that environmental risks were overemphasised as an excuse to interfere unduly with markets, and reasserted that unfettered markets would be able to solve them in the best possible way and in the shortest possible time. This sanguine view maintains that whatever attempt to reach better environmental standards within a shorter time horizon would be a dangerous, and ultimately counterproductive, interference with market self-regulation. This chapter argues that this belief is dangerously misleading.

The structure of this chapter is as follows. Section 7.2 describes the origins and consequences of the clash between the surge of environmental policy and the surge of neoliberal policy. This produced a shift from the prevailing use of command and control (CAC) policy instruments to a systematic use of market-based instruments. The latter proved to be much less efficient than expected. A case in point is the European system of tradable pollution permits (EU ETS) briefly analysed in Sect. 7.3. Environmental policy obtained a few significant successes but was unable to invert the trend towards increasing environmental unsustainability, as represented by the ecological imprint index (Sect. 7.4). Section 7.5 discusses the main reason of the growing ecological debt that resides in the energy system still dominated by the use of fossil fuels. Section 7.6 argues that policy makers may find a durable way out only by implementing a sustainable development model based on a modified technological trajectory. The concluding remarks in Sect. 7.7 point out the shortcomings of a few general objections against a systematic use of environmental policy to accelerate the transition to a low-carbon economy.

7.2 The Clash Between Environmental Policies and Neoliberal Policy Strategy

Within the liberal paradigm broadly defined, we should distinguish between two distinct approaches to environmental issues having significantly different policy implications. According to the updated liberal approach initiated by Pigou (1920), real markets are intrinsically unable to take account of many sizeable environmental costs and benefits since market prices do not register them for a host of reasons.[2] In this view, the market may succeed to reach the optimal equilibrium only if these "external" costs and benefits (also called "externalities") are "internalised" through environmental taxes or tradable pollution permits. This point of view provided the foundations for "environmental economics" that inspired the environmental policies adopted at the end of the past millennium.

The neoliberal stance that became hegemonic since the late 1970s, however, never cherished the Pigouvian approach, maintaining that the environmental externalities are not particularly significant, and in any case not easily identifiable and measurable. In particular, in this view, policy makers should avoid the use of environmental taxes because it is impossible to measure correctly the environmental costs of economic decisions so that new taxes would further distort the decentralised choices of competitive markets. Their definition and management are likely to produce damaging interferences with the working of markets whose distortional impact could be worse than that produced by the externalities to be internalised. Policy makers should instead manage externalities by completing the markets and defining the property rights on environmental resources,[3] in the conviction that the environmental problems are mainly the consequence of missing, or ill-defined, property rights.

This point of view inspired the use of a new policy instrument, tradable permits, which define indirect property rights on environmental resources and may be exchanged in the market. According to most mainstream economists, the use of this instrument is fully consistent with free-market principles. Neoliberal policy makers tolerated the use of this instrument better than its alternatives. However, a growing number of neoliberal exponents warned that also tradable permits involve arbitrary interferences of policy makers in the spontaneous working of the market. The neoliberal point of view has thus become increasingly hostile also to market-based instruments and thus to environmental policy in general, trying hard to reduce its scope and impact.

The relationship between the neoliberal trajectory of development and the surge of environmental policy is at first sight puzzling because their time profile may seem empirically correlated. With hindsight, it is evident that these two processes were independent one from the other moving in a different direction since the beginning of their diffusion. The environmental surge called for the imposition of new and stricter policy constraints on economic decisions from the point of view of sustainability, while at the same time the neoliberal surge was exerting a strong pressure towards a generalised relaxation of policy constraints. The clash between these two opposite visions became evident since the late 1990s when the pressure of public opinion in favour of the systematic adoption of environmental measures started to relent.

In the Bretton Woods period, the empirical evidence showed a good performance of industrialised economies as far as economic, financial, and social sustainability are concerned, at least as compared to previous development trajectories. The improvements obtained have been significant, though arguably insufficient in absolute terms. On the contrary, its performance in the field of environmental sustainability was definitely negative. Actually, the unprecedented average rate of growth in developed countries produced a rapid worsening of the environmental problems that assumed, for the first time in history, a global nature.

A growing awareness of the nature and gravity of the environmental problems started to emerge only in the 1970s. A significant early contribution to the environmental awareness of the public opinion was the famous report of the Club of Rome, *The Limits to Growth*.[4] The book was heavily criticised by many economists because of its alleged undervaluation of the stabilising role of markets through price flexibility and technical progress, as well as for basing the arguments on unreliable data and arbitrary functional forms. However, in consequence of this and other important contributions culminating with the influential "Brundtland Report",[5] the tide of public opinion was sufficiently aroused to exert a significant pressure on policy makers. In the 1970s, many countries, including the USA,

Germany, and then in rapid succession most developed countries, introduced for the first time in history a systematic environmental policy.
The recent assessments of researchers having a natural science background converge towards the disturbing consensus that the business-
as-usual projections of the book tend to become true.[6] For example,
Ugo Bardi concluded his recent revisitation of *The Limits to Growth* by
asserting that "the warnings that we received in 1972 … are becoming
increasingly more worrisome as reality seems to be following closely the
curves that the … scenario had generated" (Bardi 2011, 3).

The systematic adoption of environmental policy measures obtained a
few significant successes on important environmental problems through
international conventions, as well as national and local laws. Early international agreements were the Convention on Long-Range Transboundary
Air Pollution mitigation of 1979 that contributed to reduce the acid rain
transboundary pollution, and the Montreal Protocol on Substances that
Deplete the Ozone Layer of 1987 that stopped the thinning of the ozone
shield and started a process of recovery. Early national measures were, for
example, in the USA, the Clean Air Act of 1970 and the Clean Water
Act of 1972 that many other countries soon imitated. At the same time,
in many countries, the local policy authorities obtained significant results
on a host of other important environmental problems such as local pollution, garbage disposal, and energy saving.

Nevertheless, the most important steps forward remained limited
mainly to environmental issues having a significant negative impact at
the local level, whenever local pollution convinced the citizens to exert
a growing pressure on local governments to mitigate the negative externalities. On the contrary, some of the crucial factors producing global
externalities, such as the loss of biodiversity or climate change, remained
insufficiently—or inefficiently—addressed by systematic policy measures. This is true in particular in the case of global warming. A case in
point is the United Nations Framework Convention on Climate Change
(UNFCCC) agreed in 1992 during the United Nations Conference on
Environment and Development held in Rio de Janeiro. After an increasingly complex negotiation, in 1997, the parties agreed on the text of the
so-called "Kyoto Protocol", fixing emissions targets for developed countries. The achievement in 2002 of the ratification threshold brought the

UNFCCC treaty into effect as from February 2005. In the meantime, the USA—that is responsible for more than one-third of the world GHGs emissions and had signed the Protocol in 1997—did not ratify the treaty, while other countries such as Canada withdrew from it.

During the first commitment period (2008–2012), the application of the Protocol resulted increasingly weak and inefficient. A case in point is the effective management of the European system of tradable permits (EU ETS).[7] The second period of commitment (2013–2020) has not started yet in absence of a sufficient convergence towards a new agreement. Only at the end of the 2008 Doha meeting, the parties to the UNFCCC reached an agreement to extend the Protocol to 2020 and to set a date within 2015 for the development of a successor document, to be implemented from 2020. However, for a few years, the Great Recession distracted the public opinion from longer period worries and reduced the pressure on governments for a more effective environmental policy. The lobby of climate denialism, which was well-funded by contrarian industrial interests, had the opportunity of increasing its influence.[8] By the end of 2012, the USA, Japan, Russia, New Zealand, and Canada had indicated they would not sign up to a second Kyoto commitment period. The UN Conferences between 2008 and 2014 to relaunch a new and improved Kyoto commitment were a resounding failure. In 2014, however, there was a new surge of pressure on policy makers on the part of scientists,[9] public opinion, religious organisations, and NGOs taking account of the recent data showing worsening trends and reducing further residual uncertainty on the anthropogenic nature of global warming.

The 2015 United Nations Climate Change Conference, [10] also called COP 21 or CMP 11,[11] was successful, but more from the point of view of its media resonance than of its practical results, at least so far. Qualified public opinion exerted a strong pressure in favour of positive conclusions. In particular, Pope Francis published an encyclical called "Laudato si'" intended also to encourage the success of the conference.[12] Other religions took similar initiatives. Policy makers registered this new opinion climate. A particularly important case in point was the meeting on 12 November 2014 between the US President Obama and the China President Xi Jinping agreeing to limit greenhouse gases emissions. More in general, many countries committed to action, revealing under the

UN coordination their Intended Nationally Determined Contributions (INDCs). According to the official estimates, the INDCs would reduce global warming from an estimated 4–5 °C by 2100 to 2.7 °C and reduce per capita emissions of 9 % by 2030. The full implementation of these national contributions would be insufficient to stay within the 2 °C target. In addition, these sorts of commitments are hardly reliable since their violation is not subject to sanction and may be justified in many ways by a change of government, or of economic conditions. We have to conclude that it is too early to be confident in a substantial change in policy commitment aimed to tackle the issue of global warming with the necessary sense of urgency.

Summing up, the weakening of environmental policies since the late 1990s has been visible in most countries on many environmental issues and has recently deepened in consequence of the financial crisis and the ensuing Great Recession. Not surprisingly, the arguments used to withdraw from a serious environmental policy are exactly those underlying the adoption of neoliberal policies. According to the contrarian view, the environmental policy measures disturb the self-regulation mechanisms of the market, which would otherwise solve spontaneously also the environmental problems in the most efficient and timely way. That is why the surge of environmental policy, after its promising inception in the 1970s, increasingly collided in the following decades with the principles of the neoliberal policy strategy. This clash eventually succeeded to tame environmental policies. We cannot hope in a rapid convergence towards a sustainable development trajectory unless policy makers adopt a different, more long-sighted, policy paradigm.

7.3 The Delusion of Market-Based Instruments: The Case of EU ETS

Environmental policy relied first mainly on the so-called CAC instruments. Despite this daunting phrasing aims to emphasise that the use of these policy instruments deviates from laissez-faire principles, their meaning is straightforward. CAC instruments aim to prohibit actions damaging the environment and implement this prohibition through administrative and penal sanctions enforced by the legal system. The early successes obtained confirmed the effectiveness of this policy strategy. The efficacy of CAC instruments, however, has been increasingly questioned in the 1980s and 1990s when the confidence in free markets progressively surged to new heights. In consequence of this change of attitude, environmental policy shifted towards market-based instruments, such as environmental taxes and tradable permits, believed to be in principle the most efficient and less distortionary instruments. Economic theory argued that these instruments are consistent with free market principles as they internalise the negative externalities that otherwise would jeopardise the correct functioning of free markets[13] and play the crucial role of completing the markets.[14]

In recent years, however, even these instruments showed their week points. "Green taxes", believed by many environmental economists to be in principle the most efficient instrument,[15] are hardly implementable taking account of the strong rejection of new taxes by most citizens. Most policy makers abandoned early attempts to introduce "carbon taxes" in favour of tradable permits systems. However, the influential opposition of the businesses that have to buy pollution permits to continue their activity has often impaired the correct implementation of the tradable permits schemes.

A case in point is the European Emission Trading System (EU ETS) that represents the cornerstone of the European Union's policy to combat climate change, adopted since 2005. This scheme has been so far the most ambitious and comprehensive plan of this kind. However, despite being a prototype for other countries, the EU experience has shown mixed results. While the emission reduction target for 2020 (–20 %) has already been achieved by the EU, the estimated emissions reductions are likely to depend mainly on the economic recession that has significantly reduced industrial production (and consequently the resulting GHG emissions) rather than on carbon markets that have proved to be highly volatile.[16]

Notwithstanding the serious shortcomings observed in the EU application of tradable permits, many other countries adopted similar schemes, namely the Regional Greenhouse Gas Initiative, the Californian Cap and

Trade System, and the Australian Carbon Pricing Mechanism. The new plans take account of some shortcomings of the EU ETS and introduce innovations that the EU could usefully adopt to improve the performance of its own scheme. The crucial and unsolved problem, however, is that a tradable permits scheme to reduce GHGs emissions should be as global and homogeneous as possible. There are three main options. The best option would be a homogeneous worldwide ETS scheme, but not all the countries are favourable to the implementation of this ambitious plan. One could aim at least to build a global network of independent local ETS regimes hoping to contain their heterogeneity and to reduce it progressively in a second time, but even the management of a network of this kind requires some supranational authority to manage it, and many countries reject this institutional condition. One could simply device some sort of coordination between the existing local ETS schemes hoping in the progressive emergence of a more organic synthesis between them, but this gradualist approach would become really effective only in the long period after a long phase of extension of the ETS schemes to most local areas and the progressive strengthening of coordination mechanisms. For the time being, only the third option seems politically viable; however, though this approach would be better than nothing as a first step of a favourable policy escalation, the expected timing of its positive effects risks to be inconsistent with the great urgency of mitigating global warming.

Policy makers implemented the tradable pollution permits systems in the conviction that this policy instrument could incentivise the so-called eco-innovations referring to any product, process, or organisational innovation that is more environmentally friendly than the existing ones. The main hope was that carbon pricing could convince firms to invest in new technology to avoid the purchase of costly tradable permits and to sell the permits made superfluous. In addition, innovative firms could draw significant advantages from being at the forefront in the cap-and-trade market acquiring a dominant position, derived from the capacity to anticipate competitors in the implementation of environmentally friendly eco-innovations. However, the incentive to invest in law-carbon technologies vanishes when the carbon price is too low or too volatile. In the first case, after a certain threshold, it is more convenient to continue to buy pollution permits rather than to adopt less polluting technologies, while in the second case, the uncertainty on the expected advantages of eco-innovation paralyses this sort of investment. In the case of the EU ETS, the record of carbon price shows both problems. This explains why, according to most observers, the European system of pollution permits did not have a significant impact on eco-innovation.[17]

One possible way out could be the introduction of a floor and a ceiling to carbon price to maintain a minimum degree of incentives and avoid excessive fluctuations. These two boundaries of the oscillation range could progressively increase according to a pre-established progression to strengthen the incentives towards eco-innovation in a long-term time horizon. However, this sort of refurbishment of the EU ETS encounters the strong hostility of neoliberal policy makers who oppose any further constraint to the unfettered market process.

7.4 The Ecological Imprint and the Crisis: A Tale of Two Debts

The empirical evidence produced by the ecological approach confirms the pessimistic view on the unsustainability of the spontaneous evolution of the economy driven by unfettered markets. In particular, it is useful to refer here to a comprehensive measure of ecological sustainability of which we have sufficiently long time series for a long-run analysis: the "ecological footprint", standardised measure in global hectares of the amount of biologically productive land and sea area necessary to supply the resources consumed and to assimilate waste.[18] The ecological footprint has rapidly increased after World War II. Since the early 1970s, we notice a slowdown of its rate of growth due to the systematic adoption of environmental policies. This was insufficient to avoid that, in the late 1970s, our planet drifted in a situation of increasing ecological debt:

> The fact that we are using, or "spending," our natural capital stocks faster than they can be replenished, is similar to having expenditures that continuously exceed income. In planetary terms, the costs of our ecological overspending are becoming more evident by the day. Climate change—a

result of greenhouse gases being emitted faster than they can be absorbed by forests and oceans—is the most obvious and arguably pressing result. But there are others—shrinking forests, species loss, fisheries collapse, higher commodity prices. (Footprint Network 2014)

One graphic way to measure the extent of ecological debt is that of calculating the Earth Overshoot Day, namely the approximate date our resource consumption for a given year exceeds the planet's ability to replenish its stock: "in 1993, Earth Overshoot Day … fell on October 21. In 2003, Overshoot Day was on September 22. Given current trends in consumption, one thing is clear: Earth Overshoot Day arrives a few days earlier each year" (ibid.). In 2013, the Earth Overshoot Day was on August 20; in 2015, it was on August 13.

This situation of growing ecological debt has interacted and interacts with the situation of growing economic debt of states and households that has characterised the neoliberal development trajectory. The deep impact of this interaction has become evident in the origination of the subprime crisis. The overexploitation of natural resources by an unsustainable model of development reflected itself in a spike of oil and food prices from 2005 to 2008 that interacted perversely with the overindebtedness of households having a subprime mortgage or an adjustable-rate mortgage (ARM). The perverse interaction between financial and environmental sustainability observed in the period 2006–2008 was not an accident but rather an example of a more general issue that tends to become more relevant for sustainability. In the absence of a radical policy change, we should expect for the future increasing financial instability produced by unfettered financialisation and, at the same time, a growing tendency to cost inflation induced by the progressive depletion of renewables and the internalisation of external costs through green taxation and/or tradable pollution permits. In recent years, the stagnation in the European economy and the low rate of growth of the world economy kept this tendency under control. Taking account of the procyclical impact of financial speculation on natural resources consumption and their price, a vigorous and reliable recovery of the world economy would significantly revive this sort of cost inflation with its detrimental effects on the interest rate and growth sustainability.

7.5   The Unsustainability of the Energy System and Climate Change

The viewpoint of ecological imprint shows a tendency towards increased environmental unsustainability after World War II. The use of alternative methodologies confirms this trend. I restrain my analysis to one analytic approach that focuses on the energy sector that heavily affects the environmental sustainability of the existing model of development.

The growing environmental unsustainability of the last decades crucially depends on the current energy system based on fossil fuels: within the current model of development, the mere stabilisation of GHGs emissions implies the halving of the world GDP growth from about 4 % to about 2 % per year.[19] This is far from sufficient to stabilise the climate. Since the current emissions are about eight times what the biosphere may absorb, GDP growth should be severely negative for many decades. This would be unimaginable within the current model of development.

It is possible to clarify the quantitative dimensions of this delicate issue by adopting a specific version of the decomposition approach. According to the IPAT model, suggested long ago by eminent ecologists, the impact "I" of human activity on the quality of the environment depends on Population "P", Affluence "A", and Technical change "T".[20] This idea may be expressed in rigorous terms by factorising the growth rate of an index of environmental deterioration in a number of determinants.[21] We may derive the following identity:

$$ED \text{ growth} = pc \text{ income growth} + \text{intensity of } ED \text{ growth} + \text{population growth},$$

where ED is a global index of environmental degradation; income is measured by GDP; intensity of ED is measured by the ratio between ED and GDP; and pc stands for "per capita". From this identity, often called Kaya identity, we may derive a simple minimal condition of long-term emission stabilisation (ED growth = 0):[22]

$$pc \text{ income growth} = -\left(\text{intensity of } ED \text{ growth} + \text{population growth}\right).$$

This condition clarifies that a positive rate of growth of pc income may be consistent with emission stabilisation only if the rate of growth of population does not exceed the negative rate of growth of ED intensity. This condition may be satisfied only if the process of technical change is sufficiently intense and focused on increasing sustainability, and the structure of demand evolves in a greener direction. This is more likely to happen in developed countries where environmental awareness and technical progress are typically higher and demographic growth lower. However, even in the developed countries most aware of sustainability constraints, it is very difficult to comply with the conditions of stabilisation. This is certainly true in the energy field. As is well known, the existing energy system relies mainly on the consumption of fossil fuels that are heavily polluting and subject to a strong scarcity constraint.

The current emissions of GHGs are around 42 GtCO2e per year while the biosphere may absorb only about 5 GtCO2e per year without increasing their concentration in the atmosphere. This produced a growth in the concentration of GHGs in the atmosphere from 280 ppm before the industrial revolution to 430 ppm increasing the average temperature of 0.74 °C in the last century (IPCC 2014). To avoid a further increase in the average temperature, we have to reduce the GHGs emissions to less than one-eighth of its current value. On the contrary, the current projections under the "business-as-usual" scenario predict a further growth of emissions in the next decades that will bring about a further increase in the average temperature exceeding the conventional threshold of 2 °C beyond which the consequences are expected to be catastrophic. Unfortunately, the decomposition approach introduced above shows that even the intermediate objective of stabilisation of emissions is very difficult to reach.

The energy intensity is diminishing at a rate of about 2 % per year; the world population is still growing at a rate that exceeds 1 % per year, while the emission intensity of fossil fuels is currently increasing because of the substitution of coal and non-conventional fossil fuels for less polluting but scarcer conventional oil and natural gas.[23] Within the existing model of development, we may obtain a reduction of GHGs emissions only through a significant reduction of the projected, business-as-usual, per capita income growth. The climate may thus be stabilised only by shifting from the current model aimed to maximise GDP growth to a model of sustainable development based on a different energy system relying mainly on renewable energy sources and complying with the other social and environmental requisites of sustainability.

Since the Industrial Revolution, the process of financialisation spread to any field of human life, including labour, money, and land that were before, at least in part, outside the logic of market, as emphasised by Polanyi.[24] The surge of industrialisation progressively extended the logic of market from agricultural land to built environment and the biosphere in general, transforming nature from an end in itself to a mere instrument. In particular, the process of financialisation has captured since long the vital activity of energy production, distribution, and consumption (from now on "energy system"). The second financialisation strengthened the link between energy and finance by making energy resources object also of systematic financial speculation. The energy system is nowadays a crucial field of interaction between nature (environment) and finance.

This was crystal clear during the recent crisis. As I argued in Chap. 5 and recalled in Sect. 7.4, a crucial trigger factor of the subprime crisis was rooted in the interaction between the housing bubble that increased the financial vulnerability of economic units and the spike in the price of oil and food that induced cost inflation. In particular, the crisis had an impact on climate action shifting public concern and political will towards financial survival.

In addition, the Fukushima accident, which occurred in March 2011, had a significant impact on the process of convergence towards a sustainable development trajectory. This accident made evident, and further worsened, the shortcomings of the existing energy system based on fossil sources. In particular, it reduced significantly the current and prospective contribution of nuclear energy to the global supply of energy aggravating for a foreseeable future a trend characterised, according to many experts, by structural excess demand of energy. This effect is likely to last in the longer period since, in the absence of a major technological breakthrough, a new "nuclear renaissance" such as that started in the late 2000s seems unlikely, at least in the near future. In any case, the necessary upgrading of safety standards in nuclear reactors and the downsizing of their contribution to energy generation has been, and will continue to be in the foreseeable future, a significant factor of cost inflation that interacts with the ongoing recession jeopardising a durable escape from it.

The accident revealed a series of failures in the design of the Fukushima plant (unable to withstand the consequences of an earthquake such as that occurred in March 2011 and the ensuing tsunami). In addition, it revealed a short-sighted management of the crisis (late decision of using seawater to cool down the reactors), poor regulation (also due to regulatory capture), and late and contradictory reactions of policy authorities. We may find a common root of all these shortcomings in the intrinsic instability of the nuclear energy generation process due to the critical dynamic nature of the nuclear chain reaction underlying the production of energy. The structural instability of the process implies strong risks that can be only partially mitigated. This casts serious doubts on the viability of nuclear energy as cheap, clean, and secure source of energy able to contribute to the mitigation of global warming. In any case, the cost of nuclear energy is due to increase significantly in consequence of the more severe security measures that the producers have to adopt after the Fukushima accident. Only a significant technological breakthrough could relaunch the perspectives of nuclear energy in the next two decades or so.[25]

The transition from the current energy system towards a low-carbon economy will crucially depend on the evolution of energy prices. In particular, the oil price has a central role in the energy markets and thus on macroeconomic fluctuations. Since the first major oil shock in 1973, sharp increases in the oil price have been a crucial triggering factor of macroeconomic recessions.[26] A high oil price can favour the shift to a low-carbon economy, but may encourage new explorations even in areas and with techniques that involve high risks. A case in point is the rapid spreading of fracking techniques after the spike in the oil price in the period 2005–2008. This greatly increased the supply of oil in a few countries including the USA contributing to the recent plunge in the price of oil. Unfortunately, there is a serious evidence that fracking produces micro earthquakes and disrupts and pollutes the aquifers.[27] In addition, the ensuing sharp reduction in the price of oil has discouraged the private and public decisions that may favour the transition to a low-carbon economy.[28]

7.6   Technological and Development Trajectories

I discussed so far the sustainability of different development models and of their implementation in specific historical trajectories, focusing mainly on the neoliberal trajectory. I did not consider so far the technological side of development although it plays a crucial role in the determination of actual development trajectories. In order to integrate this crucial factor in the analysis, in this section I hint at the crucial interaction between technological and development trajectories.

A huge literature has extensively studied the nature and implications of technological trajectories. There is a wide agreement that technological revolutions trigger technological trajectories that last a few decades until they lose their innovative strength and are progressively superseded by a new technological trajectory. However, researchers have a different understanding of the precise nature, chronology, even the number, of such revolutions since the First Industrial Revolution. Limiting myself to mention two recent bestsellers in this field, I notice that, according to Jeremy Rifkin, the times are ripe for a Third Industrial Revolution,[29] while, according to Carlota Perez, the last technological revolution started in the 1970s is the Fifth after the Industrial Revolution.[30] Notwithstanding this and other significant differences, these two authors and most other researchers working on the nexus between the evolution of technology, economics, and society agree that the emerging technological trajectory is heading, or should head, towards a new sustainable process of development.

According to Rifkin, the creation of a renewable energy regime, partially stored in the form of hydrogen, distributed via a green electricity grid, and connected to zero-emission transport, should lead to a sustainable economy characterised by the democratisation of information, energy, manufacturing, marketing, and logistics.[31] According to Perez, the civil society has been empowered by technology of the capability to create favourable conditions for a sustainable global knowledge society.[32]

In what follows, I limit myself to refer to the neo-Schumpeterian literature, and in particular to the recent contributions by Carlota Perez, that are thoroughly rooted in this prestigious tradition.[33] I will argue that her approach is complementary to that here pursued, lending itself to what I believe to be a fruitful integration. In Perez's view, each industrial revolution triggers a typical sequence of stages. The first phase is characterised by a turbulent *installation period* of a new technological paradigm that eventually triggers a major financial and economic crisis. After the crisis, a *phase of recomposition* of the socio-institutional framework allows a more harmonic relation between technological and social conditions. This inaugurates the final *deployment phase* of the technological paradigm that lasts until its propulsive drive is exhausted. The declining effectiveness of the ruling technological paradigm stimulates the incubation of a new technological paradigm leading to a new technological revolution.[34]

The period of installation of the new techno-economic paradigm is a phase of Schumpeterian "creative destruction" forced by the tentative introduction of new technologies and business models. In this period, the investment is dominated by finance since "it is the high mobility of finance that will then enable the reallocation of available funds from the established and mature technologies and industries to the emerging ones" (Perez 2009, 781). The installation period typically leads to a deep and prolonged crisis that occurs around the middle of the technological trajectory triggered by each technological revolution.

Specific bubbles triggered each of these crises: either a major technological bubble driven by an opportunity pull or a major financial bubble driven by an easy credit push, or both. According to Perez, "in the first case it was the excitement about new technology that attracted the money into the casino … in the second it was the excitement about abundant easy money that pushed investors to get credit and to seek new objects of speculation" (Perez 2009, 794). These two kinds of bubbles are often connected, although one may occur after the other with a lag of a few years. The period that follows a major crisis is typically a phase of "creative construction" characterised by a recomposition of the tensions between the development of productive forces and the social relations of production. The re-regulation of finance and the ensuing shift of investment from finance to the real economy make it possible.

The periods of financialisation are thus recurrent phases that are associated with pathological consequences such as economic turmoil, financial speculation, and shift of investment from the real economy to finance. In these troubled periods, the financial sector plays the physiological role of facilitating the structural changes required by the introduction and diffusion of new technologies.[35] In this view, the First Financialisation has been instrumental to the introduction and diffusion of the age of automobile, oil, petrochemicals, and mass production, while the Second Financialisation facilitated the introduction and diffusion of the new techno-economic paradigm based on information and digital communication.

The first phase of creative destruction culminating in the roaring 1920s led to the Great Depression, while the phase of creative construction in the period of Bretton Woods was facilitated by a strict control and supervision of finance and implemented through Keynesian full employment policies and the progressive construction of the welfare state. The recent phase of creative destruction started in the late 1970s led to a double bubble: the "dot-com mania" collapsing in the years 2000–2001 and the housing mania triggering the subprime mortgage crisis in 2007. The first bubble was a major technological bubble driven by an opportunity pull, while the second was a major financial bubble driven by an easy credit push. What is now required to start a new sustainable techno-economic trajectory is a new phase of more harmonious growth that "will depend on the capacity of the State to restrain the financial casino … and to hand over power to production capital, allowing its longer-term horizons to guide investment once more" (Perez 2009, 790).

The technological trajectories are to some extent synchronised with development trajectories as defined in the Sect. 1.7 of this book, taking into account that the two trajectories are out of phase by about half "cycle".[36] A technological trajectory typically splits into two successive parts by a "great crisis" that is largely due to the consequence of the first disharmonic phase of its installation and sets the stage for the more harmonic phase of its deployment. Development trajectories, instead, emerge as a reaction to a great crisis and terminate in a new great crisis.[37] In the first phase, after its inception, a development trajectory sustains a relatively harmonious process of growth, while the exhaustion of its propulsive potential (typically after a few decades) leads to its second phase of gradual deterioration leading to a new great crisis.[38] The reconstruction of the actual historical evolution requires an integration between these two points of view (see Fig. 7.1 for a visual representation of the lagged synchrony between technological and development trajectories).

In consequence of the long depression of 1873–1896, a new development trajectory emerged that fostered the First Globalisation and the synergic process of the First Financialisation. In the same period, the deployment of the "age of steel and heavy engineering" was exhausting its development drive, while a new technological revolution incubated. This eventually led to the era of automobiles, oil, and petrochemicals based on the Fordist model of production. According to Perez, the emblematic date announcing the big bang of this new techno-economic paradigm is 1908 when the most celebrated early model of gasoline car, the Ford Model T, started its production. The roaring 1920s mark the major technological bubble of this technological trajectory that terminates the turbulent times of its installation eventually leading to the Great Depression. The response to this economic and social catastrophe initiates a new cycle of development based on the adoption of full employment Keynesian policies and the building of the welfare state. This allows a phase of more harmonious development characterised by a more harmonious deployment of the dominating technological paradigm. The latter starts to decline since the late 1960s in consequence of the growing turmoil in the market of labour and in the industrial relations while a new post-Fordist techno-

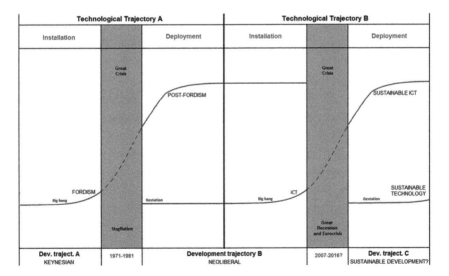

Fig. 7.1 Technological and development trajectories
Source: Elaboration by the author of Fig.1 in Vercelli (2015) based on the Figs. 4.1, 5.1, and 7.1 of Perez (2002).

logical paradigm based on mass consumerism, flexible specialisation, and a revival of small businesses starts to emerge.

The Great Stagflation of the 1970s ends the development trajectory of the Bretton Woods period leading eventually to the emergence of the neoliberal development trajectory. This new development phase is conducive to the deployment of the previous technological paradigm, while mass consumption starts to shift towards ICT appliances. The Second Financialisation provides the structural flexibility necessary for the rapid introduction of the new technologies. This process gathers momentum in the 1980s and 1990s and leads to the major technology bubble of the new economy in the late 1990s originating the dot-com crisis of 2001. The ensuing shift of investment from immaterial goods to brick-and-mortar goods starts a new major financial bubble, namely the housing bubble of 2003–2007. In this period, the regime of easy liquidity fostered by central banks nurtures the illusion that policy makers can control economic activity simply through appropriate monetary policies. In the meantime, the side effects of the neoliberal trajectory of development cumulate their disruptive effects progressively increasing the financial fragility of the system leading to the subprime financial crisis. We may interpret the ensuing Great Recession as the consequence of a phase of creative destruction characterising the systematic introduction of ICT, interacting with the contemporaneous degeneration of the neoliberal trajectory of development.

The reconstruction here sketched of the lagged synchrony between technological and development trajectories is broadly consistent with Perez's account of technological great surges with a major difference: she does not consider the Great Stagflation as a "great crisis" relevant for her analysis. I believe, on the contrary, that the Great Stagflation played a crucial role not only in the genesis of the new neoliberal trajectory of development (see retro Sects. 1.3, 5.2, and 5.3), but also in shaping the prevailing technological model of production and distribution of goods and services occurred in the same period. The technological response to such a crisis relied on the model of "flexible specialisation" and the synergic revival of small and medium businesses in the 1970s and 1980s. This new technological and organisational paradigm was instrumental to the early take-off of ICT. This new tendency, however, petered out in the late

1990s since the availability of cheap energy and cheap labour determined a revival of the old mass production model even in the ICT industries.

The analysis of the interaction between technological and development trajectories confirms that we should try hard to reconcile the disruptive effects of the ICT techno-economic paradigm with the social conditions of production and individual well-being as it has happened for other technological trajectories in the past.

The ICT sector is at the same time part of the problem, namely the unsustainability of the existing development trajectory, and part of its solution. This sector is today the most rapidly growing contributor to waste generation because of the wide range and short lifespan of digital devices.[39] In addition, the current arrangements for the disposal of electronic waste, some of which is toxic, are wanting. The GHGs emissions of the ICT sector are increasing at a rate of 6 % per annum in consequence of the growing diffusion of ICT networks and devices. This direct ecological imprint, however, may be the result of a beneficial use of ICT not only to access and elaborate information, but also to enable social and business relations that may contribute to implement a more sustainable knowledge society.

In addition, we may improve the environmental sustainability by using the ICT in a more far-sighted way. Big companies, particularly utilities, have begun to use information technology to manage energy production and distribution, transport, and other large-scale systems, with improved energy efficiency.[40] It is now urgent to exploit the potential of ICT in the direction of a more harmonious and sustainable development trajectory.[41] To this end, we should cut the vicious circle between unsustainable ICT uses and speculative financialisation by incentivising environmentally friendly ICT investment in the real economy to improve the job contents of work, full employment, and dematerialised consumption.

7.7   The Role of Public Investment

The effective transition to a sustainable development trajectory requires a huge amount of targeted investments. According to an accurate estimate, the investment required for achieving sustainable growth "stands at about US$ 5 trillion per year to 2020" (WEF 2013, 6). This huge amount of green investment is difficult to implement in particular in the case of the strategic investment required to prop up a new technological trajectory capable to support and enhance sustainability.

The most relevant investment, strategic investment, produces all its benefits only in the very long period. In addition, its benefits are typically public goods that private investors may only partially appropriate. A case in point is the badly needed investment for the mitigation of climate change.[42] Moreover, the expectations of the costs and benefits produced by the process of strategic investment typically extend along many decades and are subject to strong, even radical, uncertainty. In consequence of the process of financialisation, private investors take decisions within a progressively shorter time horizon and are strongly uncertainty averse. This explains why "from the development of aviation, nuclear energy, computers, the Internet, biotechnology, and today's development in green technology, it is, and has been, the State—not the private sector—that has kick-started and developed the engine of growth" (Mazzucato 2014, 13).

As is well known, financial markets are reluctant to finance innovation investment, the more so the more radical is the departure from existing routines. This is because the expected returns on innovative investment are not only risky but also very uncertain in the sense of Knight and Keynes.[43] This has a series of consequences that discourage innovative investment. First, credit ratings focus on the financial performance of the firm rather than on its industrial performance: "in some cases it is the most 'productive' firms that have the worst credit ratings, perhaps due to their greater spending on long-run growth investments" (Demirel and Mazzucato 2014, 51). In addition, the widespread practice of stock "buy-backs" in the interest of shareholders and top managers (particularly if the latter are endowed of generous stock options) has been found to be detrimental to R&D spending. The recent crisis increased the bias against innovative investment as the enhanced uncertainty aversion of lenders produced an increase in the cost of credit that hit the innovative firms more than the non-innovative ones (ibid.). Finally, the kind of strategic innovative investment that may accelerate the transition towards sustainable development has a long-run time horizon as its most significant returns are destined to emerge much beyond the short-term horizon of finance. This makes this sort of strategic investment unsuitable for private investment. Even venture capital that has been often credited as the mainspring of technical change in the USA and elsewhere has given a limited contribution to strategic investment focusing on projects having an expected commercial viability within a three-to-five-year period.[44]

There is only one possible way out from this problem. The government as representative of the long-term interests of all the citizens has to play the role of catalyser for the strategic innovation necessary for a new sustainable trajectory. Contrary to some well-publicised myths, this is what happened in the past: "for example, the infrastructure of the ICT revolution, laying the basis for the Internet, was lavishly funded by the State from its beginning stages until it was installed and fully functional and could be turned over for commercial use" (Perez 2013, xxii).

The government has to intervene either by investing directly in the strategic sectors to enhance sustainability or by financing—at least in part—the relevant private investment or by providing incentives and insurance for private investors and lenders to enable them to correct the distortions mentioned above. These different channels of intervention do not exclude each other and are likely to have synergic effects. In the USA, for example, the state played a crucial role in all the most significant innovations since World War II through specific agencies and initiatives. For example, the following important intervention schemes had a great impact on technological innovation: the DARPA (Defence Advanced Research Projects Agency, established in 1951) funded the development and diffusion of computers and ICT infrastructure; the SBIR (Small Business Innovation Research Program, started in 1982) provided patient capital to innovative small firms ignored by private venture capital; the ODA (Orphan Drug Act Program, established in 1984) supported research to find drugs for rare diseases that are considered too risky and unrewarding by big pharmaceutical firms and private venture capital; the NNI (National Nanotechnology Initiative, established in 2003) promoted the nanotech revolution that is now taking off; and the ARPA-E (Advanced Research Projects Agency-Energy, established in 2005) is now funding the transition to a greener energy system.

These initiatives promoted strategic innovations that changed the technological frontier in a very significant and irreversible way. The state did not limit itself, as mainstream theory prescribes, to create the conditions of market-led innovations by gently encouraging would-be innovators to act, as standard theory prescribes, but played the much more ambitious role of a Schumpeterian innovator implementing directly new strategic technologies and creating new products and markets according to a far-sighted vision. It could be objected that the case of the USA is peculiar because the initiatives mentioned above are often financed by the Federal expenditure in defence. The latter is almost equal to the joint expenditure in defence of all the other states and is so huge (about $680 billion in the Defence Department but about $1000 billion considering defence-related expenditure in other Federal department for the 2011 fiscal year) that it may easily accommodate within its different items the required patient capital to support strategic investment either directly or indirectly. However, we find a similar attitude of pro-active entrepreneurship in all the countries that succeeded, and/or try consistently to succeed, in promoting strategic technical change.

A significant example is the policy recently pursued in Germany to develop solar photovoltaics (PV) that made it the world leader in this field: "by revising its feed-in tariffs (FIT) policy in 2000 to provide better pricing for solar PV ... Germany made solar PV competitive with traditional power sources and even wind energy. At the same time, Germany also established a '100,000 roofs' programme to encourage residential and commercial investment in the technology ... Germany grew its solar PV capacity from just 62 MWs in 2000 to over 24,000 MWs by 2011. This is similar to completing 24 nuclear power plants in about 10 years" (Mazzucato 2014, 156).

Another case in point is China's twelfth "green" five-year plan (2011–2015) that aims to invest $1.5 trillion (or 5 % of GDP) in energy-saving and environmentally friendly technologies. This established Chinese solar PV manufacturing firms as prominent international players notwithstanding the tariffs introduced in many countries, including the EU, to protect domestic manufacturing firms. Analogously, China's target of 100 GW of wind power by 2015 and 1000 GW by 2050 would equal the entire electric capacity of the USA and Europe.

Public finance plays a crucial role in this field. To reach the ambitious targets mentioned above the China Development Bank (CDB) provides the necessary amount of patient capital. Analogously, the Brazilian

Development Bank (BNDES) is providing patient capital to develop bio-technology and clean technologies in Brazil. Finally, Australia's recently established Clean Energy Finance Corporation (CEFC) has announced AUD 227 million in new investment commitments. Over AUD 133 million of this is for new solar programs and projects, which will bring its total commitment to solar deployment to over AUD 200 million.

Investing in strategic technology implies uncertain returns and unavoidable mistakes. These mistakes have been sorted out and widely publicised by the supporters of unfettered markets but this is beside the point because the success of strategic investment should take account of the aggregate returns over a long period of time taking into account all the externalities.[45] Keeping in mind the strong or radical uncertainty associated by definition to strategic investment, not all the investment financed may be successful. On the contrary, it is surprising to see that the public banks providing patient capital show often very good results even in the light of mere standard accounting. The BNDES, for example, has been earning record-level returns: the return on equity (ROE) in 2010 has reached the remarkable rate of 21.2 % allowing not only the refinancing of strategic investment, but also much-needed investment in health and education.[46] Analogously, the Chinese development bank (CDB) catalysing the country's investment in the green economy obtained excellent results (ibid). Similarly, in 2012, the *Kreditanstalt für Wiederaufbau* (KfW), the German state investment bank, reported $3 billion profits.[47]

In the light of the evidence reported in this section and in the literature here cited, we may conclude that the State has a crucial role to play to support the huge investment required to converge towards a sustainable trajectory.

7.8   Concluding Remarks

There is an apparent convergence on the main features of a sustainable model of development. We may find examples of an illusory broad agreement between experts of different disciplines and policy makers of many countries in recent documents approved by the UN Assembly.[48] A similar convergence eventually emerged in the final declaration of the Paris

COP21 (see retro Sect. 7.2). Unfortunately, however, the representatives of governments often sign documents of this kind having in mind the coverage of mass media and the ensuing rate of approval of their behaviour. What is still missing is a concrete agreement on the actual implementation procedures of a reliable path of transition from the current to a sustainable model of development. This involves the difficult choice of priorities between alternative goals and of policy instruments to reach them. These choices have divergent implications for different interests and preferences and are thus highly conflictual.

During the neoliberal era, a growing number of experts and policy makers questioned the viability of environmental policy, even by means of market instruments, resorting to theoretical and empirical arguments claimed to have a general validity. These arguments are often used to stop, or at least postpone, the concrete implementation of a sustainable development trajectory. Two of them are particularly significant for our purposes: the Jevons paradox and the Sinn paradox.

Jevons, one of the most famous economists of his time, as early as in 1866, argued that "it is a confusion of ideas to suppose that the economical use of fuel is equivalent to diminished consumption. The very contrary is the truth".[49] He observed that the introduction of a more efficient steam engine had the initial effect of decreasing coal consumption leading to a drop in the price of coal; in his opinion, however, this meant not only that coal had become more affordable for the traditional uses, but also economically viable for new uses. In his opinion, this effect ultimately increased coal consumption more than technical progress had reduced it.

A few researchers have recently revived and generalised this argument under the name of "rebound effect".[50] In its more common formulation, the rebound effect asserts that an increase of efficiency in the use of energy, or a reduction of its relative price, eventually brings about an increase in the consumption of energy. We may measure the rebound effect by the difference between the projected and actual savings due to increased efficiency. Its impact depends on different factors that can follow the adoption of a more efficient device. We may distinguish between (i) direct effects if the consumer chooses to use more of the resource instead of monetising the energy cost savings; (ii) indirect effects if the consumer chooses to spend the money saved by buying other goods which use the same resource; and (iii) markets effects if the lower resource price renders new uses economically viable. Most empirical studies agree that, in developed economies, the rebound effect is significant but partial. Estimates of the rebound effect for electric end-use equipment are between 0 % and 40 %.[51] The rebound effect for house and office heating or cooling units ranges from 0 % to 50 %. Estimates for automobile fuel efficiency are between 10 % and 30 %.[52]

Researchers and policy makers often put forward the rebound effect— at least in the field of energy efficiency and climate change control—as a reason against environmental policy, claiming that, for example, an increase in the fuel efficiency of cars encourages people to drive more, or at higher speed. However, as we have seen, the empirical evidence does not corroborate this interpretation of the Jevons paradox, as the rebound effect is generally significantly less than 100 %.[53]

Summing up, in the light of the empirical evidence produced so far, the rebound effect does not imply the failure of environmental policy but only the necessity of fine-tuning its instruments to reach the desired goals. The policy measures should aim to increase the energy efficiency more than it would be otherwise sufficient, taking into account the predicted rebound effect. In addition, policy makers should keep in mind that losses in energy savings due to the rebound effect would generally be associated with gains in the consumers' quality of life. The owner of a more fuel-efficient car, for example, may choose to drive more or at higher speed without affecting the exercise costs, or may choose to use the savings on some other consumer good.

The well-known German economist Hans-Werner Sinn has recently generalised the argument based on the rebound effect to criticise the environmental policies pursued in recent decades, in particular in Europe. He argued that energy-demand reduction strategies, such as those pursued by the EU, "simply depress the world price of carbon and induce the environmental sinners to consume what the Kyoto countries have economised on. Even worse, if suppliers feel threatened by a gradual greening of economic policies in the Kyoto countries that would damage their future prices; they will extract their stocks more rapidly, thus accelerating global warming" (Sinn 2008, 360).

This "green paradox", as Sinn himself called it, casts serious doubts on the efficacy of environmental policies, at least those based on the usual demand-side approach. These policies, relying on incentives to energy saving and efficiency, risk to be "self-defeating".[54] Nevertheless, as Sinn himself emphasises, the green paradox does not deny the possibility of a more efficient environmental policy, if policy makers design it by taking into account all the economic fundamentals, including the supply conditions neglected or underplayed by the existing policy strategy. In the case of global warming, he suggests two possible solutions: either the adoption of a unified global emission trading system that would effectively put a cap on worldwide fossil fuel consumption or the adoption of a withholding tax on the capital gains resulting from financial investments of fossil fuel resource owners. Both solutions are difficult to implement. I have already discussed in Sect. 7.3 the viability of the first solution showing its current inapplicability. As for the second solution, governments do not seem to have the will, independence, and power to implement a measure that would touch the interests of very powerful states and corporations. A further solution could aim to counterbalance the rebound effect through apt policy measures such as the adoption of a flexible tax that keeps constant the cost of fuel. However, for the time being, also this alternative approach does not seem easily implementable.

Summing up, the preceding brief discussion of the rebound effect and the green paradox does not confirm the presumption that the policies of internalisation of carbon externalities pursued so far, for example, in the EU, have been futile or counterproductive, but substantiate their weakness. More in general, these paradoxes confirm the limits of an environmental policy that relies mainly on market-based instruments considered more consistent with neoliberal principles. Taking account of the shortcomings of the market-based policy instruments as experienced in their concrete application, there is a presumption that the ideal policy mix of environmental policy should resume a more systematic use of C&C instruments.[55]

Notes

1. See for example Tietenberg (1985).
2. A crucial reason for the existence of externalities is the ubiquitous incompleteness of markets (see Sect. 1.3).
3. Coase (1960).

4. Meadows et al. (1972).
5. See the "Brundtland Report" of the World Commission on Environment and Development (WCED 1987).
6. See in particular Meadows et al. (2004), and Turner (2008).
7. See Sect. 7.3.
8. Between 2002 and 2010, nearly $120 million was anonymously donated via the Donors Trust and Donors Capital Fund to more than 100 organisations seeking to undermine the public perception of the science on climate change (see Goldenberg 2013).
9. The publication of the fifth Assessment Report of IPCC greatly reduced the plausibility of climate change denialism (IPCC 2014) and increased the worries of public opinion and policy makers.
10. The conference was held in Paris from 30 November to 12 December 2015.
11. The Paris meeting was the twenty-first yearly session of the Conference of the Parties (COP) to the 1992 UNFCCC and the eleventh session of the Meeting of the Parties to the 1997 Kyoto Protocol.
12. Pope Francis (2015).
13. Pigou (1920).
14. Coase (1960).
15. See for example Nordhaus (2007).
16. See Borghesi et al. (2016).
17. See Borghesi et al. (2016); and Ekins et al. (2015).
18. See Wackernagel and Rees (1996), and Wackernagel and Galli (2007).
19. Borghesi and Vercelli (2009).
20. Holdren and Ehrlich (1974).
21. See Borghesi and Vercelli (2008 and 2009), and GEA (2012).
22. An alternative way to express the same identity equates the growth of ED to minus the growth of ED intensity. Therefore, if we want to stabilise the emissions of GHGs, the rate of growth of the world GDP cannot exceed the rate of negative growth of the emissions intensity (see Borghesi and Vercelli, 2008 and 2009).
23. See Borghesi and Vercelli (2009) in the light of the update in IPCC (2014).
24. Polanyi (1944).
25. Vercelli (2014).
26. Papandreou (2015).
27. For a recent assessment, see for example The Scottish Government (2014).
28. See for example Papandreou (2015).
29. Rifkin (2011).
30. Perez (2002 and 2009).
31. Rifkin (2011).
32. Perez (2002).

33. See in particular Freeman (2008), Freeman and Louçã (2001), and Perez (2002, 2007, 2009).
34. Perez (2009, 781).
35. See retro Chap. 4.
36. On "development trajectories", see Vercelli (2011b).
37. See retro Sect. 1.7.
38. Vercelli (2011b).
39. See Global Connectivity Group for Sustainable Development (2013).
40. The impact of "dematerialisation" of some goods such as books and music, and shifts towards homeworking and e-commerce is more controversial, since the energy costs of travel that are saved may be lost through increased heating or conditioning costs at home.
41. See Perez (2012).
42. See for example Grubb (2014), and Goldson et al. (2015).
43. See Knight (1921) and Keynes (1921, 1936).
44. Mazzucato (2014, 49).
45. The case of Concorde has been particularly emphasised in this respect. However, not all investment can be successful whether it is public or private.
46. Mazzucato (2014, 5).
47. The Kreditanstalt für Wiederaufbau ("Reconstruction Credit Institute") was established in 1948 as part of the Marshall Plan, and is owned by the Federal Republic of Germany (80 %) and the States of Germany (20 %).
48. See for example United Nations (2012).
49. Jevons (1866).
50. See for example Sorrell (2009), and Greening et al. (2000).
51. Schipper (2000, 351–353).
52. Gottron (2001).
53. The value of the rebound effect may vary by using different estimate methods. For example, Ruzzenenti and Basosi (2014) found significantly different values for the rebound effect in the European freight sector by using different approaches. However, to the best of my knowledge, none of the existing studies argues that the rebound effect completely offsets the environmental improvements obtained through environmental policies.
54. Papandreou (2015).
55. See in particular Clark and Hermele (2014).

Bibliography

Bardi, Ugo. 2011. *The Limits to Growth Revisited*. New York: Springer.

Borghesi, Simone, Massimiliano Montini, and Alessandra Barreca. 2016. *The European Emissions Trading System and its Followers: Comparative Analysis and Linking Perspectives*. New York: Springer.

Borghesi, Simone, and Alessandro Vercelli. 2008. *Global Sustainability. Social and Environmental Conditions*. Palgrave Macmillan: Basingstoke and New York.

———. 2009. Greenhouse Gas Emissions and the Energy System: Are Current Trends Sustainable? In *International Journal of Global Energy Issues*, Special Issue on 'Energy Efficiency, Environmental Performance and Sustainability', 32 (1–2):160–174.

Clark, Eric, and Kenneth Hermele. 2014. Financialisation of the Environment: A Literature Review. *FESSUD Working Paper Series* No. 32.

Coase, Ronald H 1960. The Problem of Social Cost. *Journal of Law and Economics*. 3(3): 1–44.

Demirel, Pelin, and Mariana Mazzucato. 2014. Innovation and Economic Performance (Industrial and Financial). Recent Results and Questions for Future Research. In *Innovation and Finance*, eds. Andreas Pyka, and Hans-Peter Burghof, 46–58. Abingdon and New York (NY): Routledge.

Ekins, Paul, Drummond, Paul, and Jim Watson. 2015. Economic Approaches to Energy, Environment, and Sustainability. A Survey Paper for COEURE. London: UCL Institute for Sustainable Resources (UCL ISR), University College.

Financial Stability Board. 2014. 2014 Update of Group of Global Systemically Important Banks (G-SIBs). Financial Stability Board. 6 November 2014. http://www.financialstabilityboard.org/wp-content/uploads/r_141106b.pdf

Freeman, Chris. 2008. *Systems of Innovation: Selected Essays in Evolutionary Economics*. Cheltenham: Elgar.

Freeman, Chris, and Francisco Louçã. 2001. *As Time Goes By. From the Industrial Revolutions to the Information Revolution*. Oxford: Oxford University Press.

GEA. 2012. Global Energy Assessment—Toward a Sustainable Future. Cambridge, UK, and New York, NY, USA: Cambridge University Press, and Laxenburg, Austria: the International Institute for Applied Systems Analysis.

Goldenberg, Suzanne (2013). Secret Funding Helped Build Vast Network of Climate Denial Thinktanks. *The Guardian* (14 February 2013). Retrieved 1 March 2013.

The Global Connectivity Group for Sustainable Development. 2013. *ICTS, the Internet and Sustainability. Manifesto Issued at UNESCO Conference.* https://ictstheinternetandsustainability.wordpress.com/2013/02/27/the-global-connectivity-group-for-sustainable-development-issues-a-manifesto/. Retrieved 3 March 2016.

Footprint Network. 2014. Earth Overshoot Day 2013. http://www.footprintnetwork.org/en/index.php/GFN/page/earth_overshoot_day/. Retrieved 22 December 2013.

Gottron, Frank. 2001. Energy Efficiency and the Rebound Effect: Does Increasing Efficiency Decrease Demand? CRS Report for Congress RS20981.

Gouldson, Andy, Niall Kerr, Joel Millward-Hopkins, Mark C. Freeman, Corrado Topi, and Sullivan Roren. 2015. Innovative Financing Models for Low Carbon Transitions: Exploring the case for revolving funds for domestic energy efficiency programmes. *Energy Policy* 86: 739–748.

Greening, L.A., Greene D.L., and C. Difiglio. 2000. Energy Efficiency and Consumption—The Rebound Effect—A Survey. *Energy Policy* 28: 389–401.

Grubb, Michael. 2014. *Planetary Economics: Energy, Climate Change and the Three Domains of Sustainable Development.* London/New York: Routledge.

Holdren, John P., and Paul R. Ehrlich. 1974. Human Population and the Global Environment. *American Scientist* 62(3): 282–292.

IPCC. 2014. *Fifth Assessment Report—Climate Change 2014: Mitigation of Climate Change.* Geneva Switzerland: Intergovernmental Panel on Climate Change.

Jevons, William Stanley. 1866. *The Coal Question*, 2 edn. London: Macmillan and Company.

Keynes, John Maynard. 1921. *A Treatise on Probability*. London: Macmillan.

———. 1936 [1973]. *The General Theory of Employment, Interest and Money.* (The Collected Writings of John Maynard Keynes. Volume 7). London and Cambridge: Macmillan and Cambridge University Press.

Knight, Frank A. 1921. *Risk, Uncertainty and Profit.* Boston: Houghton and Mifflin.

Mazzucato, Mariana. 2014. *The Entrepreneurial State. Debunking Public vs. Private Sectors Myths.* New York: Anthem Press.

Meadows, Donella H., Dennis L. Meadows, Jørgen Randers, and William W. Behrens III. 1972. *The Limits to Growth.* New York: Universe Books.

Meadows, Donella H., Jørgen Randers, and Dennis L. Meadows. 2004. *Limits to Growth: The 30-Year update.* White River Junction, Vermont: Chelsea Green Publishing Co.

Nordhaus, William D. 2007. To Tax or Not to Tax: Alternative Approaches to Slowing Global Warming. *Review of Environmental Economics and Policy* 1(1): 26–44.

Papandreu, Andreas. 2015. The Great Recession and the Transition to a Low-Carbon Economy, Working Paper Series No. 88.

Perez, Carlota. 2002. *Technological Revolutions and Financial Capital: The Dynamics of Bubbles and Golden Ages*. Cheltenham: Edward Elgar.

———. 2007. Finance and Technical Change: A Long-term View. In *Elgar Companion to Neo-Schumpeterian Economics*, eds. Horst Hanusch, and Andreas Pyka, 775–799. Cheltenham: Elgar.

———. 2009. The Double Bubble at the Turn of the Century: Technological Roots and Structural Implications. *Cambridge Journal of Economics* 33: 779–805.

———. 2012. Why IT and the Green Economy are the Real Answer to the Financial Crisis. Green Alliance Blog, 19 March. http://www.green-alliance.org.uk/uploadedFiles/Publications/reports/InsideTrack_30_web_spreads.pdf

———. 2013. Foreword to Mazzucato, Mariana. 2014. In *The Entrepreneurial State. Debunking Public vs. Private Sectors Myths*, xxi–xxv. New York: Anthem Press.

Pigou, Arthur C. 1920. *The Economics of Welfare*. London: Macmillan.

Polanyi, Karl. 1944. *The Great Transformation*. New York: Farrar & Rinehart.

Pope Francis. 2015. *Enccyclical Letter Laudato Si' Of The Holy father Francis On care For Our Common Home*, http://w2.vatican.va/content/francesco/en/encyclicals/documents/papa-francesco_20150524_enciclica-laudato-si.html, (Official English-language text of encyclical). Retrieved 14 February 2016.

Rifkin, Jeremy. 2011. *The Third Industrial Revolution*. Basingstoke and New York: Palgrave Macmillan.

Ruzzenenti, Franco, and Riccardo Basosi. 2014. Case Study: Paper on the Energy Efficiency Evolution in the European Road Freight Transport Sector, Working Paper Series No. 77.

Schipper, Lee. 2000. On the Rebound: The Interaction of Energy Efficiency, Energy Use and Economic Activity. An Introduction. *Energy Policy* 28: 351–353.

Sinn, H.W. 2008. Public policies against global warming. *International Tax and Public Finance*, 15, 4, 360–394.

Sorrell, Steve. 2009. Jevons' Paradox Revisited: The Evidence for Backfire from Improved Energy Efficiency. *Energy Policy* 37(4): 1456–1459.

The Scottish Government. 2014. Independent Expert Scientific Panel—Report on Unconventional Oil And Gas. http://www.gov.scot/Resource/0045/00456579.pdf. Retrieved 15 March 2016.

Tietenberg, Tom. 1985. *Emission Trading: An Exercise in Reformulating Pollution Policy*. Washington, D.C.: Resources for the Future.

Turner, Graham. 2008. A Comparison of the Limits to Growth with Thirty Years of Reality. In *SEED Working Paper 19*. Canberra, Australia: CSIRO.

United Nations. 2012. *The Future We Want*. New York: United Nations.

Vercelli, Alessandro. 2011b. Economy and Economics: The Twin Crises. In *The Global Economic Crisis. New Perspectives on the Critique of Economic Theory and Policy*, eds. Emiliano Brancaccio, and Giuseppe Fontana, 27–41. Abingdon and New York: Routledge.

———. 2014. Financial and Nuclear Meltdowns: The Fragility of Chain-Reaction Critical Processes. In *The Great Recession and the Contradictions of Contemporary Capitalism*, eds. Riccardo Bellofiore, and Giovanna Vertova, 208–220. Cheltenham: Edward Elgar.

———. 2015. The Neoliberal Trajectory, the Great Recession and Sustainable Development. *International Papers in Political Economy*, issue on "Finance and the Macroeconomics of Environmental Policies", ed. Philip Arestis and Malcolm Sawyer, 37–73.

Wackernagel, Mathis, and Alessandro Galli. 2007. An Overview on Ecological Footprint and Sustainable Development. *International Journal of Ecodynamics* 2(1): 1–9.

Wackernagel, Mathis, and William E. Rees. 1996. *Our Ecological Footprint: Reducing Human Impact on the Earth*. Philadelphia, PA.: New Society Publishers.

WCED. 1987. *Our Common Future: Report of the World Commission on Environment and Development*. New York: Oxford University Press ("Bruntland Report").

WEF. 2013. *The Green Investment Report: The Ways and Means to Unlock Private Finance for Green Growth*. Geneva: World Economic Forum.

Part III

Epilogue

8

The Eurocrisis

8.1 Introduction

A survey of the competing explanations of the subprime financial crisis concluded that the existing extensive literature overexplains and overdetermines it.[1] We can say the same of the Eurozone crisis that started in 2010 when the Great Recession was relenting elsewhere (henceforth "Eurocrisis"). The state-of-the-art reflects not only a legitimate variety of points of view but also their dependence on a causal approach looking for a single factor, or a short list of independent factors, as the cause of the crisis. In my opinion, this reductionist approach is misleading because most causal factors of the Eurocrisis are mutually correlated as parts of a system having a well-defined economic structure, institutional framework, and policy strategy. Therefore, in order to understand the crisis, it is necessary to reconstruct the origins and unfold the process that produced its conditions. To this end, I distinguish sharply the European recession occurred in 2008–2009, that is basically the European side of the subprime financial crisis and the subsequent Great Recession, from the Eurocrisis started in 2010 in the Eurozone that has been determined and made persistent by specific institutional and policy peculiarities of the EU.

© The Editor(s) (if applicable) and The Author(s) 2017   **219**
A. Vercelli, *Crisis and Sustainability*,
DOI 10.1057/978-1-137-60069-1_8

Comparing the principal macroeconomic and financial indicators in the USA, Japan, and Europe, we notice a similar behaviour until summer 2010; at the end of that year, we observe a new downturn in Europe but not in the other countries previously affected by the crisis. If we compare, for example, the indicators of real domestic demand of these areas, we see a similar pattern unfolding since the end of 2007: a marked fall until the middle of 2009 and then a slow but steady recovery until late 2010. From that point on, however, the indicator for Europe decouples sharply from those of the USA and Japan. The latter countries continue their slow but persistent recovery, while the European indicator undergoes a sharp downturn in the first quarter of 2011 initiating a negative trend that continues in the following two years.[2] The sudden decoupling of the European conjuncture from that of the USA and Japan suggests that the major change of policy strategy occurred in Europe in the second part of 2010 started a new regional turmoil that is not simply the European queue of the Great Recession but rather a new crisis. We have thus to investigate its specific triggering factors and peculiar propagation mechanism. This chapter focuses on the causes and consequences of the Eurocrisis so defined.

The next two sections briefly reconstruct the principal features of the crisis in the Eurozone discussing how it was triggered (Sect. 8.2), propagated, and reinforced by structural, institutional, and policy factors (Sect. 8.3). Section 8.4 discusses the mainstream account of the Eurocrisis showing its shortcomings, while Sect. 8.5 presents an alternative explanation. The policy implications of this paper are discussed in Sect. 8.6. Section 8.7 concludes by arguing that the current design of the common currency and its management rules are unsustainable.

8.2   The Origins of the Eurocrisis

After the bankruptcy of Lehman Brothers in September 2008, the financial contagion rapidly spread to the entire European banking system. In that period, the Eurozone exhibited all the conditions that would have rendered it susceptible to undergo a crisis in consequence of a shock, even in the absence of contagion from the subprime crisis in the USA.

The triggering shock of the international financial crisis could have originated in one of the Eurozone countries, for example, one of those characterised by a particularly significant housing bubble (such as Ireland or Spain). As for the propagation process, first it acted mainly through the interaction between the balance sheets of systemically important banks operating in the global financial markets (G-SIBs). These banks are particularly hazardous institutions because the collapse of one of them would have such large systemic repercussions to convince easily the policy authorities that they are too big and too interconnected to fail, and this would induce the use of taxpayers' money for their bailout. The list of global systemically important banks, first published by the Financial Stability Board in November 2011, includes 17 European banks and 8 US banks, showing that most G-SIBs are European.[3] The controllability of the European G-SIBs, and their potential bailout, is further jeopardised by the fact that the ratio between the turnover of these banks and the aggregate income of their countries of origin is much more unbalanced than that of the largest US banks. The failure of Lehman Brothers in September 2008 brought to everyone a vivid picture of the almost uncontrollable consequences of the bankruptcy of one of these banks. In addition, the strong and increasing potential for contagion between G-SIBs could easily create a situation in which the bailout of one of these banks would be insufficient to avoid the meltdown of the financial system.

In the years preceding the crisis, the European G-SIBs had already reached the status of major operators in the same financial markets in which also their major American counterparts were active, namely the repo market. When liquidity dried up in these markets, the European banks were gravely affected. In addition, the latter had in their balance sheets a great quantity of extremely risky derivatives whose value collapsed in consequence of the subprime crisis. The contagion influenced at the beginning mainly the British, German, and French banks undermining their economic and financial stability, spreading then to all the European banks.

In this chapter, it is enough to mention briefly the response of the German government to this delicate challenge. A first sign of the approaching storm was the crisis of the IKB, Dusseldorf-based lender that had to be bailed out in August 2007 after undergoing considerable losses in its US subprime investment. In 2008, the government had to rescue the Hypo Real Estate Bank when its mortgages to Eastern European clients, often conceded via Austrian banks, rapidly lost value, signalling a widespread problem in which most big German banks were involved. To calm the market, the German government announced the constitution of a €500 billion fund for the bailout of German banks. This did not prevent a new period of tension when at the end of 2009, several *Landesbanken*, regional development banks of crucial importance for their support to the real economy, got in trouble for their incautious investment in US toxic assets. In addition, when a collapse of exports caused a sharp decline of GDP in the fourth quarter of 2008, the government reacted by boosting family allowances and providing subsidies meant to encourage employers not to lay off workers.[4] This was sufficient for Germany to get out of the recession by resuming a moderate export-led growth since the second half of 2009. On the contrary, the USA and a few other European countries had to take much tougher measures to cope with the crisis. The US Treasury Secretary Paul Paulson, ex-CEO of the Goldman Sachs, reacted to the panic triggered by the bankruptcy of the Lehman Brothers launching an unprecedented bailout of the US financial system through the $700 billion Troubled Assets Relief Program (TARP).

The stimulus packages adopted in the USA and other countries in 2008 and 2009, including most European countries, were in contradiction with the policy prescriptions maintained by neoliberal economists in the preceding three decades. In their view, deficit spending policies to counteract a recession are nothing but a remnant of obsolete Keynesianism, while the bailout of any economic unit is believed to be inconsistent with competitive market principles. The pressure to justify these measures, then supported also by the financial and entrepreneurial world strongly hit by the crisis, produced a resurgence of ideas and policy prescriptions attributed to Keynes and Minsky in the hope that this alternative point of view could justify the heterodox measures that were then believed to be necessary. The instrumental nature of this apparent conversion of policy makers and their advisors became clear when, in the second half of 2009, the first wave of the crisis seemed to subside in consequence of the vital help provided by the stimulus packages adopted by the governments most hit by the crisis. The consensus on further stimulus measures rapidly petered out until their end was officially agreed at the Toronto meeting of the G20 in June 2010. This new orientation emerges even from the cautious final *G-20 Toronto Summit Declaration*: "sound fiscal finances are essential to sustain recovery, provide flexibility to respond to new shocks, ensure the capacity to meet the challenges of aging populations, and avoid leaving future generations with a legacy of deficits and debt" (Group of Twenty 2010).

The German Chancellor Angela Merkel strongly supported a rapid return to the orthodox point of view that rapidly became a compelling orientation for all the Eurozone. The USA, Japan, and most other countries abandoned the Keynesian language to justify their stimulus packages but continued a policy of support to aggregate demand allowing a prompt resumption of moderate but persistent rates of growth. On the contrary, since 2010 the European policy makers adopted severe austerity policies, determining a marked decoupling between the unfolding of the crisis in Europe and elsewhere. This abrupt change of policy strategy eventually triggered the second wave of the crisis centred in the Eurozone that we have suggested to call Eurocrisis.

The Eurozone repeated the same sort of mistake made by the US government in 1932, and then again in 1937, when it adopted, too soon, austerity measures that prolonged and deepened the economic depression. As the most eminent American economist of the time maintained, in 1932, "under President Hoover, recovery was apparently well started by the Federal Reserve open-market purchases, which revived prices and business from May to September 1932. The efforts were not kept up and recovery was skipped by various circumstances, including the political 'campaign of fear'"[5] (Fisher 1933, 347). Roosevelt, the new US President elected in 1933, was able to reverse the trend with his programme of extensive co-ordinated interventions in the economy that came to be known under the name of "New Deal". However, he was unable to resist beyond the middle of 1937 the pressure of conservative economists and representatives of market interests requiring the abandonment of the New Deal expansionary policies and the adoption of austerity measures to re-equilibrate the budget. Roosevelt capitulated and introduced cuts in federal spending, increases in taxes, and cuts in the New Deal job programmes, but this restrictive manoeuvre immediately interrupted the recovery plunging again the economy into a deep depression until the beginning of World War II.

This example shows clearly that the adoption of austerity measures before the complete end of a depression is a dangerous policy. A negative shock of this kind in a still very fragile economy impinges on fragile balance sheets and volatile expectations and is likely to rekindle the recession.

8.3   The Propagation of the Crisis in the Eurozone

As I suggested in the previous section, the triggering factor that produced the Eurocrisis was a specific dramatic change of macroeconomic policy. In 2010 the European policy makers, under the leadership of the German Chancellor, adopted severe austerity policies to recover the equilibrium of public accounts in the countries of the Union. This change of policy was particularly tough for the peripheral countries, in particular the PIIGS countries. The theory underlying this sharp change of policy was the theory of "expansionary austerity" maintained and advocated by a group of well-known economists very well connected with governments and mass media (I will discuss some of their ideas in Sect. 8.4).

What made the Eurocrisis particularly persistent and devastating was the mechanism of self-propagation due to peculiar institutional features and policy orientations. The process of propagation followed a sequence of stages often experienced by developing countries after the fall of the Bretton Woods system.[6] This sequence is reminiscent of the phases that characterise Minsky's theory of financial cycles as adapted to the developing countries by Taylor and Neftci.[7] In Minsky's approach the financial cycle may be affected by exogenous factors, but it is basically endogenous, in the sense that it would also occur in the absence of significant exogenous factors; the financial cycle is thus autonomously self-reproducing. On the contrary, the sequence observed in developing countries is triggered by a major change in macroeconomic policy and is thus set in motion by an exogenous cause.[8] A radical change of policy strategy typi-cally responds to some unwanted consequence of the previous macroeco-nomic policy (such as excessive inflation or devaluation of the currency exchange rate, instability of expectations, and low credibility of policy announcements), but the implementation of this change requires a major political decision that is by definition substantially exogenous. In addi-tion, the adaptation of Minsky's approach to an open economy requires the integration in the analysis of the international flows of productive and financial capital. This approach is typically called the "Taylor-Neftci cycle",[9] or "Frenkel cycle".[10] I will not use this terminology because my version of this approach aims to explain not a self-sustaining cycle, but only a sequence of stages triggered by a major exogenous factor. This cycle may be iterated in the same country only in consequence of a new major exogenous shock (such as a new change of policy strategy).

My version of this approach distinguishes four stages.[11] The first stage starts with the liberalisation of domestic and international capital move-ments, coupled with the rigid pegging of the currency exchange rate to a core currency believed to be more credible (the dollar in the case of developing countries; the euro in the case of the Eurozone). The periph-eral country obtains two short-term advantages: (i) a stabilisation of the exchange and inflation rates that may be particularly welcome in the case of previous hyperinflation and (ii) a reduction of the interest rate that relaxes the budget constraints and encourages an increase of public and private borrowing leading to more growth but also more debt. The core currency country has advantages that are more persistent and tend to cumulate: first, it avoids competition through currency devaluation from the peripheral countries pegging their currency to its own currency; sec-ond, it may lend at profitable rates to these peripheral countries avoiding exchange risk and implementing a valuable vent for the export of goods and services.

In the second stage, the increasing capital flows in the peripheral country signal improving economic parameters, interpreted as the conse-quence of more solid fundamentals. The markets are impressed not only by stable prices and a high rate of growth, but also by a diminishing debt to GDP ratio, since in this stage typically the GDP increases more than public debt. The process of growth in the peripheral country becomes thus in this phase a self-feeding bubble.

In the third stage, the illusion of improved fundamentals breaks down. The gap between the growth of prices and wages in the peripheral countries and that of the core country progressively increases because of structural reasons, feeding a cumulating foreign deficit that is the counterpart of the rising surplus in the core countries. In the peripheral country, the debt of the state and of the private sector breach the threshold of financial safety as perceived by the markets: it becomes then more difficult for the state and the most indebted private economic units to refinance their debt at reasonable interest rates.

This starts in the fourth stage a typical process of "debt-deflation" that has been first analysed by Fisher as the crucial cause of the Great Depression[12] and then subsumed by Minsky within his "financial instability hypothesis" as crucial stage of any serious financial crisis.[13] The private economic units fire sell their assets to reduce the excessive indebtedness, while a growing number of increasingly indebted units does the same; the "herd behaviour" of economic units precipitates downward the price of assets so that the ratio between debt and assets further worsens rather than improving. In the end, the private units are compelled to sell also their strategic assets determining the downsizing, often eventually the bankruptcy, of their economic activities, or their sale to more robust financial units often operating in the core countries. In the meantime, the state is also a victim of a similar vicious circle between debt and deflation. This is triggered and progressively fed by the reduction of fiscal income due to the crisis of the private sector and the sudden growth of expenditure due to the bailout of banks and other big units in severe financial distress. The ensuing increase of the spread between the rate of interest of the periphery and core countries worsens the deficit of the periphery country. The ensuing forced adoption of deflationary policies aimed to reduce the deficit and the debt/GDP ratio deepens the recession in the real economy reducing the fiscal income and increasing further the same ratio. The vicious circle between debt and deflation may go on for a long time until a change in policy thwarts it. The alternative would be appalling. In the words of Irving Fisher:

> a depression as that of 1929–33 (namely when the more the debtors pay the more they owe) tends to continue, going deeper, in a vicious spiral, for many years. There is then no tendency of the boat to stop tipping until it has capsized. Ultimately, of course, but only after almost universal bankruptcy, the indebtedness must cease to grow greater and begins to grow less … this is the so-called "natural" way out of the depression, via needless and cruel bankruptcy, unemployment, and starvation. (Fisher 1933, 346)

The four-stage qualitative model presented above fits well also in the case of the Eurocrisis. The first stage had a long gestation period spanning a couple of decades. The blueprint of the euro has been characterised from the very beginning (since the early 1980s) by the idea of coupling the liberalisation of financial markets within each Eurozone country and across them with the rigidity of exchange rates of member countries implied by the adoption of a common currency. Moreover, this plan was implemented in a particularly rigid way by imposing fixed rules of budgetary management without considering the possibility of an exit procedure. The dollar exchange standard system of the Bretton Woods period permitted more flexibility allowing, under certain conditions, for realignments in the exchange rates. As for the liberalisation of financial markets, in the early 1980s most European countries released the previous duty of their central banks of subscribing the unsold Treasury bonds at a price believed to be consistent with the sustainability of public debt. In Italy, for example, this move was often referred to with the melodramatic name of "divorce between the Treasury and the Central Bank". The growing independence of the central banks was justified by the alleged aim of assuring the independence of the latter from political pressures.[14] Analogously, commercial banks were released from their duty of assuring debt sustainability and financial stability.[15] The process of international liberalisation of capital movements started in the middle 1980s and was completed by the end of the decade contributing to the financial turbulences occurred in Europe in the early 1990s. This process prepared the terrain for the adoption of a more rigid currency agreement in 1987 (the so-called "credible European Monetary System"). The downside of this unprecedented rigidity became immediately visible in consequence of the financial turbulences of the early 1990s (culminating in the crisis of the pound in 1991 and that of the Italian lira in 1992).

When the Euro currency started in 1999, the system was ready to reap the short-term benefits typical of the second stage of the process. The peripheral countries could borrow capital at lower rates and felt encouraged to start what seemed to be then a virtuous process of growth leading to increasing private debt but also to shrinking public debt, at least in terms of debt/GDP ratio.[16] A case in point was that of Spain where the inflow of foreign capital increased from 3 % of GDP in 1999 to 10 % in 2007, while the public deficit diminished and became a surplus since 2005 because of the higher fiscal income accruing from a thriving private sector.

In the meantime, the behaviour of the German economy happened to be specular to that of peripheral countries. The private sector improved progressively its net position from a deficit of 2 % in the year 2000 to a surplus of 8 % in 2004, profiting from the increase in exports towards the peripheral countries and from an expansionary policy pursued by the government, which did not hesitate to breach the limit of 3 % from 2001 to 2006. At the same time, however, ad hoc structural reforms aimed to repress internal demand and reduce real wages according to a neomercantilist philosophy. The reforms designed in 2002 by the committee chaired by Peter Hartz, then director of personnel of the Volkswagen, and consistently implemented in the following years, succeeded in realising a severe internal devaluation to boost export-led growth. The most controversial measure of the "Hartz reforms" was the introduction of the so-called mini-jobs, precarious jobs paid as little as 400 euros per month and exempt from taxation, reducing unit labour costs for the private industry through the equivalent of a hidden subsidy. More than seven million German workers, or one in every five employees, held "mini-jobs" by September 2010. Because of these reforms, real wages fell 2.9 % between 2004 and 2011 while income inequality increased in Germany faster than in any other western European country. This enhanced the structural divergence between inflation rates of core and periphery in the Eurozone, sowing the seeds of the Eurocrisis.

The analysis summarised above shows that the third phase of the model had already started when the sudden contagion from the US subprime crisis triggered the fourth stage. In consequence of the sharply divergent dynamics of labour cost per unit of product, the peripheral countries accumulated growing deficits in foreign current accounts, while Germany accumulated growing surpluses. This structural vicious circle in the real economy was reflected by a financial vicious circle leading the peripheral countries to increase their foreign debt to finance the current deficits, while Germany increased its foreign financial surplus. The shocks of the US subprime financial crisis hit the Eurozone in this condition of growing imbalances between the core and peripheral countries triggering a deep European recession.

8.4   The Conventional Explanation

As is well known, the official explanation of the particular gravity and persistence of the Eurocrisis focuses on the allegedly excessive sovereign debt of the southern countries within the Eurozone (Portugal, Italy, Greece, and Spain). To this group of nations, often also Ireland has been added suggesting the slightly less explicitly derogatory acronym of "PIIGS" countries often used by mass media.[17] This explanation is based on four main arguments.

The first argument maintains that PIIGS countries have been particularly influenced by unsustainable Keynesian policies seeking an unreachable goal of full employment and building an overgenerous welfare state. The second argument contends that the same countries are characterised by too rigid markets of labour due to excessive guaranties obtained, and parochially managed, by powerful trade unions. The third argument maintains that a corrupt class of politicians inflates for its own advantage the excessive share of public expenditure. The forth argument maintains that the high and growing sovereign debt of these countries is related to their profligacy and excessive propensity for leisure.

Similar arguments have been put forward since long by economists, mass media, and policy makers to explain what was believed to be the ultimate cause of the so-called "eurosclerosis", the chronic illness of Europe determining a lower growth rate and a higher unemployment rate than those of more market-friendly capitalistic countries.[18] This neologism caught on as a vivid reference to the economic stagnation that in this view resulted from the alleged overregulation of markets and the over-generous social benefits policies. It was easy to resume these arguments and adapt them to the Eurocrisis started in 2010. For the same reason, the public opinion, swayed since long by a formidable mechanism aimed to manufacturing consent on these assertions,[19] found difficult to understand the shortcomings of this explanation and the existence of more plausible alternative explanations. While these arguments may contain a grain of truth, none of them—nor their combination—seems to stand up in the light of a more accurate appraisal of the empirical evidence.

A cursory examination of the official data released by the IMF immediately falsifies the general link between Keynesian policies and the growing sovereign debt of PIIGS countries. The average debt ratio of the G7 countries progressively diminished from about 70 % after World War II when Keynesian policies started to be adopted in the early 1950s to about 40 % in the middle of the 1970s when Keynesian policies started to be forsaken. In the following period, dominated by neoliberal policies inspired by new classical macroeconomics, the average debt ratio grew continuously, accelerating further in consequence of the Great Recession, and reaching again the value of about 120 % (see retro Fig. 5.1).

The G20 countries followed a similar, although less pronounced, qualitative pattern (ibid.).

As for the second argument, the empirical evidence shows that, after decades of reforms meant to make more flexible the market of labour, the index of labour market rigidity in PIIGS countries is comparable to that of most other European countries, including Germany. Since this argument relates to the rigidity of labour markets mainly to the allegedly excessive employment protection conceded by regular contracts, we may examine the OECD index of the strictness of employment protection for regular contracts. We see, for example, that in the year 2013 the Index of Employment Protection Legislation for permanent workers has the following value in PIIGS countries: Ireland 2.1, Spain 2.3, Greece 2.4, Portugal 2.7, Italy 2.8.[20] None of these countries has a value of the index that exceeds the value for Germany: 3.0. This is no doubt a partial and questionable indicator but suggests that a serious comparison between the market of labour flexibility of PIIGS countries and other countries (such as Germany) does not necessarily confirm a significant excess of rigidity of PIIGS countries in all its dimensions.

The third argument fails to demonstrate that the level reached by corruption in the Mediterranean countries is significantly different from that of most other countries, including Germany. As for the latter, significant examples are the bribery of ThyssenKrupp in Greece and the 400 billion of euros black funds of Siemens for complacent politicians.[21] The recent fraud of Volkswagen on CO_2 emissions confirms this assertion. In addition, the cross-country statistical correlation between corruption and growth rate does not show a clear pattern.[22] This is not to deny that we have to fight corruption by all means, and that a lower degree of corruption is likely to contribute in the long run to improve the sustainability of development.[23] However, there is no evidence that corruption has been a major cause of the excessive sovereign debt of the PIIGS countries since 2010.

Finally, the fourth argument does not take into account the statistics that show that Mediterranean workers (particularly in Greece) work in the average longer hours than non-Mediterranean workers.[24]

Summing up, the standard explanation of the Eurocrisis relies upon arguments that do not find support in the empirical evidence. Unfortunately, the policies pursued in the Eurozone after 2010 were heavily influenced by this unfounded interpretation of the Eurocrisis and contributed to its persistence (see Sect. 8.6).

8.5 An Alternative Explanation

According to an alternative point of view that is gathering a growing consensus, we cannot understand the Eurocrisis without starting the analysis from the faulty design of the euro and its biased and short-sighted implementation that has further worsened its performance as a common currency of the Eurozone countries.

As the Optimal Currency Area (henceforth OCA) theory has maintained since long, the benefits of a monetary union may exceed its costs only under precise conditions that are definitely not met in the Eurozone.[25]

The expected economic benefits from a monetary union mainly rely on the reduction of transaction costs, and related risks, implied by the use of the same currency. These advantages are quite visible to everyone, even simple tourists, but their quantification leads to surprisingly limited estimates. According to a study sponsored by the European Commission, the aggregate savings in transaction costs would not exceed the one-off 0.4 % of European GDP.[26] On the contrary, the disadvantages may be huge and persistent as many historical episodes have shown. The rigidity introduced by fixed exchange rates may easily sustain cumulative disequilibrium processes with devastating effects for wide areas of society. These costs may be minimised in particular by (a) labour and capital mobility across the region; (b) prices and wages flexibility; (c) actual convergence in inflation and productivity rates; (d) sufficient productive diversification; and (e) effective mechanisms of risk sharing such as fiscal transfers.

Mundell emphasised in particular the crucial importance of the first point.[27] In the Eurozone, the mobility of capital is fully liberalised while, on the contrary, the mobility of labour is still very limited because of significant linguistic, cultural, and institutional differences. This asymmetry brings about a similar power asymmetry between capitalists and workers that underlies the increasing income inequality and precariousness of labour. The flexibility of wages is limited in Europe, as elsewhere, for well-known historical and institutional reasons, while productivity growth is significantly different in European countries also for technological reasons. This is why the most coherent liberal economists suggested since long that the flexibility of currency exchange rates should be allowed to re-equilibrate the structural competitiveness gaps.[28] A mechanism of re-equilibration is necessary not only to absorb asymmetric shocks in the best possible way but also to compensate cumulative disequilibrium processes rooted in persistent structural differences between countries leading to a different trend of inflation and productivity rates.[29]

Kenen emphasised the importance that the different countries of a monetary union retain a sufficient productive diversification to withstand shocks affecting particular sectors.[30] The trouble is that, by reducing transaction costs, a monetary union tends to enhance the productive specialisation of member countries diminishing their resilience to shocks.[31] In the real world, nothing may prevent disequilibria to appear and trigger damaging cumulative processes. This requires an agreement between member countries on a mechanism for transferring funds and resources in favour of the countries or regions in difficulty. Regional disequilibria, however, are often linked to persistent structural factors; so that, differently from the mechanism of risk sharing that is typical of commercial insurance, in a monetary union, the net flows of funds tend to go for a long time in the same direction. Under these circumstances, a persistent transfer of funds from surplus countries to deficit countries would clash with the myopic self-interested attitude that is currently widespread in economics and politics, in the Eurozone not less than elsewhere. A more solidaristic policy strategy is likely to materialise only if the hegemonic power in the area under scrutiny is sufficiently far-sighted to act in the interest of all members of the monetary union. Kindleberger has convincingly argued this condition and observed that all the most severe financial crises developed in the absence of a benevolent hegemon.[32] His insights have been later confirmed and further developed by a vast interdisciplinary literature on "hegemonic stability theory".[33]

The fact that European countries do not comply with the OCA conditions has been emphasised since long by many qualified economists even before the full-fledged implementation of the common currency.[34] All of them advocated the completion of a process of structural and institutional convergence before trying to introduce a common currency. Some researchers, however, found in the empirical evidence some alleged support to the thesis that the conditions for a sustainable OCA are, at least in part, endogenous. If confirmed by the empirical evidence, this observation could give some support to a voluntarist approach to the construction of Europe such as that underlying the euro blueprint. In particular, Frankel and Rose claimed that more integration between a set of countries could lead to more intense trade among them bringing about a closer synchronisation of their business cycles.[35] In the Eurozone, however, contrary to the expectation of these and other researchers,[36] the growth of internal trade since 1999 has been limited (no more than 9 % in the first years, according to a study of Baldwin)[37] and asymmetrical: a significant increase of imports from Germany has been accompanied by stagnating exports to Germany. In any case, this argument is weak: synchronisation of business cycles may be a requisite for a common countercyclical policy in a unified currency area, if there was the willingness to adopt one, but would not affect by itself the structural problems that could even deteriorate because of persisting asymmetric trade. A case in point is the structural gap between South and North of Italy: the de-industrialisation of South was triggered by the monetary and political unification of 1861 and persisted unabated notwithstanding a continuous transfer of public resources for one and a half century. The business cycle was synchronised within Italy long ago but the structural problems did not improve.

Giavazzi and Pagano argued that, by pegging the exchange rate to a stable core currency, policy makers in the periphery of the union acquire the necessary credibility to pursue the necessary deflationary policies.[38] The trouble with this argument is that credible deflationary policies may be unavoidable under extreme conditions (a case in point could be the link to the dollar introduced in 1991 by Argentina to fight hyperinflation), but is counterproductive in different circumstances (e.g. in Argentina itself, after having conquered hyperinflation in the late 1990s, or in the European countries to counteract excessive public debt after 2010).

A third argument for the endogeneity of OCA conditions does not rely on economics but on the primacy of politics over economics. This noble vision was that of the founding fathers of Europeanism, such as Altiero Spinelli, Robert Schuman, and Jean Monnet. In this view, Europe must be unified to end an era of conflicts culminated in two devastating world wars and to release the great potential of synergies between the initiatives of European citizens living in different countries. Therefore, we should never accept that short-term economic worries slow down the implementation of this grand political project.

Whatever we may think of this generous but voluntarist approach, this perspective has not been the one pursued by the euro blueprint. On the contrary, the cart of monetary economics has been put before the horse of structural economics and politics itself. This reverse order was argued to be consistent with a pragmatic version of the argument: the shortcomings of monetary unification will force reluctant decision makers to design the necessary political institutions and persuade public opinion to accept them. Both versions of the argument did not find empirical support so far. The shortcomings of the Euro and its management have greatly increased the tensions and mistrust between European citizens living in different countries. This is the case of the citizens of PIIGS countries who felt that the appalling consequences of austerity policies were the outgrowth of priorities strongly biased in favour of the core countries of the monetary union, in particular of their banks. Also in would-be core countries such as France, the mistrust in the current design of the Euro has considerably weakened the consensus not only for the currency union but also for the EU itself. This result is exactly the opposite of that hoped by the advocates of the voluntarist strategy. In most European countries, including the core countries themselves, the belief that the official arguments in favour of the common currency conceal the underlying motivations is spreading.[39]

The process of construction of the currency union started in the late 1970s in tune with the contemporaneous neoliberal U-turn of the policy strategy. With hindsight, it is difficult to reject the suspicion that the ultimate, though undeclared, objective of the European elites was that of dismantling the peculiarities of European capitalism: the welfare state, the social security approach to labour markets and industrial relations, the full employment Keynesian policies, strict financial regulation and supervision, and the cap to the profit share deriving from the power of trade unions. Actually, from the very beginning, the driving directives of the designed monetary union were the complete removal of financial repression and the establishment of free capital movement coupled with the increasing flexibility of labour markets and industrial relations. These directives started to be implemented since the late 1970s and immediately produced an inversion of the income distribution trend that started to become more unequal after many decades of progressive equalisation. The rigidity of the exchange rates allowed Germany to avoid currency revaluations that would have capped trade surpluses in contrast to the neomercantilist beliefs of its ruling class. The currency exchange rate rigidity forced the structurally weaker countries to substitute currency devaluations with so-called internal devaluations.[40] The crucial difference is that all citizens bear the costs of currency devaluation, while mainly wage earners bear the costs of an internal devaluation. This readjustment mechanism, adopted to some extent also by the European core countries and forced upon the periphery countries, further strengthened the tendency towards increasing inequality in the distribution of income. The process of construction of the monetary union played in the reluctant countries of the Eurozone the same role of the shock therapy played by Reaganism in the USA and Thatcherism in the UK since the early1980s.[41]

8.6   Policy Implications

The policy strategy advocated in response to the Eurocrisis varies with the explanation and the approach adopted by the decision maker. As we have seen, the mainstream point of view lays the blame of the crisis mainly on the excessive public debt accumulated in the Eurozone, in particular in the PIIGS countries, and on their overregulated labour markets. In the light of the orthodox micro-founded supply economics underlying this view, there is no alternative to the reduction of public expenditure and the increase of taxation, what came to be called with moralistic over-tones an "austerity policy".[42] As is well known, this is the remedy that, since the early 2010, has been recommended to, indeed forced upon, the PIIGS countries by the institutions often called "troika" (European Commission, ECB, and IMF).

The critics immediately observed that this policy strategy would have inflicted devastating social damages to countries that were already suffering from a severe deficit of aggregate demand and high unemployment rates. In addition, the outcome of this policy strategy was predicted to entail a significant worsening of the debt/GDP ratio.[43] The mainstream point of view denied these implications maintaining that the advocated austerity policies would have been expansionary by reducing the crowding out of private investment on the part of unproductive, or in any case inefficient, public investment.[44] The critics observed that in a situation of severe recession, such as that affecting the Eurozone in recent years, private investment is constrained to stagnation not because it is crowded out by public expenditure but because the expectations are bleak. The rigid commitment of the Eurozone to austerity policy does not contribute to make them rosier but rather to darken them.[45] The trouble with the mainstream policy strategy is that the underlying models assume a supply-side view that clouds the crucial role that is played, at least in the short period, by aggregate demand. In their opinion, the positive effects of an increase in public expenditure would be at best ephemeral because the agents would immediately discount a future increase in taxation to cover the increased deficit and would save more to cope with the future occurrences.[46] This argument presupposes that the economic agents entertain rational expectations, an assumption hardly consistent with the widespread and severe market failures underlying the crisis.

Many economists and most mass media and policy makers, however, often tried to demolish any argument in favour of an increase in public expenditure by equating the latter with unproductive expenditure, if not with the growing corruption of politicians. They seemed to ignore that public expenditure immediately translates in private income and that the interaction between expenditure and income is crucial in the generation of GDP, the more so the higher the unemployment rate as confirmed by the recent empirical evidence. This basic truth had been already clearly spelled out by the expenditure multiplier of Kahn and Keynes and its underlying theory. Mainstream economists maintained, however, that the multiplier has a value that cannot exceed the unity and is thus unable to mobilise private expenditure.[47] Most econometric studies found since long, and again in recent times, that the public expenditure multiplier has a value significantly exceeding unity, the more so the higher the unemployment rate.[48] This is now admitted also by many mainstream economists but the longer period effects are still quite controversial. Many fear that the excess liquidity injected into the system by the central bank and the Treasury will have eventually serious inflationary effects. Critics emphasising the endogeneity of money creation reject this argument: an excess of liquidity is endogenously produced by banks in a booming economy, but it may be thwarted by restrictive monetary policies as soon as this becomes necessary.

Not all the critics of austerity policy believe that the abandonment of this policy and the adoption of an expansionary stance would be a sufficient move to stop the Eurocrisis. In particular, many researchers rightly observe that the adoption of an expansionary policy by a single country would only deteriorate the trade deficit believed to be the ultimate cause of the crisis.[49]

A more expansionary policy should be adopted by all the countries experiencing a trade surplus starting by Germany itself. This principle has been timidly reasserted also by the European Commission but its actual implementation did not materialise, as it would be in sharp contrast with the neomercantilist policy since long pursued by Germany, a policy that aims to boost exports by relying on a continuous internal devaluation of labour costs.[50]

8.7   Concluding Remarks

The most compelling argument in favour of free markets is that they allow decentralised decisions guaranteeing personal freedom and economic efficiency. The paradox of the Eurocrisis is that, in the name of free market doctrines, economic policy decisions have been centralised and ossified in fixed rules (such as those of the "fiscal compact"),[51] while their application has been delegated to a small number of technocrats (such as those of the "troika") designated by governments and accountable to them in an opaque way. In consequence of the policy strategy pursued by the Eurocrats, the freedom of most European citizens has been significantly limited while its political expression, democracy, has been largely suspended. The usual excuse for the appalling policy-induced consequences of the Eurocrisis advanced by the supporters of the austerity policies is a version of the classical TINA argument.[52] The specific cause of the Eurocrisis is seen in the excessive sovereign debt of PIIGS countries ascribed to structural reasons (too rigid labour markets) and policy mistakes (expansionary policies and indulgent welfare provisions inconsistent with rigid markets). Based on this explanation, the policy prescriptions are both obvious and consistent with the TINA argument: the governments of the Eurozone have to adopt severe austerity policies to reduce public debt coupled with structural reforms meant to make labour markets more flexible.

In this chapter, I have argued that the official explanation of the crisis is unfounded. The Eurocrisis was triggered by a radical change in the European macroeconomic policy occurred in 2010 that determined the decoupling of the trend of macroeconomic fundamentals of Europe from those of the USA and Japan.

Moreover, what explains the dire peculiarities of the propagation process in the Eurozone is the perverse interaction between the deep structural discrepancies of member countries that reflect themselves in their different degrees of competitiveness within an ill-conceived monetary union repressing the market forces that could re-equilibrate foreign accounts. The Eurocrisis does not depend on the rigidity of the labour markets that might have reduced instead the negative effects of the crisis, but on the unprecedented rigidity imposed upon the foreign constraints of member countries.

The Euro treaties did not provide a mechanism for the recycling of surpluses in favour of the deficit countries and—at the same time—did not contemplate any form of realignment or suspension of the rules. Finally, the management of the crisis resented the absence of a benevolent hegemon capable of mediating between conflicting interests rather than supporting mainly the interests of creditors and financial institutions. In such a situation, the single countries could not deviate from the austerity measures imposed by the troika without compromising the sustainability of budgetary rules. On the other hand, a general change of policy strategy within the Eurozone would require a radical reform of the treaties underlying the Euro Monetary Union and the abandonment of deeply entrenched attitudes of the most powerful member states such as the neomercantilist view of Germany. The inescapable conclusion descending from the preceding analysis is that the current design of the Euro and its management rules are unsustainable.

Notes

1. See Lo (2012), and the comments by Blyth (2013, 22).
2. Starting from an index 100 in the fourth quarter of 2007, the three indexes of industrial production fall to a value of about 96 in the second quarter of 2009 turning upward in the following quarter and reaching a value of about 98 in the first quarter of 2011 [see in particular the Exhibit 8 in Credit

Suisse (2013, 10)]. The gap between the European index and those of the USA and Japan, which had never exceeded 1 % before, progressively grows to 7 % as the USA and Japan indexes reach the value of 102 while Europe falls to the value of 95, lower than the preceding minimum, by the first quarter of 2013 (ibid.).

3. See also the Financial Stability Board (2014), and Blyth (2013, 49).
4. Blyth (2013, 54).
5. Hoover had cut public expenditure already in the early 1931 declaring, on 5 May 1931, that a balanced federal budget "was the most essential factor to economic recovery …" When in 1932 the re-election of Hoover as US president started to be questioned by a swing of the electorate, his supporters resorted to a campaign of fear foretelling that, if Franklin Delano Roosevelt were elected to the Presidency, catastrophic events would have occurred. They argued in particular that the interventionist policies against the crisis that Roosevelt would implement would have led to the disruption of free markets. Roosevelt reacted to this campaign of fear arguing that "as a last resort, the President, and the ex-President advance an attempt to throw political and economic tear-gas bombs among the people of the country. Now, my friends, you all know what tear gas is. It is one of the new inventions by which a few people can control many people. A few do it by blinding the eyes of the many, by causing tears to flow; and in the midst of the confusion that thus results, a determined minority seeks to accomplish its selfish purposes" (Roosevelt 1932). Similar campaigns of fear have been directed during the Eurocrisis against any proposal deviating from the orthodox point of view of austerity policies.
6. See in particular Frenkel and Rapetti (2009), and Bagnai (2012).
7. See Minsky (1982 and 1986), Taylor (1998), and Neftci (1998).
8. This is not to deny that also a developing country may be characterised by an endogenous financial cycle and that this is likely to have Minskyan features. However, the transition to a sequence characterised by a Minsky meltdown is typically set in motion by a major exogenous factor.
9. Taylor (1998).
10. Bagnai (2013).
11. Frenkel and Repetti (2009), and Bagnai (2013) distinguish seven stages of a self-sustaining cycle. We follow here the four-stage approach of Minsky's financial cycle as reconstructed in Vercelli (2011a), and Sordi and Vercelli (2012). The boundary between third and fourth stage may be defined as "Minsky moment" while the fourth stage may be defined as "Minsky process" (ibid.). In this application, however, the sequence of these four stages does not imply the endogenous self-reproduction of the cycle.

12. Fisher (1933).
13. Minsky (1982 and 1986).
14. This implies also an increased independence of the democratic control of citizens, a questionable consequence that has been often neglected or underplayed.
15. In Italy, for example, the so-called "portfolio constraint" and "maximum threshold of loans" were abolished in 1983.
16. See for example Lapavitsas et al. (2012).
17. Ireland showed in 2010 fundamentals similar to those of the Mediterranean countries although their causes and subsequent evolution were quite different. To these countries also France could be added not only because it has a Mediterranean border but also because its fundamentals have significant analogies with those of other Mediterranean countries. The analysis of similarities and differences between the periphery countries of the Eurozone is beyond the scope of this chapter.
18. See for example Giersch (1985).
19. Herman and Chomsky (1988).
20. OECD (2013b).
21. Bagnai (2012, 259).
22. Bagnai (2014, Fig. 10).
23. Rothstein and Uslaner (2005).
24. OECD (2013a).
25. As is well known, the literature on the Optimal Currency Area originated from an essay of Mundell (1961).
26. Emerson (1990).
27. Mundell (1961).
28. See for example Friedman (1953).
29. Fleming (1971).
30. Kenen (1969).
31. Krugman (1993).
32. Kindleberger (1973 and 1978).
33. See for example Eichengreen (1987).
34. Among others: Meade (1957), Kaldor (1971), Thirlwall (1991), Godley (1992), Eichengreen (1993), Dornbusch (1996), Salvatore (1997), Krugman (1998), and Parguez (1999).
35. Frankel and Rose (1996).
36. See in particular Rose (2000 and 2001).
37. Baldwin (2006).
38. Giavazzi and Pagano (1988). On the theory of "expansionary austerity", see also Alesina and Ardagna (1998), and Alesina and Perotti (1995).

39. Bagnai (2012 and 2014) has brought significant evidence of Machiavellian motivations underlying the process of monetary unification in Europe since the early 1980s by reporting explicit declarations in this sense in speeches and writings of important protagonists of the process.
40. As is well known, the so-called "internal devaluation" designates a policy strategy aiming to reduce real wages sufficiently to recover the country's competitiveness.
41. See for example Klein (2007). Mundell himself has expressed a version of this point of view, as reported by Palast (see Palast 2012).
42. Blyth (2013).
43. See for example Bagnai (2012), Krugman (2012), and Pollin (2010).
44. See Alesina and Tabellini (1990), and Giavazzi and Pagano (1990).
45. See for example Krugman (2012).
46. Influential mainstream economists such as Barro (1989) have recently revived this argument often called "Ricardian equivalence theorem."
47. Barro and Redlick (2011).
48. See Pollin (2010) and the literature there surveyed.
49. See in particular Bagnai (2012 and 2014).
50. European Commission (2012).
51. As is well known, the Fiscal Compact (i.e. the Treaty on Stability, Coordination and Governance in the Economic, and Monetary Union) is an intergovernmental treaty signed on 2 March 2012 by most member states of the EU. The member states bound by the fiscal provisions of the treaty will face annual fines up to 0.1 % of GDP, if they fail to enact a self-correcting mechanism that guarantees that their national budget is in balance or surplus under the treaty's definition and their debt-to-GDP ratio does not exceed 60.0 % or converges rapidly to this reference level.
52. See Sect. 1.4.

Bibliography

Alesina, Alberto, and Silvia Ardagna. 1998. Tales of Fiscal Adjustment. *Economic Policy* 13(27): 489–545.

Alesina, Alberto, and Roberto Perotti. 1995. Fiscal Expansions and Fiscal Adjustments in OECD Countries. *NBER Working paper 5214*, Cambridge, MA.

Alesina, Alberto, and Guido Tabellini. 1990. A Positive Theory of Fiscal Deficits and Government Debt. *Review of Economic Studies* 57: 403–414.

Bagnai, Alberto. 2012. *Il Tramonto dell'Euro. Come e perché la fine della moneta unica salverebbe democrazia e benessere in Europa*. Reggio Emilia: Imprimatur editore.

———. 2013. Unhappy families Are All Alike: Minskyan Cycles, Kaldorian Growth, and the Eurozone Peripheral Crises. In *Post-Keynesian Views of the Crisis and its Remedies*, eds. Óscar Dejuán, Eladio Febrero Paños, and Jorge Uxo Gonzalez. Abingdon and New York: Routledge.

———. 2014. *L'Italia può farcela. Equità, flessibilità, democrazia. Strategie per vivere nella globalizzazione*. Milano: Il Saggiatore.

Baldwin, Richard. 2006. The Euro's Trade Effects. Working Paper 594, European Central Bank. https://www.ecb.europa.eu/pub/pdf/scpwps/ecbwp594.pdf. Retrieved 6 April 2016.

Barro, Robert J. 1989. The Ricardian Approach to Budget Deficits. *The Journal of Economic Perspectives* 3(2): 37–54.

Barro, Robert J., and Carles J. Redlick. 2011. Macroeconomic Effects of Government Purchases and Taxes. *Quarterly Journal of Economics* 126(1): 51–102.

Blyth, Mark. 2013. *Austerity. The History of a Dangerous Idea*. Oxford: Oxford University Press.

Credit Suisse. 2013. 2014 Global Outlook. Fixed Income and Economics Research. http://www.credit-suisse.com/researchandanalytics. Retrieved 4 February 2016.

Dornbusch, Rudiger. 1996. Euro Fantasies. *Foreign Affairs* 75(5): 110–124.

Eichengreen, Barry. 1987. Hegemonic Stability Theories of the International Monetary System. In *Can Nations Agree? Issues in International Economic Cooperation*, eds. Richard Cooper, Barry Eichengreen, Gerald Holtham, Robert Putnam and Randall Henning, The Brookings Institution: 255–298.

———. 1993. European Monetary Unification. *Journal of Economic Literature* 31: 1321–1357.

Emerson, Michael. 1990. One Market, One Money. An Evaluation of the Potential Benefits and Costs of Forming an Economic and Monetary Union. *European Economy* 44: 1–347.

European Commission. 2012. Macroeconomic Imbalance Procedure. http://www.ec.europea.eu/econhttp://www.ec.europea.eu/economy_finance/economic_governance/macroeconoic_imbalance_procedure/index_en.htm. Retrieved 5 April 2016.

Financial Stability Board. 2014. 2014 Update of Group of Global Systemically Important Banks (G-SIBs). Financial Stability Board. 6 November 2014. http://www.financialstabilityboard.org/wp-content/uploads/r_141106b.pdf

Fisher, Irving. 1933. The Debt-Deflation Theory of the Great Depression. *Econometrica* 1: 337–357.

Fleming, Marcus J. 1971. On Exchange Rate Unification. *Economic Journal* 81: 467–488.

Frankel, Jeffrey A., and Andrew K. Rose. 1996. The Endogeneity of the Optimal Currency Area Criteria, *NBER Working Paper*, 5700.

Frenkel, Roberto, and Martin Rapetti. 2009. A Developing Country View of the Current Global Crisis: What Should Not Be Forgotten and What Should Be Done. *Cambridge Journal of Economics* 33: 685–702.

Friedman, Milton. 1953. The Case for Flexible Exchange Rates. In *Essays in Positive Economics*, ed. Milton Friedman, 157–203. Chicago: University of Chicago Press.

Giavazzi, Francesco, and Marco Pagano. 1988. The Advantage of Tying One's Hand: Ems Discipline and Central Bank Credibility. *European Economic Review* 32: 1055–1082.

———. 1990. Can Severe Fiscal Contractions Be Expansionary? Tales of two Small European Countries. In *NBER Macroeconomics Annual*, Cambridge, MA:75–122.

Giersch, Herbert. 1985. *Eurosclerosis*. Kieler Diskussionsbeiträge, No. 112.

Godley, Wynne. 1992. Maastricht and all that. *London Review of Books* 14(19): 3–4.

Group of Twenty. 2010. The G-20 Toronto Summit Declaration. http://epe. lac-bac.gc.ca/100/206/301/faitc-aecic/g20/2013-08-14/summit-sommet/2010/toronto-declaration-toronto1b0e.html?lang=eng. Retrieved 23 October 2015.

Herman, Edward S., and Noam Chomsky. 1988. *The Political Economy of the Mass Media*. New York: Pantheon Books.

Kaldor, Nicholas. 1971. The Dynamic Effects of the Common Market. In *The new statesman*, 12 March.

Kenen, Peter B. 1969. The Theory of Optimum Currency Areas: An Eclectic View. In *Monetary Problems of the International Economy*, eds. Robert A. Mundell, and Alexander K. Swoboda, 41–60. Chicago: Chicago University Press.

Kindleberger, Charles P. 1973. *The World in Depression, 1929–1939*. Berkeley: University of California Press.

Kindleberger, Charles P 1978. *Manias, Panics, and Crashes: A History of Financial Crises*, New York: Basic Books 1996.

Klein, Naomi. 2007. *The Shock Doctrine. The Rise of Disaster Capitalism*. Knopf Canada: Toronto.

Krugman, Paul. 1993. Target Zones and Exchange Rate Dynamics. *Quarterly Journal of Economics* 106: 669–682.

———. 1998. The Euro: Beware of What You Wish for. web.mit.edu/Krugman/www/euronote.html.

———. 2012. *End this depression now!* New York: W. W. Norton and Co.

Lapavitsas, Costas, et al. 2012. *Crisis in the Eurozone*. London: Verso.

Lo, Andrew W. 2012. Reading about the Financial Crisis: A Twenty-One-Book Review. *Journal of Economic Literature* 50(1): 151–178.

Meade, James E. 1957. The Balance-of-Payment Problems of a European Free-Trade Area. *The Economic Journal* 67: 379–396.

Minsky, Hyman P. 1982. *Can "It" Happen Again? Essays on Instability and Finance.* Armonk, NY: Sharpe.

Minsky, Hyman P 1986. *Stabilizing an Unstable Economy.* New Haven and London: Yale University Press.

Mundell, Robert. 1961. Theory of Optimum Currency Areas. *American Economic Review* 51: 657–665.

Neftci, Salih N. 1998. *FX Short Positions, Balance Sheets, and Financial Turbulence: An Interpretation of the Asian Financial Crisis.* New York: Centre for Economic Policy Analysis, New School for Social Research.

OECD. 2013a. Average Annual Working Time. *Employment and Labour Markets: Key Tables from OECD*, No. 8.

OECD. 2013b. Indicators of Employment Protection. http://www.oecd.org/employment/emp/oecdindicatorsofemploymentprotection.htm

Palast, Greg. 2012. Robert Mundell, Evil Genius of the Euro. In *The Guardian*, 26 June 2012.

Parguez, Alain. 1999. The Expected Failure of the European and Monetary Union: A False Money against the Real Economy. *Eastern Economic Journal* 25: 63–76.

Pollin, Robert. 2010. Austerity is Not a Solution: Why the Deficit Hawks Are Wrong. *Challenge* 53(6): 6–36.

Roosevelt, Franklin D. 1932. Campaign Address on the Eight Great Credit Groups of the Nation at St.Louis, Missouri, (21 October). American Presidency Project: Papers of Franklin Roosevelt. http://www.presidency.ucsb.edu/franklin_roosevelt.php. Retrieved 05 February 2016.

Rose, Andrew K. 2000. One Money, One Market: The Effects of Common Currencies on Trade. *Economic Policy* 30: 9–45.

Rose, Andrew K 2001. Currency Unions and Trade: The Effect Is Large. *Economic Policy* 33: 449–461.

Rothstein, Bo, and Eric M. Uslaner. 2005. All for all: Equality, Corruption, and Social Trust. *World Politics* 58(1): 41–72.

Salvatore, Dominick. 1997. The Common Unresolved Problems within Ems and the Emu. *American Economic Review* 87(2): 224–226.

Sordi, Serena, and Alessandro Vercelli. 2012. Heterogeneous Expectations and Strong Uncertainty in a Minskyan Model of Financial Fluctuations. *Journal of Economic Behaviour and Organization* 83(3): 558–569.

Taylor, Lance. 1998. Capital Market Crises: Liberalisation, Fixed Exchange Rates and Market-Driven Destabilization. *Cambridge Journal of Economics* 22: 663–676.

Thirlwall, Tony. 1991. EMU Is No Cure for Problems with the Balance of Payment. In *Financial Times*, 9 October.

Vercelli, Alessandro. 2011a. A Perspective on Minsky Moments: Revisiting the Core of the Financial Instability Hypothesis. *Review of Political Economy* 23(1): 49–67.

9

Concluding Remarks

9.1 Introduction

At the end of a long and demanding itinerary that tried to sketch the co-evolution of economic thought, economic policy, and economic history since the late 1970s, I just want to add a few succinct remarks on the policy implications of the interpretive narrative suggested in this book. As its underlying vision is radically alternative to that diffused by mass media, allegedly based on mainstream macroeconomics, also its policy implications are inevitably unconventional. I have already discussed some of them, particularly in Chap. 5 (unsustainability of the neoliberal policy strategy), Chap. 6 (reform of finance), Chap. 7 (reform of environmental policy), and Chap. 8 (unsustainability of the Euro institutional design). In this chapter, I intend to connect these and a few other policy insights within a framework as consistent as possible. Of course, the purpose is not that of drafting a full-fledged policy blueprint, but only that of outlining a policy vision consistent with the narrative suggested in this book. Therefore, I will not enter into the operational details of the policy suggestions because this would be inappropriate. An interpretive vision may only support a policy vision, not a full-fledged

© The Editor(s) (if applicable) and The Author(s) 2017
A. Vercelli, *Crisis and Sustainability*,
DOI 10.1057/978-1-137-60069-1_9

policy blueprint. The latter would require much more comprehensive and in-depth ethical, political, and factual foundations.

The main leitmotiv of the alternative policy vision outlined in this book is that the current evolution of market economies inspired by the neoliberal doctrine is inconsistent with the requisites of sustainable development. Therefore, what we really need is an alternative policy vision that redirects the evolutionary process towards a sustainable direction. In other words, the diagnosis of the illness suggests the most appropriate therapy. This medical analogy suggests a convenient structure for this final chapter. The narrative of this book has described the origins and evolution of a grave pervasive disease affecting the economy, the society, the biosphere, and ultimately individuals themselves. Section 9.2 summarises the diagnosis of this disease and some implications for a better therapy. Section 9.3 briefly reconstructs its aetiology, namely its main causal factors. Section 9.4 comments on the shortcomings of the current approach to therapy and clarifies a few requisites for a better one. Section 9.5 summarises the implications of neoliberalism for sustainability. Section 9.6 discusses how to escape from the neoliberal trilemma in a sustainable direction.

9.2   Implications of a Diagnosis for a Better Therapy

In this section, I briefly summarise the diagnosis of the unsustainability disease analysed in this book from the point of view of the immediate implications for its therapy. From the critical analysis deployed in the preceding chapters, it is possible to draw a few constructive suggestions on the structural modifications required to reorient the process of development in a more sustainable direction.

First, policy makers should be concerned with social sustainability, struggling hard to reduce inequality and poverty. The concept of sustainable development as defined by the Brundtland Commission is rooted in a principle of equity applied to the intertemporal distribution of resources among successive generations. For the sake of ethical coherence, this principle must apply also within each generation.[1] In addition, an extensive corpus of empirical research demonstrated that less inequality correlates with more happiness and better health.[2] It is therefore important to support social sustainability through effective policies aiming to reduce inequality and poverty.[3] For example, progressivity of taxation— that has been greatly weakened if not reversed in the last decades—should be restored, keeping in mind that this principle has been advocated also by the founding fathers of liberalism (in particular Smith himself, Stuart Mill, and Marshall). Moreover, the empirical evidence did not confirm the neoliberal belief in the existence of a trickle-down mechanism that would propagate wealth from the richest people to all layers of society.[4] Therefore, the system of systematic transfer of wealth, inclusion rights, and social security that goes under the name of welfare state should not be dismantled but rather reconstructed in a more robust and sustainable way.

One could wonder whether equity, and thus the goal of a reduction of inequality and poverty, is an ethical goal that may jeopardise the efficiency of markets. I argued that, on the contrary, a market could be really competitive only if all the competitors have access to the relevant opportunities. Otherwise, the winners of the myriad of overlapping competitions that constitute a free market will not be the best competitors but rather those having the greatest power or wealth to begin with. Moreover, they will use the proceedings deriving from their success to further increase their market power and thus their relative advantage over the other competitors. In this case, the allocation of resources is not optimal and may improve through a more egalitarian distribution of resources. In a society strongly characterised by inequality and poverty, the competition within unfettered markets would resemble more the Darwinian competition than a fair market competition as dreamed by Adam Smith, Stuart Mill, and Marshall (see retro Chap. 2).

In addition, genuine competitive markets, as conceived by the founding fathers of liberalism, require a strict regulation that assures the continuous implementation of the "rule of law", the repression of monopolistic practices, conflicts of interest, frauds, and whatever behaviour that can alter the conditions of fair competition. Corporate social responsibility (CSR) itself cannot rely only on the self-regulation of enterprises, but must be enforced by the legal system establishing a synergic relation.[5] Social sustainability is a necessary condition of economic sustainability, even if we conceive economic sustainability in the reductive sense of steady growth of the GDP (see Chap. 1). This conclusion is much more crucial and compelling if one adopts a much broader definition of sustainable development such as that adopted in this book.

The adoption of better indexes of economic sustainability would further strengthen the conclusions reached in this book. As is well known, the GDP is a misleading index of well-being since it does not include quality and depletion of social and environmental capital while it includes many spurious items (such as defensive expenditures and military expenditure). The need for a new sustainability-based economic paradigm and new welfare measures emerges clearly from the observed gap between growth indicators and self-reported happiness of individuals.[6] Beyond a minimal threshold of per capita yearly income (about $10,000), well-being and health mainly depend on social and environmental capital.[7] We have thus to abandon the fetishism of GDP growth, adopting instead more comprehensive and reliable welfare indexes that may better capture the capacity of the economic system to sustain itself and the biosphere also in the long run.[8]

Unfortunately, according to most indicators, the consistency and quality of environmental capital rapidly deteriorated since World War II. The crucial problem is the ongoing rapid climate change originated mainly from the characteristics of the current energy system based on the use of fossil fuels. To avoid a further increase in the average temperature, greenhouse gases (GHGs) emissions should be rapidly reduced to less than one-eighth of its current value. Within the existing model of development, such a consistent reduction of GHGs emissions may materialise only through a significant reduction of the rate of per capita income growth. This requires a continuous massive support to environmental sustainability in all its multiple dimensions, giving special priority to accelerating the transition to renewable energy sources.[9] The climate may be stabilised only by accelerating the transition from the current model aimed to maximise GDP growth to a model of sustainable development based on a different energy system. This system should rely mainly on renewable energy sources and comply with the other social and environmental requisites of sustainability.

I have so far suggested a few structural changes that would implement social, economic, and environmental sustainability. However, none of the measures suggested above, nor analogous measures that we might suggest, would be thoroughly implemented without acting before, or at least contemporaneously, on the sustainability of the existing financial sector. As we have seen, the radical elimination of any constraint to cross-country flows of financial capital implemented since the early 1980s has promoted a process of financialisation that has deeply impaired sustainability in all its main dimensions. In particular, it has shifted out investment from the real sector to the financial sector and has much increased the short-termism of economic choices that reduces the weight of future benefits to very little. Sustainability requires a systematic policy strategy aiming to the repression of the negative externalities originated in finance. This requires strict regulation policies meant to reduce its vulnerability and moderate its excessive influence on the social and economic decisions.[10]

A necessary, though by no means sufficient, condition to converge towards a sustainable trajectory is an effective downsizing of finance as compared to the real economy. We may attain this objective only through a coordinated set of measures. The adoption of a financial transaction tax may reduce significantly speculation without affecting the flows of capital to support the real economy. In addition, we should abandon the idea of unrestrained universal banking in favour of a new effective compartmentalisation between investment and commercial banking. To do so we have to recover and update the basic principles underlying the Glass-Steagall Act (see Appendix 1).

Analogously, the activity of revision of balance sheets should be independent of rating responsibilities, as this could eliminate the conflicts of interests that greatly contributed to the recent financial turmoil. An apt compartmentalisation would contribute to the downsizing of big banks, in particular those having a turnover superior or comparable to the aggregate income of the states where they operate. In any case, policy authorities should fix a strict dimensional cap to avoid monopolistic and oligopolistic practices, manipulation of the market, excessive influence on governments and legislators, and regulatory capture. Not only should the regulation of financial markets become much more stringent, but also their supervision should become more effective extending its grip in particular in the field of OTC derivatives and shadow banking.

Policy authorities and supervisory agencies should enforce the transparency of all financial decisions to assure the informational efficiency of financial markets and the effectiveness of legal regulation and supervision. This implies a more adequate disclosure of off-balance-sheet operations and a more suitable regulation of shadow banking.[11] As for offshore centres, international cooperation should check and reverse their growing importance intervening with the maximum energy.[12]

These and other measures should aim to repress speculation and finance for its own sake (e.g. proprietary trading and purchase of own shares), conditioning finance to develop its contribution as essential support to the real economy and in particular to investment enhancing the sustainability of development.

9.3   Aetiology: A Restricted View of Liberty and Democracy

The causal process underlying the narrative summarised in the preceding section is very complex. As I emphasised in Chap. 1, a serious analysis of the neoliberal disease should avoid causal reductionism that focuses on a single causal factor or on a short list of them. In addition, we should take into account that the concrete mechanisms connecting causes with effects evolved significantly through time in the period analysed in this book. What I aim to do in this section is simply to add a few further reflections on some relatively constant causal patterns underlying the pathology under investigation.

I see a crucial source of the causal process underlying the unsustainability of the neoliberal development trajectory in the destabilising interaction between history of facts and history of ideas started in the 1970s and progressively strengthened in the following decades.[13] I can start the reconstruction of the neoliberal vicious circle by observing that the unprecedented period of steady growth experienced by developed countries in the 1950s and 1960s, and to some extent still in the 1970s, had progressively increased the wealth and power of industry and finance to an unprecedented level. In this new environment, thriving banks felt strong enough to start a "liberation struggle" from the constraints and controls that had characterised the Bretton Woods period. They found precious allies in a growing number of economists who maintained that the time was ripe to come back to the classical principles of laissez-faire. The gradual erosion of the Keynesian hegemony underwent a sudden acceleration when the breakdown of the monetary system in 1971 and the first oil shock in 1973 started the Great Stagflation that persisted unabated until the second oil shock of 1979. By the end of this troubled period, the neoliberal point of view had accomplished what many called an anti-Keynesian counterrevolution.

We told this story in some detail in Sect. 1.3 and in Chap. 5. I just want to add here some remarks on the strength of the causal relations connecting facts and ideas. Did the shift from the Keynesian to the neo-liberal vision just reflect the change of power relations in the economy or did it play a significant autonomous role? There are many reasons to believe that the second view is the correct one. We may understand why in the light of the definition of neoliberalism suggested in Sect. 2.5. First, a new generation of rampant economists succeeded in rehabilitating the trust in unfettered markets that the Great Depression had significantly enfeebled. To this end, they worked out new arguments in support of the efficiency and rationality of free markets applying them shrewdly to the contemporaneous historical developments. In particular, they succeeded in convincing the public opinion that the Great Stagflation was a consequence of the protracted deviation from the time-honoured principles of classical liberalism and classical economics. They also managed to build up in the public opinion a profound mistrust in the state by emphasising its inefficiency, corruption, and unreliability.[14] This progressively spread the TINA fallacy, convincing most people, also those most damaged by the new policy strategy, that there is no alternative to a neoliberal policy strategy.[15] The policy makers implemented a U-turn of their policy strategy yielding to the growing pressure exerted by finance (mainly big banks) and industry (mainly big multinational corporations).

A more in-depth analysis clarifies that the influence of the new neoliberal vision was even deeper than that. It spread a very partial and distorted view of liberty reducing it to its negative side of defence of individuals from the interference of the state. This is the side of liberty that is of great concern for the most wealthy and powerful people who believe that have much to lose and very little to gain from state interference in economic decisions. Of course, they admit as exception the traditional role of the state in defence of property, contracts, and (possibly) sovereignty, as well as its modern role of privatising profits and socialising losses.

The cultural hegemony of neoliberalism succeeded to spread this distorted conception of liberty as the only possible, or correct, conception, despite the welfare of most people was strictly dependent on the positive side of liberty. Moreover, this reductionist concept of liberty further strengthened a general attitude of self-interested individualism, as any sentiment of sympathy and solidarity for other individuals may thrive only by taking seriously the positive liberty of all individuals.

Finally, the new view of markets, collective action, and liberty had the further devastating effect of undermining the concept of democracy. If unfettered markets maximise the welfare of all citizens, economic decisions lose their political nature and become a merely technical matter that policy makers may delegate to technocrats. The procedure of their appointment usually does not violate the formal rules of democracy because governments designate the technocrats in charge and parliaments approve their choice. In consequence of this long indirect procedure, however, the effective participation of the citizens in their designation is next to zero. In addition, the ensuing accountability of these powerful technocrats remains fuzzy because their activity is too distant from most citizens and the issues at stake are made often opaque by unexplained technicalities.

This new vision of liberty and democracy provided the necessary consensus for the neoliberal strategy of structural reforms leading to the liberalisation and deregulation of markets. These reforms progressively spurred the globalisation and financialisation of markets increasing further the inequality of wealth and power distribution. The new multinational elite strengthened further its cultural hegemony making easier the approval and implementation of the neoliberal structural reforms.

This vicious circle goes a long way to explain the neoliberal trajectory as reconstructed in this book, its growing unsustainability, the eventual burst of the Great Recession, and the ensuing Eurocrisis. In the co-evolving history of facts and ideas, the second process played a crucial pro-active role of justification and support of the first process. The self-interest of the most powerful decision makers gave a well-defined direction to this evolutionary process, but ideas played a crucial permissive or inspirational role and greatly contributed to promote and catalyse consensus on the neoliberal vision and policy strategy.

9.4   Therapy: Which Regulation?

A long tradition considers a competitive market as a particularly efficient device for computing and implementing the optimal allocation of resources. Von Mises developed this idea just after the October Revolution in Russia by arguing that rational economic calculation is impossible in a socialist country since central planning cannot surrogate the market by fixing a coherent system of prices.[16] This contribution started a long and hot debate on the potential viability of a socialist economy that is still alive. Dickinson soon undermined the validity of this argument claiming that central planners could easily solve a Walrasian general equilibrium model of a given socialist economy by determining the correct system of prices.[17] Hayek immediately rebutted this argument by emphasising the complexity of this kind of computation that would require a continuous unfeasible updating of the information set.[18] Lange observed, however, that central planners could circumvent this problem by adopting a "trial and error method" analogous to the Walrasian "*tâtonnement*".[19] This shifted the debate on the actual feasibility of socialism from logical to empirical arguments. Later on, Lange resumed the logical argument maintaining that an electronic computer could easily solve the problem.[20]

I have briefly recalled this famous debate because it may help to intertwine a few threads of this book in this conclusive chapter. First, the lineage starting from Mises and Hayek is an important root of the genesis of neoliberalism. Second, this debate shows how common was, and still is, the confusion between positive and normative arguments on one side and between model and reality on the other side. As we have seen in the preceding chapters (in particular in Chap. 1), this dual, often entangled, confusion still haunts the recent debate on the role and consequences of free markets and free trade. Third, the analogy between a competitive market and a computer that emerged from this debate may help to summarise and further clarify a few issues on the regulation of markets that have played a pre-eminent role in this book.

The original argument by Mises relied on two assumptions lacking rigorous foundations: first, that the persistence of a market proves its equilibrium, and second, that market equilibrium implies its optimality. Both assumptions are deeply rooted in a prestigious and influential tradition. The interpretation of a competitive market as a process gravitating towards equilibrium is a crucial viewpoint developed by Adam Smith in his masterpiece.[21] While the Physiocrats connected market equilibrium to health, Smith had in mind the Newtonian system and envisioned equilibrium as the resting point of a dynamical system. The modern mathematical theory of dynamics has subsequently clarified that the persistence of a system does not imply equilibrium as apt structural changes could preserve its persistence in consequence of a vast range of shocks. In addition, it proved that equilibrium is unlikely to be stable and unique, and does not necessarily maximise a desirable magnitude. Mises and Hayek believed on the contrary that the spontaneous order of the market epitomised by its equilibrium was optimal in the sense that collective action could not improve upon it.

The recent advances in computer science (supercomputer), artificial intelligence, and economic modelling (computable general equilibrium models) suggest that the problem of economic computation is very awkward in any kind of economy, including a capitalist one. However, if the Walrasian system is solvable by the market for a capitalist economy, it is not clear why a planner could not solve it by using an analogous algorithm. The recent artificial intelligence literature reversed the relationship between markets and computers as discussed in the debate on socialist planning. While Lange regarded markets as primitive forms of computers, computer designers tried to replicate the flexibility and adaptation capabilities of markets.[22] I feel thus authorised to liken a market to a computer and use this metaphor to clarify some of the issues discussed in this book.

The hardware of the market is rooted in the system of exchanges and its material characteristics that depend on the technology of production and trade (including the monetary technology of exchange), the preferences of decision makers, and the endowment of resources and their distribution. The software of the market is the system of rules that the market has to comply with, and depends on the institutions and legal provisions that regulate and supervise its working.

The hardware of a system is important because it sets the limits of its performance. Nevertheless, within the boundaries of what the hardware can do, the actual performance crucially depends on the software adopted. The effectiveness of a given software depends on the task we have to fulfil and the goals we want to reach. Similarly to computers, markets are instruments that help us to perform better certain tasks. In this sense, there is no reason to be against markets, and we should use all their potential to reach our goals. However, we should always see markets as means to reach given ends and never as ends in themselves, as too often happens today.

In addition, a computer cannot regulate itself by choosing and operating an appropriate software. This may happen only in the nightmares of some science fiction writer where cyborgs manage to take control of their own regulation, reproduction, and evolution to enslave the human beings to their perverse logic. Fortunately, in the real world, this scenario is still quite far-fetched. In any case, no one would dare to consider it desirable. Computers require external decision makers who operate them by choosing a well-specified software. This is true also of markets. Their performance depends on the rules of their regulation and supervision, as well as on the nature and efficiency of the institutions having this role. The self-regulation of markets so often celebrated and advocated is thus a red herring. The dilemma is not, and has never been, the choice between self-regulation of markets and their strict regulation by policy makers, but a choice between different strategies of regulation and supervision of markets. In particular, the real choice has never been between laissez-faire and regulation neither in the neoliberal era, nor before.[23] The slogan "laissez-faire" has always been used against specific forms of regulation reputed damaging or excessively severe by the economic agents constrained by its rules, or as a captivating slogan to capture the consensus of a public opinion typically hostile to any sort of constraints.

In the case of the neoliberal era, the slogan of deregulation supported the substitution of Keynesian regulation with a new approach to regulation supposed to be lighter, simpler, and less suffocating for businesses and citizens. The neoliberal style of regulation proved to be in many fields neither simpler nor lighter than before, and often even more suffocating for economic agents. A case in point is finance. The new style of regulation progressively built in the neoliberal era relies on rules increasingly complex and ad hoc. Notwithstanding the diligent work done by regulatory entities such as the BCBS, Financial Stability Board, IOSCO, central banks, and the not less daunting bureaucratic requirements imposed to financial institutions, the limits of this regulative style are intrinsically severe. A plethora of exceptions of difficult interpretation typically encumber the most important rules. Only the big financial institutions have the resources to acquire and manage the necessary skills and information. The costs for this complex task are prohibitive for small local banks that provide the main support to the real economy. In addition, as is well known since long, a too complex system of rules is ineffective because the big financial institutions that can hire the best lawyers and experts may easily discover and exploit the loopholes of the rules to circumvent them.

The paradox is that neoliberal regulation that had promised more freedom and less regulation to the economic agents has eventually established an overregulated system that is inefficient and unable to enforce the most important rules. I am inclined to call "casuistic" this style of regulation. A long tradition has maintained that a casuist system of rules risks being ineffective and unfair.[24]

9.5   Neoliberalism and Sustainability

This book has shown that neoliberalism has played a crucial role in establishing a development trajectory increasingly divergent from sustainability. This is because it played the role of orientating private and public decisions toward a convergent but unsustainable direction. The ultimate root of this failure is a narrow conception of liberty that focuses exclusively—or mainly, in the more moderate versions—on the defence of the negative liberty of individuals from the interferences of the state. This view neglects, or downplays, the crucial impact of social and economic conditions on the negative liberty of individuals, as well as the crucial influence of their positive liberty on their self-realisation and happiness.

Neoliberalism affected sustainability through direct and indirect influence channels. It exerted a powerful direct impact on the choices of individuals, organisations, and institutions—both private and public—because it provided simple, allegedly science-based, criteria of choice between alternative options. A crucial criterion adopted by the advocates of a neoliberal policy strategy is the following: what the state does but the markets can do should become a prerogative of markets to avoid the interference of the state on the negative liberty of individuals (*principle of privatisation*). Another crucial criterion of choice is that unfettered markets perform better than markets regulated by public agencies (*principle of deregulation*). A third criterion strictly related to the second one is that, whenever some sort of regulation is necessary, regulation should be the prerogative of markets themselves (*principle of self-regulation*). If most decision makers adopt these common criteria of choice, the impact on the economy is bound to be massive. This explains why the neoliberal revolution was so rapid and pervasive. The implications of these criteria for sustainability are devastating. The growing weight of self-interest and short-termism in economic decisions crowded out sustainable decision strategies that care for the well-being of the human lot also in the long period, and aim to keep the necessary equilibrium between human activity and the biosphere.

In addition, neoliberalism affected sustainability through powerful indirect channels. This book investigated two of them: globalisation and financialisation, far-reaching processes propelled by the choice criteria that I have just recalled.

The deregulation of international markets greatly accelerated the process of globalisation weakening at the same time the constraints introduced by national legislations to safeguard social and environmental sustainability. Two steps of this escalation have been particularly important. The first one was the establishment of the WTO in 1995 that rapidly became the most powerful transnational organisation. This institution has the power of imposing to a country the repeal of a law restricting trade to safeguard sustainability whenever the relevant panels or courts interpret it as an obstacle to free trade. Whenever the country does not comply with this injunction, it has to pay massive fines. The only possibility to avoid the fine is to convince the WTO that the constraints to trade are justified by sound science, a criterion that systematically excludes from acceptable justification the precautionary measures based, as is unavoidable, on probabilistic causal links.

A second step in this escalation of institutional changes that risk enfeebling further democracy and sustainability is the establishment of new ambitious trade agreements. Cases in point are the Transatlantic Trade and Investment Partnership (TTIP) between the US and the EU, and the Trans-Pacific Partnership (TPP) between the US and 11 other countries (Australia, Brunei, Canada, Chile, Japan, Malaysia, Mexico, New Zealand, Peru, Singapore and Vietnam). These agreements aim to move beyond the traditional elimination of tariffs on goods and services imposing the alignment of regulatory regimes. The expected advantages rely on the reduction of transaction costs that today mainly depend on different national regulations and rules. We have seen in Chap. 2 that these advantages are greatly overestimated. The German Federation of Industry (BDI) has recently revised the expected benefits of TTIP downsizing a previous estimate of three digit billion benefits to a negligible amount of few billion euros over the next ten years for the entire EU.[25] We have to compare these small advantages for consumers with the serious disadvantages related to increased unemployment, massive redistribution of income and wealth, downgrading of sustainability standards and enfeebled democracy (see Chap. 3).

As for sustainability standards, the main concern is the "regulatory convergence" agenda, which is likely to enforce a convergence to the lower standards. A case in point is food safety where the US standards are lower than the EU standards. European food markets could be flooded with genetically modified products and food contaminated by hormones, antibiotics and pesticides. In addition, their lower price allowed by downgraded standards could produce in Europe massive unemployment in agriculture and husbandry.

A particularly controversial provision of TTIP is the Investor-State Dispute Settlement (ISDS) clause that would give corporations the power to sue governments when policy makers introduce regulations that could curb their profits. According to UN figures, since the year 2000 US firms have sued states on 130 separate occasions under free-trade agreements earning billions of dollars. One example is Phillip Morris that has recently sued Australia and Uruguay for placing health warnings on cigarette packets. In consequence of the ISDS clause, the states would lose the sovereign power of regulating the economic activity to guarantee its compliance with sustainability criteria. This would further enfeeble democracy and enhance the unsustainability of the development trajectory.

A further major indirect influence of neoliberalism on sustainability is through the process of financialisation. As we have seen in Chap. 4, financialisation poses new challenges for achieving ecological, social and economic sustainability, regardless of whether we consider it a novel or a recurrent phase of capitalist development. The results of extensive research surveyed in this book converge to show that the process of financialisation, as occurred in the last four decades, is inconsistent with sustainability. Actually, the Second Financialisation started in the early 1980s has significantly altered the balance between the physiological and pathological functions of finance in favour of the second. We may thus reach genuine sustainability only within a model of development radically different from the existing one. We cannot implement a sustainable trajectory of development within a business-as-usual perspective, as many policy makers seem still to believe. In particular, the progressive commodification of nature has increasingly subordinated the integrity of natural environment to the financial profitability of its use. The recent process of financialisation has greatly increased this link in many fields such as land grabbing, speculation on built environment, pollution, and exhaustion of natural resources.

Financialisation as a variegated and evolutionary process has clear implications for the sustainability of development. Sustainability, in all its definitions, is about the compliance of the process of development with well-defined economic, social, and environmental constraints. Therefore, the compatibility between financialisation that is about the relaxation of constraints to economic decisions, and sustainability that is about compliance with crucial constraints, is in principle problematic. This does not imply, however, that the conflict between finance and sustainability is necessarily insurmountable. As we have seen in Chap. 7, finance could—and should—give a fundamental contribution to a rapid transition towards a trajectory of sustainable development by providing the necessary funding for its deployment. This requires, however, a radical reform of finance by repressing its growingly self-referential trajectory and by channelling its activity instead at the service of the real economy in the direction of a new trajectory of development consistent with sustainability.

9.6   The Neoliberal Trilemma

This book confirms the cogency of Rodrik's "political trilemma of the world economy".[26] In his words, "we cannot have hyperglobalization, democracy, and national self-determination all at once. We can have at most two out of three" (Rodrik 2011, 200). This trilemma is deeply rooted in the neoliberal paradigm as implemented in the recent decades. To understand this nexus I have first to clarify that the Rodrik's trilemma does not have logical foundations but semantic foundations.[27] We have to exclude one of the three horns of the trilemma not to avoid a logical contradiction but only to avoid a clash between the meanings usually assigned to each of them. In other words, globalisation may coexist with democracy and national sovereignty but only by imposing cogent constraints on the contents of each horn of the dilemma. This is what Rodrik does in its discussion of the trilemma but he does not make explicit the link between his version of the trilemma and the neoliberal policy strategy. What he says about "hyperglobalization" (that he calls also "deep globalization") is not necessarily true of any form of globalisation but only of what I have called in this book neoliberal globalisation, namely the development trajectory started in the early 1980s that aims at a complete deregulation of international markets.[28] Rodrik himself clarifies that the "managed globalisation" of the Bretton Woods period realised a viable compromise between globalisation and the usual substantive meaning of the other two horns of the trilemma.

On the other hand, as we know by experience, neoliberal globalisation does not exclude democracy in all its possible meanings. The political regime of most countries continues to be a democracy in the sense that political decisions are taken by representatives of all citizens chosen directly or indirectly through free elections. The compliance with the formal rules of democracy does not imply, however, a significant active participation of most people to the democratic process in its substantive meaning. The neoliberal development trajectory has progressively hollowed out the substantive content of democracy transferring the strategic decision power from the citizens to the markets. Not without reason, a few sociologists and political scientists maintain that we live in a post-democratic society in which the democratic forms embed an increasingly enfeebled democratic substance.[29]

Something similar can be said of national self-determination that is part and parcel of substantive democracy. Unfettered globalisation significantly hollowed out the choice set of strategic self-determination. No doubt, the higher is the degree of effective sovereignty, the larger is the set of self-determination options. The latter depends, however, on many other conditions that are more likely to be met at a local level more restricted than the national level.

At the root of the neoliberal trilemma, we find again the conflict between negative and positive liberty. Substantive democracy and self-determination are both expression and necessary condition of the positive freedom of individuals, while the prevailing focus on negative liberty underlies the ultimate justifications of neoliberal globalisation. In this book, I argued that sustainability requires the flourishing of positive liberty keeping the correct balance between positive and negative liberty. This suggests that the neoliberal paradigm is intrinsically contradictory because it aims at a rigorous defence of the individual liberty of all citizens but ends up compressing the individual liberty of most of them. This is certainly true if one believes, as I do, that individual liberty cannot flourish in a country deprived of substantive democracy and genuine rights of self-determination.

A case in point is the recent Eurocrisis. As I have argued in Chap. 8, the design of the common currency and its management rules have significantly enfeebled democracy and national self-determination, not necessarily in their formal and procedural meaning, but certainly in their substantive meaning. The policy makers pursued this strategy in the interest of the transnational European markets conforming to the neoliberal "solution" of the Rodrik's trilemma. In the ensuing Eurocrisis discussed in Chap. 8, as in a Greek tragedy, the compactness of space and time contributed to the intensity of the dramatic effect. The relentless repression by the troika of any attempt of single countries to deviate from a rigid common policy strategy clearly revealed the subordination of national self-determination to financial globalisation. The TINA mantra repeatedly intervened to repress diversity not only in the choice of policy goals but also in the choice of the instruments to realise them. The repression of diversity is a clear sign of disregard for substantive democracy and self-determination within national countries. Is this trade-off between democratic self-determination and financial globalisation justified? From the ethical point of view the answer is certainly negative, at least if one believes—as I do—that substantive democracy, self-determination and positive liberty are supreme, non-negotiable, values. Moreover, from the economic point of view the advantages, if any, are overemphasised. A recent estimate found that these benefits have an order of magnitude of one third of 1 % of the world GDP at the end of a full decade, confirming other similar estimates.[30] In addition, these advantages do not take account of the huge long-run externalities that seriously jeopardise the sustainability of development.

Summing up, we cannot dream of being able to converge towards a sustainable development trajectory without abandoning the neoliberal point of view and its policy strategy.

Notes

1. See the "Brundtland Report" (WCED 1987).
2. See a critical survey of this literature in Borghesi and Vercelli (2012).
3. See in particular Sachs (2005), and Picketty (2014).
4. Stiglitz (2012).
5. Borghesi and Vercelli (2008).
6. See for example Ng (2003).
7. Borghesi and Vercelli (2012).
8. See for example Helliwell et al. (2012); Stiglitz et al. (2010).
9. See in particular Stern (2007); and Borghesi and Vercelli (2009).
10. Stiglitz (2010).
11. See retro Chap. 6.

12. Shaxson (2011).
13. This interaction played a crucial role also before, but I refer here to a specific vicious circle that characterised the period analysed.
14. See retro Sect. 2.6.
15. I recall that TINA stands for "There Is No Alternative". See retro Sect. 1.4.
16. Mises (1920 [1935]).
17. Dickinson (1933).
18. Hayek (1935).
19. See Lange (1939). The tâtonnement ("groping") is the formalisation of an iterative auction process utilised by Léon Walras to represent how a competitive market may reach an exchange equilibrium (Walras 1877).
20. As a mature Lange (1967, 158) provocatively put it: "Were I to rewrite my essay today my task would be much simpler. My answer to Hayek and Robbins would be: so what's the trouble? Let us put the simultaneous equations on an electronic computer and we shall obtain the solution in less than a second." The recent literature shows, however, that the computability of general equilibrium is still an open problem. See for example Cottrell, Cockshot, and Michaelson (2009), and the literature there cited.
21. Smith (1776).
22. Lavoie (1981, 76).
23. This has always been clear to the most astute critics of laissez-faire. For example, Antonio Gramsci wrote long ago in *The Prison Notebooks* (1929–1935) that "it must be made clear that *laissez-faire* too is a form of state 'regulation' introduced and maintained by coercive means. It is a deliberate policy, conscious of its own ends, and not the spontaneous automatic expression of economic facts" (Gramsci 1971, 160).
24. The Oxford English Dictionary maintains that "Casuistry destroys by distinctions and exceptions, all morality, and effaces the essential difference between right and wrong". A similar criticism has been levelled against casuist systems of legal rules. Blaise Pascal maintained in his *Provincial Letters* that Jesuits were using casuistic reasoning in confession to keep the benevolence of wealthy donors, while punishing severely poor penitents (Pascal 2015 [1656–57]). The Jesuit Pope Francis has repeatedly endorsed the criticisms against casuistry in ethics.
25. To be precise, the most recent estimates of the BDI have downsized the expected benefits from TTIP to about 119 billion euros by 2027 for the entire EU, instead of about 100 billion euros a year according to its own previous estimates.
26. Rodrik (2011, 184–206).

27. Logical trilemmas are also called "inconsistent triads". They consist of three propositions of which at most two can be true.
28. This is not to deny that the Rodrik's trilemma has a certain degree of generality, but to emphasise that its precise meaning and implications are history-dependent. In particular, the trilemma is certainly visible during the First Globalisation at the turn of the nineteenth century, but democracy and national self-determination played a different role in political decisions. The universal suffrage was first implemented in the UK with the Representation of People Act of 1928.
29. See in particular Crouch (2004).
30. Rodrik (2011, 252).

Bibliography

Borghesi, Simone, and Alessandro Vercelli. 2008. *Global Sustainability. Social and Environmental Conditions*. Palgrave Macmillan: Basingstoke and New York.

——— 2009. Greenhouse gas emissions and the energy system: are current trends sustainable? In *International journal of global energy issues*, Special issue on 'Energy Efficiency, Environmental Performance and Sustainability', 32 (1–2):160–174.

——— 2012. Happiness and Health: Two Paradoxes. *Journal of Economic Surveys* 26(2): 203–233.

Cottrell, Allin, Paul Cockshot, and Greg Michaelson. 2009. Is Economic Planning Hypercomputational? The Argument from Cantor Diagonalisation. *International Journal of Unconventional Computing* 5(3–4): 223–236.

Crouch, Colin. 2004. *Post-democracy*. Chichester: John Wiley and Sons.

Dickinson, Henry D. 1933. Price Formation in a Socialist Community. *The Economic Journal* 43(170): 237–250.

Gramsci, Antonio. 1971. *Selections from the Prison Notebooks*. New York: International Publishers.

Hayek, Friedrich A. 1935. *Collectivist Economic Planning*. London: Routledge and Kegan Paul.

Helliwell John, Layard Richard, and Jeffrey Sachs. 2012. World Happiness Report. Earth Institute, Columbia University, New York.

Lange, Oskar R. 1939 [1970]. On the Economic Theory of Socialism. reprinted in Lange, Oskar R. and Fred Taylor. *On the Economic Theory of Socialism*, ed.

Benjamin E. Lippincott, 57–143. Minneapolis: University of Minnesota Press. Reprinted in New York: Augustus M. Kelley, 1970.

——— 1967. The Computer and the Market. In *Socialism, capitalism and economic growth: Essays presented to Maurice Dobb*, ed. C.H. Feinstein, 158–161. Cambridge: Cambridge University Press.

Lavoie, Don. 1981. A critique of the Standard Account of the Socialist Calculation Debate. *Journal of Libertarian Studies* 5(1): 41–87.

Mises, Ludwig von. 1920 [1935]. Economic Calculation in the Socialist Commonwealth. Reprinted in Hayek Frederick (1935, ed.) Collectivist Economic Planning: Critical Studies in the Possibilities of Socialism: 87–130. London: Routledge.

Ng, Yew-Kwang. 2003. From preference to happiness: towards a more complete welfare economics. *Social Choice and Welfare* 20: 307–350.

Pascal, Blaise. 1656–57 [2015]. *The Provincial Letters*. The University of Adelaide. https://ebooks.adelaide.edu.au/p/pascal/blaise/p27pr/index.html. Retrieved 18 March 2016.

Piketty, Thomas. 2014. *Capital in the Twenty-First Century*. Cambridge Mass: Harvard University Press.

Rodrik, Dani. 2011. *The Globalisation Paradox*. In *Why Global Markets, States, and Democracy Can't Coexist*. Oxford: Oxford University Press.

Sachs, Jeffrey. 2005. *The End of Poverty: Economic Possibilities for Our Time*. New York: Penguin Press.

Shaxson, Nicholas. 2011. *Treasure Islands. Tax Havens and the Men who Stole the World*. London: Vintage Books.

Smith, Adam. 1776 [1977]. *An Inquiry into The Nature and Causes of the Wealth of Nations*. Edited by Edwin Cannan. Chicago: University of Chicago Press.

Stern, Nicholas. 2007. *The Economics of Climate Change: The Stern Review*. Cambridge and New York: Cambridge University Press.

Stiglitz, Joseph E. 2010. *Freefall: Free Markets and the Sinking of the Global Economy*. New York: W. W. Norton & Co.

——— 2012. *The Price of Inequality. How Today's Divided Society Endangers our Future*. New York: W. W. Norton & Co.

Stiglitz, Joseph E., Amartya K. Sen, and Jean-Paul Fitoussi. 2010. *Mismeasuring our Lives. Why GDP Doesn't Add up*. New York: New Press.

Walras, Léon. 1877 [1954]. *Elements of Pure Economics*. London: Allen & Unwin.

WCED. 1987. *Our Common Future: Report of the World Commission on Environment and Development*. New York: Oxford University Press ("Bruntland Report").

Appendix 1: The Evolution of Financial Legislation: A Short Compendium[1, 2]

The US Legislation

The Banking Act of 1933, also known as Glass-Steagall Act, was passed on 16 June 1933 as an emergency response to the failure of many banks during the Great Depression. Four sections of the Act (Sections 16, 20, 21, and 32) have been of particular importance in shaping the financial system. References to "Glass-Steagall" are usually to those particular sections.

Sections 16 and 21 prevented Federal Reserve member banks from purchasing securities for their own account and from performing activities typical of investment banks such as underwriting and dealing in securities or managing corporate mergers and acquisitions. Nevertheless, banks were allowed to underwrite US Treasury securities.

On the other hand, the Act prevented investment banks from taking deposits and making loans. The Act also forbade close connections among investment and commercial banks (Sections 20 and 32) such as overlapping directorships or common ownership. In particular, Section 20 forbade member banks from affiliating with a company "engaged principally" in the "issue, flotation, underwriting, public sale, or distribution at wholesale or retail or through syndicate participation of stocks, bonds, debentures, notes, or other securities". Commercial banks could not maintain insurance affiliates, nor affiliates in non-financial commercial activity.

The Banking Act of 1933 also established the Federal Deposit Insurance Corporation (FDIC) and the Federal Open Market Committee (FOMC). Among other things, it prohibited payment of interest on demand deposits and authorised the Federal Reserve to set interest rate ceilings on time and saving deposits to limit the interest expenses of banks (Regulation Q).

This combination of "sticks" (regulations and controls) and "carrots" (limited entry, interest ceilings, and deposit insurance) produced the so-called "Quiet period" in US banking system during which no systemic event took place until 2007 (Gorton 2010).

The Financial Services Modernization Act of 1999, best known as Gramm-Leach-Bliley Act (GLBA), partially repealed the Glass-Steagall Act (it repealed Sections 20 and 32) and amended the Bank Holding Company Act (**BHCA**) thus removing the legal barriers that had prevented any combination of investment bank operations, commercial bank activities, or insurance company businesses being held by a bank holding company (BHC).

The Act allowed well-capitalised and well-managed BHCs to apply to the Federal Reserve Board to gain the status of financial holding company (FHC). This would allow them to engage, through their non-bank subsidiaries, in a wider range of activities including securities underwriting, merchant banking, and insurance underwriting.

Depository institutions, such as commercial banks, were still restricted in security and insurance underwriting and sales (Sections 16 and 21 were not repealed) but they could be part of a BHC involved in these activities.

Limitations remained on financial transactions between banks and non-bank subsidiaries (more on this later) as well as between banking, industrial, and commercial activities. Prior to the formal repeal of the Glass-Steagall Act in 1999, the Federal Reserve's interpretations of the Glass-Steagall loopholes and laws passed by Congress had already undermined the regulatory system that had emerged after the Great Depression.

In this context an important step towards deregulation was the enactment by Congress of the Monetary Control Act 1980 (MCA) which established the Depositary Institution Deregulation Committee (DIDC) to eliminate ceilings on deposit interest rates over a six-year period. The aim was to allow banks to compete with the Money Market Funds (**MMF**s) that had grown rapidly from the late 1970s (Gilbert 1986).

By the late 1970s and through the 1990s, federal banking regulators gradually extended the range of activities permissible to banks, in particular through the interpretation of Section 20 of the Glass-Steagall Act. As we have already seen, Section 20 forbids member banks from affiliating with a company "engaged principally" in activities not permitted to banks (such as securities underwriting and distribution). In 1987, the Federal Reserve allowed BHCs to underwrite and deal in corporate securities through subsidiaries (known as Section 20 subsidiaries) up to 5 % of the subsidiaries' gross annual revenue. The limit was raised to 10 % in 1989 and to 25 % in December 1996 thus "de facto" allowing even the largest securities firms to affiliate with commercial banks. This happened two years later when Travelers Insurance Company (which owned the investment bank Salomon Smith Barney) and Citicorp (the parent of Citibank) announced a merger to create Citigroup Inc., the world's largest financial services company. The Glass-Steagall Act and the BHCA had been specially designed to prevent the emergence of this type of company combining insurance underwriting, securities underwriting, and commercial banking.

Despite the merger having taken place at a time when the law still forbade it, the Federal Reserve gave its approval on the promise that unless the Congress changed the law to relax restrictions, Citigroup Inc. would have two years to divest itself of all the businesses that did not conform to the existing regulations.

At the same time, the prohibition on investment banks from taking deposits had been circumvented, in particular with the association with the so-called "non-bank banks". A "non-bank bank" is an institution that has a bank charter but it is not a bank as defined by the BHCA. In 1970, the BHCA defined a bank as an institution that both accepted demand deposits and made commercial loans, thus excluding those institutions that restricted their activities to either accepting deposits or making commercial loans. The majority of "non-bank banks" took demand deposits and made consumer loans. In the 1980s, many commercial and financial companies exploited the "non-bank bank" opportunity to take control of depository institutions (insured by the FDIC) which gave them access to a cheaper source of funds without being subjected to the supervision and restrictions imposed by the BHCA.

In 1987, Congress passed the Competitive Equality Banking Act (CEBA) that, among other things, amended the definition of a bank to tackle the problems posed to banks by the unfair competition of "non-bank banks". Therefore, the Act defined a bank either as a FDIC-insured institution or as an institution that both accepts demands deposits and makes commercial loans. The Act explicitly excluded from the definition of a bank certain categories of financial institutions: among others, credit card banks, savings associations, and industrial loan corporations, while other categories, for example, consumer and mortgage lenders, were implicitly exempted because they do not finance their operation through demand deposits.

These explicit and implicit exemptions from the definition of "bank" again gave new opportunities to non-bank banks and commercial entities to enter the market for banking services thus overcoming the division between commercial and investment banks as well as between banking and commerce (Omarova and Tayar 2011).

As with respect to product development (financial innovation), banks had gained regulatory approval to expand the range of their activities beyond those traditionally performed by banks well before the repeal of Glass-Steagall Act. In particular, the Office of the Comptroller of the Currency (OCC) from the mid-1980s to 2008, in response to requests by individual banks, pressed by competition from securities firms and other financial institutions, had used its discretionary power for gradually expanding the concept of the "business of banking" to include almost any form of financial innovation. This interpretative method allowed US commercial banks, although they were still formally prohibited from investing in commercial and financial activities, to engage in dealing and trading in an ever-growing variety of complex over the counter (**OTC**) instruments (Omarova 2009).

The increased competition from non-bank entities, the decreased regulation and the innovation in financial sectors, have transformed US commercial banks from deposit-taking and lending institutions into institutions that provide a wide range of financial instruments, including extremely complex and risky instruments.

After the approval of GLBA, Section 23A of the Federal Reserve Act (which was not repealed) was the only firewall left to insulate a depository institution from the activities, usually riskier, of non-bank subsidiaries in a holding company structure. Section 23A of the Federal Reserve Act was enacted in 1933 as an additional restriction imposed on banks. It imposed quantitative and qualitative limitations on certain "covered transactions" between banks and their non-bank affiliates. The aim was to protect depository institutions that have access to the Federal Reserve safety net from being exposed to the potential losses of their non-bank affiliates. Section 23A was supplemented in 1987 by Section 23B which stated that depository institutions should conduct affiliates' transactions on market terms. The importance of both Sections were reaffirmed by the Federal Reserve in 2002 when it issued Regulation W, which clarified how to interpret them in the aftermath of the repeal of Glass-Steagall Act.

Prior to the Dodd-Frank Act, the Federal Reserve had an exclusive power in granting exemptions from quantitative and qualitative limitations if such exemptions were in the public interest. According to some authors (Omarova 2011; Nersisyan 2015), the Federal Reserve, in granting exemptions based only on potential risks faced by individual banks, and not by the system as a whole, indirectly facilitated the growing of the shadow banking.

During the 2007 financial crisis, the Federal Reserve continued to grant exemptions from quantitative and qualitative limitations to allow financial conglomerates to finance non-bank entities through their deposit-taking entities within the FHC. This contradicted the purpose of Section 23A that was used by the proponents of the repeal of the Glass-Steagall Act as an argument to convince their opponents. It also posed a problem of legitimacy in using public funds because any bank in the Federal Reserve System can gain access to Federal Reserve funds that were not meant for investment banks.

The Dodd-Frank Wall Street Reform and Consumer Protection Act (known as Dodd-Frank Act) tried to address these problems, as we will see, introducing the so-called "Volcker rule" which instructs banks to move certain types of derivatives into their non-bank affiliates and which also makes several amendments to the requirements of Section 23A. In particular, the Act includes derivatives and securities lending and borrowing transactions in the definition of "covered transactions" and imposes limitations on the Board's authority to grant exemptions from the requirements of Section 23A.

The Dodd-Frank Act, which came into force on 21 July 2010, established a new regulatory framework whose intent was "to promote the financial stability of the United States by improving accountability and transparency in the financial system, to end 'too big to fail' to protect the American taxpayer by ending bail-outs, to protect consumers from abusive financial services practices and for other purposes".

The Act, with its more than 800 pages, covers a wide range of areas but the focus is on limiting the risk of the shadow banking system and the potential damage caused by the failure of a large financial institution (Skeel 2011). The Act brings about many significant changes in the regulation of OTC derivatives that, according to many commentators, exacerbated the 2007 financial crisis in particular due to the opacity of the market. Before the introduction of Dodd-Frank, the regulatory approach on derivatives was based essentially on self-regulation. A huge volume of contracts was traded OTC, and there was little disclosure of data, and consequently there was poor regulatory supervision.

In 1998, the Commodity Futures Trading Commission (CFTC) issued a "concept release" report calling for greater transparency in the OTC derivatives market. This was a response to cases of manipulation and fraud that had brought to light the problems related to the lack of information on this market. The other regulators, that is the Federal Reserve, the SEC (Securities and Exchange Commission), and the Treasury had an opposite view and warned that additional regulations could be catastrophic. In fact, the Commodity Futures Modernization Act (CFMA) of 2000 exempted a broad range of derivatives, including the credit default swaps (**CDS**), swaps, and mortgage-related derivatives, from CFTC and SEC regulation.

The Dodd-Frank regulatory regime requires that derivatives be cleared and traded on exchanges. The Act preserves the division of jurisdiction on derivatives between the CFTC that regulates swaps and the SEC that regulates security-based swaps (swaps dealing with stocks and other securities). The swap dealers, the entities that make a market in swaps, and the swap participants, the entities that maintain a "substantial position" in the swap markets, will be subject to registration, capital, margin, reporting, record keeping, and operational requirements.

The Act authorises the CFTC and the SEC to decide which types of derivatives are appropriate to be cleared: if it is to be cleared, it must be presented to a **clearing house** for clearing and to an exchange for trading. Dodd-Frank requires every clearing house to maintain reserves large enough to cope with the failure of its largest participant and to continue operating for at least a year after the default. Since the failure of a clearing house could be a source of potential systemic risk, the Act gives the Federal Reserve the authority to lend to the clearing houses and thus, implicitly, the capacity to bail them out.

The Act also mandates that each OTC derivatives transaction, cleared or uncleared, must be reported to a new entity known as a swap data repository. This provides a central facility for swap data reporting and record keeping, thus giving regulators better access to information.

To address systemic risk of financial collapse and to cope with the problem of large financial institutions, Dodd-Frank automatically considers any BHC with $50 billion or more in assets to be systemically important and consequently subject to a special supervision by the Federal Reserve.

For non-bank financial institutions, the Financial Stability Oversight Council (FSOC), the new systemic risk regulator, will identify systemically important domestic or foreign non-bank financial companies that could pose a risk to the financial stability of the USA. These would require more stringent supervision by the Federal Reserve. Dodd-Frank grants the Federal Reserve an almost discretionary power to impose higher capital requirements and other elements of prudential regulation on the institutions considered systemically important.

To prevent banks from undertaking risky activities, Section 619 of the Dodd-Frank Act added a new Section 13, commonly referred as the "Volcker rule" to the BHCA of 1956. Section 13 prohibits BHCs from engaging as principal in proprietary trading for buying or selling financial instruments to profit from short-term price movements. It also prohibits banks from sponsoring or investing in hedge funds or private equity funds. Non-bank financial companies singled out by the FSOC for supervision are not subject to these prohibitions, but they could be subject to additional capital requirements if they engage in certain proprietary trading activities. Section 13 contains important statutory exemptions for certain activities such as underwriting and market-making-related activities, hedging, insurance company activities, as well as trading in US government securities and on behalf of customers. An important exemption, perceived by some commentators as a watering down of the rule, permits investments in hedge funds and equity funds that "amount to not more than 3 % of the total ownership interests in any single hedge fund or equity private fund and that, in aggregate, do not exceed 3 % of the banking entity's Tier 1 capital".

To address the problem of a failure of a systemic important institution, the Dodd-Frank Act introduces a new resolution regime based on an orderly liquidation mechanism with the FDIC appointed as a receiver to seize, break up, and liquidate the financial institution whose failure threatens the financial system.

A legislative innovation created by the Act is the Consumer Financial Protection Bureau (CFPB) that with the Office of Financial Research (OFR) and the FSOC constitutes the new regulatory agencies introduced by Dodd-Frank. The aim of FSOC is to monitor and maintain the stability of the US financial system and to facilitate coordination and exchange of information among regulatory agencies. The OFR will be charged with collecting financial data to give regulators access to information about the entire financial system.

As for the CFPB, although technically part of the Federal Reserve, it has been granted an autonomous power to write and enforce rules for consumer protections. These rules relate consumer financial transactions on credit cards, mortgages, student loans, and payday loans. Insurance, employee benefit plans and, most importantly, auto loans are excluded from the CFPB oversight.

The CFPB will have exclusive regulatory power and strong enforcement power over financial institution with more than $10 billion in assets and much less authority with smaller institutions. The intent of the legislation is clearly to focus attention on the largest institutions to prevent the predatory, reckless lending that is considered to be the precursor of the 2007 financial crisis.

The Dodd-Frank Act also addresses the problems related to the perverse incentives of the securitisation process. It requires issuers of asset-backed securities (ABS), and any other entity who organise the sales of such securities, to retain at least 5 % of the credit risk of the transaction (qualified residential mortgage are excluded).

As for the credit rating agencies, the Act instructs the SEC to establish a New Office of Credit Rating to oversee and examine credit rating agencies and promulgate new rules for internal controls, independence, and transparency as well as introducing penalties for poor performance.

Finally, the Act required, for the first time, hedge funds to be registered with the SEC.

When the Act was issued in 2010, it called for a number of studies to be conducted and required regulatory agencies to issue rules to implement the many changes it introduced. After five years, many commentators argue that, in the ongoing process of rulemaking, some of its more important and controversial provisions have been weakened due to massive financial industry lobbying. On December 2014, for example, Section 716 (also known as "the swaps push-out rule" or the Lincoln Amendment) was amended and significantly narrowed in its scope. Section 716 required that banks that are swap dealers, or security-based swap dealers, should transfer all or part of their swap portfolio to separately capitalised non-bank subsidiaries. The intent was to keep banks' risky derivatives outside the FDIC-insured entities.

The amendment that was part of the Spending Bill authorised banks to continue to be a counterpart to all types of swaps, the only exemption being certain types of structured finance swaps. As for the much-debated Volcker rule, it was initially scheduled for implementation in July 2010 but was repeatedly delayed. It took effect partially in July 2015. The deadline to divest from speculative investments in private equity funds and hedge funds has been extended by the Federal Reserve to 2017 and the deadline to divest from collateralised loan obligations (**CLOs**) to 2019.

Many critics argue that the regulatory framework is too fragmented and that, on the whole, the Act has not fulfilled so far the main objective, the reining in of the big banks that are still insufficiently capitalised and increasingly exposed to risk.

The UK Legislation

The legislation that completely reshaped the UK financial system was the so-called "Big Bang" which came into force on 26 October 1986. It was part of a broader set of rules, "The financial Services Act 1986", that regulated investment business, provided investor protection, and promoted greater competition in the financial system.

The Big Bang drastically changed the way the London Stock Exchange operated. The London Stock Exchange had agreed to deregulation back in 1983 to escape prosecution for anti-competitive practices under the Restrictive Practices Act of 1956. Before the reform, the system was based on a clear separation between two kinds of firms: the "jobbers" that traded securities listed on the Stock Exchange on their own account (they acted as market makers) and the "brokers" who executed clients' buy and sell orders and were paid a fixed commission by them.

The brokers were "agents" acting in the clients' best interests whereas the jobbers were "principals" acting on their own account and dealing only with the brokers. The separation of the agency function (broker) and risk function (jobber) known as "single capacity" was meant to avoid conflict of interest: if the broker had had the possibility to act on his own account, he might have made trades in stocks to protect his own book position instead of the interests of his clients.

However, single capacity was seen as an obstacle for the city to compete with foreign banks whose numbers had increased with the emergence of the Euromarket in the 1960s. In the eve of the Big Bang, London was a leading centre in Eurocurrency deposits, underwriting and trading of Eurobonds as well as a major market for foreign exchange transactions and insurance activities.

Despite London being the fastest growing capital market in the world, the London Stock Exchange in 1985 had only 29 % of the trading volume of the New York Stock Exchange and 38 % of the trading volume of the Tokyo Stock Exchange (Brown 1986/1987). At the same time, the value of the securities traded on the London Stock Exchange was less than half the value of the Eurosecurities traded in the Euromarket (Congdon 1986). Therefore, the emergence and development of the Euromarket had created two cities "the free-wheeling, unregulated, international City of the Eurocurrency markets, and the sterling-based, cartelised, domestic City whose bastion was the Stock exchange" (quoted by Kynaston 2011a, 549). The intent of the reform was to eliminate this division.

The Big Bang's main points were the abolition of both fixed minimum commissions to introduce competition among brokers and single capacity which prohibited member firms from acting as both jobbers and brokers. Among other things, the reform also removed restrictions on the ownership of member firms so allowing the entry of outside corporations, and it put an end to the outcry system of trading in favour of a completely automated system. The Stock Exchange became a private limited company under the Companies Act 1985. As a consequence of the reform, jobbing and broking firms underwent a process of mergers and consolidations. Jobbing firms merged with broking firms or with merchant banks, and many broking firms were acquired by large commercial or international banks. All the main brokers, jobbers, and merchant banks which had existed in the UK before the Big Bang gradually disappeared, and by 2000, there remained only one independent firm (Cazenove) still engaged in the securities business (Augar 2001). JP Morgan eventually acquired Cazenove in 2009. The Financial Services Act of 1986 also abolished any oversight of the courts on derivative contracts that may have been considered speculative and thus contrary to the Gaming Act of 1845.

Several other laws addressed specifically to the banking system helped to change the structure of the UK financial system. The Banking Act of 1979 introduced the requirements for institutions to be licensed in order to accept deposits from the public. The Act was the first to introduce a regime of regulation of the sector following the secondary banking crisis of 1973–1974. That crisis made clear some weaknesses in the supervision of deposit-taking institutions. In addition, the Act was necessary to comply with the European Economic Community (EEC) Council Directive

77/780 intended to promote harmonisation in financial services. The Act created a two-tier system of "recognized banks" and "licensed institutions". Only the former had the right to call themselves "banks" and were supervised by the Bank of England on a non-statutory basis.

Both recognised banks and licensed institutions were to meet criteria regarding their legal form, prudential requirements, and management. The Act also introduced for the first time a protection scheme for depositors of failed institutions. The combined effects of this Act and the abolition of exchange controls in 1979 increased competition for UK banks from both foreign banks and from non-bank institutions.

The collapse and rescue of Johnson Matthey Bank (JMB) by the Bank of England in 1984 evidenced the deficiencies of the 1979 Act and pushed forward changes in the supervisory and legal framework. JMB was a "recognized bank" and therefore had been subject to a less stringent formal regulation than a "licensed deposit institution".

The Banking Act of 1987 repealed the Banking Act of 1979 and replaced the two-tier system of recognised and licensed institutions with a single system of authorisation and supervision for all the institutions that accept deposits in the course of business. The 1987 Act also established the Board of Banking Supervision to assist the Bank of England in the fulfilment of its increased supervisory power.

In turn, the 1987 Act was repealed by the Financial Services and Markets Act 2000 (FSMA 2000). Prior to the introduction of FSMA 2000, an important piece of legislation was the Bank of England Act 1998, which gave operational responsibility for monetary policy to the Bank of England. The 1998 Act established the Monetary Policy Committee (MPC), a nine-member body with the independent responsibility for setting interest rates to meet the government's inflation targets. Previously, the Chancellor of the Exchequer had the power to set interest rate although in consultation with the governor of the Bank of England.

The Bank quasi-independence over monetary policy was accompanied by the losing of its responsibility for banking supervision, which was transferred to the Financial Services Authority (FSA). The near collapse of Barings Bank in 1995, the collapse of the Bank of Credit and Commerce International (BCCI) in 1991, and other financial scandals that happened during the decade since the Financial Services Act 1986 had tainted the Bank of England's reputation for banking supervision as well as raising questions about the concept of self-regulation.

The FSMA 2000 established the FSA as the regulatory body to preside over the financial services market. Under this Act, the FSA had the power to grant authorisation to carry on a regulated activity in the UK providing that the applicants meet relevant criteria. The criteria were meant to ensure that only firms considered financially sound and that fulfil the additional requirements of honesty, integrity, and competence could obtain authorisation to operate in the UK.

The way the FSA exercised the regulatory power on the authorised parties was set out in the FSA handbook, an enormous document produced by the Authority itself. Although the FSA was seen by many commentators as a super-regulator with inadequate accountability, the supervisory regime was still based on light touch regulation coupled with a self-regulated approach.

Following the failure of Northern Rock in 2008, the Banking Special Provisions Act put in place a set of temporary measures to deal with the failure of the bank. The Banking Act 2009 provided a permanent regime to deal with banks in financial difficulties, the "Special Resolution Regime", a set of tools available to the Treasury, the Bank of England, and the FSA to deal with failing UK banks and building societies. It also gave the Bank of England statutory responsibilities for systemically important inter-bank payments as well as granting the Bank immunity in its capacity as a monetary authority.

The Financial Services Act 2012, which came into force on 1 April 2013, shifted supervisory power towards the Bank of England with the abolition of the FSA. In the wake of the 2007/2008 financial crisis, the tripartite system in charge of the UK financial services sector and represented by the Bank (responsible for the payment system and financial stability), the FSA (responsible for both prudential and conduct regulation), and the Treasury (responsible for the fiscal policy) was thought inadequate to cope with the problems emerged from the crisis. In particular, the division of roles had often overlapped and created friction among the Bank of England and the FSA whose responsibility was also thought to be too wide.

The 2012 Act creates a new regulatory structure consisting of the Bank's Financial Policy Committee (FPC), the Prudential Regulation Authority (PRA), and the Financial Conduct Authority (FCA). The PRA (a limited company wholly owned by the Bank of England) is responsible for prudential regulation of all institutions that accept deposits or insurance contracts (banks, building societies, credit unions, insurers, and major investment firms). These are considered "systemically important firms", namely firms that pose a risk to the financial system were they to fail.

The PRA's main objectives are to promote the safety and soundness of systemically important firms and, regarding insurers, to contribute to the securing of an appropriate degree of protection for policyholders. The PRA's prudential supervision approach is based on judgments not only focused on whether a firm complies with prudential rules today but also based on its assessment of future risks (forward-looking judgments).

The FCA is responsible for the conduct of business regulation for all authorised firms and for prudential regulation of financial firms that are considered of limited systemic importance (as for example personal investment firms, mortgage, or insurance intermediaries). It has taken over the functions of the FSA as the UK listing authority and the responsibility for the market abuse regime.

The FCA's main objectives are to promote effective competition in the interests of consumers as well as securing consumer protection.

The FPC is a committee, within the Bank of England, responsible for macro-prudential supervision. The FPC's primary objective is to preserve the UK's financial stability by identifying, monitoring, and taking policy measures to reduce systemic risk. The FPC has the power to use macro-prudential tools as, for example, setting countercyclical capital buffers, enforcing capital requirements on specific sectors or asset classes, and imposing leverage limits on banks. The FPC is required to respond to the Treasury's recommendations but may reject any recommendations it does not agree with.

The Financial Services (Banking Reform) Act 2013, also known as "Banking Reform Act", brought into law the recommendations of the Independent Commission on Banking (ICB). The commission, chaired by Sir John Vickers, was set up by Parliament in 2010 to consider structural reforms of the UK banking sector. These reforms were seen as necessary to safeguard UK retail deposits in the event of another financial crisis and to improve financial stability. The Act requires that the activity of accepting deposits, in a banking group, be placed into ring-fenced bodies (RFBs). The latter will not be allowed to engage in risky activities such as wholesale and investment bank activities and must also be financially independent from those entities of the group that undertake such activities. The RFB is designed to insulate a bank's retail deposits from shocks originating in another part of the group.

The Banking Reform Act provided the framework for the reforms of the sector; the way it would be implemented was left to secondary legislation and the PRA. In particular, the PRA is required to make rules to implement ring-fencing of core UK financial services and activities. Rules governing important aspects of ring-fenced banks, such as capital buffers, permissible relationships between ring-fenced banks and other entities of the group, are still not fully defined. All the provisions in the Act are supposed to come into force in 2019.

The EU Legislation

The influence of the EU on the banking legislation of the Member States has steadily increased since the adoption in 1977 of the First Banking Directive. The Directive 77/780/EEC on "The coordination of Laws, Regulations and Administrative Provisions Relating to the Taking up and Pursuit of the Business of Credit Institutions" was the first step towards the development of a common banking market. It allowed a Member State bank to establish branches or subsidiaries in another European Economic Area Member State. However, a bank wishing to operate in another country still had to be authorised and supervised by the host country supervisor.

The Second Banking Directive (89/646/EEC), which came into force on 1 January 1993, accelerated the process towards the integration of the European banking system by introducing both product and geographical liberalisation. The Directive obligated each Member State to recognise the banking licence of other Member States (principle of mutual recognition). Therefore, any credit institution authorised in a Member

State could operate in another Member State under its Home Member State licence ("single banking licence principle") without any further authorisation.

The Annex to the Second Directive specified the banking activities subject to mutual recognition.

The banking model adopted by the EU was the universal banking model that permits banks to undertake both commercial and investment banking activities. In particular, banks were allowed to participate in securities and derivatives transactions on their own account and for the account of customers. The Directive also incorporated the principle of "home country control" according to which a bank with a single licence is authorised and supervised by the home Member State even when it operates in the host Member State.

The Second Banking Directive together with the Directive on Liberalization of Capital Flows (88/361/EEC) and the 1992 Maastricht Treaty, which set the rules for a single currency, were fundamental for European financial integration. In 1999, the Council launched the Financial Services Action Plan (FSAP), a five-year plan with a large series of measures designed to fully integrate banking and capital markets which were still fragmented on the eve of the introduction of the Euro.

The first "Markets in Financial Instruments Directive" (2004/39/CE), which came into force on 1 November 2007, was a cornerstone of the FSAP. The primary objectives of the Directive, best known as MiFID 1, were to promote competition and enhance investor choice across Europe.

In particular, the Directive allowed investment firms to operate throughout the EU on the basis of their authorisation in their home Member State (single passport). It also abolished the "concentration rule" which required that all equity transactions should be carried out on a European-regulated market, usually the nationally regulated stock exchange. The end of the centralised marked system allowed banks and other investment institutions to compete with stock exchanges in trading financial instruments. For the first time, the Directive established a comprehensive regulated framework for the operation of a traditional stock exchange or regulated market (RM) and alternative trading venues, the so-called **multilateral trading facilities** (MTFs). The Directive also enhanced investor protection by setting rules of transparency for the intermediaries.

Following the 2008 global crisis that dramatically brought to light the inadequacy of regulation, in particular with regard to the derivatives market, the European Commission decided to review the MiFID 1 framework and on October 2011 published a proposal for a revised Directive and a new Regulation.

The recast "Markets in Financial Investments Directive", known as MiFID 2, and the Markets in Financial Investments Regulation, known as MiFIR, came into force on 2 July 2014. MiFID 2 updates the existing framework to take into account the developments of the previous years' market infrastructures and activities. The Directive and Regulation also implemented the 2009 G20 commitments to reform the derivatives market. As a response to the 2008 financial crisis, the governments and central bankers of the G20 countries agreed to review the regulatory regimes of the financial sector. The lack of banks' capital to absorb losses and the lack of transparency in the derivatives market were seen as key factors in contributing to the spread of the crisis. They aimed to create a more robust financial system by introducing a set of reforms to address the weaknesses of the system. The focus was on strengthening banks' resilience to crisis and improving the transparency of the derivatives market. In particular, G20 countries committed to having all derivatives traded on central trading facilities and to be centrally cleared, where appropriate, and all transactions were to be reported to trade repositories.

MiFID 2 aims to modernise European market infrastructures to ensure that trading, where appropriate, takes place on regulated platforms. Thus, in addition to regulated markets (RMs) and MTFs already covered by MiFID 1, a new category of trading venue, called **organised trading facilities** (OTFs) for non-equity instruments is introduced into the regulatory framework. Shares and non-equity instruments are subject to a trading obligation which means that relevant counterparties must conclude relevant transactions only on regulated markets (RMs), MTFs, and OTFs.

MiFID 2 aims also to improve market transparency to best allow investors and market participants to know at what prices they can buy and sell financial instruments (pre-trade transparency) and at what prices they have been bought and sold (post-trade transparency). Pre- and post-trade transparencies provide information to investors about trading opportunities and facilitate price formation. MiFID 2 extends pre- and post-trade transparency to equity instruments other than shares (such as depositary receipts, exchange-traded funds, and certificates) and non-equity instruments (such as bonds, structured finance products, emission allowances, and derivatives traded on a trading venue). Pre-trade transparency requirements are imposed also when equity and non-equity instruments are offered by **systematic internalisers** (SI) in OTC trading. MiFID 2 introduces a number of new rules to strengthen investor protection and reduce conflicts of interest in the provision of investment advice.

More importantly, MiFID 2 removes "**structured UCITS**" from the definition of non-complex instruments to prevent these funds being subject to less stringent rules for the protection of retail investors. MiFID 2 also introduces, among other things, a number of measures aimed at reducing systemic risk and speculative activity in commodity derivatives markets. These measures reflect the G20 commitments to address the excessive price volatility of these markets, in particular the ones related to food given the impact that higher prices had on poor countries.

As we have already noted, the derivatives market was seen as an important transmission mechanism because any defaults in trading could have a huge impact on the other activities of a bank. To limit this in future, the European Parliament and the Council issued Regulation n648/2012 on OTC derivatives, central counterparties (**CCPs**), and trade repositories (**TRs**) known as EMIR (European Market Infrastructure Regulation) which was adopted and came into force on 16 August 2012. EMIR aims to improve transparency in the OTC derivatives market through imposing a regulated regime for all participants in the market: derivatives counterparties, CCPs, and trade repositories.

According to this Regulation, entities (both financial and non-financial) that enter into any form of derivative contract (interest rate, foreign exchange, equity, credit, and commodity derivatives) should report to a trade repository every contract they enter into. This would allow the supervisory authorities to get a better overview of the market and to detect potential problems such as the accumulation of risk. This Regulation also requires certain classes of OTC derivatives that meet certain eligibility criteria to be cleared through CCPs. The classes of OTC derivatives that are subject to the clearing obligation are published in a public register held by the European Securities and Markets Authority (ESMA).

For those derivatives that are not subject to a mandatory clearing obligation and therefore are not cleared through a CCP, EMIR requires the application of risk-mitigation techniques, for example, the exchange of collateral. According to EMIR, CCPs need to be authorised to provide clearing services within the EU. EU CCPs must apply for authorisation to the competent authority in the Member State where they are established, whereas third-country CCPs need to be recognised by ESMA before providing clearing services to clearing members within the EU. EMIR also sets out a number of obligations for CCPs to ensure that they are regulated on a consistent basis, for example, organisational requirement and margin requirements.

As for TRs, the European ones need to be registered by ESMA while third-country TRs may apply to ESMA for recognition if they meet certain conditions such as the equivalence of the regulatory and supervisory framework in their country to that of the EU. TRs should also comply with certain obligations which include requirements relating transparency and data availability.

Since non-financial counterparties are supposed to use derivatives contracts only to hedge the risk associated with their business activity, they are exempted from the clearing obligation. They must comply only with reporting obligations. Non-financial counterparties should comply with the majority of EMIR requirements in cases where derivatives are not used to hedge risk and a clearing threshold is reached.

The Eurozone debt crises of 2010/2011 urged the European authorities to move quickly towards a banking union to complete the economic and monetary union and break the vicious circle of worsening finances of banks and national governments. The Capital Requirement Directive (CRD) and the Capital Requirement Regulation (CRR) together with the Directive on Bank Recovery and Resolution (BRRD) constitute a big step towards that goal.

The CRD IV (Directive 2013/36/EU) and CRR (Regulation EU n. 575/2013) adopted the new international capital standards set by the Basel Committee on Banking Supervision, known as the Basel III agreement, into EU legislation. CRR produces a single set of prudential rules which take immediate effect in all Member States. The legislation (CRR and CRD IV) aims to strengthen a bank's capital necessary to absorb losses. In fact, CRD IV requires banks and large investment firms to hold more capital of a higher quality than before. It also increases capital requirements held against securities and derivatives transactions as well as introducing, among other things, new capital buffers, new liquidity requirements, and a supplementary non-risk-based leverage ratio.

The BRRD (Directive 2014/59/EU) provides a common framework for all EU countries to deal with troubled banks. The Directive foresees a three phased approach: precautionary, early intervention, and orderly resolution. It also establishes the much-debated principle that private investors and creditors bear the first costs of troubled institutions before resolution authorities can access other sources of funding (bail-in). The BRRD has been implemented through the SRM (Single Resolution Mechanism) and the SSM (Single Supervisory Mechanism) which together with the Deposit Guarantee Scheme (DGS) constitute the pillars of the banking union.

The SRM establishes a common European process to cope with troubled banks and the steps to be taken to resolve their problems. The SRM will have a central decision-making board (SRB—Single Resolution Board) and a Single Resolution Fund (SRF) that should be built over a period of eight years through contributions from banks. The fund is due to reach a target level of at least 1 % of the amount of covered deposits of all credit institutions of the participating Member States.

The SSM aims at the centralised supervision of financial institutions giving the ECB the prudential supervision authority in cooperation with national supervisory authorities. In particular, the ECB directly supervises banks considered "significant" whereas banks "less significant" continue to be supervised by the national authorities in cooperation with the ECB.

Notwithstanding all the regulatory efforts undertaken after the financial crisis to strengthen the resilience of the banking system, according to the European Council "some significant risks in the EU's banking system remain, mainly due to the large size and complexity of some of its credit institutions and excessive risk-taking, especially in trading in highly complex financial instruments. These institutions remain too-big-to-fail and too complex to resolve in the case of failure" (European Council 2016).

To address the risk posed by large, complex, and interconnected credit institution, in June 2015, the European Council published a proposal of "Regulation on structural measures improving the resilience of EU credit institutions". The proposal of Regulation is based on the results of the Liikanen report issued by the group of experts, chaired by Erkki Liikanen, appointed by the European Commission in 2011 to examine possible structural reforms for the EU banking sector. The aim of the proposal, as with the Volcker rule and the UK "ring fencing", is to protect individual depositors against losses from risky bank activities. In fact, the proposal envisages a mandatory separation of proprietary trading from the "core" activities of credit institutions.

The decision on separation is left to the national competent authorities if the risk, according to an established set of criteria, is considered to be too high. Trading activities other than proprietary trading (e.g. market making, risky derivatives, and complex securitisation) are not subject to mandatory separation but remain subject to risk assessment by the national competent authorities. If the risk of these activities is considered excessive, the national competent authorities may decide to separate them from the "core" activities of the credit institution or impose other prudential measures to mitigate the risk. The "ring fenced" trading entities would not be allowed to take retail deposits.

The proposed Regulation will apply to credit institution identified as Globally Systemically Important Institutions as well as to other credit institutions that exceed certain thresholds in total assets (at least €30 billion) and in trading activities (at least €70 billion or 10 % of their total assets) for three consecutive years. At the time of writing, the proposal of Regulation is still to be discussed by the European Parliament.

Notes

1. The author of this Appendix is Maria Carmen Siniscalchi.

2. In this Appendix the use of bold fonts signals the first occurrence of a financial term defined in the Glossary of Financial Terms (Appendix 2).

Bibliography

Augar, Philip. 2001. *The Death of Gentlemanly Capitalism. The Rise and Fall of London's Investment Banks*. London: Penguin Books, Ltd.

Brown, Jonathan. 1986–1987. Britain's Big Bang. In *Multinational Monitor* 7/8. http://www.multinationalmonitor.org/hyper/issues/1986/12/brown.html

Congdon, Tim. 1986. Bigger than the Big Bang. In *The Spectator*, 18 october.

European Council. 2016. *Structural Reform of EU Banking Sector: Improving the Resilience of Credit Institutions*. http://www.consilium.europa.eu/en/policies/banking-structural-reform/. Retrieved 29 February 2016.

Gilbert, R. Alton. 1986. Requiem for Regulation Q: What it Did and Why It Passed Away. *Federal Reserve Bank of ST. Louis Review* 68(2): 22–37.

Gorton, Gary B. 2010. *Slapped by the Invisible Hand: the Panic of 2007*. New York: New York University Press.

ICMA (International Capital Market Association). 2013. Frequently Asked Questions on Repo. https://www.treasurers.org/ACTmedia/Repo_faqs.pdf. Retrieved 13 March 2016.

Kynaston, David. 2011a. *City of London. The History*. London: Chatto & Windus.

Kynaston, David. 2011b. Was the Big Bang Good for the City of London and Britain? In *The Telegraph*, 26 October.

Nersisyan, Yeva. 2015. The Repeal of the Glass-Steagall Act and the Federal Reserve's Extraordinary Intervention during the Global Financial Crisis. Levy Economics Institute Working Paper Collection No. 829.

Omarova, Saule T. 2009. The Quiet Methamorphosis: How Derivatives Changed the 'Business of Banking'. Cornell Law Faculty Publication. Paper 1021.

———. 2011. From-Leach-Bliley to Dodd-Frank: The Unfulfilled Promise of Section 23A of the Federal Reserve Act. *North Carolina Law Review* 89: 1685–1769.

Omarova, Saule T., and Tahyar E. Margaret. 2011. That Which We Call a Bank: Revisiting the History of Bank Holding Company Regulations in the United States. *Review of Banking and Financial Law* 31: 2011–2012.

Skeel, David. 2011. *The New Financial Deal. Understanding the Dodd-Frank Act and Its (Unintended) Consequences*. Hoboken, New Jersey: John Wiley & Sons, Inc.

Appendix 2: Glossary of Financial Terms[1]

Asset-Backed Commercial Paper (ABCP)

Asset-backed commercial paper is a short-term security whose maturity, like commercial paper, usually ranges from 90 to 180 days. However, unlike commercial paper, which is an unsecured obligation of the borrowing company, it is backed by collateral. The typical form of collateral is the company's expected future payments on auto loans, credit cards, and invoices. ABCP allows companies to raise short-term money in return for these expected future payments. They are issued by banks usually through a conduit such as a SIV.

Asset-Backed Security (ABS)

A security that is backed by a pool of assets, as for example, payments made on credit cards, automobile loans, student loans, and home equity loans. Its value derives from the underlying assets; these securities are usually created and sold through a special purpose vehicle (SPV). When the assets are a pool of mortgages, the security is known as mortgage-backed security (MBS).

© The Editor(s) (if applicable) and The Author(s) 2017
A. Vercelli, *Crisis and Sustainability*,
DOI 10.1057/978-1-137-60069-1

Bank Holding Company Act (BHCA)

This was an Act passed by the US Congress in 1956. It defined a BHC as any company that owns or controls 25 % or more of the shares of two or more banks. The Act gave the Federal Reserve regulatory power over BHCs that had to register with the Board and submit to consolidated regulation and supervision. Their investments and activities were restricted mainly to owning and managing banks and conducting activities "closely related to banking".

The definition of "bank" and the limitation of holding company status changed over time. The Congress amended the statutory definition of "bank" in 1966, 1970, and 1987. In 1970, the one-bank company was included within the scope of the BHCA.

Collateralized Debt Obligation (CDO)

It is a form of asset-backed security that is made up from different types of assets (bonds, loans, etc.). These securities are typically issued through a SPV that acquires a pool of assets from an intermediary (originator) and uses them to back the issuance of CDOs. The cash generated by the issuance of CDOs is used by the SPV to acquire the underlying assets.

The SPV issues CDOs in tranches carrying different levels of risk and repayment priorities for holders of each tranches: senior tranches rank first in the priority of payments for both capital and interest, followed by the mezzanine and equity tranches. Payments are made from the cash flow generated by the underlying assets. A higher interest rate is offered to investors willing to buy CDOs whose collateral has a high risk of non-repayment. Senior tranches, which are safer, are rated and issued in the market. Different types of collateral define different kinds of products, for example:

Collateralized loan obligations (CLOs) are backed by loans that are usually "leveraged" and have therefore a higher risk of default;

Collateralized bond obligations (CBOs) are backed by a variety of high-yield junk bonds;

Structured finance CDOs (SFCDOs) are backed by asset-backed securities (also known as CDO of ABS); and

Collateralized synthetic obligations (CSOs) are backed by credit derivatives.

Other types include:

CDO squared that are backed by tranches of CDOs; and

CDO cubed whose collateral includes tranches of CDO squared.

The process can go on to CDO^n as long as investors continue to have confidence in the collateral backing the securities.

Central Counterparties (CCPs) or Clearing Houses

They are entities that interpose themselves between counterparties to contracts traded in financial markets. They act as buyer to every seller and as seller to every buyer of the contract. This means that one counterparty is protected from the default of the other, and because the risk is taken on by the CCP, they consequently mitigate the risk in the financial system. Although CCPs can clear both securities and derivatives, given the importance that counterparty credit risk plays in derivatives transactions, CCPs play a more prominent role for the derivative market.

CCPs bear no "market" risk because when they interpose themselves between two counterparties, two new perfectly offsetting contracts are created. However, they bear "credit" risk in case one of their clearing members defaults. CCPs can manage their counterparty risk exposure through a number of reinforcing mechanism known as "risk default waterfall". They usually include access restrictions (certain standards are required to be a clearing member), risk management techniques (such as taking collateral from clearing members), loss mutualisation (by using a default fund to cover residual losses), and the use of their own capital as last line of defence.

By virtue of the risk-mitigation role they play, they are a critical component of the market in which they operate; consequently, regulation of CCPs is extremely important. A large CCP that fails could act as a channel of contagion with serious effects on the market.

Counterparty Risk

Counterparty risk is the risk that the other party in an agreement will default. In a CDS contract, a protection buyer faces a counterparty default exposure to the reference entity and to the protection seller (double default). There is an additional counterparty replacement risk on the default of the protection seller, because if the protection seller defaults, the CDS position may have to be replaced at unfavourable market prices.

The protection seller counterparty risk is the risk to lose expected premium income if the buyer defaults. One exception to the above risk allocation is the founded CDS.

Credit Default Swap (CDS)

A swap designed to transfer the credit exposure of fixed income products (bonds and loans) between parties. The purchaser of the swap (also referred as protection buyer or risk shedder) makes periodic payments, called premium, to the seller (protection seller or risk taker) who in exchange will pay the face value (par value) of the loan should the third party (reference entity) default.

In the terminology of the CDS market, the premium paid by the protection buyer to the protection seller is called spread. The market price of the premium is an indication of the perceived risk of the reference entity.

The simplest form of CDS is known as *CDS single name* in which the reference entity is an individual corporation or government. There are many variant as, for example:

Basked CDS (BCDSs), CDS with two or more reference entities (up to one hundred);

Funded CDS (called credit linked notes), CDS in which the protection seller lends the notional amount to the protection buyer to secure the settlement of any credit event. In a funded CDS, the protection buyer is not exposed to the counterparty risk of the protection seller but has to pay interest on the loan and repay the loan when the funded CDS matures;

Index CDS, CDS in which the reference entity is an index of many corporate entities. An index CDS offers protection on all entities in the index with an equal share of the notional amount. Market participants can buy or sell protection also on tranches of indices. If the credit event occurs on one of the component reference entities, the contract will not terminate and the buyer of protection will be compensated in proportion to the weight of the reference entity in the basket;

LCDS (Loan only credit default swap), CDS in which the protection is given on a syndicated secured loan rather than any loan or bond. A syndicated loan is secured when a lender from the syndicate is appointed to act as a security trustee to hold the securities placed as collateral by the borrower in trust for the benefit of all the lenders; and

CMCDS (Constant maturity credit default swap), CDS in which the premium paid by the protection buyer is not fixed as in the standard CDS but is linked to a benchmark, usually a CDS index, and is often expressed as a percentage of the reference CDS spread.

Credit Default Swap Option

A credit default swap option (also known as credit default swaption) is an option on a credit default swap that gives its holder the right, but not the obligation, to enter into a credit default swap, that is, the right to buy (call) or to sell (put) protection on a reference entity for a specified period of time and for a set spread.

CDS options can be either a payer swaption, that is, an option to buy, to obtain a credit protection paying a periodic premium, or a receiver swaption, that is, an option to provide credit protection receiving a periodic premium.

A credit default swaption protects against credit curve moves, for example, as credit risk grows, the seller of a credit default swap can protect himself against a widening CDS spread buying a CDS option. Depending on the contract, if a credit event occurs before the swaption expiry, the swaption can be knocked out (cancelled).

Credit Event

It occurs when there is a negative and significant change in a borrower's credit standing. The typical credit event in a credit derivative transaction, according to the International Swap and Derivatives Association (ISDA) definition, includes failure to pay, restructuring (except voluntary restructuring), moratorium and repudiation, obligation acceleration, and obligation default.

When a credit event occurs, the CDS buyer can either receive the face value of the debt obligation (loans and bonds), and in return, the seller takes possession of the securities or the contract can be settled in cash (cash settlement). In the latter case, the protection seller pays the difference between the face value and the market price of the debt obligation of the reference entity after an auction has taken place to determine the post default market value. The cash settlement usually happens with the naked CDS. If the credit event does not occur, the buyer continues paying premiums until the end of the contract.

International Swaps and Derivatives Association (ISDA)

It was founded in 1985 to support regulatory efforts for the safety of the financial OTC derivatives market. ISDA has produced "the ISDA Master Agreement" designed to provide standard contracts (such as payments and delivery of obligation, netting of payments, events of defaults, and liquidation) for participants in the OTC derivatives market. ISDA comprise over 800-member institutions from 60 countries. They include market participants (as corporations, governments, insurance companies, and international and regional banks) and members of the derivatives market infrastructure (e.g. CCPs) as well as service providers (such as law and accounting firms).

Although contract counterparties are free to amend the ISDA definitions, the majority of derivative trades are covered by the standard ISDA documentation.

Margin Call

A margin requirement is the minimum amount of cash or securities that need to be deposited as collateral in a trading account in order to trade in a market. The margin amount is set either by exchanges for deals transacted on exchanges or by a bank or broker for OTC deals.

The broker or exchange issues a margin call when the balance in the margin account has dropped below the margin requirement. This happens when the price of the securities moves adversely for the buyer or seller.

Money-Market Fund (MMF) or Money-Market Mutual Fund (MMMF)

A MMF is a mutual fund which is characterised by investing in short-term (usually less than one year) fixed income, high credit quality securities. These funds allow investors to participate in a diversified portfolio of assets that can include a broad range of short-term instruments such as Treasury Bills, commercial paper, and repos, depending on the type of the fund.

Federal regulations require MMFs, which are not guaranteed by the FDIC, to hold securities with very short maturities and a high credit quality in order to be able to comply with the objective of preserving the value of the funds the depositors invest even in time of market difficulties.

Monoline

A monoline is a company that is specialised in a single type of business; in the context of financial markets, the word is used to mean a company specialised as bond insurer. A monoline insurer guarantees the repayment of bonds: like any other insurance, they charge bond issuers a fee in exchange for a promise to make bond repayments if the issuer defaults.

The existence of monoline insurance makes bonds attractive to investors as the default risk is transferred from the bond holder to the monoline insurer. The latter must have a high credit rating to sustain its business.

This form of insurance first began for municipal bonds and then in the 1990s started to insure CDOs.

Multilateral Trading Facility (MTF)

A MTF is a trading system that enables multiple parties, either retail investors or investment firms, to exchange a variety of financial instruments (bonds, shares, and derivatives). These facilities, based on sophisticated electronic systems and matching software for fast order execution, are controlled by approved market operators or larger investment banks. MiFID 1 introduced MTFs within the regulatory framework setting authorisation conditions and regulatory requirements. According to MiFID 1, entities trading with financial instruments must be organised as either regulated market (RM) or a MTF.

Although the obligations for MTFs and RMs to operate under MiFID are broadly the same in terms of transparency, the financial instruments traded on a MTF have fewer restrictions for admittance than in a regulated market, thus allowing participants to exchange more exotic assets.

In September 2011, ESMA identified 143 MTFs operating in the EU and UK. With respect to national stock exchanges, these facilities offer faster trading and lower costs.

Notional Amount

The par value, in a CDS, of the protection bought by the protection buyer or sold by the protection seller. It is the amount used to calculate the premium and the recovery amount in the event of default.

Organised Trading Facility (OTF)

An OTF is a system designed to bring together buying and selling interests in financial instruments in a way that results in contracts. Introduced by MiFID 2 and MiFIR as a new category of trading venue alongside

RMs (regulated markets) and MTFs, OTFs relate only to bonds, structured finance products, emission allowances, or derivatives.

An OTF is operated by investment firms or market operators (brokers) and is designed to include segments of the market such as bilateral derivatives trades and broker-crossing networks (an internal matching system that executes client orders against each other). The execution of orders is carried out on a discretionary basis, therefore an operator of an OTF that crosses client orders may decide if, when, and how much of two or more orders he wants to match within the system.

Under MiFID 2, OTFs operators are not permitted to use their own capital to trade orders from clients (to trade against their proprietary capital) except when they trade on sovereign debt instruments for which there is no liquid market. In addition, the operators of OTFs are not permitted to be systematic internalisers.

Since most of derivatives are still traded OTC, OTFs are expected to shift more complex products to electronic platforms so that they can be monitored.

Over-the-Counter (OTC) Market

A market where traders make deals directly with each other by phone and through electronic messages. Dealers trade with end-users as well as with other dealers.

Protection Buyer

An investor (banks, hedge funds, asset managers, etc.) who, buying a CDS, hedge the risk that a borrower may default on a loan. In this case, the CDS is used to manage the risk of default that arises from being exposed to the credit risk of the reference entity. Commercial banks and other lenders are natural buyers of protection for such purposes. However, the protection buyer can buy a CDS even without owning the underlying debt (naked CDS). In fact, the main uses of CDS other than hedging are speculation and arbitrage.

Protection Seller

The protection seller takes on the credit exposure to the reference entity in a CDS contract. Protection sellers can be highly rated dealers, hedge funds, insurance companies, and regional banks who want to diversify their exposure.

Reference Entity

The reference entity is the issuer of the debt insured by the CDS contract. This includes governments, corporations, or any other legal entity such as a SPV that issues debt of any kind. The reference entity is not party to the contract.

Repurchase Agreement (Repo)

A repo is an agreement by which one party sells a security to a second party at a certain price and simultaneously agrees to buy it back at a higher price at a future date. The transaction from the point of view of the buyer of the securities is called "reverse repo".

Repos are typically short-term instruments whose maturity goes from overnight to 30 days or more. The difference between the price paid by the buyer of the security (provider of cash to the seller) at the start of the transaction, and the price he receives when he sells back the security is called the "repo rate" and represents the interest paid on the money lent. The repo rate changes according to the quality of the collateral and the terms of the loan.

Although from a legal point of view the repo is a buy and sell transaction, it plays the same economic function as a collateralised loan with the security used as collateral to mitigate the risk of the seller's default. The difference between the current market price of the security and the price at which the seller (borrower of cash) sells it at the start of the transaction is called "haircut", and it is meant to limit the credit exposure of the buyer of the security (lender of cash). The repo can either be "cash driven" when the transaction is motivated by the wish to raise short-term funds or "securities driven" when it is driven by the demand to borrow securities.

According to ICMA (International Capital Market Association 2013), the principal users of the repo market have been traditionally from the seller side (security seller-cash borrower) broker-dealers and hedge funds, from the buyer side (security buyer-cash provider) have been non-bank financial institutions (e.g. money-market funds) and some commercial banks. Since the 2008 crisis, the repo has been attracting a greater number of non-bank financial institutions as pension funds and insurance companies. Apart from its use as a cheaper source of funding, the repo market is also used to invest surplus cash, to finance a long position, to cover a short position, or to hedge.

Special Purpose Vehicle (SPV) or Special Purpose Entity (SPE)

It is a legal entity usually created by a bank (known as the sponsor or originator) to hold a portfolio of assets with the purpose of carrying out some circumscribed activities as, for example, asset securitisation. It has no physical location and from the legal point of view can take the form of a limited partnership, a limited liability company, a trust, or a corporation. Since it is a "bankrupt remote entity", if the sponsor firm goes bankrupt, the firm's creditors cannot seize the assets of the SPV and the SPV cannot become legally bankrupt.

Structured Investment Vehicles (SIV)

SIVs are limited purpose operating companies typically created by an investment bank. They are usually funded by the original investors (capital note holders) and by issuing short-term debt (CP and ABCP). SIVs then use these funds to buy highly rated medium-term fixed income assets (such as CDOs, auto loans, bank, and corporate bonds).

Unlike SPVs that are not managed but simply follow a set of pre-specified rules, SIVs are market value vehicles that undertake arbitrage activities since they issue short-term debt and invest in high-grade assets to form a diversified portfolio.

SIVs are usually highly leveraged and thus very exposed to liquidity risk in the money market. In fact, the ability of SIVs to refinance themselves depends on the investors having confidence in the assets held by them. When the subprime crisis broke out and investors, typically money-market funds, were unwilling to buy the debt issued by them, SIVs ran out of liquidity experiencing severe problems. Although many SIVs were off-balance sheet, some banks chose to bring them back onto their balance sheets, incurring huge write-downs.

Synthetic CDO (SCDO)

A synthetic CDO is a CDO backed by a portfolio of CDS. Because CDSs permit "synthetic" exposure to credit risk, a CDO backed by CDSs is called a synthetic CDO, while a CDO backed by ordinary assets is called a cash CDO (see CDO).

In a synthetic CDO, the originator (usually a bank) which owns the assets transfers the risk to investors through a SPV that is set up to act as an intermediary between the bank and the investors.

Unlike the cash CDO, the assets are not sold, in fact the originator transfers the risk by acquiring credit protection through a CDS (performs as a protection buyer). Consequently, the SPV in a synthetic CDO does not acquire the original assets but sells credit protection (performs as a protection seller) raising cash from investors to pay the originator in the event of default.

Investors purchase securities issued by the SPV (often with the help of an underwriter) in various tranches graded by risk level from higher credit quality, lower risk, lower yield tranches (senior tranches) to the higher risk, lower credit quality, and higher yield tranches (residual tranches).

The SPV invests the cash paid by investors in high-quality risk-free assets. So the cash inflow in a synthetic CDO is represented by the cash paid by the investors (to buy the tranches), by the CDS premium paid by the originator (to buy credit protection) and by the interest from the high-quality assets. This inflow forms the high-quality collateral.

A synthetic CDO can offer extremely high yields to investors but they do not have the first claim on the collateral, because the cash flow waterfall first goes to compensate the originator (protection buyer) for defaults and then goes to compensate the investors' securities according to the specific priority of the different tranches.

A SCDO can be "fully funded" when the securities issued by the SPV to raise cash are in amount sufficient to cover defaults on the underlying reference assets of the originator. In other words the investor posts the full notional amount of protection sold by the SPV. "Unfunded" SCDO or "super senior tranches" are not covered by collateral. They are usually kept by the originator bank. These tranches are supposed to be safe because they are subordinated to the funded tranches that will be the first to absorb losses in case of default, but this has not been the case as they imploded in the wake of the credit crunch.

The widespread use of SCDO highlighted the underestimation of correlation risk. We have seen that CDO is based on the technique of "pooling" and "tranching" that is to put together the payments of many bits of real estate mortgage from many different places in the same security and kept them separate by selling them in tranches to different investors. The idea was that the risk of default in the real estate market, already seen as uncorrelated, became in this way super-uncorrelated. In reality, the loans tended to default together in a greater magnitude than was expected. In particular, the super-senior tranche that was believed safe proved not to be so because its market value started to deteriorate before the default of the funded tranches.

Another problem highlighted by the use of SCDO is conflict of interest since the sponsor (usually an investment bank) who takes the position of protection buyer may assume the opposite side of a client (investor) position as in the case of Goldman Sachs "Abacus", earning enormous profits if the investor loses.

Systematic Internaliser (SI)

According to MiFID 2 and MiFIR, a systematic internaliser (SI) is "an investment firm which on an organized, frequent, systematic and substantial basis, deals on its own account by executing client orders outside a RM (regulated market), MTF or OTF without operating a multilateral system".

MiFID 2 extends the SI regime introduced by MiFID I in 2007 and applied only to shares to a broader range of instruments such as equity-like instruments (depository receipts, certificates, etc.) and non-equity instruments (derivatives, bonds, etc.).

SI are investment firms who, instead of sending client orders to a central exchange, can match them with other orders in their own book. They have to comply with certain obligations regarding, among others, pre-trade transparency (they have to show a price before a trade is made) and the disclosure of information about the transaction. They also have to state their intention of being systematic internaliser and the specific financial instruments they want to deal with.

ESMA publishes an updated list of systematic internalisers. The list represents the consolidation of national lists communicated by national competent authorities.

Trade Repository (TR)

A trade repository is an entity that centrally collects and maintains the records of derivatives transactions in a transaction register. They are supposed to enhance market transparency and identify systemic risk in the derivatives market by making market positions and potential risk concentration fully visible to regulators.

According to EMIR, the requirement to report is implemented for all derivatives and users of these derivatives. The contracts should be reported regardless of whether they are traded on a regulated market or OTC, and regardless of whether they are subject to clearing obligations or not. Both counterparties to a derivative contract have to report the details of the agreement to a trade repository of their choice.

By February 2014, there were six trade repositories registered in the EU. ESMA holds an updated list of registered trade repositories.

UCITS

UCITS stands for "undertakings for collective investment in transferable securities"; they are open-ended investment funds that raise capital from the public and collectively invest it in various financial instruments. In the EU, they are regulated through the UCITS Directive which provides a single regulatory regime across the EU for investor protection and product regulation. Therefore, UCITS funds registered in one Member State can operate freely across the EU.

Developments in financial markets have necessitated alterations to the regulatory framework. The first Directive 85/611/EC was followed by Directive 2001/108/EC (21 January 2002) which widened the investments possibilities to include new instruments such as money-market funds and derivatives and Directive 2001/107/EC which detailed minimum standards a UCITS management company should comply with in terms of capital and risk control.

In 2009, the Directive 2009/65/EC (UCITS IV) introduced a passport allowing UCITS to be managed by a company authorised and supervised in a Member State other than its home Member State. There are proposals in discussion for amendments focused mainly on the depositary functions, the introduction of rules on remuneration policies, and the harmonisation of administrative sanctions.

Note

1. The author of this Appendix is Maria Carmen Siniscalchi.

Author Index[1]

A

Abbas, Ali S. M., 128
Adrian, Tobias, 141n44, 177n25
Akerlof, George A., 177n11
Alesina, Alberto, 241n38, 242n44
Aliber, Robert Z., 22n4
Ardagna, Silvia, 241n38
Arestis, Philip, 144, 216
Arrighi, Giovanni, 94, 110n11
Ashcraft, Adam B., 135, 141n44,
    141n45, 177n25
Augar, Philip, 279

B

Bagnai, Alberto, 240n6, 240n10,
    240n11, 241n21, 241n22,
    242n39, 242n43, 242n49

Baldwin, Richard, 233, 241n37
Baran, Paul A., 110n8
Bardi, Ugo, 187
Bariviera, Aurelio F., 57n62
Barreca, Alessandra, 211n16,
    211n17
Barro, Robert J., 242n46, 242n47
Bartolini, Stefano, 140n25
Basosi, Riccardo, 212n53
Bastable, Charles F., 84n23
Baumol, William J., 84n24
Behrens III, William W., 211n4
Belhocine, Nazim, 128
Bellamy Foster, John, 110n8,
    112n43
Bellofiore, Riccardo, 216
Berlin, Isaiah, 33, 34, 43, 44, 53,
    54n6, 56n40

---

[1] Note: Page numbers followed by "n" refers to notes.

Bernanke, Ben S., 120, 140n30, 141n33, 151, 177n17
Beveridge, William, 46, 49, 57n56
Bezdek, Roger, 141n48
Bhagwati, Jagdish, 140n21, 140n23, 177n9
Blattner, Laura, 128
Blyth, Mark, 22n1, 239n1, 240n3, 240n4, 242n42
Boas, Taylor C., 47, 56n37, 56n41, 57n52, 57n53
Boesky, Hayley, 135, 141n44, 141n45, 177n25
Borghesi, Simone, 23n28, 23n31, 23n32, 23n34, 57n58, 110n21, 112n46, 139n2, 140n17, 140n19, 141n47, 179n55, 211n16, 211n17, 211n19, 211n21–3, 264n2, 264n5, 264n7, 264n9
Bourguignon, François, 127, 140n22
Brancaccio, Emiliano, 27, 115, 144, 216
Braudel, Fernand, 93, 110n10
Brenner, Robert, 110n7
Brown, Andrew, 111n23
Brown, Ellen, 111n23, 180n59
Brown, Jonathan, 279
Bryan, William J., 82n12
Burghof, Hans-Peter, 213

C

Calomiris, Charles W., 177n16
Cameron, David R., 49, 57n57
Cameron, Gavin, 139n5
Carter, Ian, 54n3, 129
Cecchetti, Stephen G., 112n42

Chichilnisky, Graciela, 27, 61, 87, 115
Chomsky, Noam, 241n19
Clark, Eric, 212n55
Coase, Ronald H., 50, 57n60, 177n8, 210n3, 211n14
Cockshot, Paul, 265n20
Congdon, Tim, 279
Cooper, Richard, 243
Cottrell, Allin, 265n20
Courtland, Shane D., 57n46
Cox, Richard, 60
Crouch, Colin, 58n64, 266n29

D

De Broeck, Mark, 128
Debreu, Gérard, 5, 22n7, 177n3
Demirel, Pelin, 204
Di Matteo, Massimo, 110n14
Diamond, Douglas W., 177n15
Diamond, Robert, 61
Dickinson, Henry D., 255, 265n17
Dixon, William, 46, 57n47
Dornbusch, Rudiger, 241n34
Driskill, Robert, 83n16, 85n31
Drummond, Paul, 211n17
Dworkin, Ronald, 54n1

E

Ehrlich, Paul R., 211n20
Eichengreen, Barry, 82n8, 241n33, 241n34
Ekins, Paul, 211n17
El-Ganainy, Asmaa, 128
Emerson, Michael, 241n26
Epstein, Gerald A., 109n3

F

Fama, Eugene, 149, 177n4, 177n5
Feinstein, Carles H., 267
Fels, Rendigs, 24n46
Fisher, Irving, 141n40, 178n40, 223,
    226, 227, 241n12
Fitoussi, Jean-Paul, 139n6, 264n8,
    264n10
Fleming, Marcus J., 241n29
Fontana, Giuseppe, 27, 115, 144,
    216
Frankel, Jeffrey A., 233, 241n35
Freeman, Chris, 110n16, 212n33
Freeman, Mark C., 214
Frenkel, Roberto, 225, 240n6,
    240n11
Friedman, Milton, vii, 6, 7, 23n16,
    23n17, 33, 34, 38, 53,
    56n23, 56n35, 123,
    140n14, 140n15, 150,
    241n28

G

Galbraith, James K., 74, 83n18,
    84n22
Galli, Alessandro, 211n18
Gans-Morse, Jordan, 47, 56n37,
    56n41, 57n52, 57n53
Garber, Peter M., 25
Gaus, Gerald F., 56n28, 57n46
Geanakoplos, John D., 55n16
Gertler, Mark, 177n17
Giavazzi, Francesco, 234, 241n38,
    242n44
Giersch, Herbert, 241n18
Gilbert, R. Alton, 271
Godley, Wynne, 241n34

Goldenberg, Suzanne, 211n8
Goldsmith, Raymond W., 89, 109n2
Gomory, Ralph E., 84n24
Goodwin, Richard, 110n14
Gorton, Gary B., 111n31, 139n10,
    157, 161, 162, 165–8,
    177n19, 177n24, 178n26,
    178n27, 178n31,
    178n33–7, 178n39,
    178n41–3, 270
Gottron, Frank, 212n52
Gouldson, Andy, 214
Graeber, David, 110n4, 111n26,
    111n28
Gramsci, Antonio, 265n23
Gray, John, 56n27
Green, Thomas H., 54n5
Greening, Lorna A., 212n50
Greenspan, Alan, 112n41, 120,
    129–32, 140n30, 141n42,
    151
Griffith-Jones, Stephany, 173,
    179n58
Grossman, Gene H., 23n31
Grubb, Michael, 212n42
Guercio, María B., 57n62

H

Hall, Peter A., 111n23
Hanusch, Horst, 215
Harvey, David, 57n48
Hayek, Friedrich A., vii, 33, 34, 46,
    53, 56n35, 56n40, 57n49,
    255, 256, 265n18, 265n20
Heal, Geoffrey, 27, 61, 87, 115
Heller, W. P., 59
Helliwell, John, 264n8

Henning, Randall, 243
Herman, Edward S., 241n19
Hermele, Kenneth, 212n55
Hicks, John, 111n29
Hilferding, Rudolf, 104, 112n35, 112n38
Hirsch, Robert L., 141n48
Hobbes, Thomas, 55n7
Holdren, John P., 211n20
Holtham, Gerald, 243
Hopkins, Antony G., 82n7
Horton, Mark, 128
Hu, Malin, 128
Hubbard, R. Glenn, 177n16

J
Jevons, William Stanley, 208, 212n49
Johnson, Robert, 54n5
Johnston, Deborah, 57n48
Jones, Robert A., 111n29

K
Kaldor, Nicholas, 241n34
Kaminsky, Graciela L., 131, 139n6, 141n32
Kenen, Peter B., 232, 241n30
Kerr, Niall, 214
Keynes, John Maynard, viii, 10, 21, 23n25, 24n47, 42, 46, 49, 53, 56n29, 57n56, 102, 112n32, 112n39, 139n9, 150, 204, 212n43, 222, 237
Kharroubi, Enisse, 112n42
Kindleberger, Charles P., 3, 4, 22n4, 233, 241n32

Klein, Naomi, 24n38, 242n41
Knight, Frank A., 204, 212n43
Kondratieff, Nikolai, 95, 110n14
Krueger, Alan B., 23n31, 140n29
Krugman, Paul, 76, 84n27, 139n6, 141n35, 241n31, 241n34, 242n43, 242n45
Kuhn, Thomas, S., 23n21
Kuznets, Simon, 13, 14, 23n29
Kydland, Finn E., 129, 140n15, 140n28, 177n7
Kynaston, David, 279

L
Lakatos, Imre, 23n22, 56n24
Lange, Oskar R., 255, 256, 265n19, 265n20
Lapavitsas, Costas, 104, 112n36, 112n44, 135, 241n16
Latouche, Serge, 16, 24n39
Latsis, Spiro J., 23n22
Lattimore, Ralph, 82n1
Lavoie, Don, 265n22
Layard, Richard, 264n8
Lenin, Vladimir I., 110n13, 112n38
Lie, Amund, 56n38, 57n50
Lippincott, Benjamin E., 267
Lipsey, Richard G., 6, 23n14
Lo, Andrew W., 22n1, 170, 239n1
Locke, John, 43, 45, 46, 57n43, 57n44
Louçã, Francisco, 110n16, 212n33
Love, Patrick, 82n1
Lucas, Robert E. Jr., 7, 23n19, 28, 55n22, 56n25, 56n36, 129, 140n14, 140n15, 148, 151
Luini, Luigi, 61, 115

M
MacCallum, Gerald C. Jr., 32, 54n2
Maddison, Angus, 140n26
Magdoff, Fred, 110n8
Magdoff, Harry, 110n8
Makasheva, Natalia A., 114
Maneschi, Andrea, 83n17
Mankiw, Gregory N., 71, 177n13
Marshall, Alfred, 20, 41, 42, 53, 249
Martell, Luke, 82n5
Martin, Henry, 83n17
Martinez, Lisana B., 57n62
Marx, Karl, 93, 110n9
Mazzucato, Mariana, 204, 206,
    212n44, 212n46
McCulley, Paul A., 177n22
McCulloch, John R., 86
Meade, James E., 241n34
Meadows, Dennis L., 211n4, 211n6
Meadows, Donella H., 211n4,
    211n6
Metrick, Andrew, 111n31, 157,
    177n19, 177n24, 178n26,
    178n27, 178n33
Michaelson, Greg, 265n20
Milanović, Branko, 23n30, 24n42,
    139n3, 140n17
Mill, John Stuart, 10, 18, 41, 43, 45,
    53, 73, 84n20, 84n23, 249
Miller, Dale E., 56n31
Millward-Hopkins, Joel, 214
Minsky, Hyman P., 131, 134,
    141n34, 141n40, 141n41,
    163, 164, 172, 179n48,
    222, 224–6, 240n7, 240n8,
    240n11, 241n13
Mirowski, Philip, 57n54
Mises, Ludwig von, vii, 34, 53,
    56n35, 255, 256, 265n16

Mishkin, Frederic S., 160, 177n10,
    177n14
Modigliani, Franco, 6, 23n13, 148
Montini, Massimiliano, 211n16,
    211n17
Morisson, Christian, 127,
    140n22
Mundell, Robert, 232, 241n25,
    241n27, 242n41
Musson, Albert E., 24n46
Muth, John F., 148, 177n2

N
Neftci, Salih N., 224, 240n7
Nersisyan, Yeva, 273
Nesvetailova, Anastasia, 177n25
Ng, Yew-Kwang, 264n6
Nordhaus, William D., 211n15
Nozick, Robert, 57n42

O
Ohlin, Bertil, 72, 84n21, 84n28
Omarova, Saule T., 177n21, 272,
    273
Orhangazy, Özgür, 112n42
Orléan, André, 112n34, 179n49
O'Rourke, Kevin H., 82n6, 82n8
Ostroy, Joseph M., 111n29
O'Toole, James, 179n51, 179n52

P
Pagano, Marco, 234, 241n38,
    242n44
Palast, Greg, 242n41
Palley, Thomas, 112n44
Panayotou, Theodore, 23n31

Papandreou, Andreas, 211n26, 211n28, 212n54
Parguez, Alain, 241n34
Pascal, Blaise, 265n24
Perelman, Chaïm, 10, 23n26
Perez, Carlota, 22n3, 95, 110n17, 110n19, 198–202, 205, 211n30, 211n32, 212n33, 212n34, 212n41
Perotti, Roberto, 241n38
Persaud, Avinash, 173, 179n58
Philippon, Thomas, 110n9
Phillips, Alban W. H., 22n10
Phillips, Kevin P., 94, 110n12
Pigou, Arthur C., 42, 53, 55n18, 56n32, 110n6, 185, 211n13
Piketty, Thomas, 23n30, 24n42, 85n31, 139n3, 140n17
Plehwe, Dieter, 57n54
Polanyi, Karl, 111n26, 196, 211n24
Polemarchakis, Heraklis M., 55n16
Pope Francis, 188, 211n12, 265n24
Popper, Karl R., 9, 22n9, 56n26
Pozsar, Zoltan, 135, 141n45
Prescott, Edward C., 129, 140n15, 140n28, 177n7
Putnam, Robert, 243
Pyka, Andreas, 213, 215

R

Randers, Jorgen, 214
Rapetti, Martin, 240n6
Redlick, Carles J., 242n47
Rees, William E., 211n18
Reinhart, Carmen M., 131, 139n6, 141n32, 178n44, 179n58

Ricardo, David, 41, 46, 57n47, 57n49, 72, 73, 78, 79, 85n30
Rifkin, Jeremy, 198, 211n29, 211n31
Ritzer, George, 144
Robbins, Lionel, 56n30, 265n20
Rodrik, Dani, 49, 57n57, 58n65, 68, 71, 73, 75, 81, 82n3, 83n15, 83n16, 84n25, 85n32, 85n33, 262, 263, 265n26, 266n28, 266n30
Rogoff, Kenneth S., 178n44, 179n58
Roosevelt, Franklin D., 223, 240n5
Roren, Sullivan, 214
Rose, Andrew K., 233, 241n35, 241n36
Rossini Favretti, Rema, 27
Rosso, Osvaldo A., 58
Rothstein, Bo, 139n3, 241n23
Ruzzenenti, Franco, 212n53

S

Saad-Filho, Alfredo, 57n48
Sachs, Jeffrey, 264n3
Saez, Emmanuel, 139n3
Salvatore, Dominick, 241n34
Samuelson, Paul A., 23n15, 73, 75
Sandri, Giorgio, 27
Sarracino, Francesco, 140n25
Sawyer, Malcolm, xvi
Scazzieri, Roberto, 27
Schipper, Lee, 212n51
Schmidtz, David, 59
Schumpeter, Joseph A., 8, 9, 23n23, 95, 101, 110n4, 110n15, 110n18, 110n19, 111n30
Selden, Thomas M., 23n31
Sen, Amartya K., 24n40

Shafik, Nemat, 23n31
Shaxson, Nicholas, 265n12
Shin, Hyun S., 141n44
Simon, Herbert, 148, 177n1
Skeel, David, 274
Skinner, Andrew S., 54n5, 55n10
Smith, Adam, 18, 20, 24n45, 34, 35, 41, 44, 55n9, 71, 72, 77, 83n17, 85n29, 85n30, 148, 176, 249, 256, 265n21
Snider, Connan A., 179n50
Solow, Robert, 23n15, 140n29
Song, Daqing, 23n31
Sordi, Serena, 240n11
Sorrell, Steve, 212n50
Soskice, David, 111n23
Spencer, David, 111n23
Sraffa, Piero, 60, 86
Starr, Ross M., 59
Starrett, D.A., 59
Stern, Nicholas, 264n9
Stiglitz, Joseph E., 23n30, 24n42, 39, 55n12, 55n21, 112n33, 112n47, 139n6, 140n19, 140n29, 177n13, 264n4, 264n8, 264n10
Stock, James H., 141n33
Stolper, Wolfgang F., 75
Suppe, Frederick, 22n6, 22n9, 23n24
Sweezy, Paul M., 100n8
Swoboda, Alexander K., 244

T
Tabellini, Guido, 242n44
Tahyar, Margaret E., 306
Taylor, Fred, 266
Taylor, Lance, 240n7, 240n9
Thirlwall, Tony, 241n34
Thorsen, Dag E., 56n38, 57n50

Tietenberg, Tom, 210n1
Tobias, Adrian, 142, 144, 180
Topi, Corrado, 214
Toporowski, Jan, 112n41
Toulmin, Stephen, 10, 23n26
Turner, Graham, 211n6

U
Uslaner, Eric M., 139n3, 241n23

V
Vercelli, Alessandro, 22n2, 22n5, 23n20, 23n28, 23n31, 23n32, 23n34, 24n40, 24n44, 54n4, 55n15, 55n20, 55n22, 56n33, 57n58, 85n34, 110n14, 110n20, 110n21, 111n25, 111n27, 112n46, 139n1, 139n2, 140n15, 140n17, 140n19, 141n47, 141n49, 177n6, 178n38, 178n40, 179n55, 179n56, 201, 211n19, 211n21, 211n22, 211n23, 211n25, 212n36, 212n38, 240n11, 264n2, 264n5, 264n7, 264n9
Veronese Passarella, Marco, 111n23
Vertova, Giovanna, 216

W
Wackernagel, Mathis, 211n18
Wallace, Christopher C., 139n5
Walras, Léon, 265n19
Warner, Carolyn M., 57n61
Watson, Jim, 213
Watson, Mark W., 141n33

Weiss, Andrew M., 177n12
Wendling, Robert, 143
Whaples, Robert, 71
Wicksell, Knut, 20, 42
Williamson, Jeffrey G.,
 82n6, 82n8
Woodham-Smith, Cecil, 84n22

Y
Yakovets, Yuri V., 114
Youle, Thomas, 179n50

Z
Zalta, Edward N., 58, 59

Subject Index[1]

A

asymmetric monetarism. *See also*
monetary, money. xi,
112n41, 130, 137, 151, 170
austerity. *See also* monetarism
expansionary, 224, 241n38
policies, 2, 107, 133, 135, 151,
223, 224, 235, 236, 237,
238, 239, 240n5

B

bank. *See also* central bank; deposits
bailout, 221, 222, 226
as catalyser, 69
charter value, 166, 167, 175
commercial bank, 101, 154, 156,
157, 175, 227, 251

dealer, 104, 166
and derivatives, 104, 105, 120,
156, 165, 170
development bank, 206, 207, 222
and financial markets, 99, 104–6,
153–6, 158, 165, 167, 171,
175, 176, 221, 227, 251
and imperialism, 69, 105
investment bank, 104, 157, 175,
207
megabank, 104, 105, 166, 170,
172, 174
public, 173–5
systemically important (SIB), 221
universal, 227, 251
banking. *See also* shadow banking
"originate-to-distribute" model,
158, 160

---

[1] Note: Page number followed by 'n' refers to notes

banking. *See also* shadow banking
    (*cont'd*)
    "originate-to-hold" model, 154,
        158
    panics, 153, 160, 162
    system, xi, 128, 135, 147, 157,
        159–64, 168, 175, 220
bankruptcy, 155, 159, 162, 178n28,
    220–2, 226, 227
    of Lehman Bros, 162
Bretton Woods
    era, 70, 120, 133, 135, 176
    monetary regime, 22, 123
    period, 2, 40, 44, 56n34, 100, 107,
        120, 122, 123, 125, 128,
        130, 133, 134, 137, 183,
        186, 202, 227, 253, 268
    phase, 70
    policy rules, 107
    system, 156, 224

C
central bank, xi, 7, 112n41, 120, 128,
    132, 135, 227, 237, 258, 285
    and asymmetric monetarism, 137,
        151, 170
    European Central Bank (ECB),
        129, 179n54, 236, 288
    and financialisation, 106, 137,
        149, 151, 165, 170, 171,
        176, 178n31, 179n53,
        179n54, 202
    independence of, 106, 171
    restrictive policies, 151
co-evolution
    of development and technological
        trajectories, 198–203
    of development paradigms, policy
        strategies and

macroeconomic theory,
    19–22, 96, 124
of economic facts, economics, and
    economic policy, ix, 2–4,
    19, 247
of financialisation and
    globalisation, ix, 57, 76, 98,
    111n23
of globalisation and trade theory,
    76
of policy strategies and
    technological trajectories,
    19, 76, 98, 124,
    198–203
of technological surges and
    macroeconomic paradigms,
    3, 98
crisis
    Asian, 131
    of the Bretton Woods era, 70,
        120, 133, 135, 176
    and capital movements, 69, 78,
        79, 122, 225, 227
    and concentration of capital, 69
    definition, ix, 2
    dot.com, 132, 200, 202
    financial. (*see* (financial crisis))
    great crisis, 19, 95, 97, 98, 138,
        200, 202. (*see also*
        Eurocrisis; Great
        Depression; Great
        Recession; Long Depression;
        Great Stagflation; subprime
        mortgage crisis)
    of mercantilism, 20
cycle
    business, 131, 140n15, 148, 149,
        151, 233, 234
    half-cycle lag, 98
    Kondratieff, 95

life-cycle of macroeconomic
   paradigms, 19–22, 97, 98
life-cycle of policy paradigms, 19,
   95, 97, 98, 124
life-cycle of technological
   paradigms, 85, 86
long, 95
Minsky's cycle, 240n8, 240n11
monetary equilibrium business
   cycle, 129, 148, 151
real business cycle, 129, 140n15,
   148, 149, 151
synchronisation, 233
"Taylor-Neftci cycle" or "Frenkel
   cycle," 225

D
debt
   collateralised debt obligations
      (CDO), 135, 157, 292–3,
      302, 303
   corporate, 161
   debt-deflation, 102, 134, 160,
      226
   debt to GDP ratio, 225–6, 228,
      236, 242n51
   ecological, 184, 192, 193
   of the economic units, 130, 163,
      164, 226
   foreign, 229
   of households, 127, 130, 136,
      167, 176, 193
   indebtedness of households, 130,
      136, 193
   information-insensitive, 154, 162,
      163, 166, 167
   leverage, 172, 292, 302
   private, 228
   public, 120, 127–9, 224, 226–8,
      234, 236, 238
   sovereign, 2, 128, 129, 133, 135,
      146, 229–31, 238, 299
   sovereign debt crisis. (*see*
      Eurocrisis)
de-growth, 11, 16, 23n37. *See also*
   growth
democracy, 33, 46, 51, 53, 54,
   57n47, 57n49, 58n65,
   109, 238, 252–5, 260–6,
   266n28
deposits.101, 156, 157, 175,
   178n35, 269–72, 279–80,
   282, 283, 288, 289. *See also*
   finance; money
   insured, 158, 159, 161, 162, 166,
      272
   and regulatory requirements, 174
   and repo market, 156, 159, 161,
      162, 164
depression. *See* Great Depression;
   Long Depression
development. *See also* development
   trajectory; sustainable
   development
   definition, 17, 250, 261
   financial, 89
   and growth, 11–17, 109n1, 133,
      136, 137, 194–6, 200, 204,
      231, 250, 252
   of market relations, 99
   model of, viii, xi, 2, 16, 70, 81,
      121, 132, 136–9, 146, 174,
      183, 193–5, 207, 250, 261
   of money, 99
   paradigm, x, 1, 3, 16, 19–22, 96,
      98, 119, 120, 124
   and trade, 50, 76, 81

development. *See also* development
    trajectory; sustainable
    development (*cont'd*)
development trajectory, ix, xi,
    121, 138, 169, 258,
    261, 262
    Bretton Woods, viii, 2, 70, 125,
        202, 262
    definition, 1, 19, 200
development trajectory (*cont.*)
    neoliberal, 1, 124, 125, 193, 202,
        252, 263
    sustainable, 1, 169, 171, 189,
        203, 208, 264
    and technological trajectory, 3,
        96, 98, 184, 198–204. (*see
        also* co-evolution)

E
ecological footprint
    definition, 193
    earth overshoot day, 193
    ecological debt, 192, 193.
        (*see also* debt)
economics
    agents, 35, 43–5, 63, 74, 90,
        100, 107, 109, 119, 149,
        164, 175, 176, 237, 258
    as autonomous discipline, 35
    behavioural approach, 147, 148,
        151, 152. (*see also* finance,
        behavioural finance)
    classical, viii, 6, 7, 21, 41, 42,
        56n29, 97, 98, 148, 253
    decisions, 44, 52, 102, 105, 185,
        186, 251, 254, 259, 261
    efficiency, 77, 238
    environmental, 16, 120
    fundamentalist, 147–52

fundamentals, 146, 148, 210
general equilibrium theory, 5, 73,
    148, 152, 153
globalisation, 63, 66, 67, 78
heterodox, 107
historical, ix, 3
Keynesian. (*see* Keynesianism)
and law-like propositions, 5
macroeconomics, viii, 5–7, 19,
    21, 38, 54, 97, 129,
    140n15, 148, 150, 152,
    230, 247
mainstream, 12, 23n37, 24n37,
    38, 39, 42, 92, 107,
    146–9, 152
motivations, 78
neoclassical, 21, 42, 56n29
new classical, viii, 7, 23n19, 42,
    98, 148, 150, 230
new Keynesian. (*see*
    Keynesianism)
policy, 3, 4, 21, 47, 67, 238, 247
primacy of politics over
    economics, 234
rationality, 148
structural, 234
supply, 236
sustainability, 120, 136, 152, 249,
    250, 261
system, 6, 69, 72, 89, 101, 102,
    106, 152, 153, 163, 176, 250
transactions, 92
units, 80, 130, 131, 134, 135,
    163, 164, 196, 222, 226
welfare, 18, 21, 34–6, 39, 44, 49,
    119, 124, 201, 238,
    250, 254
economy
    flexibility of the, 101, 102
    instability of the, 102, 103, 197

low-carbon, 184, 197
real, 3, 79, 90, 92, 93, 95, 103,
    105, 106, 120, 122, 125,
    129, 130, 133, 136, 139,
    146, 151, 155, 167, 170,
    174, 199, 203, 222, 226,
    229, 251, 252, 258, 262
EKC. *See* environmental Kuznets
    curve (EKC)
energy. *See also* Fukushima accident
    demand of, 196
    efficiency, 203, 209
    and finance, 196
    generation, 196, 197
    intensity, 195
    nuclear, 196, 197, 204
    prices, 197
    saving, 187, 206, 209
    sources, 96, 137, 138, 196, 250
    system, xi, 137, 139, 184, 194–7,
    205, 250
environment
    environmental awareness, 186, 195
    environmental capital, 250
    environmental degradation, 194
    environmental economics, 185
    environmentally friendly
        innovations, 191, 203, 206
    environmental Kuznets curve
        (EKC), 14
    environmental problems, 14, 132,
        137, 184–7, 189
    environmental standards, 74, 184
    environmental sustainability, x, xi,
        81, 103, 108, 137, 152,
        183, 186, 193, 194, 203,
        250, 251, 259
    and finance, 196
environmental Kuznets curve (EKC),
    14, 15, 23n31

environmental policy, 187
    command and control (CAC)
        instruments, xi, 184, 189,
        190, 210
    environmental externalities, 12,
        185
    green paradox, 209, 210
    green taxes, 190
    market-based instruments, xi,
        184, 189–92, 210
    and neoliberal policy strategy, xi,
        42, 119, 183, 185, 186,
        189, 208, 210, 247
    rebound effect, 208–10, 212n53
    the role of public investment,
        203–7
    tradable permits, 185, 186, 188,
        190, 191. (*see also* European
        Emission Trading System
        EU ETS)
    transition to a low carbon
        economy, 184, 197
EU ETS. *See* European Emission
    Trading System (EU ETS)
Eurocrisis, ix, 1, 51, 108, 135,
    139n7, 223, 224, 227–31,
    238, 239, 240n5, 255, 263
    and austerity policies, 223-239,
        240n5
    definition of, 220, 223, 224
    eurosclerosis, 229
    explanations, 219, 230
    and the optimal currency area
        (OCA) theory, 231, 233, 234
    origins, 219–24
    policy implications, 16, 220,
        236–8
    propagation in the Eurozone,
        220, 221, 224–9, 239
    structural factors, 233

European Emission Trading System
(EU ETS), xi, 184, 188–92
evolution. *See also* co-evolution
of capitalism, viii, ix, 1, 4, 20, 53,
95–7, 174
of financialisation, 89–112
of globalisation, 67
of liberalism, 32, 40–3, 54
of markets, 14, 19, 64, 67, 248
of neoliberalism, 43–8, 258–62
of policy strategies, 97, 98
of technology, 75, 198
externalities
definition, 13, 37, 39, 42, 75
environmental, 12, 185
financial, 175, 185, 187, 190,
207, 210, 251, 264
and free trade, 63, 74, 80
global, 187
internalisation of, 37, 42, 152,
185, 190, 193, 210
long-run, 264
measure of, 12, 13, 33, 187
and missing markets, 39
negative, 63, 109, 160, 187, 190,
251
positive, 75
and public goods, 39
and resource allocation, 37
social, 12, 251
and strategic investment, 207

F
finance. *See also* banking; debt
asymmetric information, 147, 150,
153–5, 163, 165, 167, 168
behavioural finance, 148, 149,
152

bounded rationality, 148
collateral, 154, 155, 159, 161,
162, 164, 166, 167, 176,
178n28, 295, 297, 300, 302
conduit, 127n45, 144, 265. (*see
also.* finance, special purpose
vehicle)
corporate social responsibility
(CSR), 171, 249
deregulation, xii, 123, 131, 147,
167, 175, 254
efficient market hypothesis
(EMH), 147–50
globalisation, ix, x, 58n65, 69, 79,
89, 97, 98, 111n23, 121,
126, 134, 135, 200, 254,
259, 264
and investment, 105–7, 130, 137,
199, 204, 206, 207, 210,
251, 252
leverage, 159, 169, 172, 282
liberalisation of, x, 109, 123, 134
off-balance sheet, 135, 156, 158,
160, 165, 168, 169,
252, 302
off-shore financial centres,
157, 252
permissive power of, 105
principal-agent problems, 160
rational expectations hypothesis
(REH), 140n15, 147, 148,
150, 151
reform of the financial system,
146, 168, 170, 172–4
regulation of the financial system,
98, 105, 121, 149, 151,
155–7, 167, 168, 171, 175,
235, 251, 258, 273, 282,
286

rehypothecation, 159, 161
repo market, 156, 159, 161, 162,
    164, 167, 221, 301
securitisation, xi, 101, 134, 135,
    147, 155, 158–62, 165,
    166, 175
special purpose vehicles (SPV),
    104, 158, 291, 292, 300–2
supervision of, 151, 200
and sustainability, 262
sustainable, 168–74
financial. *See also* financialisation
bubble, 102, 130, 170, 199, 200,
    202
capital, 78, 93, 95, 96, 99,
    111n24, 225, 251
contagion, 102, 120, 134, 156,
    160–4, 220, 221, 229, 293
crisis, x, 1, 120, 130, 131, 133,
    147, 151, 154, 157, 160,
    163, 173, 189, 202, 219,
    221, 226, 229, 273, 274,
    277, 281, 283, 285, 288
cycle, 224, 240n8, 240n11
detonator, xi, 132
flows, 79, 82
fragility, 120, 130, 131, 135, 137,
    156, 163, 202
globalisation, 79, 264
innovations, xii, 91, 99–102, 107,
    110n4, 111n28, 155, 176
instability, x, 3, 95, 120, 131,
    132, 153, 167, 193, 226
institutions, 2, 101, 104, 109n3,
    121, 122, 133, 135, 145,
    146, 155–7, 160, 161, 169,
    171–4, 239, 258, 272, 275,
    288, 301
investment, 106, 210, 285

market, x, 99, 104–6, 109n3,
    123, 140n30, 149, 153–6,
    158, 161, 164, 165, 167,
    168, 171, 173, 175, 176,
    204, 221, 227, 251, 252,
    293, 297, 305
propagation, 133, 134, 153, 163,
    164
sector, 3, 69, 90, 103, 122, 129,
    130, 133, 134, 137,
    140n30, 151, 176, 199,
    251, 273, 285
short-termism, 137, 251
speculation, 193, 196
stability, 98, 120, 167, 171, 175,
    179n54, 221, 227, 258,
    274, 275, 281–3
sustainability, 91, 96, 98, 102–3,
    120, 132, 137, 186, 193,
    205, 227, 251, 252, 261,
    262. (*see also*
    sustainability)
system, xi, xii, 2, 104, 106,
    112n41, 131, 134, 135,
    146, 147, 151, 155, 159,
    161, 168–77, 221, 222,
    269, 274, 276, 278, 279,
    282, 285, 293
transaction, 155, 169, 172, 251,
    270, 276
turbulences, 227, 228
vulnerability, 196
financial instability hypothesis, 226
    Financial Interrelations
    Ratio (FIR), 89, 90
financialisation. *See also* finance
bank-based *vs.* market-based, 104,
    176
channels of influence, 105

financialisation. *See also* finance
   (*cont'd*)
   de-financialisation, 91, 99, 121
   definition, 89–91
   expansion strategy of capital
      investment, 106
   and financial innovations, xii, 91,
      99–101, 107, 110n4,
      111n28, 155, 176
   and financial repression, 100,
      121, 235
   growth of speculative flows, 79
   as long-run tendency, 99–101
   and long waves, 95
   physiological and pathological
      aspects, 107
   process of, x, 58n65, 69, 90, 91,
      93, 99, 102, 103, 106–8,
      110n9, 137, 151, 152, 176,
      196, 204, 251, 261
   as reaction to decline, 93–6, 98
   as recurring phenomenon, 90–8,
      103
   role of central banks, 106
   and sustainability, 102–3, 108
   unfettered, 174, 193
   variegated, 94, 101n23, 237
Financial Transaction Tax (FTT),
      169, 172, 173,
      179n57, 251
First Financialisation, x, 69, 90, 92,
      94, 96–8, 104–7, 121, 200,
      201. *See also* Second
      Financialisation
   differences between First and
      Second Financialisation,
      103–7
First Globalisation, 76, 97, 201,
      266n28
   and free trade, 67–9

and the gold exchange standard,
      69
and the gold standard, 67–9, 121
and industrialisation, 67, 69
and labour movements, 77, 79
flexibility
   of currency exchange rates, 232
   flexibility-enhancing innovations,
      91
   of labour markets, 125, 136, 235
   and liquidity, 101
   of markets, 125, 186, 256
   structural, 95, 101, 202
   and transaction costs, 37, 232
freedom. 17, 31–58, 63, 65, 80–2,
      85n34, 102, 103, 107, 122,
      175, 238, 258, 263. *See also*
      liberty
   of bank managers, 175
   definition, 31, 32
   and free trade, 63, 65, 80, 82
   of markets, 82
   negative, 33, 47, 49, 53, 58n65,
      63
   of people, vii, 65, 80, 82
   positive, 33, 53, 54n5, 263
free trade
   forced, 68
   policies, 67–9
free trade doctrine, 80, 84n22
   consensus on, 70
   and cross-country movement of
      capital, 76–9
   and cross-country movement of
      labour, 78
   and inequality, 79
   moral implications of, 72, 73, 76,
      77
   and protectionism, 81
   and Adam Smith, 71

free trade theory
assumptions of, 73, 76
and comparative advantage, 72–5, 78, 84n22
and general equilibrium, 72, 73
and globalisation, 73, 75, 79
and income distribution, 75
limitations of, 74
Fukushima accident, 196, 197
fundamentals, 146, 148, 150, 210, 225, 226, 239, 241n17
fundamental theorems of welfare economics, 35, 36, 39

G

general equilibrium. *See* theory
Glass–Steagall Act, 121, 122, 169, 175, 251, 269–73
globalisation. *See also* co-evolution; First Globalisation; Second Globalisation
archaic, 65
definition of, 65–7
and the industrial revolution, ix, 63–7, 73, 97
modern, 65, 66
proto-globalisation, 66
Great Depression, 20, 24n46, 39, 40, 42, 66, 95–7, 121, 130, 138, 145, 169, 200, 201, 226, 253, 269, 270
Great Recession, ix–xii, 1, 2, 16, 39, 40, 51, 66, 71, 94–6, 107, 121, 124, 126, 127, 138, 145, 151, 160, 188, 189, 202, 219, 220, 230, 255
genesis, 121, 132–3, 145
propagation, 133–5, 220
Great Stagflation, 123, 138, 202, 253

green paradox, 209, 210. *See also* environmental policy; Sinn paradox
growth
a-growth, 16, 195
and corruption, 237
definition, 11–17
and development, 11–17
economic, 71, 95, 173
and environmental deterioration, 14, 15, 194
export-led growth, 222, 228
fetishism, 250
and financialisation, 99
and free trade, 68
of GHG emissions, 190
harmonious, 200
and inequality, 13, 45, 79, 85n31
and Keynesianism, 21, 222
long-term, 75
neoliberal growth regime, 133
slowdown of, 69, 127, 129, 130, 192
steady, 122, 152, 250, 252
sustainability, 193
theory, 12, 148
of the world economy, 193
of the world trade, 66, 71, 75

I

industrial relations, 125, 136, 235
industrial revolution, 72, 95, 195, 199
inequality, 3, 13, 14, 17, 18, 21, 35, 45, 55n13, 79, 85n31, 96, 103, 108, 109, 119, 125–7, 136, 146, 228, 232, 236, 248, 249, 254

information and communication
technology (ICT), 96, 98,
132, 202, 203, 205. *See also*
technology; trajectory
instability. *See also* stability
of expectations, 103, 225
financial, x, 3, 95, 120, 131, 132,
153, 167, 193, 226
structural, 197
systemic, 102, 103
investment
capital, 106
financial, 106, 210
financial *vs.* real, 130
flexibility of, 102
green, 204
industrial, 105, 106
innovative, 204
private, 106, 107, 139, 205, 236
public, 203–7, 236
real, 130
strategic, 204–7
in toxic assets, 222
invisible hand, 20, 21, 35–9, 50, 52,
55n11, 63, 64, 132, 148,
176
definition, 38
and the fundamental theorems of
welfare economics, 35, 36, 39
IPAT model, 194

J
Jevons paradox, 208, 209. *See also*
environment

K
Keynesianism
Kaya identity, 194

anti-Keynesian counter-
revolution, 54
expenditure multiplier, 237
inflationary bias, 123–5, 130, 133
Keynesian era, 125, 183
Keynesian hegemony, 253
Keynesian policies, 34, 120,
123–5, 128, 130, 138, 201,
229, 230, 235
Keynesian policy strategy, 120,
138
Keynesian revolution, 21, 42
and liberalism, 42, 53
macroeconomic paradigm, 21,
124
mainstream, 6, 21, 97, 107, 237
new Keynesian economics, 150
post-Keynesian economics, 150
uncertainty, 204
Kuznets curve, 13, 14

L
laissez faire, 3, 20, 41, 42, 47, 53,
63, 97, 138, 149, 151, 152,
189, 253, 257, 265n23
liberalism
classical, ix, 10, 20, 33, 34, 42,
43, 45–7, 77, 253
economic, 32, 34–43, 71
Fundamental Liberal Principle, 40
modern, 42, 46, 54, 56n34
ordo-liberalism, 47. (*see also*
neoliberalism)
traditional, 97
updated, 20, 42, 47
varieties of, 40–3, 49
liberty. *See also* freedom
definition (logical structure), 32
and democracy, 252–5

distinction between positive and
    negative, 34, 263
individual, 44, 49, 58n65, 80,
    263
interpretations of, 33
negative, 32–4, 43–7, 53, 259,
    263
neoliberal vision of, 254
positive, 32–4, 43–5, 47, 49, 53,
    54n5, 254, 259, 263, 264
liquidity, 101, 106, 131, 135, 151,
    154, 156, 161,.165, 168,
    172, 202, 221, 237, 302.
    See also money
liquidity-enhancing innovations. *See*
    flexibility-enhancing
    innovations
London Interbank Offered Rate
    (LIBOR), 51, 105, 170,
    179n50
Long Depression, 20, 24n46, 68, 200

M

market
    competitive, 13, 18, 34, 35, 37,
        39, 40, 55n13, 125, 185,
        222, 249, 255, 256, 265n19
    and computer, 256
    deregulation of, xii, 124, 125,
        167, 175, 259, 262
    dichotomy between market and
        state, 49, 50, 52
    efficiency, 36, 51, 105, 107,
        139n11, 149
    equilibrium, 256
    financial, x, 99, 104–6, 109n3,
        123, 139n11, 140n30, 149,
        153–6, 158, 161, 164, 165,
        167, 168, 171, 173, 175,

    176, 204, 221, 227, 251,
        252, 293, 297, 305
    free, ix, x, xii, 17–18, 20, 21,
        31–58, 63, 70, 72, 73, 77,
        80, 81, 97, 105, 148, 185,
        190, 238, 240n5, 249, 253,
        256
    gap, 38, 39
    global, 64, 77–9
    international, 64, 74, 81, 259, 262
    and the invisible hand. (*see*
        invisible hand)
    knows better, 134
    labour, 77, 119, 125, 131,
        136, 230, 235, 236,
        238, 239
    national, 63, 64, 74, 81,
        259, 262
    and optimal allocation of
        resources, 35, 40, 255
    real, 8, 13, 36–41, 50–2, 70, 149,
        185
    regulation of, 256
    as a self-regulating system, 34
    and self-regulation, 57n49, 170,
        175, 184, 189, 257
    spontaneous evolution of markets,
        14
    and sustainable development, xi,
        17–18, 248, 250
    unfettered, 1, 7, 54, 184, 192,
        207, 249, 253, 254, 259
Monetarist Disinflation, 121, 123–9
monetary
    business cycles. (*see* cycle)
    Greenspan put, 130
    innovations, 101
    policy, 106, 120, 124, 128–32,
        140n30, 141n31, 150, 151,
        280

restrictive policy, 124, 137, 151,
        237
side and real side, 6
stability, 7, 124
system, viii, 123, 253
union, 231–3, 235, 236, 239, 287
money
    creation, 154, 237
    and credit, 150
    definition of, 91, 92
    and double coincidence of wants,
        100
    evolution of, 91
    and finance, 146
    and liquidity, 101, 154, 302
    as means of exchange, 99, 100,
        111n28
    money-market mutual funds
        (MMMF), 156, 157, 166,
        175, 297
    multiplier, 159
    as quantity and as institution, 150
    and the real economy, 129, 151
    supply, 7, 23n17, 92, 110n5
    as technology, 92
    the veil of, 92, 146, 150
    wages, 5, 6, 22n12

N
neoliberalism
    development model, 3, 183, 198
    and environmental policies,
        185–9
    evolution, 43–8, 70, 124,
        147–55, 259
    genesis of, 147, 202, 255
    and negative freedom, 33, 47, 49,
        53, 58n65, 63

neo-conservatism, 3, 48
neoliberal doctrine, 10, 248
neoliberal era, 58n65, 70, 89,
        129, 134, 158, 176, 177,
        183, 208, 257, 258
neoliberal financialisation, 90,
        145–80
neoliberal inflationary bias, 3,
        133, 137
neoliberal laissez faire, 3
neoliberal model of development,
        xi, 121, 132, 133, 136–9
neoliberal paradigm. (*see*
        Paradigm)
neoliberal period, 10
neoliberal policies, ix, x, xi, 3, 7,
        46, 48, 52, 98, 108, 128,
        131, 134, 136, 137, 175,
        183, 184, 189, 192, 230
neoliberal policy strategy, x, xi, 2,
        7, 46, 63, 89, 119, 124,
        125, 127, 138, 139n12,
        176, 183, 185–9, 253,
        259, 262
neoliberal principles, 127, 129,
        210
neoliberal reforms, 46, 131
neoliberal regulation, 258
neoliberal revolution, 70, 124,
        147, 259
neoliberal revolution in finance,
        147–55
neoliberal trajectory, ix, x, 1,
        119–41, 186, 198,
        202, 255
neoliberal trilemma, 248, 262–4
nested definitions, 43, 45, 48
objection to definitions, 45, 47,
        72

standard, 44, 127, 140n15
strong, 45
and sustainability, 132, 136–9,
    183, 186, 248, 258–62
weak, 43, 45, 125

P
paradigm
    change of, 3, 19
    development, x, 3, 16, 19–22, 96,
        98, 119, 120, 124
    economic, 250
    financial, 105
    Keynesian, 2, 98. (*see also*
        Keynesianism)
    liberal, 185. (*see also* liberalism)
    macroeconomic, 19, 21, 96–8,
        124
    mainstream, 19
    methodological, 38
    neoliberal, x, xi, 1, 40, 45, 48, 98,
        125, 183, 262, 263. (*see also*
        (neoliberalism))
    new classical, 148, 150, 230
    policy, 3, 98, 189
    scientific, 8. (*see also* (vision))
    techno-economic, 96, 199–201,
        203
    technological, 95, 96, 98, 199,
        201, 202
Phillips curve, 4–7, 22n12, 125,
    129, 131, 136, 139n12,
    141n31
pluralism, 10
poverty, 17, 18, 21, 69, 78, 96, 109,
    119, 126, 127, 136, 248,
    249

R
rebound effect, 208–10, 212n53. *See
    also* environment
recession, 24n46, 102, 120, 125,
    133, 190, 197, 222, 224,
    226, 236. *See also* great
    recession
reductionism
    causal, 2, 252
    quantitative, 92
Regulation Q, 157, 175, 270
research programme. *See* paradigm;
    vision
the Roaring 1990s, 121, 124, 129–31

S
Second Financialisation, x, 90–2, 94,
    96–8, 103–9, 121–3, 134,
    141n39, 196, 200, 202,
    261. *See also* First
    Financialisation
Second Globalisation, 76–9, 97
    the Bretton Woods phase, 70
    and free trade, 70, 79
    and labour movements, 78
    the neoliberal phase, 70
securitisation, xi, 101, 134, 135,
    147, 155, 158–62, 165,
    166, 175, 277
semiotics
    pragmatics, 4
    semantics, 4
    syntactics, 4
shadow banking, xi, 101, 135, 147,
    155–62, 176, 252, 274
    growth of, 175, 273
    regulation of, 165–8

Sinn paradox, 208. *See also*
    environmental policy; green
    paradox
stability. *See also* instability
    financial, 98, 120, 167, 171, 175,
        221, 227, 274, 275, 281–3
    hegemonic theory, 233
    monetary, 7, 124
stagflation, viii, 22, 42, 54, 98, 123,
    124, 133
state, viii, xii, 17, 18, 20, 21, 32, 34,
    36, 42, 44–7, 49–54, 54n5,
    55n17, 67, 80, 111n28,
    122, 124, 166, 173, 205,
    226, 253, 254, 259,
    265n23, 304
    and market. (*see* market)
    welfare. (*see* welfare state)
subprime mortgage crisis, 135, 200
sustainability, x, xi, 3, 15–18, 54, 91,
    96, 98, 102–3, 106, 108,
    109, 120, 121, 125, 132,
    136, 138, 139, 152, 183,
    186, 192–6, 198, 203–5,
    227, 231, 239, 248–52,
    258–64. *See also*
    development; environment;
    finance; unsustainability
sustainable development, xi, 1, 11,
    16–18, 103, 147, 152, 169,
    174, 184, 189, 196, 203,
    204, 208, 248, 250, 262,
    264
    definition, 17
    economic foundations, 17
    ethical foundations, 17
    and fundamentalist economics,
        149, 152

T
technology
    evolution of, 75, 198
    technical change, 16, 67, 195,
        205, 206
    technological breakthrough, 196,
        197
    technological innovation, 125, 205
    technological paradigm, 95, 96,
        98, 199, 201, 202
    technological revolution, 95, 198,
        199, 201
    technological trajectory. (*see*
        Trajectory)
theory
    asymmetric information, 160, 163
    of comparative advantage, 72–6,
        78, 83n19
    decision, 32, 37, 55n20
    of dynamics, 256
    empirical, 4
    of expansionary austerity, 224,
        241n38
    of financial cycles, 224
    of free trade, 64, 72
    fundamentalist approach, 147, 148
    general equilibrium, 5, 13, 38, 72,
        73, 140n15, 148, 152, 153
    of hegemonic stability, 233
    interpretation of, ix, 5, 10, 39
    life-cycle, 8, 9
    macroeconomic, 19, 21, 112n39,
        123, 124
    mainstream, 147, 205
    of Optimal Currency Area (OCA),
        231, 233, 234, 241n25
    probability theory, 37
    pure, 4, 5, 8, 22n6, 39

TINA fallacy, 9–11, 253
trajectory. *See also* development
  trajectory
  of the neoliberal paradigm, 1, 98,
  262
  technological, xii, 3, 96, 98, 184,
  198–201, 204
Transatlantic Trade and Investment
  Partnership (TTIP), 81,
  260, 261, 265n25
TTIP. *See* Transatlantic Trade and
  Investment Partnership
  (TTIP)

U
unsustainability
  economic, 119, 127
  of the energy system, 194–7
  environmental, xi, 120, 184, 194
  financial, xi, 120
  of the neoliberal growth regime, 133
  of the neoliberal model of
    development, 136–9
  social, 119
  of the spontaneous evolution of
    the economy, 192

V
vision, ix, xiii, 6, 8–12, 15, 16, 20,
  24n37, 33, 43, 45, 46, 80,
  92, 97, 107, 146, 148, 152,
  174, 186, 206, 234, 247,
  248, 253–5
  of growth and development,
    11–17
  Keynesian, 107
  of liberalism, 40, 44, 56n34
  of liberty, 33, 252–5
  neoliberal, 253–5
  of the Phillips curve, 4–8
  policy, 247, 248
  pre-analytic, 8, 9

W
Washington consensus, 48
welfare state, 18, 21, 34, 44, 49,
  107, 119, 124, 125,
  128, 135, 200, 201, 229,
  235, 249

Z
the Zero Years, 121, 124, 132–3